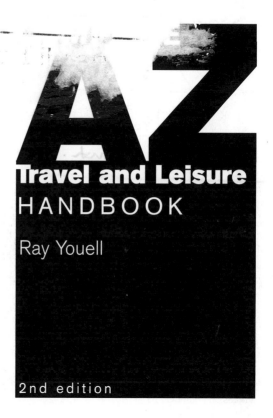

A–Z

Travel and Leisure
HANDBOOK

Ray Youell

2nd edition

Hodder & Stoughton

A B C D E F G H I J K L M N O P Q R S T U V W X Y Z

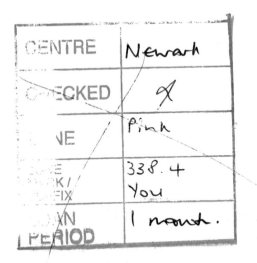
British Library Cataloguing in Publication Data
A catalogue record for this title is available from The British Library

ISBN 0 340 848936

First published 1996
Second edition 2003

Impression number 10 9 8 7 6 5 4 3 2
Year 2007 2006 2005 2004

Cover photograph: Brooke Slezak/Getty Images

Typeset by GreenGate Publishing Services, Tonbridge, Kent
Printed in Great Britain for Hodder & Stoughton Educational, a division of Hodder Headline, 338 Euston Road, London NW1 3BH by CPI Bath

CONTENTS

A
B
C
D
E
F
G
H
I
J
K
L
M
N
O
P
Q
R
S
T
U
V
W
X
Y
Z

ACKNOWLEDGEMENTS

I am indebted to the many organisations and individuals who supplied up-to-date information and examples for inclusion in the *Handbook*. Their support is greatly appreciated.

Thanks are also due to Alexia Chan at Hodder for her patience and encouragement.

As always, a big thank you to Sue, Megan and Owen, without whose support the book would never have materialised.

Ray Youell
Aberystwyth, December 2002

HOW TO USE THIS BOOK

This second edition of the *Complete A–Z Travel and Leisure Handbook* is an alphabetical textbook designed to be used easily by students and people working in the leisure, travel and tourism industries. With fully updated entries and the latest statistics, it has been developed specifically for people studying the AVCE/Vocational A levels in Leisure & Recreation and Travel & Tourism. It covers all the key topics featured in the six compulsory units associated with each of these qualifications.

Each entry in the *Handbook* contains a clear definition, with further explanation and examples where necessary. This will help the user to add precision and depth to essays, reports, test answers and case studies.

Entries are developed in line with the relative importance of the topic covered. The more important the term or organisation, the more detailed the entry. *Carnet*, for example, is covered in just a few lines, whereas *tourism* receives more in-depth analysis. The latter would provide sufficient material to enrich an essay, to clarify a point that has not yet been understood or to find out the latest statistics on a subject. Numerate topics are developed throughout, with the help of worked examples.

The study of leisure, travel and tourism can be developed further by making use of the cross-referenced entries (shown in italics throughout the book). For example, the entry for *Sport England* refers the reader to *UK Sport*. The author has limited the use of cross-referencing to important, linked concepts. Essay and report writing should, therefore, be enhanced by following the logical pathway indicated by italicised entries.

A new feature in this second edition is the inclusion of web addresses for major organisations and topics. These are included at the end of appropriate entries as 'weblinks', allowing greater depth of information to be accessed if needed.

Students of leisure, travel and tourism sometimes have difficulty with the language and jargon of the subjects. This stems from several factors:

- the diverse nature of the industries, with many different sectors
- students have often come from a variety of backgrounds
- the dynamic nature of the industries with new concepts being constantly introduced and others going out of date
- some textbooks use different terms for the same subject (such as 'green' tourism and responsible tourism).

The *A–Z Travel and Leisure Handbook* provides a single, comprehensive and up-to-date solution to these problems. In addition, the entries have sufficient detail to make the handbook a valuable reference and revision companion.

To help students with their study for the AVCE/Vocational A levels in Leisure & Recreation and Travel & Tourism, lists of the top revision topics for each compulsory unit are included at the back of the book.

I hope that the *Handbook* proves an invaluable resource for you, and is fully relevant from your first day of study and on into your working life.

Ray Youell
Head of Tourism Management
University of Wales, Aberystwyth

AA: see *Automobile Association*

AALA: see *Adventure Activities Licensing Authority*

à la carte refers to a menu in a restaurant or *hotel* from which *customers* select from a range of items, each of which is priced separately and cooked to order. (See also *table d'hôte*.)

ABC Travel Guides: a series of reference books, *gazetteers* and timetables, concerning destinations and travel planning, now made available as *OAG* publications.

above-the-line promotion refers to *marketing* and promotional activity for which a *commission* is normally paid by the chosen *media* to an *advertising agency*, e.g. *advertising* by a leisure or tourism organisation on television, at the cinema, in newspapers and magazines, or on commercial radio. (See also *below-the-line promotion*.)

ABSA: see *Association for Business Sponsorship of the Arts*

ABTA: see *Association of British Travel Agents*

ABTA bond: all *travel agent* and *tour operator* members of the *Association of British Travel Agents (ABTA)* are required to provide a bond to protect their customers in the event of financial failure. The bond can take a number of forms, but is often an insurance policy for the amount required by ABTA or a bank guarantee. This financial protection offered by the bonding scheme enables ABTA, in the event of a member's failure, to arrange for clients whose *holidays* are in progress at the time of the failure to continue their holidays, as far as possible as originally planned, and in any event to make sure that customers abroad are returned to the UK. Alternatively, customers whose holidays have not started can be reimbursed the cost of their holidays or ask ABTA to make suitable alternative arrangements.

ABTA National Training Board: see *Travel Training Company*

ABTA Tour Operators Certificate: see *ABTOC*

ABTA Travel Agents Certificate: see *ABTAC*

ABTAC stands for *Association of British Travel Agents* Certificate. It is an examination-based qualification for those working, or wishing to work, in the travel industry and was developed jointly by ABTA's Travel Agents Council and the *Travel Training Company*. Launched in September 1994, ABTAC replaces the former COTAC (Certificate of Travel Agency Competence) qualification, and is aligned to the *National Vocational Qualifications (NVQs)*. Available by distance learning and in a number of regional centres, ABTAC counts towards the staff qualifications requirement for membership of ABTA. ABTAC is to be replaced shortly by the *Certificate in Travel (Travel Agents)* qualification.

ABTOC stands for ABTA Tour Operators Certificate, an examination-based, vocational qualification which has been designed to test the knowledge, understanding and many of the skills which underpin competent performance as a tour operator. ABTOC is to be replaced shortly by the *Certificate in Travel (Tour Operators)* qualification.

Abtech: a technology advisory service offered by *ABTA* to its members, which aims to give unbiased advice on all matters relating to the use of computer systems in travel agencies and tour operations. Weblink: www.abtech.co.uk

ACAC: see *Activity Centre Advisory Committee*

ACAS: see *Advisory Conciliation and Arbitration Service*

ACC: see *Association of County Councils*

access in *leisure, travel and tourism* is an all-embracing term covering both the physical access to buildings and facilities, as well as the opportunity for all people to participate in a range of activities regardless of their gender, race, age, social status, income level, personal mobility or *special needs*. The *Sports Council* did much to widen participation in sport and recreation in the 1980s and 1990s through promotional campaigns such as *Sport for All*. Organisations such as the *Council for the Protection of Rural England* and the *Ramblers' Association* campaign strongly for the right of access to the countryside. Pressure from such bodies helped to accelerate the introduction of the *Countryside and Rights of Way Act 2000 (CROW)*.

accommodation is one of the three major components of the *travel and tourism industry*, along with *transportation* and *attractions/entertainment*. It employs around 20 per cent of the total UK tourism workforce and is a significant revenue-earner; the *British Tourist Authority* estimates that more than one-third of all expenditure by *overseas visitors* to Britain and by UK residents is for accommodation. The accommodation sector comprises a wide range of establishments, including city centre hotels, motels, cottages, caravans, lodges, farm guesthouses and country house hotels, to name but a few. Accommodation can be classified in a number of ways, for example:

- commercial or non-commercial
- *serviced* or *self-catering*
- urban or rural
- static or mobile.

Perhaps the most useful classification is into *serviced* or *self-catering*, the former including hotels and guesthouses, the latter cottages and chalets. In the UK, figures show that *self-catering* is more popular than serviced accommodation, although the single most popular type of accommodation is hotels, accounting for approximately 25 per cent of all accommodation used. *Visiting friends and relatives* is also an important category of tourist accommodation.

accommodation grading schemes are initiatives that aim to ensure consistency in the quality of service and facilities at establishments offering accommodation for business and leisure travellers. Schemes may be either compulsory, as is the case in many European countries, or voluntary, the position in the UK. The three best-known schemes in the UK are the 'star' systems administered by the *National* and *Regional Tourist Boards*, and similar schemes promoted by the *Automobile Association (AA)* and RAC (Royal Automobile Club). Tour operators sometimes devise their own classification schemes to supplement those offered by the tourist boards, e.g. the *Thomson* 'T' scheme. The use of a number of different schemes with varying criteria can lead to confusion in the minds of customers, and many in the industry are calling for a simplified scheme applicable to all establishments. At present, there is a debate within the UK tourism industry about the advantages and disadvantages of introducing a compulsory registration system for tourist accommodation.

Accor group is the biggest of the European hotel companies, operating under several *brand* names, including Novotel, Sofitel, Mercure, Ibis, Formule 1, Altea and Urbis. With headquarters in France, Accor has a stock of more than 100,000 rooms in its hotels, mainly found in France, Belgium, Germany, Italy, Spain and the UK. The bulk of Accor's expansion in the 1990s took place in the *budget hotel* sector of the market. Weblink: www.accor.com

account: a written record in which details of an organisation's financial transactions are entered. These may relate to an individual supplier, a type of expense or receipt, or a particular *asset* or *liability*. In *advertising* and sales, an 'account' is the name given to an individual organisation to whom services are provided, e.g. a travel agent that handles the business travel arrangements for J Smith Engineering Company will refer to it as the 'Smith account'.

accountability is the extent to which an individual is held responsible for his or her actions. In the workplace, managers have to accept ultimate *responsibility* for the control of their resources, including staff, plant and machinery, finance and facilities, and they are judged on the results they achieve. In the public sector, local authority employees are accountable to their *Council Tax* payers through their elected representatives, the councillors. (See also *delegation, authority*.)

account executive: an employee of an *advertising agency* who acts as the link between the clients, sometimes referred to as '*accounts*', and all the other specialist staff with the agency who will be working on particular campaigns. Working under the direction of an account director, the account executive will meet clients face-to-face and liaise with the agency's *media planners* and *media buyers*, creative teams and *market research* staff to make sure that a campaign meets its *objectives* and that the clients are satisfied with the service they receive.

accountant's pricing: see *cost-plus pricing*

accounting is the process of recording an organisation's financial transactions in accordance with standard book-keeping practice. Accounting can be divided into *financial accounting*, which is concerned with the preparation of summary reports for the *shareholders* or owners of a business, and *management accounting*, which focuses on the provision of financial information to help with business decision-making and planning. All organisations need accurate and reliable accounting systems, so that they can monitor their performance, control *costs* and meet any legal requirements for the presentation of figures.

accounting period: the period of time over which a business prepares its *profit and loss account* and at the end of which it draws up its *balance sheet*.

acculturation is the study of the reactions and impacts when people from different cultures come into contact with each other. This may be by direct contact, for example a group of UK *tourists* meeting the Masai people on a safari holiday to East Africa, or via the influence of the *mass media*.

ACE: see *Association for Conferences and Events*

acid-test ratio: see *liquidity ratio*

ACORN stands for 'a classification of residential neighbourhoods', a computer *database* developed to help organisations carry out effective *target marketing* and *direct mail* campaigns. ACORN uses the electoral register to classify individuals according to the type of residential area in which they live and can be programmed to produce names and addresses in particular postcode areas of the country for use in *direct mail* campaigns. The system can give names and addresses of people who are likely to buy particular types of *holidays* and follow certain leisure pursuits. Weblink: www.caci.co.uk

acquisition is the takeover of one company by another, e.g. in 2002 easyJet acquired the *low-cost airline* go. The company making the acquisition is usually sufficiently large to be able to finance the takeover. Acquisitions that may not be in the public interest are sometimes referred to the *Competition Commission* (formerly known as the *Monopolies and Mergers Commission*.)

ACRE: see *Action with Communities in Rural England*

acronym: a word (usually pronounced as such) formed from the first letters of other words, e.g. *ABTA = Association of British Travel Agents* and *ACORN = a classification of residential neighbourhoods*.

action plan: a statement, usually in written form, giving a series of actions to be carried out within a certain period of time. The action plan may result from a review of the *management* of a department, an *appraisal* of an individual member of staff or perhaps an evaluation of a marketing campaign. Action plans, which may form part of a wider *business plan*, should indicate who is responsible for carrying out each of the tasks identified.

Action with Communities in Rural England (ACRE): a voluntary membership organisation that represents the interests of rural areas in England, and the social and economic welfare of those living and working in them. ACRE undertakes *research* on rural issues and provides information, training and support to rural communities, including advice on *rural tourism*. Weblink: www.acre.org.uk

active leisure activity: any activity carried out in a person's *leisure time* that requires an active commitment, e.g. walking, cycling, playing football, snowboarding, etc. (See also *passive leisure activity*.)

activity: when used in a financial sense, this is a term used to assess company performance; it is a measure of how well an organisation is using its *assets*, determined by comparing *financial ratios* with previous years or comparing actual with forecast results. It can also refer to any *active leisure activity*.

Activity Centre Advisory Committee (ACAC): a group set up in 1994 to develop a voluntary *code of practice* covering the safety and welfare of those who use *outdoor activity centres*. ACAC proposed an accreditation scheme for participating centres that guaranteed to adhere to the code of practice. Centres must also agree to submit themselves to independent inspection and accept a customer complaints procedure. Members of ACAC in 1994 included the *English Tourist Board*, *CCPR*, *BAHA*, PGL Young Adventure and the *Sports Council*. Much of the ACAC's work became the basis for the establishment of the *Adventure Activities Licensing Authority*.

activity holidays have grown in popularity in the UK in recent years, due to an increased concern for health, exercise and fitness in the general population. Activity holidays range from the very intensive, e.g. off-road mountain biking, orienteering and water-skiing, to the relatively leisurely, e.g. walking and golf. *Tour operators* and hoteliers have responded to the growth in healthy pursuits by offering activity and special interest holidays and short breaks, aimed at individuals, groups and families. Activity holidays are set to be one of the growth sectors of the *leisure* and *tourism* industries in the early years of the twenty-first century.

Adair's leadership groups: a model developed by John Adair in 1983 that demonstrates the three main areas to which a leader must attend if a task is to be achieved with maximum satisfaction to all. They are:

1   achieving the task

2   building and maintaining the team

3   developing the individual.

Often, an inexperienced leader focuses his or her attention on getting the task done and is unaware that effective leadership requires him or her to consider the group and the individual as well.

ADC: see *Association of District Councils*

additional voluntary contribution (AVC): an extra payment made by a person to top-up his or her personal or company *pension*, so as to provide extra income in retirement. Some companies subsidise the payment of AVCs for their employees or even meet the full cost of the extra payments on their behalf.

add-on: something extra provided for a customer for which an additional charge is normally levied, e.g. an excursion taken while on a *package holiday* abroad, a baby seat installed in a hire car or insurance for a activity holiday in a Lake District country house hotel.

ad-hoc team: a group of people set up at short notice to investigate a particular occurrence, e.g. a sudden rise in the number of complaints to a *tour operator* about a particular *hotel* or an accident at a *tourist attraction*.

administrative systems are found throughout the *leisure* and *tourism* industries providing support to managers in their decision-making roles and staff in their everyday tasks. Administrators carry out both routine and non-routine functions. Routine functions include servicing committees, producing letters and *reports*, and preparing financial data. Non-routine functions could include providing administrative support to a one-off event or an unplanned visit by an inspector from the *Health and Safety Executive*. Leisure and tourism organisations need effective administrative systems in order to be able to:

●   record and monitor organisational performance

●   support the operation of resources – human, financial and physical

●   monitor the effectiveness and efficiency of the organisation

●   comply with relevant *legislation*.

Some of the most important areas in leisure and tourism that need administrative systems are *stock control*, the handling and recording of cash, cleaning and maintenance, health and safety, and booking systems. Nowadays, administrative systems invariably involve the use of *computers* and other *IT* equipment.

advance purchase excursion (APEX): a travel ticket purchased in advance of a journey at a discount price. APEX fares are available on a number of modes of travel, including airlines, ferries, coaches and trains. As well as having to be purchased in advance, APEX tickets sometimes have other conditions attached to them, e.g. the requirement to stay for a minimum number of nights at a destination.

Advanced Vocational Certificate in Education (AVCE): a *vocational qualification* offered in a range of subject areas from 2000, including health and social care, travel and tourism, business, and leisure and recreation. AVCEs, which replaced Advanced *GNVQs* and are sometimes referred to as Vocational A levels, were developed under the guidance of the *Qualifications and Curriculum Authority*. They are currently made available by three awarding bodies; *Edexcel, AQA* and *OCR*. Students with an AVCE have access to a wide range of career and higher education opportunities.

advantages statement: that part of the sales process in leisure and tourism, before the *customer* has made a decision whether or not to purchase, when a sales person indicates what the product or service can do for the customer, e.g. the fact that a departure time of 14.00 for a ferry crossing means that a client will not have to make an early start to reach the ferry port. An advantages statement will often follow on from a *features statement*, which gives general information about a product or service. (See also *benefits statement*.)

adventure activities are active leisure activities that involve a degree of adventure, often in an unfamiliar environment, e.g. mountain climbing, trekking, quad biking, gliding, paint balling. Operators that provide these activities for young people are policed by the *Adventure Activities Licensing Authority.*

Adventure Activities Licensing Authority (AALA): an independent, cross-departmental public authority funded by the *Department for Education and Skills (DfES)* and operating under the written guidance of the *Health and Safety Commission (HSC)*. In effect, the AALA is an independent watchdog on the delivery of outdoor adventure activities for young people. The aim of the licensing scheme is to provide assurances to the public about the safety of those activity providers who have been granted a licence. A licence indicates that the provider has been inspected by the Authority, with particular attention being paid to their safety management systems, and been able to demonstrate compliance with nationally accepted standards of *good practice* in the delivery of adventure activities to young people. Licensable activities inspected by the AALA include rock-climbing, canoeing, hill walking, caving and sailing. Weblink: www.aala.org

adventure tourism is the term used to describe a particular type of tourist activity that focuses on exploration and discovery, rather than offering a passive experience. Trekking in the Himalayas, walking in the jungles of Borneo and white-water canoeing in the Rocky Mountains would all be classified as adventure tourism. Providing adventure tourism products is a form of *niche marketing*.

advertisement: a paid insertion in the *printed* or *broadcast media* that informs readers, viewers or listeners about products and services in the hope of raising awareness and per-suading them to buy. Advertisements are also found at the cinema, on billboards, at sports stadia and on many forms of transport, including buses, taxis and the London Underground. Advertisements in newspapers and magazines can either be *classified*, which are paid for by the word or line, or display/semi-display, which are larger and charged on a pro-rata basis for space used. Current prices for advertising in all types of media can be found in the trade publication *British Rate and Data (BRAD)*.

advertising is the most visible part of an organisation's *promotional mix*. It seeks to inform and persuade existing and potential purchasers or users of products and services. Advertising is carried out in a wide range of *media*, including *television*, commercial radio, newspapers, magazines, billboards and by transport providers. The charges for advertising vary in direct proportion to the number of people who will see or hear the particular advertisement (see *opportunities to see*). Television is the most powerful, and most expensive, advertising medium, since it attracts the biggest audience. In leisure and tourism there is a distinction between trade and consumer advertising. Trade advertising is carried out on a business-to-business basis, e.g. a tour operator advertising its holidays in the Travel Trade Gazette or a sports goods distributor advertising in Leisure Management magazine. Consumer advertising is communication between an organisation and its customers, e.g. a local sports centre advertising its services on local radio or a company such as Thomson Holidays placing an advertisement in the Daily Mail. To be effective, all advertising should follow the *AIDA* principle.

advertising agency: a company that can offer a range of services to help a *leisure* or *tourism* organisation achieve maximum impact with its *advertising* budget. Large agencies employ a number of specialists, including:

- **account executives** – who are the link between the clients and all sections of the agency
- **creative teams** – who are the 'ideas people', chosen for their skill in producing effective slogans and text (copywriters), or their artistic ability (artists and graphic designers)
- **media personnel** – who both plan a media schedule and liaise with the appropriate media to buy book space or buy *airtime*
- *market research staff* – who commission or carry out *research* into new products and markets.

Agencies charge a fee for their services, depending on the nature of the work and the *media* used. Lists of advertising agencies are produced by the Institute of Practitioners in Advertising and the Advertising Agency Register. (See also *advertising, above-the-line promotion, below-the-line promotion, media buyer, media planner.*)

advertising campaign: the planning, execution and analysis of a series of events aimed at informing and persuading people to buy particular products and services. An advertising campaign, which may be carried out 'in house' or through the services of an *advertising agency*, will have specific *objectives*, e.g. raising awareness of a new product or publicising the opening of a new theme park. The campaign will often spread beyond purely *advertising* in various *media*, to include other promotional techniques such as *direct mail* and *public relations* work. It is essential that the results of any advertising campaign are closely monitored to ensure that its original *objectives* are being met.

advertising regulatory bodies are organisations that are established to monitor the standards of advertisers and to ensure that advertisers adhere to codes of practice. The most well-known in the UK is the *Advertising Standards Authority*.

Advertising Standards Authority (ASA): this is a self-regulatory body responsible for ensuring that advertisers in the various *media* conform to the British Code of Advertising Practice. The Code requires that all advertisements should be legal, decent, honest and truthful. Any material found to be contravening the Code must be withdrawn from publication. Weblink: www.asa.org.uk

Advisory Conciliation and Arbitration Service (ACAS): this body was set up under the terms of the Employment Protection Act 1975, to promote the improvement of *industrial relations* and to act as a catalyst between employers and *trade unions* in the resolution of industrial disputes. ACAS can supply conciliation officials, who listen to both parties' views and aim to mediate to bring a dispute to a speedy and acceptable conclusion. ACAS is also active in encouraging organisations to develop approved codes of practice governing, for example, the handling of disciplinary matters in the workplace. Although it is most often invited to mediate in a dispute, ACAS does have powers under the 1975 Act to intervene, where this is felt to be in the public interest. Weblink: www.acas.org.uk

after-sales service is the recognition that the *sales process* does not finish when a customer has parted with his or her money for a product or service. Any *leisure* or *tourism* organisation should expect to have to handle a number of queries and even *complaints* after a sales transaction has taken place. The more progressive organisations will follow up a proportion of its sales to establish that customers are happy with the service they received. A *travel agent*, for example, may telephone a client to enquire if her holiday went well. Attention to an efficient after-sales service is also a good *public relations* exercise.

age structure: a *demographic* factor that can have important effects on the *demand* for leisure and tourism products and services. As part of its wider *market research* activities, an organisation needs to know the current age structure of its *target markets* and how it is likely to change in the future. In general, Western countries are moving towards an ageing population, with people living longer and more active lives.

ageing population: a phenomenon of most Western industrialised nations, whose people are generally living longer and more active lifestyles. Figures from the *Office for National Statistics (ONS)* show that, for the first time ever, there are now more people aged over 65 than under 16 in the UK. The ageing of the population offers opportunities for the leisure, travel and tourism industries in terms of developing new products and services for a growing *market*.

agency agreement: a formal arrangement entered into by an agent and a *principal*, giving details of the terms under which each will operate and the scale of *commission* payable to the agent. In the case of a travel agency, it is likely to have agreements with a number of principals, including *tour operators*, airlines, car hire companies and ferry operators.

agenda: a formal list of the items to be discussed at a meeting (see figure on next page). It is helpful if the agenda is sent out before the meeting, in order to give those attending a chance to study its content, but it may be given out at the start of the meeting. A note requesting items for an agenda is sometimes sent out to all those due to attend a meeting, giving them the opportunity to have particular items discussed.

Agenda 21: see *Earth Summit*

agent: a company or individual who sells goods and services on behalf of another company (known as the *principal*) in return for a fixed payment or, more usually, a percentage of the value of the sales (known as *commission*). By using agents, a company, such as a *tour operator* or car hire firm, saves on the costs of setting up its own sales operation. It does, however, run the risk of its own products not getting sufficient exposure if the agent sells on behalf of a number of principals.

A B C D E F G H I J K L M N O P Q R S T U V W X Y Z

**Bramthorpe District Council
Leisure Services Committee**

The next meeting of the above committee will take place on Monday 6th October 2003 at 7.20pm in room B12.

AGENDA

1. Apologies for absence
2. Minutes of the last meeting
3. Matters arising
4. Chair's report
5. Secretary's report
6. National Lottery funding
7. 2003/04 budget
8. Staff training
9. AOB
10. Date of next meeting

John Sargeant
Secretary
1st September 2003

An agenda

agents of tourism development are the various individuals and organisations that facilitate or carry out tourism developments. On an international scale, commercial and government organisations work in partnership to promote their particular countries as tourist destinations, in order to reap economic, social, cultural and political benefits.

AGM: see *annual general meeting*

Agricultural Training Board (ATB): see *ATB Landbase*

AHI: see *Association for Heritage Interpretation*

AIDA stands for attention, interest, desire and action. It is a principle that should be followed when carrying out any promotional work involved with *marketing communications*. If we take the example of designing a newspaper *advertisement* for a newly opened *tourist attraction*, AIDA could be applied as follows:

- **Interest** is generated by using colour, bold headlines and a picture of a famous personality.

- **Attention** is maintained by keeping the wording as brief as possible and including language and images that the reader can easily relate to.

- A **desire** to visit the attraction is created by offering a discount voucher within the advertisement.

- **Action** is triggered by clearly stating the opening times, including a location map and printing the address, telephone number, *e-mail* address or *website* for enquiries.

AIDA is equally applicable when writing a *direct mail* letter, designing an exhibition stand or selecting *sales promotion* materials.

AIM: see *Association of Independent Museums*

aims: see *objectives*

Air Miles: a commercial, promotional scheme linked to purchases of goods and services, and the use of *credit cards*. Prospective travellers accumulate Air Miles every time they buy certain products and trade them in for flights of differing value. The scheme has proved to be extremely popular and is a good way for an airline to fill unsold capacity on aircraft. Weblink: www.airmiles.co.uk

air traffic control is concerned with guiding aircraft into and out of airports, and keeping pilots informed of weather and landing conditions. In the UK, air traffic control is the responsibility of the *Civil Aviation Authority*, which regulates military and civilian flight movements in a number of clearly defined flight zones.

air transport: see *air travel*

air travel is the category of *transportation* that includes *scheduled air services* and *charter flights*. It has grown in popularity dramatically since the end of the Second World War, coupled with the growth in *package holidays* and the movement of people from cooler northern European countries to sunny Mediterranean *destinations*. Air travel is also an important aspect of *business tourism*, with the advantages of speed, range and status. Recent developments in aircraft technology have allowed greater flight distances between stops, opening up hitherto remote parts of the world, the so-called *long haul destinations,* such as the Caribbean, Australasia, India, the Far East and countries in Africa. The use of air travel for domestic purposes has grown significantly in the UK in recent years, linked to the dramatic growth of *low-cost airlines* such as easyJet, go and Ryanair. Coupled with the steady growth in air travel has been the demand for greater capacity at airports, with extra runways and the expansion of facilities. (See also *transportation*.)

Air Travel Organiser's Licence (ATOL): a licence issued by the *Civil Aviation Authority (CAA)* and required by an individual or company selling holidays or seats on charter flights. Applicants must show that they are fit to hold an ATOL, have adequate financial arrangements and must lodge a bond with the *CAA*. In the event of company failure, the bond money is used to repatriate clients who might otherwise be stranded overseas and to refund, as far as possible, passengers who have paid in advance but not yet travelled. Where the bond is insufficient to meet all claims, the *Air Travel Trust Fund*, managed by the *CAA*, meets the shortfall. Twenty-three ATOL holders ceased trading in the year to March 2002. Weblink: www.atol.org.uk

Air Travel Reserve Fund: see *Air Travel Trust Fund (ATTF)*

Air Travel Trust Fund (ATTF): a fund set up in 1976 and administered by the *Civil Aviation Authority*. It is used when a bond lodged by the holder of an *Air Travel Organisers' Licence* is insufficient to meet all the claims against it. Previously known as the Air Travel Reserve Fund, the Trust Fund has been in deficit since 1996, but continues to protect the public using loans with the backing of a government guarantee. In the year to March 2002, £3.7 million was spent repatriating and refunding just under 20,000 passengers as a result of tour operator failures; of this total, £423,000 was contributed by the Trust, giving it an overall deficit of £8.3 million.

airline codes are unique reference symbols assigned to the worlds' airlines by the *International Civil Aviation Organisation (ICAO)* to be used in ticketing, timetables and reservations. Examples include BA (*British Airways*), BD (British Midland) and QF (Qantas).

airline deregulation is the process of withdrawing complete state control of *air travel* operations, creating a free market environment within which companies can compete with each other for business. The benefits of more private sector involvement in air travel should be better services and cheaper fares, although some people fear reductions in standards of safety and the withdrawal of loss-making routes. The USA was the first country to deregulate its airlines in 1978, leading to a rise in the number of carriers and the development of the *hub and spoke system*, as a way of reducing costs. Airline deregulation in Europe has yet to be fully achieved, with pressure from countries with existing state airlines, including France and Italy, to delay deregulation indefinitely.

airtime: the name given to time bought on radio or television as part of an *advertising campaign*. Airtime rates vary greatly, depending on the size of the audience and the region of the country used.

AITO: see *Association of Independent Tour Operators*

Albemarle Report: an influential report published in 1960 with the full title 'The Youth Service in England and Wales', which stressed the need for a greater range and distribution of better quality facilities for *sport* and indoor *recreation* for young people.

allocation: a block of airline seats, hotel rooms or *self-catering accommodation* that is reserved for the exclusive use of a particular *tour operator* or *travel agent*, under the terms of an agreement. The operator or agent has first call on their allocation until a specified release date, after which the seats or accommodation may be freely sold to other companies or individuals.

allocentric: one of a number of types of tourist behaviour developed by Plog in 1977 as part of a research study for airline companies. Allocentrics were people who enjoyed travel and cultural exploration, were in above average income groups, independent in mind and body, and adventurous. (See also *psychocentric, mid-centric*).

alternative tourism: see *green tourism*

Alton Towers is one of the UK's most popular *tourist attractions* for which an entrance fee is charged. Owned by the *Tussauds Group*, the Alton Towers *theme park* includes a number of *white knuckle rides* and catering outlets. Located close to the M6 motorway, it has a regional and even national *catchment area*. Weblink: www.alton-towers.co.uk

ALVA: see *Association of Leading Visitor Attractions*

AMA: see *Association of Metropolitan Authorities*

Amadeus: a *computerised reservation system (CRS)* operated by a number of European airlines including Iberia, Lufthansa and Air France, set up in 1987 to compete directly with the US *Sabre* and *Apollo* systems. Weblink: www.amadeus.com

American Express (Amex): a multinational corporation that, like *Thomas Cook*, was one of the founding companies in the worldwide *travel and tourism industry*. It initiated *traveller's cheques* in the late nineteenth century in the USA and became involved in travel operations early in the twentieth century. American Express has concentrated primarily on providing services for business travellers and in currency exchange. The company is also well known for its *charge card*, which is managed by a separate business unit within the corporation. Weblink: www.americanexpress.co.uk

American Plan: an accommodation arrangement based on full board, with a room and three meals per day provided. (See also *Modified American Plan, Continental Plan, European Plan*.)

American Society of Travel Agents (ASTA) is a representative body for *travel agents* and *tour operators* based in the USA. ASTA undertakes a similar role in its own country to that taken by *ABTA* in Britain, but it has a wider geographical sphere of influence given the importance of the USA as a major tourist-generating country. ASTA has in the region of 20,000 members in 125 countries around the world. Weblink: www.astanet.com

Amex: see *American Express*

Amtrak is the official government-funded rail service operated in the USA. Weblink: www.amtrak.com

animateur: see *animator*

animator: a person who takes on the role of an entertainer of *tourists*, by becoming directly involved in the experience they are enjoying, e.g. a costumed guide at a *heritage museum* such as Ironbridge Gorge, or a person acting the role of a Victorian teacher at the Wigan Pier attraction. Derived from the French word animateur, they become part of the tourist experience and are sometimes used as *visitor management* tools, e.g. actors and jugglers entertaining people queuing to get into Jorvik Viking Centre in York.

annual general meeting (AGM): a gathering held every twelve months to which members of a *company*, society, *charity* or similar organisation are invited, often to elect new *directors* or officials. It is a legal requirement for a limited company to hold an AGM, to which all *shareholders* are invited, in order to approve the *accounts* for the year, take part in the election of directors and ask questions of the chairman and other board members.

annual report: a document which looks back over the previous twelve-month period of a *limited company* or other organisation, highlighting successes and achievements. By law, limited companies must publish an annual report and accounts, which must be sent to every *shareholder*. It must contain a *balance sheet*, a *profit and loss account*, and a *cash-flow statement*. Large *leisure* and *tourism* companies, such as Manchester United, *British Airways* and the *Rank Group*, produce glossy annual reports to contribute towards their image building. *Public sector organisations*, such as the *British Tourist Authority, Sport England* and the *Countryside Agency*, also produce annual reports, to give interested parties details of their activities and achievements.

annual percentage rate (APR) is a figure that gives the true cost of a *loan*, in percentage terms, based on the amount of the loan outstanding. Under the terms of the *Consumer Credit Act 1974*, lenders are legally obliged to quote the APR on loans, rather than the often misleading flat interest rate figure, which can make a loan seem cheaper than it really is. By comparing one APR with another, a borrower can identify the cheapest loan that meets his or her needs.

annual spending on sport: see *sport*

Ansoff's matrix is a model that can be used by an organisation to develop the most profitable range of *products* and services it offers to its customers, sometimes referred to as its *product portfolio*. It is a type of *portfolio analysis* that allows an organisation to examine what it can do to its products and the markets they are sold in, so as to expand its operation (see figure on next page).

MARKET

	Existing	New

Ansoff's matrix

The figure shows that an organisation has four possible courses of action. It can focus on existing customers by either modifying an existing product (sector 1) or introducing new products to them (sector 2), or concentrate on attracting new markets, with either new products (sector 3) or by repositioning an existing product (sector 4). All four courses of action has a degree of risk attached to them, although launching a new product to a new market is likely to be the highest risk scenario of them all.

ANTOR: see *Association of National Tourist Office Representatives in Great Britain*

AONB: see *Area of Outstanding Natural Beauty*

apartotel: a term used to describe a type of *accommodation* which is a mixture of an apartment and a *hotel*, e.g. providing furnished accommodation plus optional services such as a restaurant or maid service.

APEX: see *advance purchase excursion*

Apollo: a *computerised reservation system (CRS)* developed by United Airlines in the USA and made available to agents in Europe from 1987. (See also *Galileo*.)

appraisal: see *staff appraisal*

appropriate tourism: see *green tourism*

APR: see *annual percentage rate*

AQA: see *Assessment and Qualifications Alliance*

arbitration is the practice of resolving a dispute by inviting an independent person to listen to both sides of an argument and make a judgement as to a fair resolution of the problem. Disputes in the workplace, perhaps concerning working conditions or pay, are often resolved through arbitration, sometimes involving experts from the *Advisory Conciliation and Arbitration Service (ACAS)*. Arbitration is sometimes known as conciliation or mediation.

Area of Outstanding Natural Beauty (AONB): set up under the 1949 National Parks and Access to the Countryside Act, there are currently 37 AONBs in England and Wales, given protected status on account of their scenic beauty (see figure accompanying *National Parks*). They range from the *green belt* countryside of the Surrey Hills to the open moorlands of the North Pennines. Many AONBs are popular destinations for *leisure* and *tourism*, although, unlike *National Parks*, they are not designated primarily for their recreational value. The *Countryside Agency* is responsible for designating AONBs and providing advice to government and others on how they should be protected and managed. Weblink: www.countryside.gov.uk/aonb

arena: a large, purpose-built indoor facility with the flexibility to be used for a variety of purposes, including *sports* events, exhibitions, concerts and circuses. Most large UK cities have at least one arena, e.g. the MEN Arena in Manchester, Sheffield Arena, Birmingham Arena at the *NEC* and Wembley Arena.

arithmetic average: see *mean*

ARR: see *average room rate*

Articles of Association: one of the two documents that *limited companies* must produce under the terms of the *Companies Act* 1985, the other being the *Memorandum of Association*. The Articles of Association is akin to the company's set of rules, outlining details regarding the frequency of meetings, types of shares, voting procedures, the names of *directors* and their powers, and other company matters.

arts and entertainment: an important sector within the UK *leisure and recreation industry*, covering a wide range of activities, including:

- visiting art galleries
- going to music concerts
- visits to the *cinema* and theatre
- attending exhibitions
- playing computer games at home
- playing bingo at a social club
- watching sports events
- taking evening classes
- following hobbies in the home
- visiting a pub or wine bar.

While *public* and *voluntary sector* organisations are responsible for providing a range of arts and cultural facilities in their local communities, e.g. art galleries, *museums*, theatres, etc., the majority of arts and entertainment facilities are important revenue-earners for the *private sector*, with companies such as *Rank*, Virgin and Granada being major players in the sector. (See also *Metier*.)

Arts Council of England is an independent, non-political body working at arm's length from the government to encourage and promote all aspects of the arts in England. On 1st April 2002 the Arts Council of England and the ten *Regional Arts Boards (RABs)* joined together to form a single development organisation for the arts. The new organisation is responsible for developing, sustaining and promoting the arts in England. The Council is funded by the *Department of Culture, Media and Sport (DCMS)*; its grant in 2002-2003 amounted to £295 million. In addition, it received £208 million from *National Lottery* proceeds. (See also *Arts Council of Wales, Arts Council of Northern Ireland, Scottish Arts Council*). Weblink: www.artscouncil.org.uk

Arts Council of Northern Ireland: the prime distributor of public support for the arts in Northern Ireland. It was established in 1962 as a successor to the Committee for the Encouragement of Music and the Arts, and became a statutory body on 1 September 1995. Its functions include the development and improvement of knowledge, appreciation and practice of the arts, and increasing public access to, and participation in, the arts. Weblink: www.artscouncil-ni.org

Arts Council of Wales: the body responsible for funding and developing the arts in Wales. It became accountable to the *National Assembly for Wales* on 1 July 1999. The Council receives funding from the National Assembly and from the *National Lottery*, via the *Department for Culture, Media and Sport*. The Council works with many partners in carrying out its duties, including the professional, community and voluntary arts, *local authorities* and other sectors. Weblink: www.artswales.org.uk

ASA: see *Advertising Standards Authority*

assertiveness training is concerned with developing a degree of self-confidence in an individual, so that he or she is able to put across a point of view without appearing to be unduly aggressive. In the work environment, it is important for staff to be able to control their emotions, particularly in circumstances where they are in regular contact with the general public.

Assessment and Qualifications Alliance (AQA): an independent awarding and examinations company that offers a range of educational qualifications, including *vocational qualifications* in leisure, travel and tourism. AQA came into existence in April 2000 following the merger of the Associated Examining Board and the Northern Examinations and Assessment Board. It is the largest of the three unitary awarding bodies and is accountable to the *Qualifications and Curriculum Authority*. (See also *Edexcel, OCR*.) Weblink: www.aqa.org.uk

asset: an item that is owned by an individual or organisation and which has a certain value. In *leisure* and *tourism* businesses, assets are normally divided into those intended for long-term use (*fixed assets*), e.g. buildings, land, equipment and machinery, and those readily convertible into cash (*current assets*), e.g. stock such as food and drink.

Association of British Travel Agents (ABTA) is the trade body that currently represents 6698 travel agency members and 999 tour operator members, with a combined turnover of £36 billion. Ninety per cent of the UK's *package holidays* are sold through ABTA members. The Association was formed in 1950, when new aircraft technology and greater personal freedom were giving people the means to travel further afield. ABTA's principal aims are to:

- establish an organisation which is fully representative of travel agents and tour operators in the UK

- promote and develop the general interests of all its members
- establish and maintain *codes of conduct* between members and the general public, with the object that membership of ABTA will be recognised as a guarantee of integrity, competence and high standards of service
- discourage unfair competition without interfering with initiative and enterprise based on fair trading
- promote friendly relations with others in the *travel industry*
- liaise with other bodies concerned with the development of travel in the UK and abroad.

The Association is a self-regulatory body run by its membership, via a network of councils and committees, with members appointed by member travel agents and tour operators. Members of ABTA are required to adhere to strict rules governing their business practice. These are contained in ABTA's Codes of Conduct which regulate all aspects of tour operators' and travel agents' relationships with their customers and which have been drawn up in conjunction with the *Office of Fair Trading*. In addition to its Codes of Conduct, ABTA seeks to protect the interests of the travelling public through its conciliation and arbitration schemes, which provide opportunities for travellers who have reason to complain, to have their problems investigated and appropriate action taken. In 2001 ABTA dealt with 17,500 complaints and paid out £2.2 million in respect of travel agents' failures and £90,000 to cover the failure of tour operators. (See also *Stabiliser*, *ABTA bond*, *Tour Operators' Code of Conduct* and *Travel Agents' Code of Conduct*.) Weblink: www.abta.com

Association of County Councils (ACC): the former independent organisation which represented the shire *county councils* in England and Wales, on matters such as transport policies, European legislation and economic development. The ACC ceased to exist in 1997, but its work continues within *the Local Government Association (LGA.)*

Association of District Councils (ADC): the former independent body which represented the interests of the non-metropolitan *district councils* in England and Wales, on matters ranging from environmental policy, *Uniform Business Rates* to *compulsory competitive tendering*. The ADC sought to promote local government and work towards forging partnerships between *local* and *central government*. The ADC was also active in promoting the value of *leisure* services and *tourism* at local level. It ceased to exist in 1997, but its work continues within *the Local Government Association*.

Association of Independent Museums (AIM) was established in 1977 to provide a forum for *museums* not directly administered by central or local government. AIM endeavours to further the cause of independent museums, to continue to increase professional standards and promote self-help among its members, and generally increase museum awareness. The Association is run on a voluntary basis by members, with subscription fees kept as low as possible. Current AIM members include the London Transport Museum and the National Tramway Museum. Weblink: www.museums.org.uk

Association of Independent Tour Operators (AITO) is an alliance of over 150 smaller, specialist tour operating companies in the UK. Established in 1976, AITO's *objectives* include helping member companies to market more effectively, ensuring the public can book members' holidays with confidence, promoting *sustainable tourism*, keeping members up to date with the issues of the day and encouraging higher standards and greater professionalism among its members. (See also *Campaign for Real Travel Agents*.) Weblink: www.aito.co.uk

Association of Leading Visitor Attractions (ALVA): an independent membership organisation that was set up in 1990 to fill a perceived gap in the framework of national tourism bodies. ALVA's mission is 'to represent to government, the tourism industry, the *media* and the public, the views and achievements of the country's foremost visitor attractions in matters which concern the effectiveness of *UK tourism* and the interests of the Association, whilst promoting co-operation and high standards of visitor management among its members'. Current members of ALVA include Blackpool Tower, the British Museum, Buckingham Palace and York Minster. In total, ALVA member *attractions* welcome some 85 million visitors per year. Weblink: www.alva.org.uk

Association of Metropolitan Authorities (AMA): the former independent body which represented Metropolitan Districts in England, the London Boroughs and the Corporation of the City of London. AMA ceased to exist in 1997, but its work continues within *the Local Government Association*.

Association of National Tourist Office Representatives in Great Britain (ANTOR) is a voluntary body representing more than 80 National Tourist Offices (NTOs) based in Britain. It acts as a forum for the exchange of ideas among its members and works with the *travel trade* to promote its member countries. ANTOR produces its own World Travel Guide annually. Weblink: www.tourist-offices.org.uk

Association of Tourism Teachers and Trainers (ATTT): established in 1975 as the Association of Teachers of Tourism, with the aim of helping its members to be more effective teachers of tourism subjects, the ATTT is a specialist section within the *Tourism Society*. ATTT provides a forum for discussion of matters relating to tourism education and training at all levels. It acts as a *pressure group* to promote high standards of professionalism in tourism education and training, as well as extending links between employers and tourism educators and trainers. The affairs of the ATTT are organised by a voluntary committee elected from the Tourism Society membership. Weblink: www.tourismsociety.org

Association for Conferences and Events (ACE) is a trading name of the Association of Conference Executives Ltd., which was established in 1971 to act as a forum for member organisations who are involved in all facets of the industry. ACE offers a range of services to its members, including a helpline for advice and information, mailings of job vacancies, a regular letter and a series of workshops. In 1992, ACE was involved in the development of *National Vocational Qualifications* for the business travel sector and has since been involved in extending the NVQ system into the events services sector.

Association for Heritage Interpretation (AHI): a key UK forum for anyone interested in *interpretation*, which it defines as 'the art of helping people explore and appreciate our world'. Founded in 1975 as the *Society for the Interpretation of Britain's Heritage*, AHI aims to promote high standards in the provision of interpretation and to gain wider recognition of interpretation as a professional activity. It runs events, publishes a journal and runs a respected awards scheme. Weblink: www.heritageinterpretation.org.uk

Association for Tourism in Higher Education (ATHE) is a consortium of providers of tourism in higher education, which continues the work of the former *National Liaison Group for Tourism in Higher Education*, originally established in 1993. ATHE was formed in December 2000 with a number of objectives, including developing and promoting links between tourism education and industry, advancing the recognition of tourism as a subject of study and encouraging high standards in tourism course provision. ATHE members include many of the leading UK higher education institutions with interests in tourism, including the University of Surrey, Sheffield Hallam University and the University of Plymouth. Weblink: www.athe.org.uk

ASTA: see *American Society of Travel Agents*

ATB: see *ATB Landbase*

ATB Landbase: an organisation formerly involved in assessing training needs and providing courses for the land-based industries, such as agriculture, horticulture, equine management, *rural tourism* and *recreation*, *conservation* and forestry. Previously known as the Agricultural Training Board, ATB Landbase worked with *Training and Enterprise Councils (TECs)* and colleges to meet the need at local level for practical, supervisory and management training. On April 1 1998, ATB Landbase became part of *Lantra*, the *National Training Organisation* (NTO) for the land-based sector.

ATHE: see *Association for Tourism in Higher Education*

ATLAS: see *European Association for Education in Tourism, Leisure and the Arts*

ATOL: see *Air Travel Organisers' Licence*

ATTF: see *Air Travel Trust Fund*

attitude of the staff working in leisure, travel and tourism is vital to the success of an organisation, whatever its size. Employees must have a positive attitude to their duties, a friendly yet professional manner with customers and a determination to succeed. An outgoing *personality* is often an advantage for anybody seeking employment in leisure, travel and tourism.

attractions are one of the three core components of the *tourism* industry, along with *transportation* and *accommodation*; indeed they are often the very reason why visitors decide to venture out. In 2001, the British Airways London Eye was the most popular UK paid attraction with 3.85 million visitors. However, the free entry to Blackpool Pleasure Beach made it the number one UK tourist attraction in the same year with 6.5 million visitors. Attractions can be classified into those that are naturally occurring and those that are man-made. Throughout time, *natural attractions* have always been a powerful motivating force behind people's desire to travel. On an international scale, the Himalayas, the Amazon rain forest, the Sahara Desert, the Alps, the Black Sea, the Rocky Mountains and the Victoria Falls (to name but a few) have all welcomed visitors in their millions. Closer to home, the *National Parks* in England and Wales, the Scottish Highlands and the Giant's Causeway, are still important visitor destinations. *Man-made attractions* are purpose-built facilities designed to provide fun, excitement and entertainment.

ATTT: see *Association of Tourism Teachers and Trainers*

audit: an independent investigation into the financial or operational aspects of an organisation, often prior to a change in *policy* or operation, or in response to a problem. Audits are most often associated with the financial resources of an organisation, but may also be concerned with environmental or health and safety matters. (See also *environmental audit*.)

Audit Commission: a government agency responsible for ensuring that *local authorities*, *quangos* and other national bodies receiving public funds are effectively and efficiently managed, and that the public is getting value for money from the provision of a range of services, including *leisure* and *recreation* facilities. Weblink: www.audit-commission.gov.uk

authoritarian leadership: see *autocratic leadership*

authority: the right to take actions and make decisions. In the workplace, authority is often delegated from managers to their subordinates, but managers are, at the end of the day, accountable for their own actions and ultimately responsible for the actions of the staff under their control. (See also *delegation, accountability, responsibility*.)

autocratic leadership is a leadership style most commonly associated with *centralised, hierarchical organisational structures* (*steep pyramids*), where decision making rests with a small number of senior staff. This may be because senior managers distrust their staff or because they are unwilling to delegate responsibility down the hierarchy. Autocratic leadership, sometimes called authoritarian leadership, can often lead to a demoralised workforce.

Automobile Association (AA): one of the foremost motoring organisations in Europe, which, in 1912, introduced a star rating system for *hotels* and other *accommodation* in the UK. Today the AA *accommodation grading scheme* has developed to encompass one to five star appointments for hotels and a 'listing' category for private hotels, guesthouses, farmhouses and inns. AA inspectors make unannounced visits on an annual basis to accommodation establishments within the classification scheme, in order to ensure that standards of service and quality of facilities are being maintained. Hotels that consistently provide outstanding levels of hospitality, service, food and comfort are recognised by the awarding of one to five red stars, the AA's ultimate accolade for quality. Weblink: www.theaa.com

AVC: see *additional voluntary contribution*

AVCE: see *Advanced Vocational Certificate in Education*

average room rate (ARR) is an important *performance indicator* used in the *management* of *hotels* and other *accommodation* establishments, since it shows the average price paid by guests on a particular day or other period of time. It is calculated by dividing the value of rooms sold by the total number of rooms occupied, e.g.

$$\frac{£2400}{40 \text{ rooms}} = \text{an ARR of } £60$$

Once the ARR has been calculated, comparisons can be made between different time periods and even different establishments.

What other subjects are you studying?

A–Zs cover 18 different subjects. See the inside back cover for a list of all the titles in the series and how to order.

BAA: see *British Airports Authority*

BABA: see *book-a-bed-ahead*

back of house: see *back office*

back office is a term used to denote certain organisational functions that are carried out 'behind the scenes', away from direct contact with customers and the public in general. Sometimes referred to as 'back of house', these functions include accounting, security, maintenance, *stock control* and *marketing*. There must be a strong link between these back office functions and the *front office*, denoting the reception point in a leisure or tourism facility. For example, when a guest books into a hotel at reception, information must be conveyed, either manually but more likely via a *computer* system, to other departments that need to know, such as housekeeping, accounts, food and beverage, laundry and marketing. The concept of a back office is widespread in leisure and tourism, not just in hotels but also in *leisure centres*, entertainment complexes and *tourist information centres*.

back-to-back: the practice of a single *charter* aircraft flying to an overseas *destination* with a full load of passengers and returning with another full load of passengers who have just completed their holiday. Back-to-back arrangements ensure that an airline maximises its capacity at all times, thereby reducing its costs.

BACT: see *British Association of Conference Towns*

bad debt: an unpaid bill or account that has not been settled and which is unlikely ever to be repaid, perhaps because the *debtor* has ceased trading. It is important for organisations to keep a tight control of its debtor situation by chasing late payments and not granting credit too freely. Bad debtor control can have a serious effect on a company's *cash-flow* position.

baggage allowance is the weight of luggage that airline passengers are allowed to take with them without incurring an excess charge. Currently the allowance is 20kg (44lb) for economy passengers and 30kg (66lb) for those travelling first class with scheduled carriers, but other allowances may be set by *low-cost airlines*.

BAHA: see *British Activity Holiday Association*

balance of payments is a statement of the inflows and outflows of currency to and from a particular country earned from its *imports* and *exports*. A nation's balance of payments is divided into its capital account and current account, which can be thought of as being similar to an individual's savings and current accounts. The capital account is made up of investments, grants and loans, while the current account is sub-divided into 'visible' and 'invisible' items. Travel, tourism and leisure are 'invisible' items on the current account. The difference between a country's receipts from *incoming tourism* and the expenditure by its residents on travel abroad is shown separately as the *travel* (or tourism) *balance*.

balance sheet: a statement of an organisation's *assets*, *liabilities* and *capital* and a summary of its financial position at a given point in time, usually the last day of the financial year (see figure below). Balance sheets are constructed at least on an annual basis and often more frequently than this, depending on an organisation's financial systems. An organisation's ability to pay off outstanding debts can be assessed by comparing *current assets* with *current liabilities*, as shown in the balance sheet. It can also be used to determine the extent to which an organisation is able to borrow funds from external sources without straining its capability to service its debts.

Balance sheet for 'Spangles' café

	£	£
FIXED ASSETS		
Lease on premises	25,000	
Fixtures and fittings	7,000	
Kitchen equipment	4,000	
Van	3,500	39,500
CURRENT ASSETS		
Stock	2,000	
Debtors	1,500	
Bank	6,000	
Cash	200	
Total current assets	9,700	
CURRENT LIABILITIES		
Creditors	3,000	
Total current liabilities	3,000	
NET CURRENT ASSETS		6,700
TERM LOAN		(3,000)
		43,200
OWNER'S CAPITAL EMPLOYED		
At start	15,000	
Profit for period	28,200	
		43,200

banker's draft: a *cheque* drawn by a bank, as distinct from a personal cheque written by an account holder. Sometimes called certified cheques, they give the payee a greater degree of security, particularly when payment is needed quickly and there is no time to go through the normal cheque clearing process. Banker's drafts are also an easy way of accepting payment in a foreign currency.

Bank Holidays were first introduced in the UK during the *Industrial Revolution*, under the Bank Holiday Act of 1871, which created four public holidays per year. They became the magnet for trips to the countryside and coast, with resorts such as Brighton, Scarborough and Margate welcoming thousands of visitors on Bank Holdays. Today, changes in working practices, greater mobility and changes in trading laws mean that Bank Holidays are no longer viewed by many people as a time to relax, but rather a chance to indulge in some DIY or go *shopping* to the many out-of-town retail complexes around the country, e.g. Lakeside, Bluewater, Meadowhall and Metrocentre.

bar chart: a useful way of presenting data to give an immediate comparison between variables, e.g. the trend in overseas visits to a country or the monthly sales figures for a *leisure centre*. Bar charts can be drawn either vertically or horizontally, with the heights of the bars corresponding to the values indicated (see figure below).

County of origin of visitors to theme park

BATO: see *British Association of Tourism Officers*

BCC: see *Bus and Coach Council*

BCG: see *Boston Consulting Group matrix*

bed and breakfast is a type of *serviced accommodation* offered in private households, popular because it offers excellent value for money and allows guests to experience the way of life of the owners of the establishment. It is particularly popular with *overseas visitors* to Britain who want to sample the 'real' British way of life, whether it is on a Welsh or Scottish farm or in an historic city such as York or Bath. Bed and breakfast is also an accommodation and meal arrangement offered by all types of serviced accommodation comprising a room and British or continental breakfast. (See also *Continental Plan*.)

Belbin's team types: a theory concerned with the development of effectives teams. Based on research with over 200 teams conducting management business games at the Administrative Staff College at Henley, Belbin identified the following nine team types: co-ordinator, resource investigator, team worker, shaper, company worker/implementer, completer finisher, plant, monitor/evaluator and specialist. Members of teams will almost always represent a mix of roles and will play dominant and sub-dominant roles from time to time.

below-the-line promotion refers to marketing activity for which *commission* is not normally paid to an *advertising agency*, but the work is carried out on a fee basis instead, e.g. an agency may charge a fee of £8000 to carry out a small *direct mail* campaign for a travel company. As well as *direct mail*, other below-the-line activities include *public relations*, *sales promotions* and *merchandising*.

benchmarking is a process of setting industry standards of performance based on the achievements of the most efficient companies in the sector. It is beginning to be applied to the *UK tourism* industry, under an initiatives developed by the *Confederation of British Industry* and *English Tourism Council.*

benefits statement: part of the *sales process* in *leisure* and *tourism* when a sales person indicates specifically what a product or service can do for an individual customer. The information given is selected on the basis of the customer's *needs* and should, if presented in a positive fashion, persuade him or her to commit to a sale. The sales person can then make the necessary arrangements to *close the sale*. (See also *features statement*, *advantages statement*.)

Bermuda Agreement: an *air travel* protocol developed between Britain and the USA, which restricted air carriage between the two countries to the national carriers alone. Agreed initially in 1946, soon after the *Chicago Convention on Civil Aviation*, the Bermuda Agreement was subsequently modified in 1977.

berth: the term used to describe a bedspace on a ship or train. May also be used to mean the place where a ship comes to rest in a harbour.

Best Value: a statutory initiative introduced under the 1999 Local Government Act. Since 1 April 2000 all *local authorities* have been obliged to implement Best Value, which requires them to '...secure continuous improvement in the way functions are carried out having regard to a combination of economy, efficiency and effectiveness'. The Best Value initiative's effect on the provision of leisure and tourism facilities will call for councils to measure the performance of their services and explore the best ways that they can be delivered.

BFI: see *British Film Institute*

BHTS: see *British Home Tourism Survey*

BISL: see *Business in Sport and Leisure*

BITOA: see *British Incoming Tour Operators' Association*

Blue Badge guides: individuals registered with a *Regional Tourist Board* and able to offer a range of *guiding services* to visitors, after completion of a training course. In the most important development since the introduction of the Blue Badge qualification in the early 1950s, the Institute of Tourist Guiding (ITG) was launched in April 2002 as the standard-setting body not only for Blue Badge tourist guides but for the whole tourist guiding sector.

Blue Flag Campaign: a scheme that provides a comparison between standards of cleanliness and *management* at European resort beaches. Launched in 1987, the European Year of the Environment, a Blue Flag is awarded to resort beaches which have achieved the guideline standard of the *EU Bathing Water Directive*. There is some concern in the UK at the way in which the Directive has been implemented, and tourism organisations are pressing for a simplified system of operation for the future. The Blue Flag scheme is co-ordinated in the UK by ENCAMs, a body concerned with environmental campaigns. (See also *Seaside Award*.) Weblink: www.seasideawards.org.uk

BOA: see *British Olympic Association*

boarding pass: authorisation issued to a traveller to allow him or her to board an aircraft, cruise ship, train or ferry. Passengers are sometimes required to show their boarding passes when making *duty-free* purchases on board. Boarding passes used on ships are sometimes called embarkation passes.

body language is a common type of *non-verbal communication*, involving the transmission of messages through gestures of the body, such as a shrug of the shoulders to show indifference, banging a table to display anger, a particular facial expression, eye contact or bodily contact.

booking systems are an essential requirement in the leisure, travel and tourism industries, as a way of monitoring sales, controlling access to facilities and *events*, and ensuring financial and other *resources* are used effectively. Booking systems may be either manual, based on charts and card files, or computerised. Many organisations that formerly used manual systems have transferred their *data* onto *computers*, because of the greater speed and storage capacity they offer.

bonding is concerned with providing financial security in order to compensate travellers in the event of a *company* failure. *ABTA tour operators* and *travel agents*, for example, must deposit a bond on joining the Association, so that travellers can be financially compensated should there be a problem with a holiday. (See also *ABTA bond*.)

bonus: a regular or one-off payment to an employee in appreciation of hard work and effort, or in relation to the completion of a specific project or campaign. *Overseas representatives* may be paid a bonus by their *tour operator* at the end of the season, hotel workers sometimes receive a bonus at Christmas and a manager of a major *tourist attraction* may be paid a bonus at the end of an exceptionally successful year.

book-a-bed-ahead (BABA): a booking service offered by *tourist information centres (TICs)* in the UK, whose staff will make a reservation in a hotel or other type of *accommodation* through another TIC or direct with an establishment anywhere in the country, in return for a small fee or *commission* (normally 10 per cent).

borough council: see *district council*

Boston box: see *Boston Consulting Group matrix*

Boston Consulting Group (BCG) matrix: a model that can be used by *marketing* managers to analyse their likely *strategies* for future survival and expansion. Developed in the early 1960s in the USA, and sometimes also referred to as the Boston box or the Boston matrix, the BCG is a type of *portfolio analysis* that allows an organisation to judge how its current products and services are performing and what changes, if any, need to be made to its *product portfolio*, to ensure future success (see figure on next page).

The figure shows that the matrix compares the rate of market growth of particular products with their relative share of the market. 'Stars' are those products and services that enjoy a high market growth rate and a high *market share*, while at the other end of the spectrum, 'dogs' have both a low market growth rate and a low share of the market. In between are the *'cash cows'*, products that have a high share of a stable market, and 'question marks', where the rate of growth is high but market share is low.

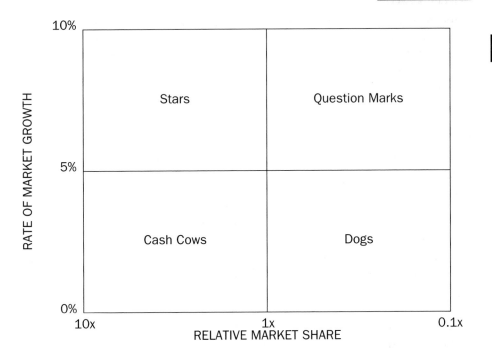

Boston Consulting Group matrix

Boston matrix: see *Boston Consulting Group matrix*

BR: see *British Rail*

BRA: see *British Resorts Association*

BRAD: see *British Rate and Data*

brainstorming is a way for members of a group to solve problems or develop new ideas by saying the first things that come into their heads. This spontaneous action sometimes leads to innovative ideas and solutions, which standard *management* decision-making practices may miss. Having 'brainstormed' a list of ideas, the group members can then consider each in detail and make further recommendations for action.

brand: an identifiable product or service name or *image* offered by a company, e.g. Virgin, Harvester, Reebok or Avis. Customers often buy leisure and tourism products and services from companies with well-known brand names, since there is an expectation of a degree of quality and consistency often attached to the brand.

brand awareness is the extent to which a customer recognises one particular *brand* over another, e.g. the fact that a customer is aware of the difference between *British Airways'* First Class service and Virgin Atlantic's Upper Class service. Brand awareness is measured through *surveys* and other *market research* techniques and can lead to alterations in the way that products and services are promoted.

brand leader: the product or service that has the greatest volume of sales in its particular product category. Eurocamp, for example, is the brand leader in self-drive camping holidays to the Continent, since it sells more of this type of holiday than any other operator. In order to remain the brand leader, an organisation must hold on to its *market share*.

brand loyalty is shown when *customers* continue to purchase a particular product or service on a regular basis. A couple, for example, may book their annual holiday with the same *tour operator* every year, or choose the same car hire firm for business trips. Encouraging brand loyalty makes very good business sense, since research in the USA has shown that it takes five times as much effort, time and money to attract a new customer than it does to keep an existing customer. Companies may offer incentives to existing customers to develop their brand loyalty, e.g. airline *frequent flyer programmes* or discounted prices.

branding is the practice of giving a product or service a distinctive name or logo, in the hope that it will become easily identifiable from its competitors and take on a certain identity. Branding is linked to the concept of *market segmentation*, with *brands* being developed to meet the needs of different segments of the market. Common brand names used in leisure and tourism include Harvester, Avis, Reebok, Holiday Inn, Sky and Slazenger, to name but a few. Organisations hope that customers will show *brand loyalty*, by buying their particular products above all others.

breakeven denotes the point at which an organisation's sales generate just enough *revenue* to cover *fixed* and *variable costs*, with no *profit* nor any loss. The break-even point is often shown on a break-even chart, as shown in the figure below.

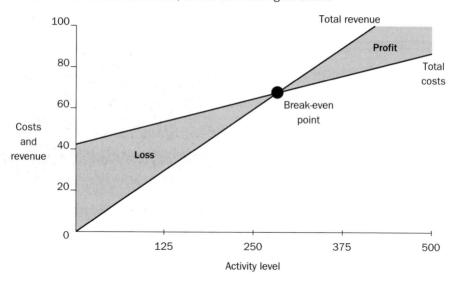

break-even load factor is a measure of the number of seats that need to be sold on an airline flight, as a proportion of total seats available, before all operating, *marketing* and administrative costs are covered. It is not uncommon on charter flights for the break-even factor to be set as high as 90-95 per cent, so as to bring down the actual cost per seat to a level which will encourage people to buy. It is only when the break-even load figure has been reached that the airline will begin to make a profit on the flight.

bridleway: a *public right of way* suitable for use by horse riders, walkers and cyclists, but not by vehicles.

briefing: a meeting at which an individual or group of people are given information prior to taking part in an *event* or attending a meeting. A briefing session will not only convey factual information, but may also advise which course of action to take if particular circumstances occur, e.g. an emergency at an outdoor event. (See also *debriefing*.)

Britain consists of England, Wales, Scotland and Northern Ireland, and is sometimes more fully described as Great Britain. Islands around Britain that are part of the *United Kingdom* include the Orkneys, Shetlands, Isles of Scilly, Anglesey and the Isle of Wight. The Isle of Man and Channel Islands have their own administrations.

Britain in Bloom is an annual environmental enhancement competition co-ordinated by the Royal Horticultural Society (RHS). The scheme is divided into a number of different categories depending on the population size of a city, town or rural area. Weblink: www.rhs.org.uk/britaininbloom

British Activity Holiday Association (BAHA) was formed by a number of *outdoor activity centre* operators in 1986, with the express intention of establishing operating guidelines for the safe and efficient management of activity centres. Since that time, BAHA has developed a *code of practice* for members, activity guidelines and an inspection scheme. The Association has also contributed to the debate on safety at outdoor activity centres generally and was a member of the *Activity Centre Advisory Committee (ACAC)*. Members of BAHA include PGL Adventure and Kingswood Learning and Leisure. Weblink: www.baha.org.uk

British Airports Authority (BAA) is a former government-controlled organisation that was privatised in 1987. Now a *public limited company*, BAA owns and operates seven UK airports – Heathrow, Gatwick, Stansted, Glasgow, Edinburgh, Aberdeen and Southampton, with management interests in airports in the USA, Italy, Oman and Australia. Every year, BAA takes responsibility for nearly 200 million passengers travelling through its airports, including over 120 million in the UK. Heathrow alone handles some 54 million passengers per year using more than 200 scheduled routes, confirming its status as the world's busiest international airport. BAA also manages the commercial facilities at its airports, including shops, restaurants, bars, bureaux de change and car parks. BAA is campaigning hard to ensure the construction of a fifth terminal at Heathrow to increase the airport's capacity by a further 30 million passengers a year. Weblink: www.baa.co.uk

British Airways (BA) is the world's biggest international passenger airline, carrying more passengers from one country to another than any of its competitors. In 2001, more than 48 million passengers chose to fly on the 53,000 flights that the company operated. BA has a worldwide route network covering some 263 destinations in 97 countries. BA employs 60,000 staff in around 100 countries. In seeking to achieve its mission of being 'the undisputed leader in world travel' BA has embarked upon a major *globalisation* programme, which it calls its Global Alliance. As part of this project, it helped to establish the One World alliance in 1999, with a number of airlines including Aer Lingus, American Airlines, Iberia and Qantas. Unlike many of the world's airlines, British Airways is owned entirely by private investors, with more than a quarter of a million *shareholders*. Weblink: www.britishairways.com

British Association of Conference Destinations: see *British Association of Conference Towns (BACT)*

British Association of Conference Towns (BACT) is a professional association representing all the major, and many of the smaller, conference *destinations* in the British Isles. Founded in 1969, BACT is now known as the British Association of Conference Destinations

(BACD) and represents more than 100 destinations and more than 3000 venues throughout the UK. The Association's primary objective is to promote the British Isles as a destination for conferences, exhibitions and *incentive travel*. The Association also organises *CONFER*, an exhibition currently held annually in London. Weblink: www.bacd.org.uk

British Association of Tourism Officers (BATO) is the former network of *tourism* professionals based in the *United Kingdom*, whose main common purpose was to come together and share best practice in the tourism industry, discuss topical issues and matters of concern, develop new ideas and act as an advisory organisation to government and other agencies. Most members of BATO worked in local authority tourism departments and other *public sector* bodies. BATO was dissolved in 1996 and replaced by the new *Tourism Management Institute* in April 1997.

British Film Institute (BFI): an independent organisation that aims to encourage the development of the art of film in Great Britain and Northern Ireland, and to promote its use as a record of contemporary life. Established in 1933, the BFI also seeks to encourage the best use of *television* in the United Kingdom and to foster the study and appreciation of films for television and television programmes generally. Weblink: www.bfi.org.uk

British Holiday and Home Parks Association: the nationally recognised representative body of the parks industry, including park homes, caravan holiday homes, chalets, touring caravans, tents and all forms of park *self-catering accommodation*. The Association works for the benefit of park owners and managers, servicing and representing their interests and promoting the *image* of the industry as a whole. It is a strong lobbying organisation, with access to decision makers in Westminster, Whitehall, Brussels, Strasbourg and *local authority* offices. Weblink: www.bhhpa.org.uk

British Home Tourism Survey (BHTS): a former consumer survey now replaced by the *United Kingdom Tourism Survey*.

British Hospitality Association (BHA): formerly the British Hotels, Restaurateurs and Caterers' Association, the BHA is an independent organisation established in 1910 to represent the interests of its members and the wider *hospitality industry*. The BHA lobbies government and the *European Commission* on matters of specific relevance to the industry, including taxation, proposed domestic legislation, the *Package Travel Directive* and changes to the *accommodation grading* systems. BHA acts as a campaigning voice for its members by liaising with the *trade press*, organising mailshots to members and co-ordinating stands at major exhibitions. Weblink: www.bha-online.org.uk

British Incoming Tour Operators' Association (BITOA) is an independent membership organisation representing around 100 *incoming tour operators* in the UK. Founded in 1977, BITOA aims to provide a forum for the exchange of information and ideas, to follow an accepted *code of conduct* and to act as a *pressure group* in dealing with government and other bodies in the UK with a common interest in tourism matters. Weblink: www.bitoa.co.uk

British Isles: this means the *United Kingdom* and the Republic of Ireland. (See also *Britain*.)

British Olympic Association (BOA): a national, voluntary organisation made up of representatives of the UK governing bodies of the sports included in the *Olympic Games*. Founded in 1905, the BOA aims to encourage, particularly in the young, the ideals of the Olympic movement, to co-ordinate British participation in the Games and to assist the governing bodies in their preparation. The BOA also acts as a forum for consultation on issues related to the Games, including drug abuse and the introduction of new Olympic sports. Weblink: www.olympics.org.uk

British Rail (BR): the former public corporation that used to own the UK rail network and was responsible for providing passenger and freight services nationwide. BR was privatised in the mid-1990s, with the establishment of *Railtrack* and a number of *train operating companies*. The government of the day believed that a *private sector* railway system would offer the travelling public a more efficient service than had hitherto been provided by the public sector. Opponents of rail privatisation considered that rural rail lines and others used infrequently would disappear, since they would not be an attractive investment for the private sector.

British Rate and Data (BRAD) is a monthly publication that contains up-to-date information on *advertising* opportunities in a wide range of *media*, including national and provincial newspapers, magazines, transport advertising, commercial radio and television, billboards and *direct mail*. BRAD, which is used extensively by *advertising agencies*, lists detailed information on prices, contacts, copy deadlines and circulation figures. Some libraries hold copies of BRAD, but it is an expensive item.

British Resorts Association (BRA): an independent organisation representing *local authorities*, *tourist boards* and other organisations with common aims within the UK, Isle of Man and Channel Islands. Formed in 1921, the aim of the Association is to function as a national organisation promoting the mutual interests of all member resorts and tourist regions. Membership is currently 60 local authorities, 10 tourist boards and 14 commercial organisations. BRA provides an information service to members on such matters as European *legislation*, *marketing* and customer care, and is active in *lobbying* interested parties to highlight the economic importance of tourism. Weblink www.britishresorts.co.uk

British Sky Broadcasting Group: see *Sky Television*

British Spas Federation (BSF) celebrated its 75th anniversary in 1996. Led originally by the British Medical Association, more recently the work of the BSF has been funded and co-ordinated by its 13 spa town members, with interest from private health resorts. The aim of BSF is to promote British spas as centres for *tourism*, *leisure* and health, while at the same time increasing the awareness of mineral waters and preserving the historic fabric of the spa towns. Weblink: www.britishspas.co.uk

British Sports Association for the Disabled (BSAD) was established in 1961 to provide and encourage *sport* and *recreation* for people with disabilities. With over 50,000 individual members in approximately 550 clubs, schools and associations throughout England, and a further 14,000 members in Wales, Scotland and Northern Ireland, BSAD (now known as Disability Sport England) works in partnership with other organisations, such as the British Paralympic Association, *Sport England* and *governing bodies* of sport in order to achieve its aims. Weblink: www.disabilitysport.org.uk

British Sports Trust (BST): the charitable arm of the *Central Council of Physical Recreation* responsible for the operation of the *Community Sports Leaders Award*. Weblink: www.bst.org.uk

British Standards Institution (BSI): an organisation, funded through government and voluntary subscription, which sets minimum standards for quality and safety of products and services. Organisations are awarded BSI 'kitemarks' for products and services that meet these minimum requirements. In *leisure* and *tourism*, the increasing importance of quality has meant that many organisations have sought *British Standard (BS) 5750*, now more commonly known as *BS EN ISO 9000*.

British tourism: see *UK tourism*

British Tourism Survey Monthly (BTSM): a former consumer survey now replaced by the *United Kingdom Tourism Survey*.

British Tourist Authority (BTA): established under the 1969 *Development of Tourism Act*, the BTA is responsible for promoting *Britain* to *overseas visitors*. Its mission is to 'build the value of inbound tourism to *Britain*, generating additional tourism revenue throughout Britain, throughout the year'. Its principal *objectives* are:

- to maximise the benefits of tourism to Britain from abroad, while working in *partnership* with the *private* and *public* sector organisations involved in the industry and the *English Tourism Council*, *Northern Ireland Tourist Board*, *VisitScotland* and the *Wales Tourist Board*

- to identify the requirements of *visitors* to Britain, whatever their origin

- to stimulate the improvement of the quality of tourism *products* on offer

- to spread the economic benefits of tourism to Britain more widely, particularly to areas with tourism potential and higher than average levels of unemployment

- to encourage tourism to Britain in *off-peak* periods

- to make the most cost-effective use of its *resources* in pursuing its *objectives*.

In order to meet these objectives, BTA works in close co-operation with N*ational* and *Regional Tourist Boards (RTBs)*, *local authorities*, *media* and the *travel trade* (see figure below). As well as running the British Travel Centre in London, BTA operates in 27 overseas markets to promote Britain as a tourism destination. BTA is funded by the *Department for Culture, Media and Sport (DCMS)*, with funding of £35.5 million for the year 2002–2003. Partnership support from airlines, hotels, car rental companies, National and Regional Tourist Boards (RTBs), and local authorities increases marketing resources by some £15 million each year. At the time of writing, the government is consulting on a probable merger of the BTA with the English Tourism Council (ETC) to form a unified body. Weblink: www.visitbritain.com

BTA's network

British Travel Educational Trust: an educational charity formed in 1970 with the aim of promoting education in *tourism* in its widest context. The Trust provides funding for both international research projects undertaken by individuals and projects related to tourism education undertaken by organisations. Those working in any sector of the *British tourism* industry or holding an academic post at a further or higher education establishment in the UK are eligible to apply for Trust funding.

British Travel Trade Fair (BTTF) is the UK's premier, annual business-to-business *travel trade* exhibition focusing on *UK tourism* products. Attracting over 500 exhibitors and 3000 domestic and international travel trade professionals, it gives the suppliers of a wide range of UK products, including hotels, *destinations*, travel companies and *attractions*, the chance to meet with potential buyers, who may be conference organisers, coach operators, overseas buyers, *tour operators* or *travel agents*. The buyers need up-to-date information on new products on offer and the Fair is a cost-effective way of doing business. BTTF is organised by Reed Travel Exhibitions on behalf of the *English Tourism Council*, Tourism Ireland, *VisitScotland*, the *Wales Tourist Board* and the *British Tourist Authority*. Weblink: www.britishtraveltradefair.com

British Trust for Conservation Volunteers (BTCV): founded in 1959, BTCV is a voluntary body that offers people the chance to take practical steps to improve their environment. It provides advice, training and support to more than 130,000 volunteers each year, working on environmental projects throughout Britain, including repairs to dry stone walls, footpath clearance and beach cleaning. BTCV also operates a programme of *conservation* holidays each year, which it calls 'Natural Breaks'. Weblink: www.btcv.org

British Universities Accommodation Consortium (BUAC) was set up in 1971 to promote the residential/non-residential exhibition, catering and meeting facilities available at member Universities or University Colleges throughout England, Wales, Scotland and Northern Ireland. Now known as Venuemasters, the organisation is funded entirely from membership subscriptions. Weblink: www.venuemasters.co.uk

British Waterways Board (BWB) is a public corporation sponsored by the *Department for the Environment, Food and Rural Affairs*. Often referred to simply as British Waterways, the mission of BWB is the efficient management of the inland waterways system in Britain for the increasing benefit of the nation. The carrying of freight is still important on the 2000 mile network of canals managed by BWB, but their future lies increasingly in the fields of *leisure* and *recreation*, specifically fishing and cruising. Britain's canal network welcomes more than 10 million visitors each year, supporting 55,000 jobs. Every year Britain's inland waterways generate more than £1.5 billion in visitor income. Weblink: www.britishwaterways.co.uk

Britrail Pass: a rail ticket giving *overseas visitors* to Britain unlimited travel on train services. The ticket is not available in the UK, but must be purchased in the visitors' home country before travelling to Britain. It is aimed mainly at the independent traveller who wishes to explore the lesser-known parts of the country by public transport.

broadcast media: generally refers to *television* (terrestrial, cable and satellite) and commercial radio, but is increasingly being used to include global communications systems such as the *Internet*.

brochure: an essential promotional tool for most leisure, travel and tourism organisations, since they are mainly involved in selling *intangible* products, such as holidays, *short breaks* and coaching sessions. Brochures must be both informative and persuasive, and should follow the *AIDA* principle in their design. A well-designed brochure should aim to convert an enquiry into a sale.

brunch: a meal taken mid-way between breakfast and lunch times. First conceived in the USA, brunches are now commonplace in *hotels* throughout the world, particularly at weekends when many people prefer to get up late in the mornings and so miss normal breakfast serving times.

Brundtland Report: an influential document which resulted from the World Commission on Environment and Development, organised by the *United Nations* in 1987, which focused on the concept of global sustainability and the threats to the world environment. The report, named after the Norwegian Prime Minister who chaired the Commission, defined sustainable development as 'meeting the needs of the present without compromising the ability of future generations to meet their own needs'. The report is significant in being the first attempt to address global environmental problems. It has been a major influence on the development of the concept of *sustainable tourism*. (See also *Earth Summit*.)

BS 5750: see *BS EN ISO 9000*

BS 7750: a *BSI* Standard that focuses on *environmental management* systems. Following similar processes to *BS 5750*, BS 7750 requires an organisation to document all its systems and measure its environmental performance. The Standard is designed to be equally applicable to service industries, such as leisure and tourism, and manufacturing concerns. Central to certification to BS 7750 is the need to consider the whole organisation, which means that the environmental management systems can be based on many of the principles of *total quality management (TQM)*.

BS EN ISO 9000: a quality standard (also known as BS 5750) that aims to ensure consistently high levels of product and service delivery. Developed initially for manufacturing industry, this British Standard (BS) is now increasingly applied to service industries, including *leisure* and *tourism*. The underlying objective of BS EN ISO 9000 is to make sure that all administrative and management systems are fully documented and audited, leading to high standards of quality at all times. Critics of the Standard argue that it is overly bureaucratic and that simply having well documented procedures does not necessarily lead to high quality standards.

BSAD: see *British Sports Association for the Disabled*

BSF: see *British Spas Federation*

BSI: see *British Standards Institution*

BSkyB: see *Sky Television*

BST: see *British Sports Trust*

BTA: see *British Tourist Authority*

BTCV: see *British Trust for Conservation Volunteers*

BTEC: see *Business and Technology Education Council*

BTSM: see *British Tourism Survey Monthly*

BTTF: see *British Travel Trade Fair*

BUAC: see *British Universities Accommodation Consortium*

bucket shop: a non-appointed *travel agency* that specialises in selling discounted air tickets, for both *charter* and *scheduled services*. Commonplace in the 1970s and 1980s, bucket shops were used by major airlines to sell off seats at short notice (a process known as 'dumping'). The role of bucket shops has declined markedly in recent years, particularly since discounted fares are now made available legitimately to *ABTA* and *IATA* appointed agents and specialist brokers.

budget: a forecast of expected income and expenditure over a given period of time. At an organisational level it is an action plan for the coming financial period, which can be used to delegate *responsibility* to departmental managers. In practice, it is likely that a leisure or tourism organisation will have many budget heads, i.e. many products and activities that will attract *income* and incur *costs*. Each of these budgets will be consolidated into one master budget for the organisation, which will detail its overall short-term financial plan. The budget is the principal tool for allowing managers to co-ordinate and control the activities of their organisation. Two of the most useful financial control measures are the *sales budget* and the *expenditure budget*. (See also *budgetary control*.)

budget airline: see *low-cost airline*

budget hotel: a type of *accommodation* that has grown rapidly in recent years, a result of low prices, flexibility and convenience. Aimed at both leisure travellers and the business market, successful *brands* include Travelodge, Holiday Inn Express and Comfort Inn.

budgetary control is the process of comparing actual *costs* or expenditure with budgeted figures to identify any *variances*, and taking appropriate action to put matters right. Budgeting control is an essential part of the job of a manager in leisure and tourism. The investigation of any deviations from the budgeted figures is known as *variance analysis*.

budgeting: see *budgetary control* and *budget*

built attractions: see *man-made attractions*

Bus and Coach Council (BCC): see *Confederation of Passenger Transport UK (CPT)*

'bus stop' arrangement: a term used in aviation when an aircraft takes off from one airport and stops at another to pick up passengers, before flying on to its final destination airport. This arrangement is carried out in order to maximise capacity on the aircraft and may be preferable to *consolidation*, which would involve one set of passengers travelling by road to meet their flight at another airport.

Business and Technology Education Council (BTEC): see *Edexcel*

business environment: a general term used to denote the local, regional, national and international world in which an organisation functions and the factors that will have some bearing on its operation. The business environment is often divided into those internal influences over which an organisation has some degree of control (the *micro environment*) and those that form part of the wider world and which are normally outside of its control (the *macro environment*).

business house agency: a *travel agency* that specialises in providing a range of services for business clients, including airline tickets, *visas* and currency requirements.

Business in Sport and Leisure (BISL) was established in 1991 with the aim of *lobbying* for changes to the *fiscal* and *statutory* climate for sporting and leisure developments in the UK. It is an independent umbrella organisation, representing more than 50 private sector companies in *sport* and *leisure* and acts as a forum for the exchange of information between members.

business objectives are the commercial aims that an organisation sets itself, as opposed to any *social objectives* it may be seeking to achieve. They will relate to *profitability*, *sales revenue*, *market share*, etc., and will be the basis on which the organisation's overall *strategy* and *business plans* are developed.

business plan: a document that sets out the future financial and operational aspects of a current or proposed venture. Business plans are commonly prepared by new businesses seeking external funding and support, as a way of convincing external agencies, such as banks, planning authorities and potential sponsors, that a project is viable. Large organisations will prepare overall business plans, plus plans for different departments within the organisation. A business plan should include detailed information about:

- the *objectives* of the venture
- financial *costs* and revenues
- market *demand*
- legal aspects
- *management* expertise.

While an organisation's *strategic planning* process will give a blue print of its overall aims, business plans should be seen as short- to medium-term working documents, reviewed on an annual basis and constantly monitored.

business skills are essential requirements for anybody considering working in a management role in the leisure, travel and tourism industries. They include expertise in finance, *marketing*, *human resource management*, purchasing and administration.

business tourism is the category of the *travel and tourism industry* concerned with travel for business purposes, rather than travel for leisure purposes (*leisure tourism*). Business tourism includes travel for meetings, exhibitions, trade fairs, conferences, conventions and *incentive travel*. Business tourism is an increasingly important sector of the industry since it is often high value, earning hoteliers, carriers and caterers, significant revenue. The events of *September 11* 2001 had a major impact on international business travel, with many countries only just returning to their former market positions. Some travel agents specialise in dealing with business travel and are known as *business house agents*.

business travel: see *business tourism*

Butlin's: the name of the world's pioneer in *holiday camps*. The first holiday camp was opened in Skegness in 1936 by Billy Butlin. Butlin's camps soon spread across the country, working on the principle that if the children were happy, their parents would be as well. Today, Butlin's holiday centres (known as Butlin's Holiday Worlds) attract around 500,000 holiday-makers every year, in accommodation that has been updated to meet current demands. Butlin's also operates hotels and is the leading contractor of star entertainers in the UK.

BWB: see *British Waterways Board*

bye-laws are local regulations implemented by *district* and *county councils*, covering the proper use of *public open spaces*, footpaths and recreation grounds.

CAA: see *Civil Aviation Authority*

CAB: see *Citizens' Advice Bureau*

cabotage refers to airline and shipping routes within a country's national territory, e.g. flights between London and Glasgow, and even London and Gibraltar. Such routes are not subject to international agreements on fares, making residents of the country eligible for reduced rate tariffs, sometimes called cabotage fares. It is intended that when full *airline deregulation* occurs in the *European Union (EU)*, the routes between member states will be considered cabotage routes.

Cadw is responsible for the protection, *conservation* and appreciation of the built *heritage* in Wales. Created in 1984, and now funded by the *National Assembly for Wales (NAW)*, Cadw performs similar functions in Wales to those undertaken by *English Heritage* in England. Its duties include *planning* responsibilities for ancient monuments and historic buildings, grant-aiding their repair and managing 129 ancient monuments in Wales, including Chepstow Castle, Tintern Abbey and Conwy Castle. Weblink: www.cadw.wales.gov.uk

Camelot: the company chosen by *OFLOT* to operate the *National Lottery*, from a final short list of eight applicants. Camelot Group PLC is a consortium of the following companies – Cadbury Schweppes, De La Rue, G Tech, Racal and ICL. Weblink: www.camelotgroup.co.uk

campaign has two meanings in *leisure* and *tourism*. The first is concerned with *advertising* and *promotion,* and is a planned activity aimed at increasing sales of products and services, e.g. an *advertising campaign* tied in with a major sporting event. The second is an activity undertaken by a *pressure group* to highlight an issue or stop a planned development, e.g. the campaign to halt the expansion of Stansted Airport in Essex.

Campaign for Real Travel Agents (CARTA): an alliance of specialist, owner-managed/directed travel agencies offering independent advice to customers. CARTA was established by the *Association of Independent Tour Operators (AITO)* to ensure that their holidays were available locally in the UK through a network of experienced travel agents. Weblink: www.realholidays.co.uk

Campaign for the Protection of Rural Wales (CPRW) is a national charity founded in 1928 as the Council for the Protection of Rural Wales. Today it organises concerted action to protect the beauty of the coast and countryside in Wales. CPRW has branches throughout Wales, whose aim is to protect the local environment while encouraging sustainable rural development. Funded by members' subscriptions and supporters' donations, CPRW is a source of information and guidance on *conservation* issues in Wales to politicians, the *media* and rural bodies. Weblink: www.cprw.org.uk

capital represents the funds invested in a business in order to acquire the *assets* which it needs to be able to trade. The principal sources of capital are from *shareholders* and lenders (*loan capital*).

capital allowance: the proportion of the cost of *fixed assets* that can be charged to profit each year, thereby reducing a company's tax liability, e.g. a company vehicle costing £10,000 may be eligible for a 25 per cent capital allowance per year, resulting in the business being able to offset £2500 against its taxable income.

capital costs: see *capital expenditure*

capital expenditure represents expenditure on the acquisition or improvement of *fixed assets*, such as buildings, machinery and plant. (See also *revenue expenditure*.)

capital gearing: see *gearing*

car ownership has risen dramatically since the end of the Second World War. There were 2.3 million cars on the roads in 1950, 11 million in 1970 and around 24 million in 2002. The private car is the predominant mode of travel for tourists in Britain, whether UK residents or *overseas visitors*. The car accounted for 73 per cent of all holiday trips by UK residents in 2001. The growth in car use is putting severe strain on Britain's main tourist areas, including the *National Parks*, historic cities and *seaside resorts*.

Caravan Club: founded in 1907, the Caravan Club represents the interests of over 850,000 members and their families in the UK. It operates the largest private network of sites in the British Isles, with 200 Club sites and over 3000 *Certificated Locations (CLs)*. The Club offers a comprehensive range of services to its members, including a travel and insurance service, and places environmental and safety issues to the fore in its work. Weblink: www.caravanclub.co.uk

caravanning is a popular type of *self-catering* holiday, accounting for 17 per cent of all UK holidays taken by the British in 2001 and contributing £1.2 billion to the national economy. Caravan holidays use either towed vehicles or take place in static vans on holiday parks. Many caravanners are members of the *Caravan Club* or Camping and Caravanning Club of Great Britain.

career development is the process of progressing in employment in a structured manner. People who manage to plan their career development successfully have clear employment and lifestyle objectives in mind and take full advantage of *staff training* opportunities made available by their employers. They also take an active role in *staff appraisal*. (See also *staff development*.)

career opportunities: see *careers in leisure, travel and tourism*

careers in leisure, travel and tourism offer a variety of benefits, including job satisfaction to those who like helping other people make the best use of their *leisure time*, opportunities for travel at home and abroad, excellent prospects for promotion and scope for initiative, flair and imagination. In return, the industries look for staff who like working with people, who are not afraid of hard work (when most people are 'at leisure'), who are prepared to learn quickly, to whom *personal presentation* and *personal hygiene* are important, and who can take on *responsibility*, often at a young age. There are many different career opportunities as shown in the following table. (See also *employment in leisure, travel and tourism*.)

- Hotel management
- Sports coaching
- Casino/betting shop management
- Sports administration
- Contract catering
- Event management
- Teaching/lecturing
- Airlines and airports
- Tour operators
- Tourist attractions
- Coach operators
- Tourist information centres
- Ferry and cruise companies
- Arts administration
- Pub or restaurant management
- Countryside management
- Outdoor pursuits
- Conference planning
- Leisure centre management
- Sportsman/woman
- Travel agencies
- Local authority tourism departments
- Hotels and other accommodation
- Car hire companies
- Guiding
- Training

The wide range of possible careers in leisure, travel and tourism

carnet: a French term describing an official document that allows the temporary importation of goods into a foreign country, without the payment of any levies or duties. This could be related to a vehicle, promotional items of no commercial value or *duty-free* goods.

carrier: the term used in the *travel and tourism industry* to denote any individual or *company* that offers transportation services for passengers or goods. Airlines, car hire companies, coach operators, taxi firms, railway operators and ferry companies all fall within the category of 'carrier'.

carrying capacity: the maximum number of people that a resort, site or other tourist area can sustain, before there is a reduction in the quality of the visitor experience or adverse effects on either the physical environment or the *host community*. The concept is at the heart of the debate surrounding *sustainable tourism*. It is a difficult concept to put into practice, because people will have different threshold levels above or below which the quality of their experience will fall. Carrying capacity is sometimes divided into distinct types:

- Physical capacity – the most straightforward type indicated, for example, by a finite number of bedspaces or car parking spaces
- Psychological or perceptual capacity – relates to a decline in the quality of the visitors' experience
- Biological capacity – concerns environmental damage to flora and fauna
- Social capacity – relates to adverse pressures on the host community.

CARTA: see *Campaign for Real Travel Agents*

cartel: an arrangement whereby a number of providers of goods and services agree to either regulate supply or fix prices in order to maintain their *profitability*. An example in the *travel and tourism industry* would be two ferry companies operating on the same route both agreeing to keep their prices artificially high, rather than getting involved in a price war. A cartel is a form of restrictive practice that is outlawed in most countries, since it is considered to be against the public interest. In the UK, the *Competition Commission* can intervene in the case of a suspected cartel arrangement, if it considers that the public interest is being jeopardised.

cascading is the process of disseminating information and ideas within an organisation down the hierarchy. Often associated with *staff development* and *training*, cascading is a cost-effective way of informing a large number of people from a small initial base. An example of cascading would be a senior manager in a leisure or tourism organisation attending a training course on new *computer* systems, and running a session for other managers within the organisation on his return. They in turn would brief their staff, thereby ensuring that everybody who needs to know is made aware of the details.

cash cow: a product or service that enjoys a high relative share of a market that is either static or declining. The cash cow generates surplus cash that can be invested in other areas to help other products and services grow. Organisations will try to maximise the prices of their 'cash cows', while keeping expenditure to a minimum. The term is used in *portfolio analysis*, in particular the *Boston Consulting Group matrix*.

cash-flow is the money coming into a business from sales receipts and other *revenue* sources, and going out of the business in the form of *fixed* and *variable costs*, such as payments to suppliers, employees and interest charges.

cash-flow forecast: an estimate of the expected future cash inflows and outflows of an organisation, usually presented on a monthly basis (see figure below). Banks and other lenders will expect to see a cash-flow forecast before granting a *loan* or extending an organisation's *overdraft* facility.

	October (£000s)	November (£000s)	December (£000s)
Cash at start	52	62	72
Total cash inflows	180	160	140
Total cash outflows	170	150	170
Net cash-flow	+10	+10	−30
Cumulative cash	62	72	42

Quarterly cash-flow forecast

cash-flow statement: a statement of the flow of funds into and out of a business for a given period of time, usually twelve months. An organisation's cash-flow statement provides a link between its *profit and loss account* and its *balance sheet*. It forms part of the audited accounts and shows the funds that have entered a company, how they have been used and how any net surplus or deficit in short- and long-term funds has been applied.

catchment area: the geographical limit from within which a leisure or tourism facility draws its customers. The size of the catchment area will depend on a number of factors, such as the availability and quality of transport links, the uniqueness of the facility and the population density of the area. The use of *market research* data will enable a facility to estimate the total size of a *target market* in its catchment area.

catering: the sector of *leisure* and *tourism* that is concerned with the preparation, distribution and serving of food. It includes cafés, *fast-food outlets*, restaurants, motorway service areas, pubs, school meals and contract catering services. (See also *hospitality*.)

CBA: see *cost-benefit analysis*

CBI: see *Confederation of British Industry*

CCETs: see *ELWA – Education and Learning Wales*

CCPR: see *Central Council of Physical Recreation*

CCT: see *compulsory competitive tendering*

CCTV: see *closed-circuit television*

CCW: see *Countryside Council for Wales*

CD-ROM stands for 'compact disc read-only memory'. It is a method of information storage and retrieval using a *personal computer (PC)* with the appropriate hardware and software. Increasingly, *secondary research* information, including newspapers, directories, encyclopaedias and *databases* are being made available on CD-ROM. Computers installed with a CD-ROM drive can accept advanced software with sound and video effects superior to normal *floppy disk software*.

CDW: see *collision damage waiver*

CEI: see *Centre for Environmental Interpretation*

census: a survey in which data about every individual in a 'population' is recorded, as distinct from *sampling*, when only a proportion is surveyed. In the UK, the Census of Population is carried out every ten years and is managed by the *Office for National Statistics (ONS)*. The most recent was undertaken in 2001 and revealed a total UK population of 58.8 million. The census provides useful data for leisure and tourism organisations on such matters such as the economic and social characteristics of the population, e.g. levels of *car ownership*, number of one-parent families, etc.

Center Parcs is a company with its origins dating back to the late 1960s in the Netherlands, when the idea of 'a villa in a forest' was born. The Center Parcs' concept revolves around providing a relaxing, high quality, natural holiday environment, where city dwellers can escape from the pressures of everyday life. The company now operates four sites in the UK, near Nottingham, Cambridge and at Longleat in Wiltshire, plus the former Oasis Village in the Lake District. All Center Parcs have covered leisure pools and *self-catering accommodation* in woodland settings, plus a range of active leisure pursuits. Weblink: www.centerparcs.co.uk

Central Council of Physical Recreation (CCPR) was founded in 1935 with three particular objectives:

- to encourage as many people as possible to participate in all forms of *sport* and *recreation*
- to provide the separate *governing bodies* of the individual sports with a central organisation that would represent and promote their interests
- to increase public knowledge and awareness of the importance of sport.

CCPR claims to be 'the voice of sport', since it is the only organisation that speaks for the interests of some twenty million British sportsmen and women. It is a non-governmental voluntary organisation, which is largely self-financing and whose officers and Executive Committee are elected by the membership as a whole. At present, the membership of the CCPR includes the Football Association, the Royal Yachting Association and the Institute of Swimming Teachers and Coaches, to name but a few. The CCPR also provides a number of services for its member bodies, including a press service, help with *sponsorship*, legal advice and assistance with fund-raising. In 1982, the CCPR launched the *Community Sports*

Leaders Award to harness greater community involvement in sport. This aspect of its work is now operated by CCPR's charitable arm, the *British Sports Trust (BST)*. Weblink: www.ccpr.org.uk

central government: another name for national government, denoting the body that has overall control over a particular country's affairs, such as its monetary policy, foreign affairs, defence, social services and employment policies.

central reservation system: a centralised booking facility used by leisure and tourism companies to offer an efficient service to the *customer*, while at the same time minimising its costs. Examples include central reservation systems operated by hotel chains, *tour operators* and airlines. Such systems are usually computerised, so as to be able to offer greater flexibility of choice to the customer and provide links with other network systems. (See also *computerised reservation systems*.)

centralised structures: *organisational structures* in which power and decision making rest with a small number of senior managers. Organisations with this type of *'steep' pyramid* structure are often run on very centralised lines, with many tiers of management, often powerless to make decisions on a day-to-day basis. Centralised structures can lead to a demoralised workforce and a senior management team that is out of touch with its staff. They are also criticised for being too bureaucratic. Advocates of centralised structures argue that they have the advantage of promoting a clear *corporate identity* for an organisation and facilitate the implementation of common policies across very large enterprises. (See also *decentralisation*.)

Centre for Alternative Technology (CAT): an environmentally-based *tourist attraction* in Wales, which is unusual in that it is a *public limited company (PLC)*. It decided to change its status and issue shares to the public as a way of financing a capital building programme. Weblink: www.cat.org.uk

Centre for Environmental Interpretation (CEI): the former non-profit making organisation set up in 1980 by the Carnegie UK Trust as a national centre for environmental and heritage *interpretation*. With offices in Manchester and Edinburgh, CEI held the largest UK collection of published and unpublished information on the subject of interpretation. CEI staff ran a series of short courses on the subject throughout the UK and provided in-house training for a range of agencies including the *National Trust*, *Groundwork Trusts* and *local authorities*.

Certificate in Travel (Tour Operators): a *vocational qualification* designed for people working, or wishing to work, for a *tour operator*. It will shortly replace the *ABTA Tour Operators Certificate (ABTOC)*. Primary and Advanced levels under ABTOC will be known as Levels 2 and 3 under the Certificate in Travel (Tour Operators).

Certificate in Travel (Travel Agents): a *vocational qualification* designed for people working, or wishing to work, in a travel agency. It will shortly replace the *ABTA Travel Agents Certificate (ABTAC)*. Primary and Advanced levels under ABTAC will be known as Levels 2 and 3 under the Certificate in Travel (Travel Agents).

Certificate of Travel Agency Competence (COTAC): the former examination-based, UK qualification for those working, or seeking employment, in the *travel industry*. Awarded by City and Guilds, COTAC was replaced in 1994 by the *ABTA Travel Agents Certificate (ABTAC)*, bringing the qualification more in line with *National Vocational Qualifications (NVQs)*.

Certificated Location (CL): a network of 2700 caravan sites in Britain, licensed by the *Caravan Club*. CLs originated when the *Caravan Club* was granted exemption under the 1960 Caravan Sites and Control of Development Act, which allowed the Club to grant certificates to landowners to provide these small, informal sites for not more than five vans at any one time. Found mostly on farms, CLs offer a range of basic facilities and an opportunity to 'get away from it all' for Caravan Club members, as well as useful extra income for their operators.

certified cheque: see *banker's draft*

chain of command: the declared lines of *authority* within an organisation through which *communication* takes place and decisions are conveyed. In large private sector organisations with a *hierarchical* structure, the chain of command begins at the top with the *directors*, through senior managers and middle managers, to the employees.

chain of distribution: see *distribution channels*

chair: see *chairman*

chair of board: see *chairman*

chairman: an individual who takes on the role of chairing the meetings of an organisation. The chairman of a *company* will have a much wider role than simply chairing meetings of the board of directors. He or she may also take responsibility for developing the *mission* and *policies* that the company will follow, in conjunction with other directors and senior staff. In many leisure and tourism organisations, the chairman, (sometimes known simply as the chair or chair of board) becomes the public face of the organisation, e.g. Richard Branson of Virgin and Stelios Haji-Ioannou of easyJet.

Champion Coaching is a *National Coaching Foundation (NCF)* government-funded initiative which aims to deliver quality coaching to children between the ages of 11 and 14 who show an above average level of ability in a particular *sport* or sports. The mission of Champion Coaching is 'promote quality-assured youth sport coaching for performance-motivated children within a co-ordinated community structure'. Begun originally in 1991/92 as a pilot study, the initiative has spread to cover a wide range of sports, including volleyball, cricket, tennis and hockey. The children recruited on to the scheme are nominated by their school's PE teacher and attend for a period of six weeks, normally in out-of-school hours. As well as developing a range of useful skills, they are given the chance of gaining various coaching awards.

change management is the process of anticipating, investigating, *planning* and managing enforced or unenforced changes to any of an organisation's *resources* and operating mechanisms. Managing change is a constant process in the dynamic leisure and tourism industries, where customer needs and expectations constantly alter, and competitive pressures force companies to adopt new working practices and management styles. People are inherently resistant to change, making change management a process that must be undertaken with a very sensitive touch. Factors in an organisation's *internal* and *external* *environment* will combine to trigger change on a regular basis in virtually all leisure and tourism organisations.

Channel Tunnel: one of the biggest civil engineering projects of the twentieth century, opened to passenger and freight traffic in 1994. Built by *Eurotunnel*, a joint English-French consortium of construction companies, the Tunnel offers a rail passenger service, known as

Eurostar, linking London with Paris, Brussels, Lille and other major European cities. The Tunnel also operates a passenger and vehicle-carrying facility, called *Le Shuttle*, where cars, coaches and lorries are loaded onto shuttle trains running every 15 minutes at peak times. The Channel Tunnel has proved popular with travellers and fierce competition for ferry companies, capturing nearly 50 per cent of all cross-Channel traffic by the end of 2000.

charge cards allow payment by plastic card on *credit* in place of cash, but, unlike *credit cards* they offer no extended credit facility, i.e. accounts must be settled in full each month. Their use in leisure and tourism facilities is mainly for business and corporate customers. Diners Club and *American Express* are two of the best known charge cards, accepted across the world.

charity: an organisation established to campaign for a particular cause or help those in most need in our society. In leisure and tourism, many environmental and *heritage* organisations are registered as charities.

charter flight: an aircraft commissioned for a set period of time, flying to a particular destination and able to offer reduced fares by setting high *load factors*. Most *package holidays* that include air travel will use charter flights; this arrangement is known as *inclusive tours by charter*. (See also *scheduled air services*.)

Charter Mark: an award scheme set up by the government to reward excellence in public services, including *leisure* and *recreation*, under the *Citizens' Charter* initiative. Applicants have to demonstrate to the satisfaction of the Prime Minister's Advisory Panel on the Charter that they have achieved measurable improvements in the quality of their service over the previous two years, and that their customers are satisfied with their services. Winners of a Charter Mark keep it for three years and can gain useful publicity for their organisation. Weblink: www.chartermark.gov.uk

Chartered Institute of Marketing (CIM) was founded in 1911 and is the leading organisation for *marketing* and sales professionals in Europe, with over 50,000 members and registered students worldwide. Awarded a Royal Charter in 1989, the principal aim of CIM is to establish marketing as a universally recognised, understood and accepted profession, reflecting the levels of quality, standards and principles expected of a chartered body. It has more than 40 industry groups, including CIMTIG, the *Chartered Institute of Marketing Travel Industry Group*. Weblink: www.cim.co.uk

Chartered Institute of Marketing Travel Industry Group (CIMTIG) is one of 40 sector groups belonging to the *Chartered Institute of Marketing (CIM)*. Made up of CIM members working in *public* and *private sector travel* and *tourism*, CIMTIG holds regular meetings for members and non-members on issues of relating to sales and marketing in the industry. Weblink: www.cimtig.org

Chartered Institute of Public Finance and Accountancy (CIPFA) is a professional body representing accountants and financial administrators working in the public sector. Every year CIPFA publishes comparative data on the operating costs of *public sector leisure* service departments and leisure facilities across the country.

check-in is the procedure of registering a guest at a *hotel* or other *accommodation* establishment on his or her arrival. Check-in can also mean the process of completing the necessary formalities before travelling on an airline, some forms of rail travel (e.g. *Eurostar*), boarding a ferry or cruise ship, or picking up a hire car.

check-out: the procedure for guests vacating their rooms, paying their bills and leaving a hotel or other *accommodation* establishment. Some hotels offer a fast check-out facility, particularly suited to the needs of business travellers wishing to depart early in the morning.

cheque: a method of payment without the use of cash, used by both individuals and businesses. Cheques are a relatively convenient way of paying for goods and services, backed up by a *cheque guarantee card*. The use of *debit cards*, such as Switch and Delta, is having a considerable impact on the number of cheques issued.

cheque guarantee card: a card used in conjunction with a *cheque* to guarantee that the amount written on the cheque, assuming it is less than the face value of the card, will be paid by the bank or building society which issued the card. Most cards honour cheques up to the value of £50, but it is becoming increasingly common to find £100 cheque guarantee cards. Staff should only accept cheques that are accompanied by a current card, with the same signature as on the accompanying cheque.

Chicago Convention on Civil Aviation: an international symposium held in 1944 which agreed the five *freedoms of the air* and established the *International Civil Aviation Organisation (ICAO)*. (See also *Bermuda Agreement*.)

Children Act 1989: government legislation that contained new regulations affecting everybody who has responsibility for planning, managing and delivering services to children. The main impact on the *leisure and recreation industry* is the need to ensure consistent standards of care and common frameworks for provision, which include powers to ensure that staff working with children receive appropriate training. Activities such as summer play schemes, children's couriers on campsites, sports coaching and adventure holidays all fall within the scope of the Children Act.

CHNTO: see *Cultural Heritage National Training Organisation*

CIM: see *Chartered Institute of Marketing*

CIMTIG: see *Chartered Institute of Marketing Travel Industry Group*

cinema attendances have been rising steadily since the mid-1980s, with record attendances of 156 million at the UK's 750 cinemas in 2001 and industry projections of 182 million for 2003. These figures have to be viewed in the context of a long-term downward trend in visits that began in the 1960s. The growth in audiences has coincided with the introduction of *multiplex* cinemas, which now account for over 65 per cent of all screens. Total cinema screens in the UK in 2002 stood at 3333, of which 2188 were in multiplex facilities. There has been significant industry investment to upgrade facilities and provide customers with a more comfortable environment.

CIPFA: see *Chartered Institute of Public Finance and Accountancy*

circulation: the number of copies of a newspaper or magazine distributed by its publishers. Advertisers need to know circulation figures when devising *advertising campaigns*, as well as the socio-economic profile of the readers, in order to target customers most effectively. It is generally the case that the larger the circulation of a newspaper the more expensive its costs of advertising. In Britain currently, the highest daily circulation is held by the 'Sun', while the most popular Sunday newspaper is 'The News of the World'. The 'Readers' Digest' has the highest circulation of any magazine. Details of circulation figures can be found in *British Rate and Data*.

Citizens' Advice Bureau (CAB): a voluntary organisation that operates a chain of centres throughout the country offering free advice on a range of matters including legal disputes, financial problems and housing issues. People who have had problems with products and services, for example faulty *sporting goods* or *holidays* that have gone wrong, sometimes visit a CAB to find out how to complain and investigate their consumer rights. Weblink: www.nacab.org.uk

Citizens' Charter: a scheme launched by the government in 1991 with the aim of raising the standard of public services and making them more responsive to the needs of consumers. Although successful in some areas, critics of the scheme consider it to be more of a *public relations* exercise than a genuine attempt to raise standards. (See also *Charter Mark*.)

City Challenge: a competition operated by the *Department of the Environment (DoE)* in the 1980s and 1990s to stimulate investment in *urban regeneration* projects in England. Cities were encouraged to develop projects, which often included leisure and tourism facilities, and bid on a competitive basis for City Challenge funds.

city farm: a facility that allows people living in towns and cities to have first-hand experience of looking after animals and learning about nature. Schools will often use the city farm as a learning resource.

Civic Trust: a charitable organisation that aims to improve and regenerate the environment where people live and work, particularly in urban areas, and to promote high standards of *planning*, design and *conservation*. With the help of a network of local groups, the Trust makes annual awards for appropriate development of all kinds. Weblink: www.civictrust.org.uk

Civil Aviation Authority (CAA): a body that has been serving the needs of UK air travellers since it was established under the Civil Aviation Act of 1971. It is both a public service enterprise and a regulatory body, whose responsibilities include:

* air safety – air worthiness and operational safety
* air traffic control and telecommunications
* economic regulation – including air transport licensing and *Air Travel Organisers' Licences (ATOLs)*
* advice to government on civil aviation matters
* consumer interests in relation to civil aviation.

The CAA is financed by the users of its services and does not receive any subsidy from government. Weblink: www.caa.co.uk

civil prosecution: an action concerned with offences that do not automatically lead to prosecution by the police. Civil law gives an individual the right to pursue a grievance with another person or organisation through the courts. (See also *criminal prosecution*.)

CL: see *Certificated Location*

class: see *social class*

classified advertisement: an announcement in the *trade* or *consumer press* usually charged on a per line or per word basis (see figure on following page). It is a relatively cheap form of *advertising*, since, unlike *display advertisements*, no pictures or headlines are included. Many smaller leisure and tourism companies advertise their services in the classified advertisements of newspapers and magazines.

> **Majorca:** self-catering villa close to Arenal. Sleeps 6. Available July–Oct. From £320 per wk. Tel. 0171 682 6225
> **Majorca:** cheap flights and villas. Call (0162) 71835
> **Menorca:** luxury villas and apartments. From £450 inc. pools and maid service. Menorca Alive. Tel. 0182 68665

Example of a classified advertisement

climate plays a crucial role in how people use their *leisure time*. British people will often travel thousands of miles to escape this country's cool temperate climate, in favour of 'guaranteed' sunshine. Within Britain itself, there are marked differences in climate, with the west and south generally experiencing warmer summers and less severe winters than the north. This is due in part to the warming effects of the Gulf Stream, a warm ocean current that originates in the Gulf of Mexico and passes along the west of Britain on its way north. Mild Atlantic winds re-inforce this effect.

climatic changes are identifiable long-term alterations in the earth's climate, for example *global warming*. It is predicted that climatic changes will have profound effects on *tourist destinations* and *recreational activities* in the future.

closed-circuit television (CCTV) has a number of uses in leisure and tourism, including helping organisations improve the security of their buildings, equipment and staff. CCTV is also a useful management tool, particularly in large leisure and tourism facilities, where it can be used to observe visitor and traffic flows, e.g. in a *theme park* or large outdoor event. It is also useful for staff training sessions, for example *interviewing* and *interpersonal skills* training.

closed question: one that invites a specific reply, often negative, from within a small selection of responses, rather than allowing a respondent to give an expanded reply, as is the case with an *open question*. Examples of closed questions are 'can I help you?' and 'can I get a brochure for you?', both of which invite the reply yes or no. In a sales situation, the use of closed questions makes it difficult to establish rapport with the customer. Closed questions are, however, useful for *questionnaire* surveys, since they can speed up the analysis stage of the survey.

'closed shop': an arrangement in the workplace whereby employees must join a trade union when taking up their post. The Employment Acts of 1980, 1982, 1988 and 1990, plus other related employment legislation, contained clauses to outlaw the 'closed shop' arrangement, which was considered to be undemocratic.

closing a sale is a selling technique used to persuade a *customer* to make a commitment to purchase a particular product or service. It is a key stage in the *sales process*, when staff should be looking for buying signals from the customer to trigger the process of closing the sale. Statements from the customer such as 'that sounds fine' or 'yes I like that', clearly indicate a desire to purchase. When such signals are evident, the member of staff should begin to finalise the deal, perhaps by taking a customer's money, cheque or credit card details. Sales staff should always remember, however, that customers should never be forced into a sale that they may later regret. Closing the sale is all about helping a customer move from 'I'd like' to 'I'll buy'.

coach travel is a relatively cheap form of transportation, favoured by students, young people, and senior citizens. Young people use the scheduled services operated by companies such as *National Express*, while older people use these services, but also go on organised coach holidays to scenic parts of Britain, including the Lake District, Snowdonia and the Highlands of Scotland, organised by companies such as Shearings and Frames Rickards.

code of conduct: a set of voluntary guidelines that an industry association or regulatory body devises, laying down minimum standards within which its members will operate, or face sanctions if they transgress. In leisure and tourism, the *Association of British Travel Agents (ABTA)* operates codes of conduct for both *travel agency* and *tour operator* members, governing their relationship with the paying customer. The *Office of Fair Trading (OFT)* advises industry organisations on the content and implementation of codes of conduct.

code of practice: see *code of conduct*

collateral is the American term for the *security* that is usually required before a *loan* can be made by a financial institution.

collision damage waiver (CDW): an extra *insurance* payment made by a person hiring a motor vehicle, in order to exempt the hirer from further costs in the event of an accident resulting in damage to the vehicle.

commercial mortgage: a long-term *loan* from a bank or building society for the purchase of land and buildings, which are used as *security* in case the lender defaults on the agreement. A leisure or tourism organisation may take out a commercial mortgage for the purchase or extension of retail premises, new holiday *accommodation*, a sports facility or other business premises.

commercial organisations are *private sector enterprises* that have profit maximisation as their prime *objective*. The majority of leisure, travel and tourism organisations operate in the commercial world. (See also *non-commercial organisations*.)

commission is a payment made to an agent for selling the products and services of a *principal*, e.g. a *travel agent* is paid a commission for selling a t*our operator*'s package holidays. The commission is usually an agreed percentage of the selling price, which may be increased for higher sales levels (*override commission*). Sales staff in a company may be paid commission in addition to their basic salary, as an incentive to increase sales.

Commission for Racial Equality (CRE) was established under the *Race Relations Act of 1976*, combining the functions of the two former statutory bodies, the Race Relations Board and the Community Relations Commission. The CRE works towards the elimination of discrimination, promoting equality of opportunity and good relations between different racial groups generally. Weblink: www.cre.gov.uk

committee: a group of people who work together to achieve a common purpose, operating under a set of rules (the constitution) and with elected officials. As a minimum, a committee can operate with two officials, a *chairman* to control meetings and a secretary to take the minutes of meetings and handle correspondence. In reality, it is likely that the committee will also need a treasurer and people to organise publicity and fund-raising. If a committee has been formed to organise an *event,* it is a good idea to invite *sponsors* on to the committee, as well as representatives of the emergency services.

commoditisation is the notion that *tourism* products and even *destinations* can be sold in the same way as other commodities. Tour operators' brochures depict resorts from Bali to the Bahamas using similar *images* and descriptions. The 'packaging' and selling of tourist *destinations*, however, can have long-term environmental and socio-cultural effects on *host communities*; sensitive planning and management is needed to ensure their future well-being and the sustainability of the enterprise.

communication is the interaction between individuals and their exchange of information and opinions. Service industries, such as leisure, travel and tourism, rely heavily on effective communication both within organisations (*internal communication*) and with the outside world (*external communication*). Communication may be either *formal*, such as a letter to a client, or *informal*, for example a chance conversation with a colleague in the corridor. Communication does not only involve written and spoken words. *Non-verbal communication (NVC)* is when we use gestures and body language to make our feelings known or emphasise a point. (See also *one-way communication, two-way communication, marketing communications*.)

communication barrier: an obstacle preventing the smooth flow of information through an organisation. Examples include distortion to messages as they pass through many layers of bureaucracy, managers with poor *interpersonal skills* and individuals suffering from *information overload*.

communication channels: the routes through which individuals communicate with one another. Typical communication channels in leisure and tourism organisations include formal meetings and staff liaison committees.

communication networks are charts that show the communication structure within an organisation. Three of the most common networks are the circle, the chain and the wheel (see figure below). The wheel is considered to be the most effective for simple tasks, the chain the slowest, but the circle tends to give employees the most job satisfaction, as it gives the greatest amount of interaction between employees.

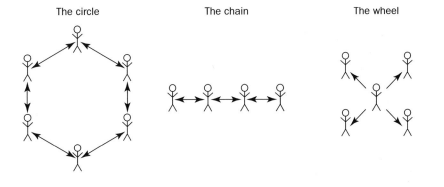

The circle   The chain   The wheel

communication skills are an essential requirement for employees in the leisure, travel and tourism industries. Staff must be competent in dealing with customers and colleagues face-to-face, in writing, by *e-mail*, on the telephone, at presentations, etc. Effective communication skills can help staff when handling *complaints* and in sales situations.

communication systems: the equipment and procedures that an organisation uses to disseminate information between employees and to maintain contact with outside agencies. The main types of communication systems used by leisure and tourism organisations include *written*, *verbal* and *electronic* communication systems. They help an organisation to manage its flow of information, act as an aid to decision making, help monitor organisational performance and facilitate links with external bodies.

community arts is made up of individuals, organisations and practices that give all members of a community the opportunity to take a full part in their local arts scene and express themselves creatively. In England, community arts organisations are funded by *local authorities*, the *Arts Council of England* and the *Regional Arts Boards (RABs)*, often benefiting from *National Lottery* proceeds.

community charge: a tax which replaced household rates and which was levied on individuals rather than being related to the value of their house. Colloquially known as the 'poll tax', the community charge was introduced by the Conservative government in 1990 and levied on all adults over the age of eighteen, with reductions for students, pensioners and people on state benefits. The tax proved very unpopular, not least because the very wealthy were often paying the same community charge as the very poor. The Government scrapped the tax in 1992–93 in favour of the *council tax*, again based on the value of property.

Community Consortia for Education and Training (CCETs): see *ELWA – Education and Learning Wales*

community council: the lowest tier of local government, coming below *county* and *district councils*, and the one which many would say is the closest to the people it represents, namely those living in small rural or urban communities. Sometimes referred to as a parish council, the community council is responsible for managing some local facilities, such as sports fields, but generally lacks the power and resources of either the district or county councils to be able to get things done. Instead, the role of the community council is often that of a local sounding board, bringing items for attention to the notice of the respective authorities and elected representatives of the people.

community group: any collection of individuals that comes together to improve aspects of the quality of life in their community. This could be setting up a group to develop tourism in the area, improving leisure facilities, planning an event or entering the *Britain in Bloom* competition. Community groups often seek *funding* from *local authorities* and the *National Lottery* to help their work.

community recreation is an important sector of the UK *leisure and recreation industry,* concerned with meeting the leisure needs of all members of society, irrespective of class, income, gender, age, religion, education, ethnic origin, ability or mobility. Studies conducted from the 1970s onwards have shown that the majority of users of leisure facilities tend to be white, male, car-borne and middle class. Bodies such as the *Sports Council* (now *UK Sport*) have sought to redress the balance through campaigns such as *'Sport for All'*, while the *CCPR* introduced its *Community Sports Leaders Award* in 1982. (See also *sports equity*.)

Community Sports Leaders Award (CSLA): created by the *Central Council of Physical Recreation* in 1982 in recognition of the contribution of sport to the social well-being as well as the sporting life of the nation. The idea behind the CSLA is to develop existing voluntary effort by recruiting from local communities people who might care to extend their involvement by training to become leaders in their own chosen activity. It is awarded at three progressive levels and is recognised as a qualification for the voluntary service element of the *Duke of Edinburgh's Award Scheme*. Operation of the Award is now carried out by the *British Sports Trust*.

Companies Act 1985: the principal piece of UK legislation concerning the formation of *companies* and their operation. The Act stipulates the documentation and records that all limited companies must keep, including the *Memorandum of Association* and *Articles of Association*. Parts of the 1985 Act were amended in 1989 to bring them into line with European legislation.

company: see *limited company*

compensation: money or other benefits given to an individual as a result of poor service, problems with products and services, or to make up for inconvenience or anxiety. In leisure and tourism, *tour operators*, airlines, leisure operators, etc. will, from time to time, agree to pay compensation to aggrieved customers, sometimes under the terms of a *customer charter* or *code of conduct*.

competition is a common feature of the *leisure, travel* and *tourism* industries, especially since the majority of organisations operate in the private sector, with profit maximisation as their primary *objective*. In an attempt to increase their *market share*, companies with sometimes enter into merger talks with potential partner organisations, leading sometimes to *vertical* or *horizontal integration* in the industries. The government has sought to encourage competition within leisure, travel and tourism through *privatisation* and *compulsory competitive tendering*.

Competition Commission: an independent public body, established under the Competition Act 1998, with two distinct functions. On its reporting side, the Commission has taken on the former *Monopolies and Merger Commission* role of carrying out inquiries into matters of unfair competition concerning monopolies, mergers and the economic regulation of the utility companies. Secondly, the newly established appeals tribunals hear appeals against decisions of the Director General of Fair Trading and the Regulators of utilities in respect of infringements of the prohibitions contained in the Act concerning anti-competitive agreements and abuse of a dominant position. Weblink: www.competition-commission.org.uk

competitive advantage is a position that an organisation strives to achieve over its competitors, perhaps through a wider range of products, more effective *promotion* or higher standards of *customer service*.

competitive pricing: a pricing method, sometimes referred to as 'the going rate', which assumes that, where products and services are similar, the organisation will match the prices of its competitors. This method often leads to very low profit margins and, in the long run, the collapse of some organisations, e.g. *tour operators*, who find that their *profitability* is too low.

competitive tendering is the process of inviting bids for the provision of goods and services. It is common practice in both *private* and *public sector leisure and tourism* to ask suppliers to tender, often to find the supplier who can do the job for the lowest price. As part of a general move towards privatisation and the contracting out of services, local councils are required to invite tenders for a range of their services which were previously provided by council employees, a practice known as *compulsory competitive tendering*.

competitor activity must be monitored constantly if a leisure, travel or tourism enterprise is to maximise its effectiveness. *Competition* is fierce and knowledge of what competitors are doing in terms of pricing, product development or marketing can make the difference between success and failure.

complaints are adverse reactions or comments by *customers* who are unhappy about a product or service they have bought, or the standard of service they have received. Common areas for complaints in leisure and tourism include tour operators changing details of package holidays at the last minute, retail staff being unhelpful towards customers and problems in getting through on the telephone to a company. All staff must be trained in handling customer complaints and learn to treat them as a form of *feedback* which will help improve standards in the future.

compulsory competitive tendering (CCT) is the process of inviting tenders from commercial operators for the management of services and facilities that were previously carried out by public agencies. CCT was first adopted following the Local Government and Planning Act 1980, which required competition for building and highways construction and maintenance. The Local Government Act of 1988 extended the 1980 Act by requiring local authorities to subject a number of services to competitive tendering, including:

* refuse collection
* schools and welfare catering
* vehicle maintenance
* management of sports and leisure facilities.

Facilities falling within the scope of CCT include sports centres, leisure centres, athletics grounds, cycle tracks, bowling greens, artificial ski slopes and golf courses. The principle underlying CCT is that increased competition should provide an improved service and better value for money for the local population. Critics of CCT argue that it may lead to certain services and facilities being phased out since they are unprofitable, but nonetheless fulfil an important local need, e.g. facilities for disabled people. There is no doubt that CCT has provided *local authorities* with major challenges, not least in terms of the efficiency of organisational structures, as well as cost and revenue factors. (See also *Best Value*.)

computerised reservation system (CRS): an automated facility that allows leisure and tourism companies to provide up-to-date information on product availability and offer customers the opportunity of finalising a purchase of a range of products, including holidays, flights and car hire. Specialist leisure and tourism companies will have 'stand alone' systems, often operating on tailor-made software, e.g. *leisure centres*, coach companies and specialist *tour operators*. Larger organisations, such as airlines and mass market tour operators, have extensive systems that can often be accessed directly by travel agents using a *'gateway'* facility, in order to check availability and make reservations. Such systems are interactive, ensuring that there is constant updating of product availability and no problem of the same stock being offered for sale by more than one person at a time.

Airlines have invested heavily in global computerised reservation systems, which provide not only accurate data on airline flights and costs, but also information on other travel services, including car hire, resort information, exchange rates, weather data, sporting events and resort excursions. Probably the best known system is American Airline's *Sabre* CRS, although there is competition from European systems such as *Galileo* and *Amadeus*.

computers: see *personal computer (PC)*

concentrated marketing: a type of *marketing strategy* where an organisation chooses to compete in only one sector of a market, developing the most effective *marketing mix* for that sector. Many smaller operators in leisure and tourism choose this option and gain in-depth information on their *customers* and their requirements. Eurocamp is a UK company that adopts a concentrated marketing strategy, focusing on a narrow sector of the market for family camping holidays.

concentration ratio refers to the share of the market taken by the largest companies in a particular industry, e.g. between them, *Thomson*, My Travel, JMC Holidays and First Choice Holidays have around 60 percent of the total market for outbound *package holidays*.

concession: an individual or organisation that is given the opportunity to trade within an existing facility, such as a *tourist attraction* or *hotel*, in return for a fixed fee or percentage of their profits being given to the facility owner. Concessionaires are also found at *events*, providing services such as catering and retail units. The owners and operators of facilities need to ensure that the concessionaires meet certain minimum quality and safety standards to make sure that their own reputation is not compromised.

concierge: a French term used to denote a member of hotel staff with responsibility for the movement and storage of guests' luggage, car parking and the provision of information.

conciliation: another name for *arbitration*.

conditions of employment: details such as salary, holiday arrangements, hours of work, *pension* entitlement, etc. that are included in an employee's *contract of employment*.

condominium: an apartment in which individual living units are owned separately, but the land and building in which they are housed is in the collective ownership of the residents. Condominiums are often found in resort areas and may be used as *second homes*.

Confederation of British Industry (CBI) is the representative body for industry in *Britain*, embracing the manufacturing and service sectors of the economy. Its mission is to promote the long-run competitiveness of British business. It is seen by government and the *European Commission* as the principal mouthpiece for industry in Britain across the whole range of policy issues. The CBI is a key player in the *Tourism Alliance*, developed as a single voice for tourism in the UK. Weblink: www.cbi.org.uk

Confederation of Passenger Transport UK (CPT) is an independent association representing the interests of UK bus and coach operators. Formed in 1974 as the Bus and Coach Council (BCC), CPT acts as the voice of the bus and coach industry in representations at national and European level. It has drawn up a *code of conduct* for professional operators, covering bonding arrangements and safety. Weblink: www.cpt-uk.org

CONFER: an annual trade exhibition organised by the *British Association of Conference Destinations*. The aim of the exhibition is to give organisers of conferences, exhibitions and *incentive travel*, the opportunity to obtain up-to-date information on the services and facilities offered by BACD member destinations.

conference: a gathering of people for the purpose of information exchange, analysis and discussion. Academics and people working in the *leisure* and *tourism* industries hold regular conferences, sometimes called conventions or congresses, in order to keep up-to-date on industry developments and maintain contacts. Conferences in general, across all sectors of industry, are an important element in *business tourism*, bringing economic benefits to regions and countries around the world.

conflict in teams can have serious implications for an organisation if it is not managed effectively. Conflict can be either inter-team, i.e. between two or more teams in the same organisation, or intra-team, i.e. develops within a team. It can lead to a number of problems, including high staff turnover, increased staff absenteeism, reduced staff morale and poor levels of *customer service*.

conglomerate is the name given to a large organisation that owns and operates a number of smaller subsidiary enterprises, each of which contributes to overall profitability. In leisure and tourism, the *Tussauds Group* is a good example; it operates Madame Tussaud's, *Alton Towers* and Warwick Castle (and many other attractions) as independent business units, with a co-ordinating role for itself as the parent company. (See also *multinational corporation*.)

congress: see *conference*

conservation: the practice of protecting artefacts, buildings, habitats and natural landscapes for future generations to enjoy and appreciate. *Tourism* and *recreation* often come into conflict with *conservation*, leading to problems of *erosion*, pollution and the spoiling of landscapes. Careful management is needed to ensure that visitors do not destroy the very thing they have come to enjoy. Organisations such as the *Countryside Agency* and the *British Trust for Conservation Volunteers* offer practical solutions to countryside conservation problems, while the *Civic Trust* promotes the conservation of urban areas.

consolidation: the practice in the *charter* airline industry of combining the passengers on a flight from one departure airport with those from another departure airport, so as to produce one plane-load of passengers. Consolidation occurs when the take-up of seats on an aircraft is low, i.e. there is a low *load factor*. It is in the interest of the airline or tour operator to consolidate, since it helps their productivity. Passengers, however, are often inconvenienced by the practice, particularly when the *transportation* to another departure airport results in a delay in them catching their flight or starting their holiday.

consortium: a grouping of independent businesses or other organisations working together for a common purpose or benefit. A group of farmhouse *accommodation* owners, for example, may pool their resources to develop a *joint marketing* scheme or buy their collective supplies in bulk at discount prices. Best Western Hotels is a good example of a marketing consortium in the leisure and tourism industries; individual hoteliers pay to become members of the consortium and benefit from inclusion in a national *brochure*, *advertising* and *promotion*, and the services of a *central reservation system*. Consortia are also found in the visitor attractions sector, e.g. the *Association of Leading Visitor Attractions*.

constraint: a factor that limits the extent to which an organisation is able to achieve its full potential. Constraints may be *internal*, over which the organisation has some degree of control, or *external*, i.e. those that occur in the wider world and over which it has little control.

consultancy: a firm that is employed to carry out work on behalf of another organisation, perhaps because of their expertise in a particular sector or subject. Consultants are frequently used by leisure, travel and tourism organisations to, for example, develop *marketing plans*, produce *feasibility studies* or draw up plans for new facilities or events.

consumer: the end user of a product or service, but not necessarily the person who bought it in the first place (the *customer*). For example, a mother may treat her son to a course of golfing lessons; the son will be the *consumer* and the mother the *customer*. Marketers of leisure, travel and tourism products and services must bear this distinction in mind when devising *marketing campaigns*.

Consumer Credit Act 1974: government *legislation* designed to protect *customers* who enter into a credit agreement when buying products and services. The Act has a wide scope and covers *credit cards*, *hire purchase* arrangements, any type of cash *loan* and bank *overdrafts*. One important part of the Act is the requirement that all publicity material concerning a credit arrangement must clearly state the *annual percentage rate (APR)* charged by the lender.

consumer demand: a measure of the willingness of people to buy or use goods and services. Demand by consumers for leisure, travel and tourism products and services will be influenced by a variety of factors, including the state of the economy, *fashions and trends*.

consumer needs: see *needs*

consumer press refers to magazines, newspapers and journals targeted at members of the general public. (See also *trade press*.)

consumer protection: the process of ensuring that consumers are treated fairly, honestly and safely when they buy goods and services. Consumer protection is most commonly achieved through government legislation, but can be carried out on a voluntary basis, e.g. a voluntary code of practice or *code of conduct*. Legislation designed to protect consumers includes the *Consumer Protection Act 1987*, the *Trades Description Act 1968* and the *Food Safety Act 1990*. Consumer protection legislation is enforced by *central government* and local authority officials, including *Environmental Health Officers* and *Trading Standards Officers*. There is an increasing amount of consumer legislation coming from the *European Commission*, e.g. the *Package Travel Directive*.

Consumer Protection Act 1987: government legislation that addresses a number of consumer issues, including the clear display of prices for good and services, the safety of products and the liability of suppliers if things go wrong. In the case of travel and tourism, many of these issues are now contained in the *Package Travel Directive*.

consumer spending refers to the different amounts that individuals and households spend on products and services in the course of their daily lives. Research data in *Social Trends* shows that British people spend more on leisure activities than any other item of household expenditure, including food, housing and travel. In 1999, the average British household expenditure per week was as follows:

- £60 on leisure goods and services
- £59 on food and non-alcoholic drinks
- £57 on housing

- £52 on motoring
- £22 on clothing
- £14 on alcohol
- £12 on fuel and power
- £9 on tobacco
- £8 on fares and travel.

Besides leisure, which includes items such as holidays, sports, cinema and electrical items, the UK's other passion appears to be computers; in 2000, one in three households in the UK owned their own computer.

consumerism is a developing movement which encourages people to be better informed of their legal rights as consumers and empowers them to challenge suppliers of goods and services. The popularity of *television* and radio programmes such as Watchdog and You and Yours, plus the growth of groups such as the *Consumers' Association*, is evidence that people are no longer willing to accept poor standards of products and service. This applies equally well to leisure and tourism products and services, whose providers need to be constantly aware of consumer tastes and preferences.

Consumers' Association: a membership organisation that champions consumer rights and carries out independent testing on a range of products and services, to determine safety levels, reliability and value for money. Perhaps best known for its monthly publication *Which?*, the Association also carries out extensive research on holidays and associated leisure products, with these results published in a sister publication called *Holiday Which?* The Association also campaigns on behalf of its members for changes to government *legislation.* Weblink: www.which.net

Continental Plan: an accommodation arrangement consisting of bed and continental breakfast. (See also *American Plan, Modified American Plan, European Plan*.)

contingency plan: a set of procedures, planned in advance of an event, which can be put into operation if certain circumstances arise, e.g. the failure of the electricity supply at a major outdoor event, the failure of a key member of staff to turn up or an accident to visitors. All event organisers must ensure that they have plans in place to deal with a range of contingencies, particularly those affecting health and safety.

continuing professional development (CPD): the practice of giving employees the opportunity, through different types of *staff training* and development, to improve their work skills and develop themselves as individuals. When linked to *staff appraisal*, CPD can be an effective way of developing an organisation's human resources and empowering individuals to be effective members of staff. As part of a planned programme of continuing professional development, staff may attend in-house training courses, go to conferences and seminars, 'shadow' other members of staff or study for formal qualifications.

contract of employment: a written, legal document that sets out the terms and conditions under which a member of staff is expected to work. Under the Trade Union Reform and Employment Rights Act of 1993, employees who are eligible to be given a contract of employment must receive it within two months of starting their employment. The contract will contain details of a number of conditions of employment, including the names of both parties to the contract, the job title, the date when employment began, details of remuneration, hours of work, holiday entitlement, termination arrangements and *grievance procedures*. The current trend in UK employment is away from permanent contracts for employees in leisure and tourism, towards short-term contracts and casual working.

contribution pricing: the practice of setting prices for products and services on the basis that as long as the prices set cover the *variable costs*, then the product or service is making a contribution towards the *overheads* of the business. It is sometimes referred to as marginal costing. (See also *loss leader*.)

Control of Substances Hazardous to Health (COSHH): a set of regulations that add to an employer's duties concerning the use of harmful substances, as laid down in the *Health and Safety at Work, etc. Act*. Under the COSHH Regulations 1999, employers must assess the likely exposure to all hazardous substances on their premises and put in place control measures and monitoring procedures as appropriate. A 'hazardous substance' can be solid, liquid, gaseous, vapour, dust or fumes. The use of chemicals in the leisure and tourism industries falls within the scope of the Regulations, for example the treatment of swimming pool water, storing and using disinfectants, controlling insects and vermin, and the marking and management of sports fields.

convention: see *conference*

convention bureau: an organisation responsible for promoting an area to *tourists*. Convention bureaux in the UK, e.g. Sheffield Visitor and Convention Bureau and Manchester Visitor and Convention Bureau, are often *partnerships* between *public* and *private sector organisations*, pooling their resources to gain maximum impact. Most convention bureaux will offer an *accommodation* reservation service, arrange conferences and offer *tourist information*. Many bureaux are members of the *British Association of Conference Destinations (BACD)*.

conversion rate: a term used in *marketing* to denote the ratio of enquiries that are converted into sales in response to a promotional *campaign*, e.g. 20 holiday bookings arising out of 200 enquiries for brochures would give a conversion rate of 1:10.

co-operative: a type of business enterprise which is owned and managed by its workforce and operated on democratic lines. The number of co-operatives in leisure and tourism is small, but they are to be found in community ventures such as art galleries, music workshops, street theatre and countryside groups. They operate on the basis of one person, one vote, with *objectives* being determined by the workforce and any profits distributed equitably.

co-operative marketing: an arrangement between two or more organisations which agree to pool their resources and share costs, in the hope of achieving a better response to a promotional *campaign* than if they advertised individually. Sometimes called joint marketing, it is best suited to sectors of the leisure and tourism industries that are not in direct competition with each other, e.g. hotels and airlines, tourist boards and ferry companies. Fifty/fifty marketing is a particular type of co-operation in which, for example, travel agents and tour operators share advertising space in the *consumer* or *trade press*, each paying half of the total cost.

corporate fitness describes a company's efforts to improve the fitness levels of its employees, in the hope that fitter staff will work more effectively and ultimately bring benefits to the organisation. This could include the provision of sports grounds, fitness suites, facilities for bicycle storage and indoor gyms.

corporate hospitality refers to entertaining existing and potential business clients with the expectation of making new contacts and increased business *opportunities*. Corporate hospitality events range from lavish occasions at Wimbledon or Henley Regatta, to the owner of a business inviting his bank manager for a meal in a local restaurant.

corporate identity is the image that an organisation portrays to the outside world, as shown by its *logo*, business stationery, vehicles, staff uniforms, premises and *advertising*, all of which should be co-ordinated to reinforce the identity. Establishing a corporate identity helps to project an image that is easily recognised and establish a consistent level of quality and service in the minds of *customers*. Establishing an effective corporate identity can help to increase *brand loyalty*.

corporate image: another name for *corporate identity*

corporate objectives: see *business objectives*

corporation tax is a direct tax paid by *companies* on their profits, in the same way that individuals pay *income tax* on their income and investments. There is a lower rate of corporation tax for small and medium-sized businesses.

corrective maintenance: see *maintenance*

COSHH: see *Control of Substances Hazardous to Health*

cost-based pricing is a pricing policy that sets the prices of products and services purely on the basis of the cost of their production, taking no account of market factors and conditions. In the highly competitive leisure and tourism industries such a policy rarely exists, except where there is little direct *competition*. *Market-led pricing* is the norm in leisure and tourism. (See also *cost-plus pricing*.)

cost-benefit analysis (CBA) is a planning process which considers all the financial, operational, environmental and social costs and benefits of a proposed project or other course of action. It is a systematic technique that tries to look beyond the purely commercial costs and benefits and into the wider social and community issues that may arise. A CBA of a major airport expansion, for example, would certainly consider the extra *revenue* and jobs that the project would generate, plus the extra costs, but also the effects on the local people of extra noise and disturbance, the loss of amenity land and the likelihood of extra accidents and their associated costs. These costs, which may be hard to quantify, are sometimes known as *social costs*.

cost centre: a readily identifiable location, department or function within an organisation, against which its *costs* of operation can be charged. Taking as an example the *marketing* department of a large *tour operator*, it is likely to have a number of cost centres including:

- *market research*
- brochure production
- brochure distribution
- agency sales support
- agency marketing
- *merchandising*.

Each cost centre will be allocated a unique cost code to make sure that all its costs are correctly identified.

cost control is the process of managing an organisation's expenditure within pre-determined limits. *Budgeting* allows the comparison of actual and budgeted *costs* and allows management to take corrective action over any *variances* found.

cost-plus pricing is a simplistic pricing method that totals all an organisation's *fixed* and *variable costs* and adds a small profit margin to arrive at the final price to charge. Sometimes called 'accountant's pricing', cost-plus pricing assumes that an organisation can calculate its costs accurately, which a large leisure complex, for example, may find difficult. It also ignores market conditions, thereby denying an organisation a potential profit opportunity. It does, however, have the advantage of protecting a firm's profit margin, since it assumes that any increases in costs will be passed on to the customer.

costs are the items of expenditure incurred by an organisation in the production of its goods and services. Costs may be classified by nature, i.e. *fixed* (remaining constant despite the level of business activity), or *variable* (changing in proportion to the level of activity). Classification by type is also common, dividing costs into *direct* and *indirect*. For purposes of *budgeting*, costs are sometimes allocated to *cost centres* or the departments that incur them. *Cost control* is an essential element of the work of managers in leisure and tourism.

COTAC: see *Certificate of Travel Agency Competence*

couchette: basic sleeping *accommodation* provided on trains in some continental European countries and consisting of a *berth* in a shared compartment, with a supply of linen but no en-suite washing or toilet facilities.

Council of Europe: this was established in 1949 with the aim of promoting greater unity between its members and achieving economic and social progress. The Council is not a *European Union* body, but many of its members are EU member states, including the *United Kingdom*, Spain, Greece and Germany. The Council promotes co-operation in a number of areas, including health and social services, youth activities, *consumer protection* and the harmonisation of laws within Europe.

Council of Ministers: an important institution of the *European Union* which decides on all the laws that establish Union policies. The Council consists of government ministers from the fifteen member states, accountable to their own parliaments, representing national interests on the subjects under discussion, e.g. trade, agriculture, social policy, etc. Each member state takes a six-month turn to hold the Presidency of the Council, setting the agenda and chairing meetings.

Council for Museums, Archives and Libraries: see *Resource*

Council for National Parks: a body established in 1936, before Britain's *National Parks* were designated, as the Standing Committee for National Parks. It was a way of ensuring that the environment within the National Parks was both protected and made available for the public to enjoy. Today the Council works to continue the original aims of the Standing Committee by campaigning for protection of the National Parks, fighting issues of national importance, such as mineral extraction in the National Parks, and encouraging *good practice*, including environmentally-friendly farming projects and schemes to protect the cultural *heritage* of local communities. Weblink: www.cnp.org.uk

Council for the Protection of Rural England (CPRE): established in 1926, CPRE is an independent environmental group working for the protection of the English countryside. It fights against the onset of urban development in the countryside, works for better *conservation*

measures and a stronger system for the protection of the landscape. CPRE also encourages better *management* of woodland and farmland, and advocates more efficient use of energy resources. Its 59,000 supporters are drawn from all over the country, with a branch in every county, eight regional groups and more than 200 local groups. Weblink: www.cpre.org.uk

council tax: a tax levied by local authorities on people living in their area, in order to supplement *central government* funding for local services. Council tax, which replaced the unpopular *community charge* (poll tax) in 1992–93, is used by *local authorities* to provide a range of services, including refuse collection, library services and *leisure* facilities. The amount of council tax a person pays is based on the value of the property in which they live; the higher the value of the property, the greater the council tax.

country park: an area designated for outdoor *recreation* and located close to urban areas. Country parks were established under the *Countryside Act of 1968* as a way of giving town-dwellers a chance to enjoy their leisure in the open without travelling too far and adding to congestion on the roads. The designation of country parks is the responsibility of the *Countryside Agency* and *Countryside Council for Wales*, although they are maintained by *local authorities*.

Countryside Act 1968: government *legislation* concerned with *conservation* and *access* to the countryside for leisure and recreation. The Act established the *Countryside Commission* (now the *Countryside Agency*) and designated *country parks*, nature trails, picnic sites and bird sanctuaries.

Countryside Agency: the statutory body working to make life better for people in the countryside and to improve the quality of the countryside for everyone. It has a wide-ranging programme of work, including running demonstration projects of *good practice* in countryside management, advising on strategy for the *National Parks,* working with local authorities to protect the *Areas of Outstanding Natural Beauty*, supporting practical work on the *Heritage Coasts*, establishing *National Trails* and developing Community Forests close to major towns and cities. The Countryside Agency resulted from the merger of the *Countryside Commission* and the *Rural Development Commission*. Weblink: www.countryside.gov.uk

Countryside and Rights of Way Act 2000 (CROW): government legislation that aims to give people greater freedom to explore open countryside, reflecting many years of pressure for such an Act. When fully in force, CROW will create a new right of *access* to mountain, moor, heath, down and common land. It will reform and improve public rights of way in England and Wales, give greater powers to *English Nature* to conserve biodiversity and protect *Sites of Special Scientific Interest* and improve the management of *Areas of Outstanding Natural Beauty*.

Countryside Commission: the former government-funded *quango* that was established under the *Countryside Act of 1968* with the following broad aims:

- to conserve and enhance the scenic, natural, historic and cultural qualities of the whole countryside
- to secure and extend opportunities for people to enjoy and use the countryside for open air recreation
- to promote understanding of the countryside, its life and work.

The Commission's work is now carried out by the *Countryside Agency*.

Countryside Council for Wales (CCW) is the government-funded body formed as a result of the merger between the Nature Conservancy Council and the Countryside Commission in Wales. With its headquarters in Bangor, the Council is the statutory adviser to government on sustaining natural beauty, wildlife and the opportunity for outdoor enjoyment in rural Wales and its inshore waters. The purposes of CCW are to conserve the quality of the Welsh landscape and its inshore waters, conserve the variety of wildlife and habitats, create opportunities for everyone to enjoy and understand the countryside, and to consider the culture and economy of Wales in all its day-to-day work. Weblink: www.ccw.gov.uk

countryside recreation is a growing sector of the UK *leisure and recreation industry*, encompassing both informal and formal activities. Informal activities, such as walking and rambling are among the most popular pastimes in Britain, while the growing interest in health and fitness has encouraged many people to take up formal recreational pursuits in the countryside, for example mountain biking, orienteering and rock climbing. The increasing number of people seeking enjoyment and recreation in the countryside is putting some rural areas of Britain under extreme pressure, especially the *National Parks*, where managers are constantly trying to maintain a balance between the needs of the visitors and the *conservation* of the natural environment.

Countryside Recreation Network (CRN) is a network providing an easy means of access to individuals and agencies concerned with countryside and related *recreation* matters. The Network reaches a variety of organisations and individuals in the public, private and voluntary sectors. It assists the work of agencies and individuals by helping to meet the needs of its members for advice, information and research. CRN also promotes co-operation between member agencies and encourages the dissemination of good practice in *countryside recreation*, through a series of conferences, training events and its regular publication Countryside Recreation Network News. It is funded by a number of government departments, agencies and other bodies which share an interest in countryside recreation issues. Weblink: www.countrysiderecreation.org.uk

county council: the tier of local government responsible for providing services to the people and businesses in one of the 34 county councils in England and Wales. County councils tend to operate at more of a strategic level than *district councils*, and are responsible for developing *Structure Plans*, the provision of roads, education and social services facilities, and *tourism policy*. (*See also Local Government Association*.)

courier: a representative of a travel company who is employed to assist *customers* during their holiday or business trip. Couriers, sometimes called resort representatives, are most usually associated with *tour operators*, where they take responsibility for the care of clients on a package holiday abroad. Typical courier duties include arranging transfers between airports and *accommodation*, organising excursions from resorts and generally helping to provide customers with an enjoyable experience. Couriers are usually only employed for the holiday season and may be specifically recruited to work with children on holiday.

cover is a term used in the catering industry to denote the number of places available for customers who are eating in a restaurant or *hotel*, i.e. a restaurant with 100 covers will seat 100 customers.

CPD: see *continuing professional development*

CPRE: see *Council for the Protection of Rural England*

CPRW: see *Campaign for the Protection of Rural Wales*

CPT: see *Confederation of Passenger Transport UK*

Crafts Council: a government funded body established in 1979 to promote contemporary crafts in Britain and ensure that crafts can be enjoyed by as wide a cross-section of the public as possible. The Council works with the *Regional Arts Boards (RABs)* and provides funding for crafts in the regions. It also advises crafts people on such matters as business development and training, and represents the interests of crafts generally at government level. Weblink: www.craftscouncil.org.uk

CRE: see *Commission for Racial Equality*

credit is when goods and services are supplied but the request for payment is delayed. The actual period of time granted is known as the *credit period*. Credit is accepted practice in all dealings between organisations and sometimes between *companies* and their *customers*. Credit may be given freely (the so-called 'free credit' often seen on consumer purchases) or may attract an interest payment. *Credit cards* offer a free credit period before settlement is due.

credit card: a plastic card, issued by banks and other financial organisations, that gives its holder a period of free credit, subject to certain conditions. Credit cards are a convenient way of making a large purchase, and are in widespread use in *hotels*, restaurants and other catering outlets, and for booking *holidays* and flights. Credit cards can also be used for postal, *Internet* and telephone bookings, allowing instant purchases of, for example, theatre and concert tickets. The two most common cards in use in Britain are operated by Mastercard and Visa.

credit control: the process of managing an organisation's *debtors* so as to minimise *bad debts* and the time within which payments are due.

credit period: the amount of time granted by a supplier within which payment is expected to be made. Credit periods are typically 30, 60 or 90 days, depending on the value of the goods and services supplied and the working relationship between the two parties concerned.

creditor: a person or individual to whom money is owed for the supply of goods and services. Creditors form part of an organisation's *current liabilities*, as shown on its *balance sheet*. It is common practice in leisure and tourism for companies to grant periods of *credit* before payment is due.

criminal prosecution: an action inflicted on those who commit a criminal offence, e.g. fraud or arson. Such offenders are pursued by the police and prosecuted on behalf of the public if it is believed they are guilty of an offence.

crisis management is the response of an organisation to an unexpected or unplanned event or incident, such as a fire or major accident. All organisations should have *contingency plans* to cover such occurrences, with clear lines of *responsibility* and *communication*, so as to implement emergency procedures as quickly as possible. In the event of an incident of national importance, an organisation should have prepared a *public relations* plan to minimise adverse publicity.

critical path analysis (CPA): a technique used in *operations management* to simplify decision making by breaking a project into its component activities. CPA sets out to:

- identify all the tasks and activities involved in the project
- place them in an appropriate sequence
- set timescales and allocate work tasks
- calculate the best critical time path for the project.

By so doing, CPA can be used to plan, schedule, monitor and control the project. It is used particularly in the *management* of large building projects, such as the development of a new *theme park* or *hotel* complex. It is also applicable to planning *marketing campaigns* and developing new products.

CRN: see *Countryside Recreation Network*

CROW: see *Countryside and Rights of Way Act 2000*

Crown Classification Scheme: a voluntary national *accommodation grading scheme* for *serviced accommodation* in *Britain* that was launched in 1987. The scheme classified the facilities offered by establishments into one of six categories, from 'listed' for basic, clean facilities to 'five crowns' for hotels with en-suite facilities in all bedrooms, a restaurant serving breakfast, lunch and dinner, the availability of a night porter, room service, etc. In 1990, the Crown Scheme was refined to include an assessment of the quality of the accommodation as well as the 'listed' and one to five crown ratings. The quality gradings were as follows:

- approved – an acceptable overall standard of quality
- commended – a good overall standard of quality
- highly commended – a very good overall standard of quality
- deluxe – an excellent overall standard of quality.

The scheme has since been superseded by the *Star accommodation grading scheme*. (See also *Key classification scheme*.)

CRS: see *computerised reservation system*

cruising is considered by many to be the ultimate *holiday* in a 'floating hotel'. It is currently experiencing something of a revival, with new generation ships and mass market tour operators beginning to offer cruise holidays at affordable prices to a new segment of the market. The cruise market in Britain has grown rapidly in recent years to become second only to that of the United States. Nearly 800,000 UK passengers take cruises every year. Apart from round-the-world cruises, the most popular destinations are the Caribbean, the Mediterranean and the Baltic. (See also *fly-cruise*, *Passenger Shipping Association*.)

CSLA: see *Community Sports Leaders Award*

CSQ: see *customer service questionnaire*

CTC: see *Cyclists' Touring Club*

cultural destination: a tourist *destination* renowned for its rich historical, architectural, literary, linguistic, artistic or musical associations. As tourists become more discerning in their tastes, cultural destinations offer new and enriching experiences for individuals and groups. Popular cultural destinations include Rome, Vienna, Paris, London and Prague.

Cultural Heritage National Training Organisation (CHNTO): one of a national network of over 70 *National Training Organisations (NTOs)*, CHNTO has responsibility for all education and training matters relating to the UK cultural heritage sector, including *museums*, galleries, heritage organisations, botanical gardens, zoos and aquaria. Weblink: www.chnto.co.uk

cultural identity: the mixture of a variety of real and perceived symbols and traditions that give a country or region its unique identity. Effective *tourism management* is concerned with ensuring that destinations do not lose their cultural identities when developed for *tourism*.

cultural recreation: see *arts and entertainment*

cultural tourism is 'travel with a purpose', for those seeking artistic and cultural inspiration. It includes history tours, *museum* visits, wine and food appreciation holidays, trips to art galleries and music tours.

Cumbria Tourist Board is the official *Regional Tourist Board* covering the county of Cumbria, centred on the Lake District *National Park*. Weblink: www.cumbria-the-lake-district.co.uk

currency refers to notes and coins used as the medium of exchange in a country. Some countries impose restrictions on the amount of currency that can be taken into and out of the country, so as to protect their exchange rate. Many countries in Europe have recently adopted the *Euro* as their currency. (See also *hard currency*.)

currency fluctuation: changes in *the rate of exchange* between one *currency* and another. Fluctuations in international currencies can have a marked effect on the demand for tourism; for example a fall in the US dollar against the pound sterling will make US holidays more expensive for British people.

current assets are items owned by a business, where the value is constantly changing, for example stock, cash and *debtors* (those who owe money to an organisation), and which are likely to be converted into cash before the date of the next *balance sheet*, generally within twelve months. The balance of current assets over current liabilities is known as the *working capital*, which finances an organisation's everyday operations.

current liabilities are amounts owed by an organisation that are likely to be repaid before the date of the next *balance sheet*, usually within twelve months. Typical current liabilities include *creditors* (those to whom money is owed), loans, overdrafts and dividends.

current ratio: see *liquidity ratio*

curriculum vitae (CV): a written statement of an individual's career history, which may be sent to a prospective employer in response to a job advertisement. Some organisations prefer to ask for a CV rather than a completed job application form, while others make it very clear that a CV is not acceptable in place of an application form. A complete CV should include the following:

• Name	• Employment record
• Address	• Skills
• Telephone number	• Notable achievements
• Date of birth	• Interests and hobbies
• Education to date	• Names and addresses of referees
• Academic and vocational qualifications	

customer: a individual with a unique set of characteristics who buys or uses *leisure* and *tourism products* and services. Customers are the lifeblood of an organisation and usually the very reason for its existence. Customers will have very different needs and will expect high levels of *customer service* from leisure and tourism providers. (See also *consumer, internal customer*.)

customer care: a specific component of *customer service* that focuses on training staff to provide *customers* with a high quality service at all times. High standards in customer care will give an organisation a competitive edge, while at the same time reducing the burden on *management* associated with customer and staff dissatisfaction.

customer charter: a written document that sets out the minimum levels of service and standards of facilities that *customers* can expect when they use a facility or buy a particular product or service. The charter will indicate clearly what the organisation is trying to achieve and sometimes what is expected of customers in return. Customer charters are gaining in popularity in all sectors of the UK economy, even at government level with the introduction of the *Citizens' Charter* and the awarding of *Charter Marks*.

customer comment form: a technique for giving visitors an immediate opportunity to tell the management what they think of the service and facilities they have used. Unlike *customer service questionnaires (CSQs)*, which give people the chance to comment in-depth, customer comment forms often contain only a few questions and can be found in a wide range of leisure and tourism facilities, including hotels, restaurants, fast-food outlets, visitor attractions, ferries and leisure centres. The forms are regularly checked by management and appropriate action taken as necessary to improve standards. See figure on page 64 for an example.

customer loyalty is shown when customers continue to use the services of a particular facility or company, e.g. returning to the same hotel every year on holiday or using a particular *health club* on a regular basis. This kind of *repeat business* is very important to leisure, travel and tourism organisations, since it can reduce their marketing and promotional costs.

customer needs: see *needs*

customer orientation is the *management* philosophy and practice that puts *customers* at the heart of the operation of any leisure, travel or tourism organisation. Rather than focusing purely on what is supplied to customers (*product orientation*), customer orientation is concerned with making sure that all levels within an organisation have a clear commitment to providing products and services that customers will want, as well as excellence in the standards of *customer service* offered.

customer profile: the precise characteristics of the *customers* who buy a particular product or service, such as age, gender, employment status and income level. Customer profile information is a vital starting point for *product development* and *promotion*.

customer satisfaction questionnaire (CSQ): an important *market research* tool used by most leisure and tourism organisations. CSQs invite customers to make comments on the quality of service and standards of facilities they have experienced on their holidays or other leisure or travel arrangements. It is common practice for airlines, *tour operators* and hotel companies to use CSQs in order to improve the levels of service they offer their customers. CSQs are sometimes referred to as 'customer service questionnaires'.

PASSENGER AREA AND TOILETS	1	2	3	4	5
Passenger area – overall impression					
– decor					
– seating availability					
– storage of baggage					
– signposting					
– cleanliness					
– disabled facility					
Toilets – overall impression					
– cleanliness					
– hygiene facilities					
– disabled facilities					

With the exception of the journey you are making, how often have you travelled with Star Travel on this particular route over the past 12 months?

Not at all ☐ 0   Once ☐ 1   Twice ☐ 2   3-4 times ☐ 3

5-6 times ☐ 4   7-10 times ☐ 5   3-4 times ☐ 6

Age:

-14 ☐ 1   15-19 ☐ 2   20-24 ☐ 3   25-34 ☐ 4   35-44 ☐ 5

45-54 ☐ 6   55-59 ☐ 7   60-64 ☐ 8   65+ ☐ 9

Sex: Male ☐ 1   Female ☐ 2

Nationality:

British ☐ 1   French ☐ 2   Spanish ☐ 3   German ☐ 4

Italian ☐ 5   Other ☐ 6   *Please specify* _____

Example of a customer comment form

customer service concerns all aspects of the interface between a *customer* and an organisation (see figure on following page). Recognition of its importance is relatively new to leisure and tourism, although most organisations now offer some form of *customer care* training. The key issues to be addressed by any organisation that is committed to the highest standards of customer service include:

- identification of customer *needs*
- developing the right mix of products and services
- ensuring high quality delivery systems
- measuring customer satisfaction
- carrying out staff *training*.

Obstacles to good customer service include poor *communication* within an organisation, lack of management commitment and inadequate *resources*.

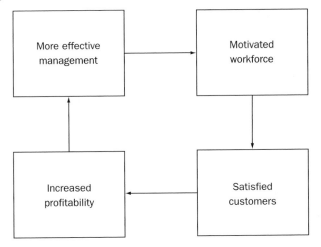

The benefits of developing a customer service approach

customer service questionnaire: see *customer satisfaction questionnaire*

Cyclists' Touring Club (CTC): established in 1878, the CTC is Britain's largest cycling organisation, promoting recreational and utility cycling. It provides its members with technical advice, touring services, *insurance* and legal aid. The CTC campaigns to improve facilities and opportunities for all cyclists and has been active in the development of the *National Cycle Network*. Weblink: www.ctc.org.uk

CV: see *curriculum vitae*

Do you know we also have A–Zs for:

- **Geography**
- **Business Studies**
- **ICT and Computing**
- **Geography Coursework?**

Ask for them in your local bookshop or see the inside back cover for ordering details.

data: factual information of any kind, including statistics, financial information and details on markets. The term is often used in connection with *computer* programmes and systems.

data analysis is an important aspect of both *research* and *management* in leisure, travel and tourism, involving the analysis of information collected for a specific purpose, e.g. data associated with a *survey* of visitors to a *National Park* or *health club*. Large volumes of data are likely to be analysed using a computer program such as SPSS.

database: a collection of files, *data* and records, stored manually or on a computer-based or electronic system, and used for a range of *management* purposes. Common uses of databases in leisure and tourism are travel companies compiling lists of their customers and leisure centres holding details of their suppliers on computer. The main advantage of using a computerised database, such as Microsoft Access, is that once data has been entered onto the system, it can be easily retrieved, amended or sorted, much more quickly than by using a manual system. Also, searches of the database can be made for specific purposes, for example the details of all customers living in a particular town or taking a short break in a particular country.

database marketing is the use of information held in a *database*, usually computerised, for *marketing* and promotional purposes. An example of database marketing would be a tour operator sending a *brochure* to all the clients who travelled to a particular destination the previous year. It is a rapidly growing part of the marketing industry, helped by advances in computer *software* and networks.

Data Protection Act (DPA): government *legislation* introduced in 1984 (and updated in 1998) to safeguard the public from problems relating to the inaccuracy of any information held about them on *computer* records. Under the terms of the Act, all organisations that hold data about individuals on automated systems must register with the Data Protection Registrar and comply with a set of Data Protection Principles, which are a set of *good practice* guidelines. Individuals who have computer data held on them have a number of rights in civil law, including right of access to the data, rights to *compensation* for inaccuracy of data or its wrongful disclosure, and rights to have any inaccuracies in the data rectified.

Date Line: see *International Date Line*

day visitor: see *excursionist*

DCF: see *discounted cash flow*

DCMS: see *Department for Culture, Media and Sport*

DDA: see *Disability Discrimination Act 1995*

debenture: a method by which a company can finance long-term *capital* projects. It is a form of long-term *loan* at a fixed annual rate of interest, secured on the *assets* of a company, often land and buildings. Debentures are sometimes issued by golf clubs and operators of stadia, as a way of financing their expansion plans. If the company defaults on the loan, the *security* can be sold to repay the lender.

debit card: a card used in place of a *cheque*, with the cardholder's bank account being debited usually within three working days. Debit cards offer greater convenience than writing a cheque and, since their introduction, the number of cheques written by current account holders has fallen dramatically. Debit cards should not be confused with *credit cards*, since they offer no free credit period. Examples of debit cards are Switch and Delta. (See also *cheque guarantee card*.)

debriefing is the practice of reflecting on an *event* or meeting after is has finished and sometimes relaying information to a third party. It is important that debriefing sessions take place immediately after the event or meeting, while information and views are still fresh in the mind.

debtor is an individual or organisation that owes you money. Debtors form part of an organisation's *current assets*, i.e. those items whose value is constantly changing and which will be converted into cash in the normal course of trading. It is important for organisations to keep tight control of their debtor situation by chasing late payments and not granting *credit* too freely. Bad debt control can have a serious effect on a company's *cash-flow* position. (See also *creditor*.)

decentralisation: the process of distributing power and *responsibility* away from a central source to smaller management units, e.g. the head office of a major travel agency chain deciding to allow its branch managers to take some management decisions that were previously the responsibility of head office personnel. Within an organisational structure, senior managers may introduce a more decentralised or 'hands off' approach to management, by shedding layers of bureaucracy and creating a *'flat' pyramid* structure. If managed properly, decentralisation can lead to faster decision making, better *communication*, more senior management involvement in day-to-day activities and improved staff motivation and morale. In large, multi-centre enterprises, decentralisation can, however, lead to a lack of uniformity of business operation, which may prove less cost effective.

DEE: see *Department for Education and Employment*

deferred demand consists of those people who are not currently using or buying a particular product or service, because of a problem on the supply side. This could be a lack of *accommodation* in the resort of their choice, no tickets left for the theatre or a fire at a restaurant that has forced the management to close. At some stage in the future, it is expected that the customers will get what they want, i.e. deferred demand, sometimes called latent demand, will be converted into *effective demand*. (See also *potential demand*.)

DEFRA: see *Department for Environment, Food and Rural Affairs*

delegation: the process of assigning work tasks to subordinates. Delegation is an essential element of *management*, but one which many managers find difficult to carry out effectively. The structure of an organisation will have a bearing on the degree of delegation that takes place; a *centralised structure* will limit the extent of delegation, since the senior managers will be unwilling to pass decision-making powers down the hierarchy. While specific tasks can be delegated to subordinates, it must be remembered that the *responsibility* for ensuring that they are carried out satisfactorily must lie with the manager. (See also *authority*.)

delivery note: a form sent by a *supplier* to a *customer* at the time of delivery giving details of items supplied. The person receiving the goods is asked to sign the delivery note, which acts as confirmation of delivery and receipt. An *invoice*, showing the costs of the items supplied, usually follows the delivery.

Delphi technique: an approach to the long-term *forecasting* of events based on the combined judgements of a group of experts, rather than by using more objective statistical methods. The technique could be used, for example, to predict the likely trends in *tourism development* in a number of countries.

demand is considered by economists to be one half of a marketplace for goods and services, supply being the other. It is the driving force of a market economy, with producers developing goods and services to satisfy the demand. Demand for leisure and tourism products will be influenced by a number of factors, often categorised into *determinants* and *motivators*. The actual number of people buying or using a product or service is known as *effective demand*, while *suppressed demand* is made up of individuals who are currently not buying or using a particular product or service, either because there is a problem on the supply side (*deferred demand*) or because their current circumstances do not allow them to buy or use a particular product (*potential demand*).

demarketing is the technique of withdrawing *marketing* activity from a product or service so as to dissuade *customers* and thereby reduce *demand*. In leisure and tourism, demarketing can be applied to a *destination* that has become too popular and is giving rise to complaints of overcrowding and damage to the environment. Demarketing usually goes hand-in-hand with increased marketing effort for other products, facilities or destinations so as to switch demand.

demographic changes: see *demographics*

demographics are factors concerning the characteristics of the population of a country or region, e.g. *age structure*, proportion of males and females, social class, level of income and employment status. Researching the demographic profile is an important step in *market segmentation* and can also be used to forecast changes in demand, e.g. the trends for people to live longer and retire from work earlier will affect the demand for holidays and other travel products in the future. Demographic data is available from a number of sources, including *Social Trends*, the *General Household Survey* and specialist leisure and tourism *consultancy* reports.

demonstration effect: this is seen most often in *developing countries*, when members of the *host communities* begin to imitate the patterns of behaviour of their (generally) wealthier visitors. Some residents are curious about, and may yearn for, the consumer goods belonging to the tourists, e.g. cameras, personal stereos and radios. At its worst, the demonstration effect can lead the hosts into crime and violent behaviour against the tourists.

Department for Culture, Media and Sport (DCMS) was created in July 1997 and it took over the work of the former *Department of National Heritage*. The DCMS aims to improve the quality of life for all, through cultural and sporting activities, and through the strengthening of the cultural industries in Britain. It is headed by a Cabinet Minister, the Secretary of State for Culture, Media and Sport. DCMS has responsibility for:

- broadcasting
- the arts
- *sport*
- *tourism*
- national heritage
- the film industry
- the *National Lottery*
- creative industries
- museums and galleries
- libraries.

More than 50 public bodies receive funding from DCMS, including the *British Tourist Authority, English Tourism Council* and *UK Sport*. The DCMS budget for 2000–2001 was £1 billion. Weblink www.culture.gov.uk

Department for Education and Employment (DEE): former government department formed from the merger of the previous Education Department and Employment Department. The DEE's responsibilities are now carried out by the *Department for Education and Skills (DfES)*.

Department for Education and Skills (DfES): previously the *Department for Education and Employment,* the main areas of responsibility of the DfES include schools and further/higher education policy, vocational education and training, plus the work of a number of agencies, including the *Advisory Conciliation and Arbitration Service*. Weblink: www.dfes.gov.uk

Department for Environment, Food and Rural Affairs (DEFRA) was formed in June 2001 from the former *Department of Environment, Transport and the Regions* and *Ministry of Agriculture, Fisheries and Food*. DEFR's Countryside Division is responsible for policies on National Parks, AONBs, tourism, commons and the coast. DEFRA also sponsors the *Countryside Agency*, National Park Authorities and the *British Trust for Conservation Volunteers*. Weblink: www.defra.gov.uk

Department of Environment, Transport and the Regions (DETR): the former government department responsible for a variety of issues, including *planning*, new towns, inner cities, countryside issues, environmental protection, regional policy and *conservation*. Particular responsibilities of the DETR included the *National Parks, Areas of Outstanding Natural Beauty* and *public rights of way*. It ceased to exist in 2001 and was replaced by the *Department for Environment, Food and Rural Affairs (DEFRA)*.

Department of National Heritage (DNH): created after the 1992 general election as a totally new ministry, the DNH aimed to co-ordinate the many different activities that go to make up *leisure* and *tourism* in Britain. The DNH had responsibility for:

- broadcasting
- the arts

- *sport*
- *tourism*
- national *heritage*
- the film industry
- *the Millennium Fund.*

Before the DNH was formed, these activities were the responsibility of many different government departments. The DNH was superseded by the *Department for Culture, Media and Sport* in July 1997.

Department of Trade and Industry (DTI): government department with a very wide sphere of activities, including *grants* to industry and small businesses, export promotion, *European Union* initiatives, *consumer protection* and company legislation. The DTI works in partnership with the *Regional Development Agencies* in England. Weblink: www.dti.gov.uk

departmental structures: *organisational structures* based on clearly defined functions and activities. A mass market *tour operator*, for example, will have a structure based on a number of departments, including marketing, research, contracting, flights, brochure production and reservations. These types of structures benefit from a clear division of *responsibilities*, but this may hamper inter-departmental liaison.

deplane is the term used to describe passengers leaving an aircraft. (See also *enplane*.)

depreciation: a measure of the falling cash value of *fixed assets* over a period of time. For tax purposes, assets such as equipment and vehicles are able to be 'written off' over an agreed number of years, with tax relief claimable on their depreciating value.

deregulation is the withdrawal of local or *central government* control over industries to encourage greater *competition* between companies. Although its advocates argue that deregulation (sometimes referred to as liberalisation) will provide *customers* with better products and services, some people fear that deregulated industries will lose interest in achieving *social objectives* and be concerned only with generating profits. *Airline deregulation* in Europe is high on the agenda currently, following on from the experience in the USA, where the Airline Deregulation Act was passed in 1978. The UK operates a deregulated coach travel industry.

desk research: see *secondary research*

desktop publishing (DTP) is a sophisticated *wordprocessing* system that is capable of producing very high quality documents from a standard *personal computer*. DTP allows the user to manipulate text, pictures and graphics on screen and download the finished result to a printer. By so doing, it is possible to arrange printed pages in the same format as a newspaper or magazine. New wordprocessing software now incorporates many features that were once only found in DTP packages.

destination life cycle: a *model* based on the *product life cycle* concept, but applied to the way that destinations grow and/or decline over time. Sometimes referred to as the tourist area life cycle (TALC), the destination life cycle suggests that all tourist regions will undergo a similar pattern of growth over a given period of time. They will pass through a number of stages, from initial exploration, through *development*, into stagnation and eventual decline. Majorca is considered to be a classic example of the destination life cycle concept, having enjoyed steady growth between the mid-1970s and the end of the 1980s, only to be faced with a decline in visitor numbers at the beginning of the 1990s. It was considered that

Majorca had reached the stagnation point in the cycle. The tourist authorities have responded to the drop in popularity by investing in *hotels* and *infrastructure* to help regain its appeal as British travellers' most popular overseas holiday destination. Like the product life cycle concept, the major weakness of the destination life cycle is that it describes what has already taken place and cannot be an accurate *forecasting tool*.

destination management system (DMS): a computer-based system for providing up-to-date information on the availability of tourism facilities and services in a destination, for example *accommodation*, *events* and *attractions*. The latest DMS systems on offer are Internet-based, e.g. visitwales.com, launched by the Wales Tourist Board in 2002.

destination marketing: the processes and techniques concerned with attracting visitors to a *destination*, whether it be a continent, country, region, town, country area or single *visitor attraction*. Destination marketing is a complex issue, often undertaken by *public sector* agencies, since it involves the *promotion* of many different leisure and tourism products in the same area, most of which will be under different ownership and control.

destinations are the end points of people's journeys, whether they are travelling for leisure or business purposes. It is often a destination, its *images* and the way in which it is promoted, that stimulates an individual to want to visit, thus energising the whole of the *travel and tourism industry*. Destinations are the focus of much tourist activity and the point at which many components of leisure, travel and tourism come together. Attracting visitors to destinations is a very competitive business, given the economic and social benefits that tourism can bring to a wide range of national, regional and local destinations.

determinants are the economic, social, political and technological factors that influence a person's *demand* for travel and leisure products, irrespective of any motivations they may have. These will include:

* the political regime under which they live
* *demographic* factors, e.g. an ageing population
* socio-cultural factors, e.g. types of community (urban/rural)
* geographical factors, e.g. living in cold or hot climates
* economic factors, e.g. the wealth of a country as measured by its *GDP/GNP.*

Determinants can be regarded as the 'base' factors that influence travel; people living in a *developing country* with a low GNP are unlikely to have the necessary financial *resources* to travel abroad, when compared with, say, people living in the UK or Germany. Determinants are usually considered along with *motivators*, the inner feelings and needs of individuals.

DETR: see *Department of Environment, Transport and the Regions*

developed countries: the world's most advanced nations with high per capita incomes.

developing countries: nations of the world with relatively low levels of economic development and low standards of living. They are, however, visited in increasing numbers by tourists from developed nations and are beginning to realise that tourism can bring economic and social benefits if planned and managed properly. However, in developing countries (sometimes known as Third World nations) there are concerns about the harmful *environmental* and *socio-cultural impacts* of unplanned tourism *development*.

development: a wide-ranging term that can mean both the building of a single facility, such as a hotel or leisure complex, or the longer-term process of a country acquiring *infrastructure* and *superstructure* developments as part of its *economic development*. Development can be a very emotive term, with individuals and groups campaigning against new road developments and large facilities, while *developing countries* often criticise the role played by *multinational corporations* in exploiting their resources for development. Most leisure and tourism developments are regulated, to a greater or lesser extent, by central and local governments.

development agencies: *public sector organisations* that provide advice and often grant aid for *economic development* projects, which could include leisure, travel and tourism developments. In Wales, the *Welsh Development Agency* assists firms wishing to relocate or establish new business ventures in the Principality, while England has nine *Regional Development Agencies* which promote *economic regeneration* in their specific regions, working closely with the *Regional Tourist Boards*.

Development Commission: see *Rural Development Commission*

development control: see *planning control*

Development of Tourism Act 1969: the first, and to date only, piece of UK *legislation* dealing specifically with *tourism*. The Act covers four main areas:

- the establishment of the *British Tourist Authority, English Tourist Board* (now *English Tourism Council*), *Wales Tourist Board* and *Scottish Tourist Board* (now *VisitScotland*)

- the introduction of *'section 4 grants'* for tourist developments

- the establishment of the hotel development grants scheme

- legislation to introduce a compulsory registration scheme for *accommodation*.

The part of the Act concerning compulsory registration of accommodation has not been fully implemented, with the industry instead preferring to follow a system of voluntary *accommodation grading*. The *Northern Ireland Tourist Board* was not included in the 1969 Development of Tourism Act, having already established its own *tourist board* under the Development of Tourist Traffic Act (N Ireland) in 1948.

development plan: a term which has a number of meanings in *leisure* and *tourism*, including a detailed scheme for a single project (e.g. the building of a major *tourist attraction*) or an overall long-term plan for land use developments in a country or region. Development plans are drawn up by private and public sector bodies, and are constantly reviewed in the light of changing circumstances. Some agencies include reference to techniques such as *critical path analysis* and *PERT* in their development plans.

DfES: see *Department for Education and Skills*

DG Enterprise: the Directorate General (DG) of the *European Commission* that includes *tourism* amongst its responsibilities. It has a separate Tourism Unit which works to improve the quality, competitiveness and sustainability of European tourism and its enterprises, the great majority of which are classed as *micro-businesses*.

DG XXIII is the former department of the *European Commission* with special responsibility for *tourism*. It is now known as the *DG Enterprise* or the Enterprise Directorate.

differentiated marketing is a type of *marketing strategy* that tailors specific marketing approaches and activities to different sectors of a market, rather than adopting the same approach to everybody, as is the case with *undifferentiated marketing*. A mass market *tour operator*, for example, will have different strategies for reaching families, young couples and senior citizens, and will develop a range of products to suit each groups' individual *needs*.

differential pricing: a technique used to influence *demand* for products and services, and ultimately maximise *revenue*, by offering variable prices at different times or for different market segments. It is common, for example, for leisure facilities to offer discounted prices outside of peak times, in the same way that holidays are often more expensive in the *peak season*.

dinky: stands for 'double income no kids', a term first used widely in Britain during the Thatcher years of the 1980s. 'Dinkies' are couples where both partners follow professional careers and do not, by choice or otherwise, have children. They enjoy an affluent lifestyle, with high *disposable incomes* to spend on a range of consumer durables and expensive leisure pursuits. Dinkies are an important target market for some leisure and tourism organisations. (See also *yuppie*.)

direct costs relate to expenditure incurred as a direct result of the production of an organisation's products and services. Sometimes called 'prime costs', an example of direct costs would be the expenditure associated with running an extra series of health and fitness courses, e.g. the wages for an extra instructor, publicity, postage, telephone costs, etc. (See also *overheads*.)

direct mail is the most common and fastest-growing type of *direct marketing* used in leisure and tourism. It is a technique that uses a *mailing list* of names and addresses to send *promotional materials* to selected individuals or organisations. Its uses in leisure, travel and tourism are extensive, for example:

- a *tourist attraction* sending details of its group rates to selected coach operators
- a *travel agent* mailing a newsletter to existing clients
- a *local authority* sending out leaflets about its leisure facilities with *Council Tax* bills.

Large direct mail campaigns can make use of sophisticated *database marketing* systems, such as *ACORN*, as a way of targeting customers more effectively.

direct marketing is the term used to describe the various techniques that an organisation can use to sell its products and services on a personalised basis direct to the *consumer*, without the need for an *intermediary*. It is an important element of *promotion* in leisure and tourism, with the benefit of being able to target *customers* effectively and precisely. The most common direct marketing techniques used in leisure and tourism include *direct mail, telemarketing, door-to-door distribution* and *direct response advertising*.

direct response advertising is any type of *advertising*, in any medium, that asks a customer to respond in some way, perhaps by ringing a telephone number, completing a coupon or calling in to a shop to pick up a *brochure* or free gift. Some organisations use 'freecall' numbers such as 0800, reduced-rate numbers or a freepost address, in order to stimulate more responses to the advertising.

direct sell is when an organisation sells its products and services direct to the consumer, rather than through an *intermediary*, sometimes called a 'middle man'. A hotelier, for example, may choose to advertise his establishment in local and national newspapers and handle all enquiries and bookings himself, rather than using the services of an agent. The hotelier will not have to pay any fee or *commission* to an agent when he sells direct, but he will have to pay the costs of *advertising* and staff time for handling enquiries and taking bookings. In the *package holiday* industry, direct sell operators, such as Portland Holidays, suggest that they can sell holidays more cheaply since they don't have to pay any commission to travel agents.

direct services organisation (DSO): a *local authority* in-house team that submits a *tender*, in competition with commercial organisations, for the right to manage leisure services and facilities. Under the terms of *compulsory competitive tendering* legislation, the DSO must keep separate accounts for this aspect of the local authority's work. Successful DSOs may bid for the management of facilities in nearby districts, thereby increasing their sphere of activity.

direct tax is a levy on a person's income and the profits of an organisation. Individuals pay *income tax*, while companies pay *corporation tax* on their profits. Since 1979, the burden of *taxation* has shifted away from direct to *indirect taxes*, such as *value added tax (VAT)*.

director: a senior manager within an organisation, elected by the *shareholders* as their representative on the board of directors, the main policy-making committee. The duties of directors, who may be *executive* or *non-executive*, are to exercise their power, influence and authority for the good of the organisation. They are expected to act in a professional manner at all times when managing the affairs of the organisation.

Disability Discrimination Act 1995 (DDA): *government legislation* designed to protect disabled people from discrimination in employment and to increase *access* to goods, facilities and services, including leisure, travel and tourism products and services. Since 1999 service providers have had to make 'reasonable adjustments' for disabled people. From 2004, they will have to consider making alterations to the built environment, e.g. access to buildings and the ability to move freely inside buildings. This will have an important impact on many leisure, travel and tourism businesses.

Disability Sport England: the new name for the *British Sports Association for the Disabled (BSAD)*.

disadvantaged groups: categories of people who, for a number of reasons generally outside of their control, are unable to participate fully in leisure activities and tourist trips. These groups, which *research* shows include many women, ethnic minorities, disabled people, rural dwellers and unemployed people, have been targeted for priority treatment by bodies such as the *Sports Council* (now *UK Sport*), the *Holiday Care Service* and *Countryside Agency*. (See also *community recreation*.)

disciplinary procedures: the steps that the *management* of an organisation takes to deal with staff whose behaviour, work performance or absenteeism are giving cause for concern. The process normally starts with a *verbal warning*, followed by a *written warning*. If the problem persists, the management may issue a final written warning, which may ultimately lead to *dismissal*. It is important that organisations follow the disciplinary procedures to the letter, so as to ensure fairness for the employee and to reduce the likelihood of a claim for *unfair dismissal*.

discount: a reduction on the published price or *rack rate* for a product or service. Discounts are normally available for bulk purchases, so that a *tour operator* will be able to negotiate discounted rates for *accommodation* with hoteliers, on the basis of a high volume of business.

discounted cash-flow (DCF): a method of *investment appraisal* used to measure the desirability of an investment project, by converting future monetary values into current figures.

discretionary income: see *disposable income*

dismissal: the termination of an employee's *contract of employment* by his or her employer, with or without notice. This may be as a result of *gross misconduct* or *redundancy*. (See also *unfair dismissal*.)

Disney: arguably the most successful *leisure* corporation of all time, based on the world's most popular *theme parks* founded by Walt Disney in the USA, the first being opened in California in 1955. Today, Disneyworld in Florida welcomes more than 25 million visitors every year, making it the world's number one tourist attraction. Disney ventured into the European theme park market in 1993 with the opening of *Disneyland Paris*, originally known as EuroDisney. Disney resorts and theme parks have set the industry standard for levels of *customer service* and *customer care*. Weblink: www.disney.co.uk

Disneyland Paris: the *Disney* resort opened in 1993 near Paris (originally known as EuroDisney). After a disastrous start from a financial viewpoint, the theme park is beginning to show signs of improvement, both in visitor numbers and revenue. Disney has had problems in selling an essentially American concept to the European market. Weblink: www.disney.co.uk

displacement effect is when tourism *development* has the effect of taking employment and other economic *resources* away from other industries, e.g. the development of tourism is some Mediterranean countries has taken jobs away from *primary sector* industries, such as fishing and agriculture. This may have long-term consequences for the health of a nation's economy.

display advertisement: an announcement in the *consumer* or trade *press* that includes headlines, graphics and/or pictures to create an impression with readers. Display adver- tisements tend to be larger than *classified advertisements* and are more expensive, being charged on a pro-rata basis for the space they take up.

display screen equipment: the Health and Safety (Display Screen Equipment) Regulations 1992 were developed as a direct result of the *EU Directives on health and safety*, to cover the safe use of such equipment as *computers* and *VDUs*. Work with display screens is not generally high risk, but it can lead to muscular and other physical problems, eye fatigue and mental stress. Under the regulations, employers have a duty to:

- assess workstations and reduce risks that are discovered

- make sure that workstations meet minimum requirements

- plan work so that there are breaks or changes of activity

- provide information and training for staff who use display screen equipment.

Given that many staff in the leisure and tourism industries use computers and VDUs on a daily basis, these particular regulations have serious implications for particular organisations.

disposable income is the amount of money left over when all necessary household and personal expenses have been met. Disposable income (sometimes called discretionary income) is money that people can choose to spend as they wish, for example on *leisure* pursuits and *holidays*.

distance learning: a type of *off-the-job training* that involves study without the need for face-to-face contact with teachers or trainers. It can involve the use of written study materials, videos, the *Internet*, audio cassettes, radio and television programmes. Sometimes referred to as a correspondence course, distance learning gives the student the advantage of working at his or her own pace. Some distance learning programmes, such as those run by the Open University, offer students telephone and *e-mail* support from tutors, refresher seminars and summer schools.

distribution channels are the methods used to make products and services available to *customers*. Since many leisure and tourism products are *intangible*, with consumption taking place at the point of production, there is no need for a standard distribution system, as would be the case with, for example, sports goods or food. The way that *package holidays* are sold shows clearly how distribution channels operate in leisure and tourism. *Tour operators* liaise with hoteliers and airlines to buy hotel bedspaces and airline seats. They then produce a *brochure* of their holidays which is stocked by travel agents, who sell the packages for a *commission*. Customers book their holidays from the travel agents or can sometimes book direct with *direct sell* operators. In this process, the tour operator acts as the wholesaler and the travel agent as the retailer.

district council: the tier of local government concerned with providing services to people living in one of the 238 shire districts in England and Wales. District councils are responsible for providing a wide range of services, including libraries, refuse disposal, environmental health, planning and building control. District councils, some of which are known as borough councils, also play a vital role in the provision of leisure and tourism facilities, such as sports and *leisure centres*, parks and gardens, playing fields, museums, *tourist information centres* and theatres. Some of these may be dual use or *joint use*, when a facility is shared between the local community and schools or colleges to maximise its use. (*See also Local Government Association*.)

diversification is the process of introducing new facilities, products and services into an organisation in order to increase sales and/or reduce the reliance on too narrow a range of products. There are many examples of diversification in leisure and tourism, including a tour operator buying a chain of hotels or a leisure centre offering to carry out fitness testing for employees of a nearby firm. Three distinct levels of diversification can be identified in leisure and tourism:

● diversification into and out of the industry – e.g. Lord Thomson initially built his empire on publishing, but diversified into tour operations in 1965

● diversification into different sectors of leisure and tourism – e.g. the Virgin Group has interests in cinemas, airlines, holidays, hotels, entertainments and leisure

● diversification within an individual organisation – e.g. a couple running a farm *bed and breakfast* enterprise deciding to convert a redundant building into *self-catering accommodation*.

An important aspect of diversification is that an organisation is able to spread its risks across a number of different operations, thereby reducing the likelihood of overall business failure.

dividend: a payment to a *shareholder* from the profits of a *company*. Dividends are paid on both *ordinary shares* and *preference shares*, and are a type of investment from which the shareholder hopes to benefit, although there is no guarantee of a fixed return with ordinary shares. Dividends on *ordinary shares* will vary from one year to another, depending on the profitability of the company.

DMS: see *destination management system*

DNH: see *Department of National Heritage*

'dogs': see *Boston Consulting Group matrix*

domestic tourism is when people take holidays, *short breaks* and business trips in their own country. For example, a family from Worcester taking a two-week holiday in a caravan in Wales or a group of academics from London attending a conference in Sheffield are both examples of domestic tourism. Figures from the Star UK website show that British people took 63.8 million holidays of 1–3 nights and 28.9 million holidays of 4–7 nights in Britain in 2001. In the same year, the *Heart of England Tourist Board* region was the most popular with UK residents, capturing 22.2 per cent of long holidays. The domestic tourism industry in the UK has faced fierce competition in recent years from overseas package holidays. There is a general belief that many UK tourist regions have not invested sufficiently in accommodation, *infrastructure*, training and product development, and that they must be flexible enough to respond to the changing nature of the market for UK holidays. (See also *UK tourism*.)

domestic tourists: see *visitor*

domestic visitors: see *visitor*

door-to-door distribution: a method of *direct marketing* that involves the distribution of leaflets or other *promotional materials* to selected households. Door-to-door distribution is popular with hotels, restaurants, attractions and leisure facilities that are keen to capture a local market. A certain amount of *market segmentation* is possible with this distribution method, with particular postcode areas being targeted in terms of social class, income levels, age characteristics, family composition, etc. Local free newspapers often offer a leaflet distribution service to local companies.

DPA: see *Data Protection Act*

drugs in sport is a key issue in *sport* today. Since the 1960s, drugs have become a major concern in international sport, with increasing numbers of sports people choosing to use performance-enhancing substances rather than relying on training, diet and dedication. The huge rewards for success are often cited as the main reason why many people are prepared to take the risks associated with taking drugs in sport. Organisations such as *UK Sport* and the *International Olympic Committee (IOC)* are dedicated to ending drug misuse in sport.

DSO: see *direct services organisation*

DTI: see *Department of Trade and Industry*

DTP: see *desktop publishing*

dual use: see *joint use*

Duke of Edinburgh's Award Scheme: a voluntary scheme aimed at encouraging young people between the ages of 14 and 25 to develop their talents, help their local communities, make new friends and learn new skills. They can progress from the Bronze Award, through Silver to the Duke of Edinburgh Gold Award, by completing specific tasks, service duties and expeditions. Weblink: www.theaward.org

duty-free refers to goods that are purchased free of all taxation (duty). The sale of duty-free items, such as cigarettes, alcohol and consumer goods, used to provide welcome extra funds for a variety of UK travel companies until, on June 30 1999, the sale of such items in airports and at sea was halted throughout the *European Union*. Purchases for consumption on board ferries and aircraft remain duty-free, and passengers on journeys to destinations outside the EU are still allowed to buy duty-free items.

A B C D E F G H I J K L M N O P Q R S T U V W X Y Z

Earth Summit: a major international conference on *sustainable development*, the first of which was held in Rio de Janiero in 1992 to consider global development and its impact on the world environment. Attended by the majority of world leaders, the Summit was a natural progression from the World Commission on Environment and Development held in 1987, which gave rise to the *Brundtland Report*. The Summit agreed a set of principles for future sustainable development, known as Agenda 21, which has since been interpreted and expanded at national, regional and local level in many of the world's countries. Many communities in the UK have developed their own action plans, referred to as Local Agenda 21. The role of tourism in global economic development was debated at the Earth Summit, leading to further debate on the concept of *sustainable tourism*. The second Earth Summit took place in Johannesburg in 2002.

East of England Tourist Board is the official *Regional Tourist Board* covering the counties of Essex, Suffolk, Norfolk, Cambridgeshire, Bedfordshire, Lincolnshire and Hertfordshire. Weblink: www.eastofenglandtouristboard.com

EC stands for European Community, the grouping of member states renamed the *European Union* in 1993. The European Community was originally called the European Economic Community (EEC) when it was established in 1958.

economic and monetary union (EMU): the process by which all members states of the *European Union* agree to a single interest rate and exchange rate policy, rather than each country determining its own. At the final stage, there was a *single currency* for all participating countries. As part of the EMU process, 12 European countries adopted the *Euro* as their currency in January 2002. At the time of writing, Britain has still to decide whether or not to introduce the Euro in place of the pound.

economic development is the goal of countries, regions, urban and rural areas all over the world. Through planned growth, economic development aims to improve the quality of life in areas and communities by increasing employment opportunities and wealth creation. Tourism and leisure developments are often seen as an effective way of achieving economic development, either by themselves, e.g. a *developing country* deciding to introduce tourist facilities, or in conjunction with other economic sectors, e.g. as part of an *urban regeneration* scheme.

economic impact of sport: see *sport*

economic impacts of leisure, travel and tourism refers to the positive and negative effects of the industries on national and local communities. One of the principle positive impacts is income generation for private individuals, *local authorities*, companies, voluntary bodies and *national governments*. Leisure and tourism also create jobs, with tourism alone employing more than 120 million people worldwide. Investment in leisure and tourism can also help *urban regeneration* projects and economic development, as well as adding to regional and national prosperity. Negative economic effects include the fact that local people may resent paying part of their taxes to provide facilities for visitors and land and property prices may rise as a result of tourist activity in an area.

economic regeneration: the process of revitalising derelict urban and rural areas, often involving *partnership* arrangements between *public* and *private sector* organisations. Leisure and tourism often plays a significant part in regeneration projects, helping to create employment and add to an enhanced quality of life for residents and better facilities for tourists. Notable examples of regeneration schemes in the UK include Bristol Docks and Cardiff Bay. (See also *economic development, urban regeneration*.)

economies of scale: the benefits that a large organisation gains by virtue of its size and scale of operation. *Multinational corporations*, for example, are able to pool the resources of their subsidiary companies and gain favourable discounts from *suppliers*. Smaller enterprises that enter into *co-operative marketing* activities can do likewise.

ecotourism is defined by the *Ecotourism Society* as 'purposeful travel to natural areas to understand the cultural and natural history of the environment, taking care not to alter the integrity of the ecosystem, whilst producing economic opportunities that make the conservation of natural resources financially beneficial to local citizens'. There is some concern that ecotourism, rather than being beneficial to local communities, can, because of its exploratory nature, actually have a more harmful effect than *mass tourism*, whose harmful impacts tend to be confined to small areas of a country or destination area.

Ecotourism Society: an independent membership organisation that promotes the concept and practice of *sustainable tourism*, aimed particularly at visitors to natural areas of the world who wish to explore cultural and natural history. Weblink: www.ecotourism.org

ECU: see *European Currency Unit*

Eden Project: one of the most successful tourist attractions of recent years, the Eden Project near St Austell in Cornwall welcomed 1.7 million visitors in 2001, its first full year of operation. Based on the theme of gardens and ecosystems from around the world, the attraction is built in a former china clay quarry and features futuristic glass-domed structures called biomes, which house the plants. Weblink: www.edenproject.com

Edexcel is an independent awarding and examinations body that offers a range of educational qualifications, including *vocational qualifications* in leisure, travel and tourism. Accountable to the *Qualifications and Curriculum Authority (QCA)*, Edexcel (formerly known as *BTEC*) is a major partner in the development of *National Vocational Qualifications (NVQs)* and *General National Vocational Qualifications (GNVQs)*. (See also *AQA, OCR*.) Weblink: www.edexcel.org.uk

educational trip: see *familiarisation trip*

Education and Learning Wales: see *ELWA*

EEA: see *European Economic Area*

EEC: European Economic Community. See *EC*

EFCT: see *European Federation of Conference Towns*

effective demand is the actual number of people using or buying a particular product or service, e.g. the number of people visiting a *theme park* over a six-week period or the number of people buying *package holidays* to Greece. Commercial organisations aim to increase the effective demand for their products so as to increase their *market share*. (See also *suppressed demand*.)

effectiveness is a measure of how well an organisation has met its *objectives*. Measuring effectiveness presupposes that the organisation has developed *objectives* that are both realistic and measurable (see *SMART objectives*.) Measurement is undertaken by developing and implementing a range of *performance indicators* and *financial ratios*. Effectiveness is also a function of *management style* and *leadership*.

efficiency is the wise use of an organisation's *resources*, i.e. the maximum output from the resources used. It can be measured in many ways, including by using *performance indicators* (e.g. the number of visitors per member of staff at a *tourist attraction*) and *financial ratios* (e.g. the *return on capital employed*). By using techniques such as these, an organisation can measure its financial efficiency, operational efficiency and overall efficiency.

EFTA: see *European Free Trade Association*

EFTPOS: see *electronic funds transfer at point-of-sale*

EHO: see *Environmental Health Officer*

EIA: see *environmental impact assessment*

EIB: see *European Investment Bank*

eighty/twenty rule: see *Pareto principle*

EIS: see *English Institute of Sport*

elasticity of demand: an economics term that measures how much the *demand* for a product or service is affected by changes in its *price*. Goods and services whose demand stays constant even if prices rise are said to be 'demand inelastic', e.g. staple foods such as bread. Those whose demand falls when the price rises are said to be 'demand elastic', e.g. some leisure and tourism products, such as entry prices at *tourist attractions* and *package holidays*.

Electricity at Work Regulations 1989: a set of statutory regulations that cover all aspects of electrical installations, equipment and maintenance in all places of work, including leisure and tourism premises. The regulations cover such items as earthing, connections, isolation of supply, protection from excess current and the competence of members of staff. *Management* must follow a clear programme of action to minimise risks from electrical plant and installations, including regular inspections, *risk assessments* and *training* for staff.

electronic communication: a range of techniques and equipment that allow the rapid transfer and receipt of information. Based on the premise that electronic communication is faster and more efficient than paper-based alternatives, worldwide communications are now available to all leisure and tourism organisations, regardless of their size. Electronic communication systems allow organisations to communicate internally and externally, using facilities such as *electronic mail*, *facsimile (fax) transmissions*, *ISDN* and the *Internet*. Electronic communication is set to transform business operations in the twenty-first century.

electronic funds transfer at point-of-sale (EFTPOS) is an electronic payment system, triggered by a plastic card, that automatically transfers money from a customers bank account and credits the sum of money to the company selling the goods or services. The transaction is carried out at the *point-of-sale*, providing the *customer* with greater convenience and the retailer with greater security, since there is less cash to handle. EFTPOS systems accept both *credit cards* and *debit cards*.

electronic mail (e-mail) is a computer-based system that allows the transfer of messages and information between registered e-mail users on a *network*. Today, e-mail systems are found in most leisure, travel and tourism organisations, such as the headquarters of airlines, tour operators, tourist boards, hotels and travel agencies. E-mail is also used extensively in the home, through *Internet service providers* such as AoL, BT and Claranet. E-mail provides instantaneous communication and also cuts down on the amount of paper used in an organisation.

electronic point-of-sale (EPOS): an electronic sales and *stock control* system that automates many of the tasks previously performed by sales staff, allowing them to concentrate on providing high levels of *customer service*. EPOS systems are commonplace in shops and supermarkets, where they will perform all of the normal functions of a cash register, but also log all transactions with time, date, items sold, cost, method of payment and the name of the member of staff who served the customer. In leisure and tourism, EPOS systems are found in pubs, clubs, arenas, entertainment complexes, cinemas, bars and fast-food outlets, where staff use 'touchpads', small touch-sensitive panels located behind the bar or counter and pre-programmed with prices. EPOS also allows automated control of stock and re-ordering procedures.

electronic ticketing: see *e-ticketing*

ELWA (Education and Learning Wales): a partnership organisation responsible for all post-16 education and training in Wales. It comprises the National Council for Education and Training for Wales and the Higher Education Funding Council for Wales. ELWA superseded the *Training and Enterprise Councils (TECs)* in Wales in 2001 and established Community Consortia for Education and Training (CCETS) to deliver its services in local areas. (See also *Education and Skills Council.*) Weblink: www.elwa.ac.uk

e-mail: see *electronic mail*

e-mail survey: the collection of data from a sample of respondents using *e-mail*, as opposed to a *telephone survey* or *face-to-face interview* technique. An e-mail survey has the advantage of being relatively cheap and can be set up very quickly.

embargo: refers most commonly in leisure and tourism to a date or time before which a *press release* cannot be used. For example, a press release about the launch of a new tourism initiative may be circulated to the news media 24 hours before it actually takes place, with an instruction that the contents of the release should not be made public until after the launch has actually taken place. More generally, an embargo may be an order forbidding trade with a particular country or a stop on the release of information.

embarkation pass: see *boarding pass*

employment application form: a form completed by job applicants. (See also *curriculum vitae.*)

employment contract: see *contract of employment*

Employment Gazette: government publication that lists current employment statistics by *Standard Industrial Classification* categories.

employment in leisure, travel and tourism is one of the principal *economic impacts* that countries and local areas gain from investment in the industries. Figures from the *World Travel and Tourism Council* estimate that there are approximately 118 million people working in the tourism industry worldwide. In the *European Union*, some 8 million people are directly employed in tourism, representing roughly 5 per cent of total employment. When employment in other sectors such as transport and distributive trades is added to this, this figure rises to 20 million jobs. Closer to home, there were an estimated 2.12 million people employed in tourism-related industries in 2001 (including the self-employed), which included 410,000 in hotels and other accommodation and 414,000 in sport and other recreational activities. Recent trends suggest that employment in the leisure, travel and tourism industries will continue to rise in the early years of the twenty-first century. (See also *careers in leisure, travel and tourism*.)

employment in sport: see *sport*

empty leg: an airline flight that has no passengers aboard. 'Empty legs' are the usual consequence of a *flight series charter* arrangement, when there will be an empty flight home at the beginning of a season, having dropped passengers off, and an empty flight out at the end of the same season to pick up passengers.

empty nester: a term used by leisure and tourism marketers to denote couples whose children have left home ('flown the nest'), thereby increasing the couple's *disposable income* available to spend on leisure, travel and tourism products and services.

EMS: see *European Monetary System*

empowerment is the process of giving individuals ownership of the means to improve their personal and work-related development. Empowering people in the workplace can result in a more motivated and effective workforce, with greater confidence to try new ideas and exploit any new *opportunities* that may come along.

EMU: see *Economic and Monetary Union*

enclave: see *tourist enclave*

English Heritage is the government's official adviser on *conservation* legislation concerning historic buildings and ancient monuments. Established under the National Heritage Act 1983, it provides the major source of public funds for rescue archaeology, town schemes, and repairs to historic buildings and ancient monuments. It is also responsible for preserving and presenting around 400 national historic properties, including Stonehenge, Dover Castle, Battle Abbey and Tintagel Castle. Financed mainly from government funds, English Heritage has a membership of around 300,000 and is the largest independent organisation responsible for heritage conservation in the country. Weblink: www.english-heritage.org.uk

English Institute of Sport (EIS): a nationwide network of the best training facilities and support services for sport, aimed at raising standards of performance to world class levels. It co-ordinates support to world-class performers and co-operates with a range of partners, including *national governing bodies of sport*, performance directors and coaches. EIS has nine multi-sport hub sites: Bisham Abbey *National Sports Centre*, Gateshead International Stadium, Holme Pierrepoint National Watersports Centre, Lilleshall National Sports Centre, Loughborough University, Manchester Sport City/Belle Vue, University of Bath, University of East Anglia and the Don Valley Stadium in Sheffield. There are also 35 smaller satellite centres specialising in particular aspects of sport. The EIS network is due to be fully operational by the end of 2003, with funding of more than £120 million. Weblink: www.eis2win.co.uk

English Nature is the government agency that champions the conservation of wildlife and natural features throughout England. It was established under the Environmental Protection Act of 1990, replacing the former Nature Conservancy Council. English Nature has a wide range of responsibilities, including *National Nature Reserves, Sites of Special Scientific Interest*, Biodiversity Action Plans, Local Nature Reserves, European Heathlands and the UK Marine Special Areas of Conservation Project. Weblink: www.english-nature.org.uk

English Sports Council (ESC): one of the bodies that in 1996 replaced the *Sports Council*. The ESC (now called *Sport England*) concentrates its resources on helping grass-roots sport and the *governing bodies* of sport to achieve their objectives.

English Tourism Council (ETC) was established in July 1999 at the successor to the *English Tourist Board (ETB)*, with the following mission:

'We will drive forward the quality, competitiveness and wise growth of England's tourism, by providing intelligence, setting standards, creating partnerships and ensuring coherence.'

The aims of the ETC fall into three distinct areas, namely quality, competitiveness and wise growth. In terms of quality, the ETC has stated that it will:

- set, develop and promote the highest standards through the existing schemes for *accommodation* in England
- evaluate whether other quality initiatives are needed to improve the product, customer service standards and environment that make up England's tourism experience
- identify examples of *best practice* and interpret them for the benefit of the industry
- champion the development of national initiatives such as resort regeneration in England.

To ensure competitiveness, the ETC will:

- provide the industry with relevant *market research* and forecasts
- champion and develop standards for common systems and techniques to help businesses and other agencies reach consumers more efficiently
- publish business advice and information on how legislative change may impact on tourism
- identify the big issues facing tourism, publicise the opportunities and threats and champion possible solutions
- research growth sectors in tourism and signal how the industry can take advantage of them.

In terms of wise growth, the ETC will:

- provide the framework for the successful delivery of the government's tourism strategy, *Tomorrow's Tourism*, and fund England's *Regional Tourist Boards* to deliver their part
- raise *sustainability* on the tourism industry's agenda, set measurable targets and audit progress
- champion the value of and interests of English tourism wherever possible, particularly the social, economic and job creation benefits

- represent industry interests to advise government and provide advice on policy issues which affect the ability of tourism to flourish

- promote opportunities to make tourism accessible to all.

In order to achieve its aims, the ETC works in *partnership* with a range of organisations, including the *Department for Culture, Media and Sport*, *local authorities*, the tourist industry, other government departments and the *British Tourist Authority* (see figure below). At the time of writing, the government is consulting on a probable merger between the ETC and the British Tourist Authority to form a unified organisation. Weblink: www.englishtourism.org.uk

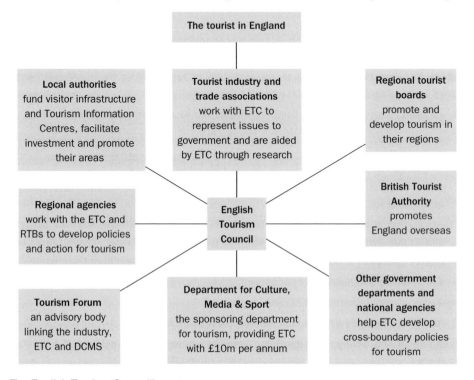

The English Tourism Council's partners

English Tourist Board (ETB) was, until July 1999, the official *tourist board* for England, established under the *1969 Development of Tourism Act*. With its headquarters in London, shared with the *BTA*, its principal objectives were to:

- encourage people living in the UK to take holidays in England

- stimulate the provision and improvement of facilities for tourists to England

- advise government and public bodies on all matters concerning tourism in England

- produce and distribute information on tourism to the travel trade and consumers

- ensure that England's character and heritage was protected through the sensitive management of tourism.

In order to achieve these objectives, ETB engaged in a wide-ranging programme of work with *public* and *private sector* organisations, which included *marketing* to the public and the *travel trade*, co-ordinating the network of *tourist information centres* and advising on national and local tourism planning and development. The ETB also undertook and commissioned *research*, publishing a range of statistical data related to tourism. Throughout the 1990s, ETB's *grant-in-aid* from government was cut severely and it was replaced in 1999 by the *English Tourism Council*.

enplane is the term used to denote passengers boarding an aircraft. (See also *deplane*.)

Enterprise Neptune is the *National Trust's* campaign to save Britain's threatened coastline. Launched by the Duke of Edinburgh in 1965, with a target of raising £2 million towards the purchase of the remaining 900 miles of unspoilt coastline in England, Wales and Northern Ireland, Enterprise Neptune (renamed the Neptune Coastline Campaign in 1999) had raised £36 million by 2002, allowing 413 miles of coastline to be conserved. As well as raising funds to acquire coastline, the campaign also aims to draw attention to the pressures facing this threatened habitat.

entertainment facilities: a wide-ranging term used to describe a variety of products and services offered by public, private and voluntary sector *leisure* and *recreation* providers. They can be divided into those facilities provided outside the home, e.g. cinemas, bingo halls, social clubs, theatres, etc., and a range of *home-based leisure* facilities and products, such as television, board games, computer games, video recorders, hi-fi systems, etc. Private sector entertainment facilities can be further sub-divided into those that require active participation, including dance halls, ballrooms, nightclubs, etc., and those that offer performances to audiences, e.g. arenas, concert halls, theatres, etc. (See also *arts and entertainment, community recreation*.)

entrepreneur: an individual who is prepared to take a risk and accept a challenge or undertake a venture that has no guarantee of success. Entrepreneurs often run their own businesses and can be an inspiration to others to follow the route of enterprise. Richard Branson, *chairman* of the Virgin Group, is often cited as a good example of a successful entrepreneur.

environmental audit: an investigation of an organisation's *policies*, *management* and practices from the point of view of their impact on the local and global environment. Many leisure, travel and tourism organisations, large and small, are beginning to look at their activities and put in place measures to reduce their environmental impact, e.g. the use of low energy lighting systems, unleaded fuels, recycling programmes and bio-degradable materials. Although often a voluntary exercise, many companies are, nonetheless, keen to display their 'green' awareness, as well as using their concern for the environment as a *marketing* tool.

environmental auditing: the practice of carrying out an *environmental audit*.

environmental education: instilling in people of all ages knowledge about the environment in the hope of engendering respect for its future conservation.

Environmental Health Officer (EHO): an official employed by a *local authority* to monitor a range of environmental issues in a locality, including the handling and storage of food in shops, restaurants and hotels, air and water pollution, and excessive noise at events such as outdoor concerts and sporting matches.

environmental impact analysis: see *environmental impact assessment*

environmental impact assessment (EIA): a technique for carrying out an appraisal of the costs and benefits of a particular development from an environmental point of view.

Sometimes called an environmental impact analysis, an EIA may be necessary before the building of a major *hotel* or leisure complex is given the approval to proceed. The EIA is a structured process which aims to establish who will lose and who will gain if a development goes ahead, examine alternative courses of action and their likely impacts, and consider ways of reducing impacts if a project is given the green light. Increasing concern for the environment will mean that EIAs will become more common in determining future leisure and *tourism* projects.

environmental impacts of leisure, travel and tourism can be both positive and negative. On the positive side, we see initiatives such as the *Britain in Bloom* competition and the *Seaside Award* helping to improve local environments for both local people and visitors. Problems associated with the environmental impacts of leisure and tourism include litter, pollution, physical *erosion* and loss of habitats. Careful visitor and traffic management can go some way towards minimising many of these problems, although areas such as the *National Parks* are under particular pressures.

environmental issues, such as deforestation of the world's rain forests, global warming, loss of habitats, spreading urbanisation and traffic growth, are becoming of increasing concern to individuals and governments. Initiatives such as the *Earth Summit* seek to highlight their importance and devise strategies for reducing their impacts and fostering *sustainable development*.

environmental management: the practice of managing *resources* in such a way as to cause least harm to the environment and promoting *sustainability*. This may involve organisations in carrying out an *environmental audit*, *environmental impact assessment* or applying for external certification under *BS 7750*.

Environmentally Sensitive Area (ESA): an area of countryside where the *Department for Environment, Food and Rural Affairs (DEFRA)* is working with farmers and other landowners to conserve characteristic landscapes, wildlife habitats and historic features. The ESA scheme was introduced in 1987, with ten designated areas, including Breckland, Clun, North Peak and the South Downs. After several years of operation, the original schemes have been enhanced and expanded, and now include provision for public access for walking on enclosed farmland.

EOC: see *Equal Opportunites Commission*

EPOS: see *electronic point-of-sale*

equal opportunities is concerned with giving all people, regardless of their gender, age, race, religion, ability, employment status, income level and mobility, equal rights in society. This extends to equal rights in the workplace and employment issues generally, as well as equal access to *leisure* and *tourism* facilities and opportunities. *Legislation* such as the *Equal Pay Act*, *Race Relations Act* and *Disability Discrimination Act*, have sought to make discrimination illegal, while bodies like *Sport England,* the *English Tourism Council* and *Countryside Agency* are actively promoting equal access for all.

Equal Opportunities Commission (EOC): an organisation set up under the auspices of the *Sex Discrimination Act 1975* to promote *good practice* in eliminating discrimination in the workplace on the grounds of gender. The EOC now has a wider remit, being involved with a range of equality issues and advising individuals and employers on the development of codes of practice and other mechanisms for reducing discrimination.

Equal Pay Act 1970: legislation introduced to abolish discrimination between men and women in pay and other terms of their *contracts of employment*. The Act was amended in 1983 to give all workers the right to equal pay for work of equal value when:

● the work being carried out by both male and female employees is the same or broadly similar (this is known as 'like work')

● the work of employees undertaking different jobs is of 'equal value'

● a *job evaluation study (JES)* has been carried out.

Employees who feel that they should be receiving equal pay can apply to an *industrial tribunal* at any time during their employment, or up to six months after leaving.

equity is a financial term referring to the owners' stake in a business as *shareholders*, plus the profits from previous years that have not been distributed. Equity is a form of risk capital, since there is no guarantee that shareholders will receive any dividend on their investment in a company. Principal sources of equity are a company's owners, private shareholders, banks and providers of *venture capital*.

ERDF: see *European Regional Development Fund*

ERM: See *Exchange Rate Mechanism*

erosion: the physical wearing away of ground through excessive trampling or vehicle movements. Some tourist and recreational use of land, particularly in popular *'honey pot'* areas such as *National Parks*, can result in surface erosion which must be managed to ensure no long-term damage. Some *adventure activities*, for example quad biking, off-road cycling and 4 x 4 driving, can have serious effects on the landscape.

ESA: see *Environmentally Sensitive Area*

ESF: see *European Social Fund*

estimates are projections made by *local authorities* of their likely *revenue* and expenditure for the forthcoming year. Councillors debate whether estimates for particular departments will need amending and must agree the estimates before the officers can begin preparing their operating budgets. The estimates are usually based on the previous year's budgets, with an adjustment made for *inflation*.

ETB: see *English Tourist Board*

ETC: see *English Tourism Council, European Travel Commission*

ethics: the moral codes and values that should underpin any decision-making by individuals and organisations. They represent an acceptance that a *company* decision which would generate most profit is not necessarily in the best interests of society as a whole. A *tour operator*, for example, may identify an opportunity to develop *package holidays* to a remote part of South America, which would prove financially profitable in the long-term. There may, however, be risk of environmental or cultural damage to the indigenous people. It may decide not to go ahead on ethical grounds. *Sponsorship* is another area that sometimes causes ethical problems. Should a sports club or individual sportsman or woman accept sponsorship money from a company that promotes smoking or other harmful practices? *Pressure groups* sometimes become involved in these situations and force companies to think again.

ethnic minority: the term used to describe a small number of people of a particular cultural background living in an area or country where the majority of the population follows a different cultural or religious code. There is general concern that ethnic minorities in Britain may not be getting equal access to *leisure* and *sport* facilities. Bodies such as *Sport England* and the *Countryside Agency* have targeted people from within these groups as priorities for action to improve the situation.

e-ticketing: a practice pioneered by airlines, particularly the *low-cost airlines*, that allows passengers to make a reservation without the need to have a paper ticket as confirmation of their booking. E-ticketing is particularly useful for the increasing numbers of bookings for holidays and other leisure, travel and tourism products and services that are made on the *Internet*.

EU: see *European Union*

EU Bathing Water Directive: this *EU Directive* and its associated regulations set quality standards for bathing waters in all member countries of the *European Union*. The Directive requires each country to identify the stretches of coastline most popular with holidaymakers and these are regularly tested during the bathing season. In the UK, the testing is carried out by the Environment Agency. All EU countries have to make sure that their bathing waters meet the standards set down in the Directive and take measures to rectify any deficiencies. The results of tests are made available to the general public. In 2002, 481 sites were tested in England and Wales, with a compliance rate of 97.1 per cent, a figure that has been growing steadily since the tests first began. (See also *Blue Flag Campaign*.)

EU Directive: a law or regulation which is binding on all member states of the *European Union*. Proposals for EU Directives come initially from the *European Commission*, are debated by the *European Parliament* and given final approval by the *Council of Ministers*, after consideration by their national parliaments. Examples of EU Directives are the *Package Travel Directive* and the *EU Bathing Water Directive*.

EU Directives on health and safety: six sets of health and safety at work regulations that came into force at the beginning of 1993, to meet the requirements of six European Union (EU) Directives on health and safety. The Directives are part of the EU's programme of action on health and safety, which is an essential ingredient of the move towards a *Single Market* in Europe. Most of the requirements of the Directives are not completely new, meaning that any leisure or tourism organisation that is already complying with the *Health and Safety at Work, etc. Act* should not find the regulations daunting. The regulations cover:

- *health and safety management*
- *work equipment safety*
- *manual handling of loads*
- *workplace conditions*
- *personal protective equipment*
- *display screen equipment*.

All leisure and tourism organisations are likely to be affected in some way by one or more of the regulations, with implications on finance, staffing and *management*.

EU Package Travel Directive: see *Package Travel Directive*

Euro: the currency adopted on January 1 2002 as part of *Economic and Monetary Union* by the following 12 countries: Austria, Germany, Luxembourg, Belgium, Greece, the Netherlands, Finland, Italy, Portugal, France, Ireland and Spain. The introduction of the Euro was an historic day for these countries and saw the demise of currencies such as the French franc, Spanish peseta and Italian lira. At the time of writing, Britain has still to decide whether or not to adopt the Euro instead of the pound.

Eurocheque: a form of *currency* that was used throughout Europe until its withdrawal in 2002. It allowed the holder to withdraw money from banks and write *cheques* in any local currency. Just as with a standard cheque used in the UK, Eurocheques had to be supported by a valid Eurocheque guarantee card. Eurocheques were not used extensively by UK travellers who tend to find *travellers' cheques* and *credit cards* more convenient.

European Association for Education in Tourism, Leisure and the Arts (ATLAS) is an association of higher education institutions throughout Europe that provide courses in *tourism, leisure* and the arts. Established in 1991, ATLAS exists to:

● promote the teaching of tourism, leisure and the arts throughout Europe

● encourage the exchange of staff and students between member institutions

● promote links between professional bodies in tourism, leisure and the arts and liaise on issues, curriculum development and professional recognition of courses

● promote transnational research which helps to underpin the development of appropriate curricula throughout Europe.

Membership of ATLAS is open to any institution of higher education or professional body in Europe with an interest in these areas. Weblink: www.atlas-euro.org

European Capital of Culture: conceived as a way of bringing European citizens closer together, the European City of Culture initiative was launched on 13 June 1985 by the *Council of Ministers*. In 1999 the European City of Culture was renamed the European Capital of Culture. In 2002 the accolade was awarded to Bruges and Salamanca; Cork has been designated for 2005. At the time of writing, a number of UK cities are campaigning hard to be nominated as European Capital of Culture 2008.

European Commission: an important institution in the *European Union*, which makes proposals for European laws and ensures that EU policies and practices are followed by member states. The Commission fulfils a similar role to that of the civil service in the UK, except that the Commission actually proposes *legislation*. Any proposals for new EU laws or regulations pass from the Commission to the *European Parliament* for debate and then on to the *Council of Ministers* for approval or rejection. The Commission is made up of a number of separate departments, known as Directorates General (DGs). The department concerned most with tourism issues is *DG Enterprise*, although the work of many other DGs has a bearing on the industry. Weblink: www.europa.eu.int

European Community (EC): the former name of the grouping of European countries now known as the *European Union*.

European Council is the name given to the European Union Heads of State or Government, which usually meets twice a year to give overall direction to the Union's work. The Heads of State take it in turns to chair the meetings of the European Council. (See also *Council of Ministers*.)

European Court of Justice: a *European Union* institution that interprets and adjudicates on Union law. There are fifteen judges, one from each member state, plus one extra to prevent deadlock, and six Advocates General who advise the Court. The Court is assisted by a Court of First Instance, which handles certain cases brought by individuals and companies.

European Currency Unit (ECU): an artificial currency made up of the trade-weighted averages of the currencies of the *EU* member states. The ECU was the basis on which the *European Union's* transactions used to be carried out. It is now replaced by the *Euro*.

European Economic Area (EEA): the trading zone set up under an agreement signed in 1992 by the member states of the *European Union (EU)* and the *European Free Trade Association (EFTA)*. The agreement allows greater access to EU countries for EFTA members, while at the same time promoting the harmonisation of legislation between countries belonging to the two organisations. The EEA comprises the EU Member States, plus Iceland, Liechtenstein and Norway. Negotiations on the accession of the 10 future EU Member States to the EEA were launched in Brussels in 2002.

European Economic Community (EEC): see *European Union*

European Federation of Conference Towns (EFCT) is a Brussels-based membership organisation representing the interests of more than 100 leading conference cities in more than 35 European countries. EFCT provides advice and guidance to meeting planners and conference and incentive group organisers who seek a venue anywhere in Europe. For conference towns which meet its criteria, EFCT membership is a resource which helps to spread information about their *destinations*, centres, hotels and services. In 2002, EFCT members in the UK were London, Aberdeen, Glasgow, Manchester, Belfast and Bournemouth. Weblink: www.efct.com

European Free Trade Association (EFTA): set up in 1960 to encourage the free movement of goods between its member countries, which originally included the *UK*, Austria, Finland, Iceland, Denmark, Norway, Sweden and Switzerland. Since countries cannot be members of both EFTA and the *European Union*, the UK, Denmark, Austria and Sweden have subsequently left the Association. In many respects EFTA is a rival organisation to the European Union, but there is close co-operation on matters concerning the movement of people, goods, services and capital and both bodies have agreed to work towards the formation of an integrated trading zone known as the *European Economic Area*.

European Investment Bank (EIB) is the *European Union's* bank for financing capital investment projects that promote the balanced development of Europe. The Bank works with both public and private sector organisations and has funded a variety of *tourism* projects throughout the EU.

European Monetary System (EMS): a system introduced in 1979 that aims to harmonise the currencies of the member states of the *European Union* prior to full *Economic and Monetary Union*. The two principal elements of the EMS are the *ECU (European Currency Unit)* and the *Exchange Rate Mechanism (ERM)*. (See also *Euro*.)

European Parliament: the institution in the *European Union* which debates and amends legislation put forward by the *European Commission*. Currently, the Parliament is made up of 626 Members of the European Parliament (MEPs), directly elected every five years from within the member states. Seats are shared out between member states broadly according to the size of the country. The Parliament sits in both Brussels and Strasbourg. Weblink: www.europarl.eu.int

European Plan: an *accommodation* arrangement consisting of a room only, with no meals included in the tariff. (See also *American Plan, Modified American Plan, Continental Plan*.)

European Regional Development Fund (ERDF): a *European Union* structural fund that is primarily used by member states to improve the *infrastructure* in their countries. Eligible tourism and leisure projects include airport developments, hotel building and extensions, road projects, conference centres, museums, sports centres, archaeological sites and leisure developments. The ERDF is only able to support capital projects in designated areas of the UK.

European Social Fund (ESF): a *European Union* training fund, which concentrates on helping young people who are out of work and the long-term unemployed in the EU member states. Certain ESF projects are connected with leisure and tourism, for example skills *training* in the hotel and catering sector.

European Travel Commission (ETC): a voluntary body established in 1948 to promote the whole of Europe as a single tourist destination to the rest of the world. ETC's stated aims are to increase the level of *tourism* from other parts of the world to Europe, as a result of its marketing activities, and to provide a forum for individual member countries to exchange ideas and experiences for the benefit of each member of the group. The work of the ETC is supported by the *European Commission*, which sees tourism as an industry of growing economic importance throughout Europe and beyond. Weblink: www.etc-europe-travel.org

European Union (EU): a grouping of fifteen countries, known as member states, which have joined together to safeguard peace and promote economic and social progress in Europe. The EU originated in 1957 as the European Economic Community (EEC) with six original members: France, Italy, West Germany, Belgium, the Netherlands and Luxembourg. Membership increased to nine in 1973 when Ireland, the United Kingdom and Denmark joined. In 1981 Greece became the tenth member state, followed by Spain and Portugal in 1986. The most recent members are Austria, Finland and Sweden who became full members in 1995. With a population in excess of 400 million, the EU is the world's largest trading entity. The EU is made up of a number of inter-linked institutions, the most important of which are the *European Commission*, the *Council of Ministers, the European Parliament, the European Council* and the *European Court of Justice*. The Treaty of Rome sets out the Union's legal framework. It was amended by the Single European Act in 1986, while the Treaty of Maastricht incorporated further changes. The EU is involved with a number of issues which concern leisure and tourism in Europe, including the abolition of frontier controls, liberalisation of air travel, the *Package Travel Directive*, harmonisation of *VAT* rates and the deregulation of coach travel. At the time of writing, plans are well advanced for the expansion of the EU by a further 10 countries, namely Estonia, Latvia, Lithuania, Poland, Czech Republic, Slovakia, Hungary, Slovenia, Malta and Cyprus. Weblink: www.europa.eu.int

European Year of Tourism 1990 was conceived by the *European Commission* with the general aim of promoting greater knowledge among *EU* citizens of the cultures and lifestyles of other member states. Specific objectives of the initiative were the staggering of holidays, the development of new tourist destinations, the creation of alternatives to mass tourism, the promotion of tourism within EU member states and the development of tourism to Europe from non-EU countries. Altogether there were more than 2000 events held in the UK alone in support of the initiative.

Eurostar is the passenger train service that operates through the *Channel Tunnel*, as opposed to *le Shuttle*, which is the vehicle-carrying service using shuttle trains. Eurostar reaches Paris in three hours and Brussels in three hours and fifteen minutes from the Waterloo International Terminal in London. These timings are likely to reduce considerably when the high-speed rail link between London and the Channel Tunnel is completed. Eurostar offers a range of *APEX* and standard fares and some *tour operators* are now featuring short breaks on the continent travelling on the service. Weblink: www.eurostar.com

Eurostat is the official body that collects, analyses and publishes statistical data on matters concerning the *European Commission* and member states of the *European Union*. Officially known as the Statistical Office of the European Communities, Eurostat publishes two main sets of documents:

● statistical documents – comprehensive, reference data intended for specialists and made available in paper form or on diskette, magnetic tape, CD-ROM or via the *Internet*

● general publications – intended for a wider audience and grouped in subject areas, including education, health, transport, travel and tourism.

Eurostat also publishes a variety of yearbooks which are a useful starting point for initial research. Eurostat's data on tourism shows which are the main *generating* and *receiving* countries in Europe. Weblink: www.eurostat.com

Eurotunnel: the joint English–French consortium of companies that built and now operate the *Channel Tunnel*. (See also *Eurostar, Le Shuttle*.)

evaluation is the process of looking back on an event or management decision to gauge if, with the benefit of hindsight, matters were handled as effectively as possible. In *leisure* and *tourism*, there are many circumstances in which evaluation is undertaken, including:

● to see if an event has met its *objectives*

● to establish whether visitors are happy with a facility or standard of service

● to find out whether financial and staffing *resources* are being used to best effect

● to compare performance with competitor organisations

● to identify weaknesses and strengths in *management* and administrative systems.

Evaluation is often the final stage of a cyclical management process, for example *management by objectives*.

evaluation process: see *evaluation*

event co-ordinator: a person who takes the lead role in overseeing the *planning* and organisation of an event. Events play an important part in leisure and tourism, making the appointment of an effective co-ordinator a very important decision. Although every event is unique, there are basic skills and qualities that any good co-ordinator should possess, including excellent leadership qualities, good written and oral *communication skills*, persuasive negotiation skills and the ability to delegate. The co-ordinator will often chair the planning meetings set up to ensure the smooth running of an event.

event evaluation is the process of reflecting on the planning and staging of an event to analyse whether its *objectives* were met and *resources* were used to best effect. It tries to answer a number of questions, such as 'was the organisational structure workable?', 'were those who attended satisfied with the event?' and 'were all eventualities covered?' The event organiser and organising committee should hold a *debriefing* session with all staff and helpers after the event, before a final *report* on the event is prepared and distributed to interested parties, with one copy being retained for future reference.

event management: all aspects of planning, organising, directing, co-ordinating and reviewing an event, in order to make the most effective use of resources and ensure that the event achieves its objectives.

event objectives are the aims that an individual or organisation will hope to achieve from running an event. Event organisers need to be clear at the outset exactly why an event is being staged and what outcomes are expected of them and their helpers. As with all goals, event objectives need to be measurable, realistic and achievable (see *SMART objectives*). Precise objectives vary depending on the nature of the event and whether the organiser lies in the *public, private* or *voluntary sector*. Public sector organisations stage events to fulfil their social and community objectives, rather than attempting to make a profit. Local councils, for example, often feel that events improve the quality of life for local people. Private companies will usually be looking to make a profit from running an event, although an event in itself may be seen as a good way of promoting a facility or product. Voluntary bodies organise events to raise funds and publicise a specific cause, perhaps a local playgroup or an environmental concern.

event planning is a crucial early phase in the running of a successful event. Once a decision to proceed has been made, an individual or, more commonly a group of people, will get together to plan timescales and the best use of their *resources*. The key stages in the planning process for a large event are likely to include:

- making the decision widely known
- setting budgets
- appointing a co-ordinator
- assembling a *committee*
- creating an organisational structure
- clarifying *objectives*
- setting timescales and deadlines
- devising *contingency plans*.

It is sometimes helpful if the plan is set out as a *critical path analysis*, indicating the precise order of tasks and where responsibilities lie.

events are an important part of the leisure and tourism scene worldwide, ranging in complexity from the *Olympic Games* to a local neighbourhood fête. The definition of an event would include the fact that it is a 'one off', or at least occurs infrequently, and that it is an opportunity for the public to enjoy its leisure time, or business people to meet, while at the same time allowing the organisers to achieve their objectives. While it is true that events are not a new phenomenon (the Olympic Games originated in 776 BC), the scope of events held today goes well beyond celebrating a religious festival or recognising the cultural importance of a date in the calendar. Nowadays, events can be staged very quickly to meet ever-changing needs, tastes and fashions, and areas can develop *events-led strategies* to help towards economic and social development.

events-led strategy: a promotional programme that uses a series of events, either existing or newly created, to raise the awareness of an area and attract visitors to it. An events-led strategy is seen as a way of contributing to the economic and social development of both rural and urban areas, e.g. the many events promoted in the *Mid-Wales Festival of the Countryside* and Cardiff City Council in its bid to become *European Capital of Culture* 2008. Such a strategy is particularly attractive to an area that has few inherent *natural* or *man-made visitor attractions*.

exchange rate fluctuation: see *currency fluctuation*

Exchange Rate Mechanism (ERM): an important arrangement, part of the *European Monetary System*, which was established in 1978 to limit fluctuations in the currencies of the member states of the *European Union*. Political and economic tensions between countries led in 1992 to the UK suspending its membership of the ERM.

exchange rates: see *rate of exchange*

excursion fare: see *APEX, PEX*

excursionist: a term which originated in North America to describe an individual who makes a visit which doesn't involve an overnight stay away from their normal place of residence. In Britain an excursionist would be called a day visitor. For statistical purposes, excursionists include travellers in transit and those on ocean cruises who do not use *accommodation* in the country visited.

executive director: a full-time employee of an organisation who sits on its board of directors, thereby helping to determine *policy*. An executive director is normally responsible for a department or group of departments within an organisation, and has a number of managers working under his or her leadership. (See also *non-executive director.*)

existing market: see *market*

expatriate: a person who chooses to live in a country other than that of which he or she is a citizen. The move is not necessarily permanent, but is usually relatively long-term.

expenditure budget: a chart which shows the spending limits that must be adhered to so that a department or whole organisation achieves its financial targets. It will include all the *fixed* and *variable costs* that are attributable over a given period of time, which could be a month or a year. Showing monthly expenditure allows management to swiftly rectify any *variances* between the budgeted and actual expenditure by taking the appropriate action. The performance of the expenditure budget cannot be divorced from the figures contained in the *sales budget* and it is a matter of preference whether or not the two budgets are combined or kept separate. (See also *budgetary control.*)

exports are goods and services sent overseas from their original country of origin. They may be either *'visible'* or *'invisible'* items and the flows of currency associated with exports are shown in a country's *balance of payments*. The earnings from *overseas visitors* coming to Britain is considered an export, since they are bringing money into the country, in the same way that a British car manufacturer does when it earns money from exporting its vehicles.

external communication is liaison between an organisation and a range of outside bodies. In leisure and tourism, these will include *customers*, the Inland Revenue, trade associations such as *ABTA*, professional bodies such as the *Tourism Society*, the *Health and Safety Executive (HSE)*, the police, neighbours and other organisations in the many sectors of the industry.

external constraint: something outside an organisation's immediate control that limits its ability to achieve its full potential. Typical external constraints in the leisure and tourism industries are economic factors, such as changing *rates of exchange* or *interest rate* rises, social factors, including the rise in one-parent families, political considerations, such as a change in the government, and technological developments, including the introduction of new global communications systems. (See also *internal constraint*.)

external cost: see *social cost*

external environment: see *macro environment*

external recruitment: the process of identifying and employing the most suitable person from outside an organisation to fill a job vacancy.

externalities are those costs or benefits of an organisation's operation that are borne by the wider community or society in general, rather than by the organisation itself, e.g. one external benefit of building a fifth terminal at Heathrow may be that the energy costs for the airport as a whole are reduced, but an *external cost* may be that local people will have to put up with more noise from aircraft. (See also *internal costs*.)

extra product is a common *sales promotion* technique in leisure and tourism, when a *customer* is given additional benefits when buying a product or service, at no extra cost, e.g. three weeks for the price of two on a holiday.

extrapolation is the technique of *forecasting* future events based on an analysis of past performance. Tour operators, for example, will plot past sales figures for particular products and destinations on a graph and attempt to forecast future sales on the same graph. Extrapolation can only give a short-term guide to likely future trends. (See the figure below.)

face-to-face communication is the most common way that individuals communicate with each other. For staff working in leisure and tourism, the type of occasions when they will be communicating face-to-face is very diverse, e.g. a travel agency clerk advising a client, a coach teaching children how to play tennis or a concierge directing hotel guests to the nearest railway station. Information and decisions within an organisation are often communicated on a face-to-face basis, although it does have the disadvantage of being an informal technique, so there is no written confirmation of what was said. For this reason, decisions made in a face-to-face situation (for example a meeting or briefing event) will often be confirmed in writing. Face-to-face communication allows an individual to see how a person reacts to a situation and observe any *non-verbal communication*.

face-to-face interview: a *survey* that involves an *interviewer* asking questions of a member of the general public, known as the *respondent*, and recording his or her answers on a *questionnaire*. This type of survey is very common in all sectors of the leisure and tourism industries, from leisure centres to *seaside resorts*, and is a good way of obtaining both *qualitative* and *quantitative data*. Face-to-face interviews can be carried out in a number of different locations, such as at the respondent's home, in the street, at a leisure or tourism facility, en route to a *destination* or at work. Such interviews have a number of advantages over other *survey* techniques, for example:

- the interviewer can explain difficult questions
- visual aids can be used
- the interviewer can prompt the respondent for further detail
- initial interest on the part of the respondent is aroused.

The principal disadvantages of face-to-face interviews are that they are expensive, since interviewers have to be recruited and fully trained, and that they are time-consuming when compared with other techniques, e.g. *telephone and e-mail surveys*.

facsimile transmission (fax): the sending of written documents nationally and internationally using fax machines or computers connected by telephone lines. It combines the speed of the telephone with the accuracy of the printed word and is, therefore, particularly suited to the needs of *travel agents*, *tour operators* and airlines, who operate globally, often across different *time zones*.

factoring is the practice of selling off *bad debts* at a reduced rate to an agency which specialises in their collection. For the organisation, selling off the debts has the advantage of eliminating the time and effort needed to chase outstanding payments, plus any legal fees and interest payments associated with them, but the price at which the debts are passed on is considerably less than their face value.

factory tourism: a particular type of tourist activity where working factories open their doors to members of the public, either as individuals or in organised groups. Examples in the UK include Cadbury World and Wedgewood Pottery.

'fam' trip: see *familiarisation trip*

familiarisation trip: an educational visit which gives *travel agents, tour operators* and other members of the *travel trade*, the opportunity of trying facilities and services first hand, so that they are in the best position to advise clients on their holiday choices. Also referred to as 'fam' trips or educational trips, they are an important part of both *sales promotion* and *public relations*.

Farm Holiday Bureau: a network organisation whose primary function is to promote the concept of *farm tourism* in the UK. Now branded as Farmstay UK, it represents the interests of more than 1000 independent farmers who offer hospitality to visitors either in the farmhouse, as bed, breakfast and evening meal, or in *self-catering accommodation*. The Bureau produces an annual guide, ensures high standards of accommodation in conjunction with the National Tourist Boards and acts as a forum for debate. An increasing number of bookings made with Farmstay UK are via the *Internet*. Weblink: www.farmstayuk.co.uk

farm open day: an event held on a working farm to which the general public are invited as a way of educating them in the work of the farming community, as well as providing an extra source of revenue for the farmer. The open day is a type of *interpretation*, in that it is providing visitors with items such as demonstrations, self-guided trails and guided walks that are designed to enhance their enjoyment and understanding.

farm tourism: a type of *rural tourism* centred on working farms. It takes many forms, but is most commonly associated with *accommodation*, including farmhouse bed and breakfast and self-catering accommodation in cottages and converted, redundant farm buildings. Farm tourism provides a welcome alternative source of income for farmers and their families and can help stop rural depopulation, particularly loss of young people. Farms also provide facilities for day visitors, including *farm open days* and rare breeds centres.

Farmstay UK: see *Farm Holiday Bureau*

fashions and trends have an important role to play in leisure, travel and tourism, since they often influence *consumer demand*. Young people especially are likely to be swayed in their leisure purchasing habits by fashions and trends, often wanting the latest computer games, sports equipment and accessories.

fast-food outlet: a limited-menu catering enterprise that offers food and drink for consumption on or off the premises. Fast-food outlets aim to serve a high volume of *customers* in as short a time as possible, thereby maximising revenue. Many are part of multinational chains, such as BurgerKing and KFC, and operate on uniform recipes, procedures and products.

fast-moving consumer goods (FMCGs) are products that sell in volume through a network of sales outlets. FMCGs include food, toiletries, clothes and cars. Much of the early work in *marketing* was focused on FMCGs, particularly in the USA. Techniques such as *market segmentation, niche marketing* and *target marketing* were applied first to the FMCG sector and have only latterly been applied to *service sector* industries, including leisure, travel and tourism.

Fastrak: a *viewdata system* used in travel agencies to access *principal's computerised reservation systems* using a *VDU* plus either a telephone line or cable connection. Its main rival is *Istel*.

fax: see *facsimile transmission*

feasibility study: a systematic analysis of a possible project or development to determine whether it is sensible to go ahead, both financially and operationally. The study, whether carried out in-house or by external consultants, should include information on the *capital* and revenue costs of the proposal, the likely market, any environmental consequences, an assessment of the *competition* locally and any legal constraints that may cause a problem. After careful analysis of the facts, the feasibility study should include a recommendation on whether or not the proposal should be given the go-ahead. (See also *pre-feasibility study*.)

features statement: that part of the *sales process* in leisure and tourism, before the *customer* has made a decision whether or not to purchase, when a sales person highlights the features of a particular service or product. This could be the number of rooms in a hotel, the frequency of flights from a particular airport or the type of equipment available in a health and fitness club. Often a customer shows a degree of indifference at this stage, making it necessary to introduce an *advantages statement* or *benefits statement* in the hope of finally *closing a sale*.

Federation of Tour Operators (FTO): an independent membership body representing the interests of the leading British tour operating companies. Formerly the Tour Operators' Study Group (TOSG), the FTO is active in lobbying government for changes to *legislation* that affects its members' interests. (See also *International Federation of Tour Operators*.) Weblink: www.fto.co.uk

feedback: the process of inviting and collecting comments, suggestions and complaints from a variety of sources and using the information to influence future *policies* and *strategies*. Feedback is an essential aspect of any *communication* process in leisure and tourism, and is given by customers, staff, volunteers, local people, politicians, pressure groups, councillors, etc. Feedback from customers can be either formal or informal, and can be obtained from surveys, customer comment forms, *customer satisfaction questionnaires*, suggestion boxes, *focus groups* and 'mystery shopper' techniques. The feedback obtained will help determine future products, services and *customer service* standards.

feelgood factor: the notion that people have to feel confident in themselves before a nation's economy can prosper, irrespective of how positive any economic indicators show the economy to be.

ferry services: shipping that carries passengers, freight and vehicles on relatively short-duration trips, linking one land mass with another. The most popular ferry services in the UK are those concentrated on the English Channel, especially the Dover–Calais route. Other important services link the UK with Ireland and Scandinavia. Growth in the popularity of ferry travel in recent years has seen the introduction of longer crossings from the UK to Spain, with P&O operating to Bilbao and Brittany Ferries to Santander. Ferries operating on the Dover–Calais route are facing competition from the *Eurostar* and *Le Shuttle* services using the *Channel Tunnel*. Ferry companies are responding to increased competition in a number of ways, for example the introduction of new, faster ferries, improvements to the quality of ship accommodation and price reductions.

field research: see *primary research*

fifty/fifty marketing: see *joint marketing*

financial accounting is concerned with the preparation of the financial information an organisation is required to produce by law. In the private sector, these statutory accounts are:

- the *profit and loss account*
- the *balance sheet*
- the *cash-flow statement*.

Financial accountants are bound by legislation contained in the various Companies' Acts concerning the method of presentation of financial data and the disclosure of certain information. Financial accounts are prepared to meet the needs of owners, managers, *shareholders*, the Inland Revenue, H M Customs and Excise (in the case of *VAT*), the Registrar of Companies and any providers of finance to the organisation. (See also *management accounting*.)

financial performance of a leisure or tourism organisation will be affected by a number of external and internal factors. External factors, outside the immediate control of the organisation, could include the general state of the economy, changes in *fashions* and tastes, government *legislation*, industrial disputes, *competitor activity* or *seasonality*. Internal factors might include low sales volume, high levels of *credit*, poor *stock control* or high *fixed* and *variable costs*.

financial ratios are a means by which managers can measure the financial *effectiveness* and *efficiency* of their organisation. Common ratios used in leisure and tourism include the *return on capital employed*, *gross profit/sales ratio* and the *net profit/sales ratio*. When combined with *performance indicators*, financial ratios provide essential information for *planning* and *management* purposes.

Fire Certificate: a statutory document issued by local fire authorities to regulate the use of public premises and specify certain minimum standards of fire equipment and procedures that must be adhered to. A Fire Certificate will list a number of conditions that the owner or operator of the premises will need to comply with, including:

- keeping escape routes clear in case of emergency
- providing employees with fire safety training
- limits to the number of people allowed on the premises
- carrying out fire drills at specified times
- keeping records relating to fire safety matters.

Fire Precautions Act 1971: legislation to regulate the use of premises and reduce risks to the public from fire-related incidents. Under the terms of the Act, the operator of any premises providing entertainment, *recreation* or use by a club or association, where there are more than twenty employees on the ground floor or more than ten above ground floor level, must apply for a *Fire Certificate* from the local fire authorities. *Hotels* and other *serviced accommodation* also fall within the scope of the Act, with a *Fire Certificate* necessary if the accommodation sleeps more than six guests at first floor level or just one guest at either second floor level or below ground.

Fire Safety and Safety of Places of Sport Act 1987: government *legislation* prompted by the tragic events at Bradford City Football Club in 1985, when 56 spectators lost their lives in a fire. The Act deals with means of escape in the event of a fire and the means for fighting fires. It modified *the Fire Precautions Act 1971* by reducing the need for certification of premises considered to have a low fire risk, allowing fire authorities to grant exemptions in these cases. It did, however, extend the *Safety of Sports Grounds Act 1975* to include all sports grounds (previously only applicable to sports stadia).

first aid refers to treatment procedures that can be carried out immediately at the scene of an accident, prior to the emergency services arriving to take control of the situation. The *Health and Safety at Work, etc. Act* and its associated regulations, in particular the *Health and Safety (First Aid) Regulations 1981*, place a duty on employers to provide adequate first aid for both employees and non-employees, which in the case of leisure and tourism would include guests, visitors, spectators, customers and contractors.

fiscal: a term used to describe anything to do with *taxation*, e.g. fiscal *legislation* would be Acts of Parliament dealing with tax matters.

fixed assets are items of a monetary value that have a long-term function in an organisation and can be used repeatedly. Fixed assets, which include land, buildings, facilities, vehicles, equipment and machinery, are not primarily held for conversion into cash, but to further an organisation's trading activities in the long term. They not only provide the basis on which trading activity is carried out, but can also be used as *security* for additional *loans*. Fixed assets are shown in an organisation's *balance sheet*. (See also *current assets*.)

fixed costs: expenditure that remains constant despite an organisation's level of business activity (see figure below). A museum, for example, will need to pay rates, rent and salaries, whether it has 20,000 or 200,000 visitors through its doors. Other examples of fixed costs in leisure and tourism include energy costs, fixtures and fittings, *depreciation*, interest charges, equipment *leasing* costs and *insurance*. The costs that fluctuate in line with the level of business activity are known as *variable costs*.

FLA: see *Football Licensing Authority*

flag of convenience: the arrangement when ship owners register vessels in a country other than their own, so as to avoid, among other things, paying government taxes, paying agreed wage rates and meeting health and safety requirements. Ships flying under flags of convenience are often considered by the owners of legitimately registered fleets to be a threat to their livelihoods and a constant danger on the high seas.

flat hierarchy: see *flat pyramid*

flat pyramid: a type of *hierarchical* structure in which there is a wide span of control, i.e. decision making is delegated downwards within the organisation, rather than resting with a few senior managers, as is the case with *steep pyramid* structures. A flat pyramid structure, sometimes called a 'flat hierarchy', is a form of *decentralisation*, often resulting in faster decision making, better *communication* and a positive effect on staff morale (see figure below).

flexi-time is a working arrangement that enables staff to complete a set number of hours of work per week, but on a flexible rather than fixed basis. A *travel clerk*, for example, may be required to work 40 hours in a standard week. Whereas this would normally be made up of five days work at eight hours per day, a flexi-time arrangement would allow, for example, four days at ten hours per day, thereby giving one day off. Flexi-time is particularly suitable for working parents with young children.

flight series charter: a type of *charter flight* arrangement used by tour operators where they contract with an airline for a fixed number of flights to a particular *destination* on a specific time each day or week. The disadvantage of this arrangement over, for example, *time series charter*, is that there will be *'empty legs'* at the beginning and end of the season.

floppy disk: a device for storing and retrieving *data* files outside of a computer's hard disk. Many software packages and *computer* games are sold on floppy disks and loaded into the computer before use. Floppy disks are also a good way of storing data so as not to overload a computer's internal memory, thereby slowing it down. Back-up copies of files can also be stored on floppy disks to prevent data loss resulting from failure of the main memory.

flotilla: a collection of boats, often yachts, sailing as a fleet under the guidance of a lead boat. Flotilla sailing is a popular product in the Mediterranean, especially around the Greek Islands, offered by a number of specialist UK-based *tour operators*.

flume: the name given to a slide or chute found in many modern swimming pools and leisure centres.

fly-cruise: a holiday arrangement combining a *charter* or *scheduled flight* to and/or from a port with a sea cruise. It is possible, for example, to fly from London to New York on Concorde and sail back to the UK on a luxury cruise liner such as the Queen Elizabeth II (QE2).

fly-drive: a holiday arrangement combining a charter or *scheduled flight* with car hire. It is normally sold as a package with either *serviced* or *self-catering accommodation* included. Some fly-drive packages include a set itinerary for clients to follow, with pre-booked *accommodation* en-route.

FMCG: see *fast-moving consumer goods*

focus group: a research technique used to collect in-depth information on *customers'* habits and to explore the reasons why they choose one product or service instead of another. A focus group meeting usually consists of up to ten consumers under the guidance of a skilled interviewer, who will use a number of techniques to delve into the innermost thoughts and values of the members of the group. The sessions are usually recorded for future analysis and will often cause an organisation to change its product range or promotional activities as a direct result of the outcomes of the meeting.

Food Hygiene Regulations: a set of regulations introduced under the Food Safety Act 1990 to regulate all aspects of food offered for sale. The Regulations lay great emphasis on cleanliness and sanitation, as well as the correct storage and preparation of food. *Local authorities* enforce the Food Hygiene Regulations through teams of inspectors, who have wide-ranging powers, including the right to enter premises at any reasonable hour of the day to check whether the Regulations are being complied with. Penalties for breaching the Regulations are severe, including heavy fines for the original offence and additional daily fines for each day the breach continues. In exceptional circumstances, the establishment could be banned from serving food altogether until measures to rectify the situation are completed.

Food Safety Act 1990: see *Food Hygiene Regulations*

foot and mouth disease (FMD) was detected in the UK towards the end of February 2001 and was to have a dramatic impact not just on farming but also on *domestic* and *incoming tourism*. Large tracts of countryside in infected areas of the country were closed to visitors, causing severe difficulties for leisure, travel and tourism businesses. The government provided funding packages to help rescue the situation, but many enterprises had little income in their 2001–2002 season. The *British Tourist Authority* estimates that, in the six-month period following outbreak of the disease, overseas visitor numbers to the UK fell by 9 per cent compared to the same period in 2000. This equated to a loss of 1.3 million visits. Spending also fell by some 12 per cent in the same period, down from £7.6 million in 2000 to £6.6 million in 2001. The UK tourism industry was dealt a second major blow in 2001 when terrorists attacked the twin towers in New York on *September 11*.

Football Licensing Authority (FLA): established under the Football Spectators Act of 1989, the FLA is concerned with ensuring the safety of football grounds. It operates a licensing scheme for football grounds, advises government on the introduction of all-seated accommodation in stadia and keeps under review the safety standards of football terracing. Weblink: www.flaweb.org.uk

Football Trust: established in 1990, the Trust helps football at all levels, from national stadia and Premier League clubs to the grass roots of the sport. The *grants* it is able to give are funded by the reduction in pools betting duty and donations from 'spot the ball' competitions. (See also *Taylor Report*.)

forecasting: the technique of estimating a future likely outcome, based on the best possible information available. This may be achieved by carrying out *market research*, *extrapolation* or by seeking expert opinion (known as the *Delphi technique*).

foreign exchange: another word for foreign *currency*.

Forestry Commission: a government department responsible for the protection and expansion of Britain's forests and woodlands. More than 70 per cent of all adults have visited British forests in the last few years. They make around 350 million day trips from their homes, in addition to visits by regular users and holidaymakers. Established in 1919 to help reduce timber shortage problems experienced during the First World War, the Commission now has two Divisions, Forest Enterprise and Forest Research. Forest Enterprise is responsible for the management of 800,000 hectares of forests and woodlands, which provide a variety of opportunities for *recreation* and *leisure*, including walking, cycling, orienteering, horse riding, camping, fishing and birdwatching. Forest Research aims to deliver high quality scientific research and surveys. Weblink: www.forestry.gov.uk

formal communication is *communication* between two or more parties that is the result of a pre-planned course of action. This could be a letter to an aggrieved customer, a company *report* on financial performance, a *staff appraisal*, a *memorandum* or the *minutes* of a meeting. Formal communication methods may be either written, verbal or electronic, and are used to establish efficient working methods within organisations and between outside agencies. (See also *informal communication*.)

forming is the initial stage of team development, when the *objectives* and team roles are being clarified. Team members are likely to feel anxious at this stage and will be trying to establish their credentials and create an impression on both the *team leader* and other members of the group. (See also *storming, norming, performing*.)

Foundation for Sport and the Arts (FSA): set up by the pools promoters after the 1991 Budget, FSA was created through a reduction in the pools betting levy. This released around £20 million, to which a contribution of £40 million was added by the Pools Promoters' Association. FSA donated approximately £60 million annually in its first years of operation, but this has dropped significantly as a result of the falling appeal of the pools. In 1998, some £12.6 million was distributed to a wide range of projects established by sports and arts organisations and individuals.

four Ps: refers to the four elements of the *marketing mix*, namely *price, product, place* and *promotion* (see figure below).

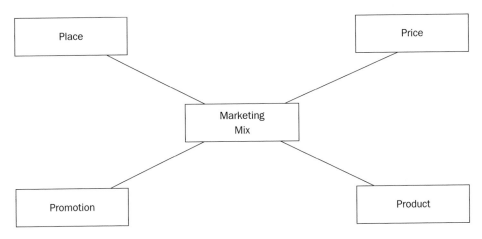

The four Ps of the marketing mix

franchising: an arrangement between two companies where the principal company (the franchisor) permits the other company (the franchisee) the right to use its trading name and methods in return for an agreed payment. Franchise operations in *leisure* and *tourism* include Budget Rent-a-Car and KFC Restaurants. The benefit for the franchisee is that the company name is already well established and he or she will have access to the advice, expertise and promotional activities of the franchisor. The franchisor gains financially, from an initial start-up payment and an annual fee, and can expand its operations relatively quickly and cheaply.

fraud is a serious concern for many leisure, travel and tourism businesses. Organisations must establish effective security measures to ensure that the risks of fraud from within and outside the business are minimised. These could include the use of *CCTV*, security guards and *staff training*.

freedoms of the air: a set of five airline operating procedures that were agreed at the *Chicago Convention on Civil Aviation* in 1944. These so-called 'five freedoms of the air' are:

1   The right to fly across another country without landing

2   The right to land in a country, for example to refuel

3   The right to off-load freight, mail or passengers from an aircraft of the country from which they originated

4   The right to load freight, mail or passengers on to an aircraft of the country for which they are destined

5   The right to load or off-load freight, mail and passengers on aircraft other than those of the country of destination or origin.

These principles provided a framework for agreements between countries and ensured that the flights operating between one country and another would be restricted to the carriers of the two countries concerned.

freelance describes a person who is not employed full-time by any one organisation, but works on a number of different projects for different people on a contract basis. Self-employed freelancers work in many support services to the *leisure, travel* and *tourism* industries, e.g. *public relations*, design, photography, *marketing*, project feasibility, *consul-tancy* and *training*. Employing freelance staff is sometimes seen by an organisation as a way of cutting costs, since there are less overhead costs involved.

freesale: an agreement that allows *tour operators* to sell an agreed number of rooms in a *hotel* without first checking availability with the hotelier. The tour operator simply confirms the sales by telephone, e-mail, telex or fax, in return for which the hotel agrees to make the specified accommodation available. Freesale differs from an *allocation* of rooms, since the hotel is likely to 'block out' certain busy periods in the year and not offer rooms at these times.

frequent flyer programmes are *incentives* operated by most major airlines to reward *customers* who use their services regularly. They work by collecting points for journeys made, with more points for longer journeys. Once a certain number have been collected, the traveller can exchange them for free flights or other gift items. Frequent flyer programmes are a very good way of maintaining *brand loyalty*.

fringe benefit: see *perks*

front of house: see *front office*

front office is a term used to denote the point at which *customers* and the public in general come into contact with staff in a leisure or tourism facility, e.g. the reception area in a *leisure centre* or a *hotel*. Sometimes called the 'front of house', staff working in the front office carry out a range of clearly defined functions, including welcoming visitors, taking bookings, handling cash, providing information, issuing equipment, controlling entry and promoting services. Unlike *back office* functions, which take place 'behind the scenes', the duties of front office staff bring them into direct contact with the public on a regular basis. It is important, therefore, that front office employees are chosen for their excellent *customer service* skills.

FSA: see *Foundation for Sport and the Arts*

FTO: see *Federation of Tour Operators*

full board: an *accommodation* arrangement, sometimes known as *American Plan*, consisting of a room and three meals per day. (See also *half board*.)

functional structures are *management* structures based around the main functions carried out by an organisation. A *national tourism organisation*, for example, may operate a functional structure based on the following departments:

- *marketing*
- *development*
- *research* and corporate planning
- finance and administration.

Although it is relatively easy to allocate job roles in these types of organisations, some critics point to a lack of flexibility with functional structures; this can sometimes be overcome by implementing a *matrix organisation*.

funding of leisure, travel and tourism is a complex issue, involving a host of *private, public* and *voluntary sector* organisations. Private sector operators receive the bulk of their start-up funding from commercial sources, principally the banks. They may apply for funding from *central* or *local government*, or even European sources, in the form of grants or low-interest loans. Public sector organisations receive their funding from central government sources, principally the *Department for Culture, Media and Sport*, and from their local *Council Tax* payers. Voluntary bodies rely on donations, subscriptions and bequests, along with *sponsorship* from commercial companies and grants from central and local government organisations.

funding of sport: see *sport*

Do you need revision help and advice?

Go to pages 265–75 for a range of revision appendices that include plenty of exam advice and tips.

Galileo: a *computerised reservation system (CRS)* pioneered by *British Airways* and other major European airlines to compete directly with the American Airlines' *Sabre* CRS. Galileo has now merged with United Airlines' *Apollo* CRS. Weblink: www.galileo.com

gateway has two meanings in leisure, travel and tourism. Firstly, it is the word used for an interactive computer facility that allows selected *travel agents* to access the *computerised reservation systems* of major *principals*, including airlines, hotel companies and tour operators, in order to check product availability and make bookings. Access is gained via the travel agent's *visual display unit* connected to a telephone line.

The second meaning is an entry city to a country, normally an airport, border crossing or port, that is used by visiting tourists. Most countries have more than one gateway.

GATT: see *General Agreement on Tariffs and Trade*

gazetteer: a geographical index or reference manual used by those wanting detailed information on countries and the facilities available at tourist *destinations*.

GDP: see *gross domestic product*

GDS: see *global distribution systems*

gearing: a financial term used to describe the proportion of a company's *capital* that is supplied by long-term borrowing, Generally speaking, the higher the gearing the higher the risk the company is taking. A company that has a greater than 50 per cent proportion of its capital as borrowed funds is referred to as 'highly geared'.

General Agreement on Tariffs and Trade (GATT) is a series of trade agreements which, since 1947, have established strict procedures for international trade. Some 96 countries are parties to the GATT discussions and agreements, which together account for more than 80 per cent of total world trade. The underlying principle of GATT is that its members should enjoy favourable trading terms between each other, provided that home producers are not disadvantaged.

General Household Survey (GHS): a survey undertaken by the *Office for National Statistics* to discover factual information about the habits and possessions of households in Britain. Started in 1971, the GHS collects data about, for example, the number of households that have televisions or dishwashers, as well as information about participation in *leisure* and sporting activities. (See also *Social Trends*.)

General National Vocational Qualifications (GNVQs) are knowledge-based, work-related qualifications designed to offer a choice of opportunities in employment or higher education. GNVQs are available in a number of occupational areas, including leisure and tourism, and are part of the *National Vocational Qualification* framework, endorsed by the government, *CBI* and *TUC*. GNVQs offer students a flexible qualification based around mandatory, optional, additional and core skill units. They are currently available from three awarding bodies, *Edexcel, OCR* and *AQA*. Advanced GNVQs were replaced from 2000 onwards by the *Advanced Vocational Certificate in Education (AVCE)*.

general sales agent (GSA): an individual or organisation that is appointed by a travel company, usually an airline or *tour operator*, to represent them in a particular country. The company benefits by not having to set up a sales operation of its own, thereby saving costs. A GSA often represents more than one company and can handle a range of functions, including *marketing*, reservations, ticketing and handling enquiries. The GSA will usually operate on a *commission* basis plus an initial fee for start-up costs.

generating country: see *tourist generating country*

ghetto tourism: a term describing the policy of restricting *mass tourism* to a small number of selected resorts, so as to minimise its *socio-cultural impacts* on a wider area. Some people consider this approach to be more sustainable than allowing tourists free movement within a country. (See also *tourist enclave*.)

GHS: see *General Household Survey*

global distribution systems (GDS) is the name sometimes used to describe the major *computerised reservation* systems that have been developed by the world's biggest airlines, e.g. *Sabre* and *Worldspan*. The main feature of a GDS system is that it gives the user access to a wide range of related travel services, not just airline information.

global warming refers to long-term changes to the earth's climate brought about, in part, by increased carbon dioxide emissions from vehicles and aircraft. Scientists suggest that the earth's temperature is rising, with potentially damaging consequences for tourist *destinations* in the long-term, e.g. the loss of marginal ski resorts, rise in water levels in low-lying countries and increased algal growth in warmer seas.

globalisation: the process of striving for world dominance in an industry sector, through company takeovers, strategic alliances, *vertical* and *horizontal integration*. *Multinational corporations* seek to achieve *economies of scale* by operating at a global level. Improved electronic communication methods, such as the *Internet* and *global distribution systems* facilitate the movement of airlines, hotel companies and travel companies towards globalisation.

GMT: see *Greenwich Mean Time*

GNP: see *gross national product*

GNVQ: see *General National Vocational Qualifications*

goals: a term that originated in the USA and means the same as *objectives*. Goals are targets that an individual or organisation seeks to achieve by implementing a number of different strategies. The goal of *British Airways*, for example, is 'to be the undisputed leader in world travel'.

good practice is a term used to highlight activities, organisations and initiatives that are considered to be particularly successful in their operation. By publicising examples of good practice, organisations hope to raise standards of operation generally across an industry sector, including leisure, travel and tourism. Good practice examples are often used as the starting point for a *benchmarking* exercise.

governing body of sport: each organised *sport* in Britain has a governing body whose job it is to represent the interests of that particular sport. Governing bodies draft and amend the rules and laws of the sport, organise local and national competitions, as well as selecting teams for international competitions such as the *Olympic Games*. They also keep players and participants informed about their particular sport and maintain relations with the media. The national governing bodies are all members of the *Central Council of Physical Recreation (CCPR)* and are grouped into six main divisions; games and sports, interested organisations, major spectator sports, movement and dance, outdoor pursuits and water recreation. Around 200 governing bodies are members of the CCPR, including the British Darts Organisation, Welsh Chess Union and the Lawn Tennis Association.

government legislation: see *legislation*

GP referral scheme: an initiative started in the mid-1990s to link the patients of General Practitioners with nearby sports and leisure facilities as a way of improving the health and fitness of individuals. Most areas of the country now operate GP referral schemes.

Grand Tour: the name given to a circuit of the major cultural centres in Europe undertaken by young aristocrats from a number of countries from the seventeenth century onwards. The original aim of the Grand Tour was to widen the young men's education and cultural awareness prior to seeking positions at court on their return home. Cities such as Paris, Venice, Florence, Rome and Geneva gave these gentlemen the opportunity to sample different cultures, societies and experiences. Most of those from Britain who took part in the Grand Tour were drawn from the ranks of the landed classes of peers and gentry.

grant: see *grant aid*

grant aid: sums of money made available to *leisure* and *tourism* organisations from *central* and *local government* bodies, such as local authorities, *Sport England* and the *Arts Council*. The granting of the funding is usually tied to satisfying certain *objectives* and subject to certain criteria, e.g. no one individual should be allowed to gain financially from the grant aid. Sometimes referred to as grant-in-aid, it is often given for *capital* projects only and not for *revenue* purposes.

grant-in-aid: see *grant aid*

gratuity: a payment made to a member of staff by a *customer* for services rendered. Gratuities, often called tips, are commonly paid to staff working in hotels, restaurants and for taxi firms. (See also *service charge*.)

Great Britain: see *Britain*

green belt is the name given to areas of land surrounding urban areas for which there is some degree of protection against further *development*, particularly house building. The idea of green belt policies, which incidentally have applied to London since 1938, is to restrict the size of towns and cities, by controlling the spread of built-up areas, while at the same time providing open spaces for *leisure* and *recreation*. In Britain, there are green belts around most major urban areas, including London, Birmingham, Manchester and Bristol. In many respects, green belt policies have failed to meet their aims, with new development 'leap-frogging' the protected areas.

Green Flag International (GFI) is a non-profit making *conservation* company working with the *travel and tourism industry* to help improve its environmental performance and to establish conservation projects at tourism *destinations*. Members of GFI include a number of specialist tour operators, including Eurocamp, Saga Holidays, Cox & Kings, Sunvil Travel and Simply Crete. Services to members include an environmental advice service, training on environmental issues and *environmental audits*.

Green Globe: a worldwide *environmental management* and awareness programme for, and led by, the *travel and tourism industry*. Its prime *objective* is to provide a low-cost, practical means for all *travel* and *tourism companies* to undertake improvements in their environmental practice. Green Globe helps a company to develop an environmental programme and provides advice and information on a range of environmental issues to its members. It can also be applied to *tourist destinations* with the award of Green Globe status.

green tourism: a general term used to describe a type of tourist activity which aims to be respectful of the environment in which it takes place and the communities that live there. Variously described as *sustainable tourism*, alternative tourism, appropriate tourism, intelligent tourism, soft tourism, responsible tourism and *ecotourism*, green tourism is characterised as small scale activities which make use of local labour and produce to deliver a holiday experience that is an alternative to *mass tourism*. Green tourism has developed from an environmental standpoint, whereas the evolving notion of *sustainable tourism* argues that both *environmental* and *socio-cultural* issues need to be addressed.

Greenwich Mean Time (GMT) is the local time at the *Greenwich Meridian*, from which standard times around the world are calculated, e.g. 0900 hours GMT will equate to 0400 hours New York time and 1000 hours Paris time.

Greenwich Meridian: the point on the globe representing 0° longitude and on which world *time zones* are based.

grievance procedures: the steps that an employee can take to raise objections to the treatment he or she is receiving at work. Details of the procedures are often set out in a staff handbook and should be included in an organisation's induction training. (See also *industrial tribunal*.)

gross domestic product (GDP) is a measure of the size and value of a nation's economy, usually expressed as the total value of all goods and services produced during a specified time period, usually one year. GDP is made up of a number of items, found in the manufacturing and *service sector* of an economy. Earnings from tourism contributes to a country's GDP, with those nations relying heavily on tourism revenue having the highest percentage contributions to GDP, e.g. tourism accounts for more than 25 per cent of Malta's GDP, while the figure for the UK is in the region of 4.5 per cent. (See also *gross national product*.)

gross margin: a calculation of the proportion of a company's *sales revenue* that is *gross profit*. It is calculated as follows:

$$\text{gross margin} = \frac{\text{gross profit}}{\text{sales revenue}} \times 100$$

gross misconduct: any action by an employee that is so serious as to warrant instant *dismissal*. Such actions would be detailed in a *contract of employment* and include being drunk on duty, theft, fraud, assault, causing damage to property, insubordination and the misuse of equipment.

gross national product (GNP) is a measure of a country's economic growth, calculated by adding the value of all goods and services produced to the net revenue from abroad. *Tourism* can play a significant role in contributing to a country's GNP through extra expenditure in the economy on goods and services. (See also *gross domestic product*.)

gross profit is the difference between a company's *sales revenue* and the cost of its sales.

gross profit/sales ratio is an important measure of an organisation's financial performance. Sometimes called the gross profit percentage, it shows how much *profit* an organisation is making as a percentage of sales. It is calculated as follows:

$$\frac{\text{gross profit}}{\text{sales}} \times 100$$

A fall in the gross profit/sales ratio may be the result of increased *competition*, forcing a reduction in the prices for facilities and services. (See also *net profit/sales ratio*.)

gross profit percentage: see *gross profit/sales ratio*

ground arrangements: the range of local services provided for *tourists* at *destinations*, such as transfers to and from their accommodation and airport, excursions and car hire arrangements. They are often provided by specialist companies, known as ground handling agents, working on behalf of *tour operators* and airlines.

Groundwork: an independent charitable organisation that helps people to improve their local environment and the prospects for their local economy, through a sustainable approach to *development* and *management*. Local Groundwork Trusts have been set up across the country, working in partnership with private, public and voluntary sectors of all communities, enabling them all to take action for a better local environment. Weblink: www.groundwork.org.uk

group dynamics: the way in which individuals interrelate with each other when in a group situation. Establishing a group of people to work on a project can bring benefits to an organisation, but it can also cause management some problems, such as conflict between team members and personality clashes. It takes an effective *team leader* to cope with such problems and to steer all group members to achieving their *objectives*.

group motivation is the way that team members inspire each other, and are inspired by their leader, to work together as an effective unit to achieve the group's goals. The leader should aim to maintain a cycle of motivation and success, since one feeds on the other. When appropriate, group members should be praised for their efforts and given tangible rewards for their hard work.

GSA: see *general sales agent*

guided walk: a type of *interpretation* where a guide leads an individual or group of people around an area pointing out and explaining points of interest en route. Guided walks can greatly enhance a person's understanding and enjoyment of the place they are visiting.

guiding services: the range of services provided to tourists to help them get maximum enjoyment from their visit to a *tourist destination*, e.g. a *guided walk*, a chauffeur driven tour, accompanied holiday, etc. Many of these services are provided by registered *Blue Badge guides*.

Guild of Business Travel Agents (GBTA): When it was formed in 1967, GBTA's six original members sought special attention for the needs of business *travel agents*, which it considered were not properly represented by the existing national organisation. Today, the Guild is called upon as an adviser in every sphere of travel, technical, commercial or political, and, with the help of a parliamentary consultant, it maintains a continual pressure on the legislators to make special provision for business travellers. The Guild has nearly 40 members, including large multiples like *Thomas Cook* and Carlson Wagonlit Travel, medium-sized, multi-branch agencies, and small independents. Collectively, GBTA members handle 80 per cent of agents' business house air traffic in the UK and had a combined turnover in 2000 of £6.9 billion. Weblink: www.gbta-guild.com

Gulf Stream: see *climate*

Gulf War: the war in Kuwait and Iraq broke out in the winter of 1991 and was to have long-lasting and far-reaching effects on world *travel and tourism*. By the time it ended in the spring of 1992, many prospective holidaymakers had decided to cancel their trips, particularly those travelling from North America. The majority of US corporations withdrew their staff from world travel for fear of terrorist attacks and unrest, leaving many *business tourism* companies at an all-time low, with airlines and hotel companies bearing the brunt of the problem. Although worldwide leisure travel quickly returned to its former pre-Gulf War state, the war, plus other terrorist attacks during the 1990s and more recently, have changed the nature of business travel forever. (See also *September 11.*)

What other subjects are you studying?

A–Zs cover 18 different subjects. See the inside back cover for a list of all the titles in the series and how to order.

half board: an *accommodation* and meal arrangement consisting of a room and breakfast plus either a midday or evening meal. It is sometimes referred to as *Modified American Plan*.

hard currency: the term used to denote a *currency* in high *demand* and with a stable or rising rate of exchange. The opening up of the former Eastern Bloc countries since the late 1980s has led to a high demand for hard currencies, particularly US dollars, in hotels and shops there.

hard disk: the permanent, high capacity memory installed inside a *computer*. Computer programs that are used frequently, such as *wordprocessing, database* and *spreadsheet* packages, will be installed on the hard disk for speed and convenience, rather than stored on *floppy disks* and loaded each time the computer is used. Documents created on the computer can also be stored on the hard disk. The storage capacity of the hard disk is measured in megabytes (Mb); a memory of 270 Mb means it can hold about 270 million bytes of data, one byte being equivalent to a single character.

hard sell refers to an aggressive sales technique used by sales people who will try to *close a sale* at all costs. In leisure and tourism, selling *timeshare* and other leisure products, particularly by telephone, are often considered as examples of hard sell.

hardware refers to the *computer* equipment which houses and operates a range of computer programs (the *software*). *Personal computers (PCs)* are the most common type of hardware available, for business, home and leisure uses.

haute cuisine: a French term to describe food of the highest culinary quality, served in elegant surroundings.

hazards: identifiable health and safety problems in the workplace that could lead to accidents to staff and visitors. Hazards should be identified by means of health and safety inspections and *risk assessments*. Once identified, remedial actions need to be carried out to reduce the risks of personal injury.

HCIMA: see *Hotel, Catering and International Management Association*

HCTC: see *Hotel and Catering Training Company*

headhunter: an individual or organisation that specialises in identifying suitable applicants for jobs, rather than waiting for those individuals to make applications themselves. Headhunters are often recruited by large organisations which are looking to fill senior positions. The advantage of using the services of a headhunter is that he or she takes the initiative in making contact with suitable applicants, who may not necessarily be looking for another position and would, therefore, not see the job advertised.

health and fitness is an important element of leisure and tourism, since it can have a bearing on how people choose to use their *leisure time* and the type of *holidays* they buy.

There has been a general increase in people's concern for their health in recent years, evidenced by the growth in *health clubs*, aerobics classes and *activity holidays*.

Health and Safety at Work, etc. Act 1974 was introduced to promote and encourage high standards of health and safety in the workplace. Part 1 of the Act, the part that concerns *leisure* and *tourism* organisations the most, aims to:

● secure the health, safety and welfare of people at work

● protect other people against risks to health and safety

● control the storage and use of dangerous substances, e.g. chemicals;

● control the emission of noxious or offensive substances from premises.

The Act places duties on both employers and employees. Employers must safeguard, so far as is reasonably practicable, the health, safety and welfare of all those in their employment. In practice, this will include such matters as providing information and *training* to all staff in health and safety matters, providing plant and equipment that is not a risk to health and providing a written safety policy (applies only to those employing five or more staff). Employees must take reasonable care to avoid injury to themselves and others in the workplace, co-operate with their employers to make sure that the Act is enforced and not interfere with or misuse anything provided to protect their health, safety and welfare.

The Act is enforced by inspectors appointed by the *Health and Safety Executive*, who have wide-ranging powers to enter premises and inspect records. If an inspector discovers that the Act is not being fully implemented, he or she can, as a last resort, close down the premises until such time as action to rectify the situation is completed.

Many of the requirements of the Health and Safety at Work, etc. Act have been clarified and updated by the *EU Directives on health and safety* which came into operation on 1 January 1993.

Health and Safety Commission (HSC): a government-funded body responsible to the Secretary of State for Employment and Skills for taking the necessary steps to secure the health, welfare and safety of people at work and also to protect the public against those risks to health and safety arising out of a work situation. The HSC was established in 1974 under the *Health and Safety at Work, etc. Act* and its membership is made up of employers, *trade unions* and *local authority* representatives. Weblink: www.hse.gov.uk

Health and Safety Executive (HSE) is the operating arm of the *Health and Safety Commission* and is responsible for enforcing the legislation under the *Health and Safety at Work, etc. Act*. HSE appoints teams of inspectors who have wide powers to enter premises and examine records and staff to check that the Act is being complied with. Inspectors can also investigate accidents that take place on premises, not only to employees but also visitors. This could include, for example, accidents at sports centres, *theme parks* and other leisure and tourism facilities. Weblink: www.hse.gov.uk

Health and Safety (First Aid) Regulations 1981 place a general duty on employers to make, or ensure there is made, adequate first aid provision for their employees if they are injured or become ill at work. This includes providing equipment and facilities for first aid and ensuring sufficient numbers of staff are trained in first aid procedures.

health and safety management: the Management of Health and Safety at Work Regulations 1992 were developed as a direct result of the *EU Directives on health and safety*. The regulations are aimed at encouraging employers to take a more systematic approach to health and safety by, among others things, drawing up a *risk assessment*. Once risks have been identified, measures must be put in place to rectify the situation. The regulations also require employers to appoint competent people to devise and apply the health and safety measures, provide training in health and safety matters, set up emergency procedures and co-operate with other employers who may share the same work site.

health club: a purpose-built facility designed to provide a variety of health and fitness equipment and services for the growing numbers of people in the UK who are committed to developing and maintaining a healthy lifestyle.

Heart of England Tourist Board is the official *Regional Tourist Board* covering the counties of Derbyshire, Gloucestershire, Herefordshire, Worcestershire, Leicestershire, Northamptonshire, Nottinghamshire, Rutland, Warwickshire, West Midlands, Staffordshire, Shropshire and also represents the districts of Cherwell and West Oxfordshire. Weblink: www.hetb.co.uk

heritage is an all-embracing term that is increasingly used to describe anything that has some kind of link, however tenuous, with past events. The more traditional uses of the word relate to the natural and man-made world in which we live, for example 'our natural heritage', to include mountains, moors, lakes and rivers, and the 'built heritage', relating to monuments, buildings and artefacts. People also talk of 'cultural heritage', referring to customs and traditions of the past, including the arts and music. In present day leisure and tourism, we are all familiar with heritage centres and heritage museums, but some people are concerned that the term 'heritage' is being exploited for commercial advantage, thereby losing its authenticity. The use of the term 'heritage' is closely allied to the ways in which *museums* and other attractions are redefining their roles so as to offer the visitor an 'experience' rather than merely an educational or pleasurable trip.

Heritage Coasts are among the most precious assets for wildlife and landscape, as well as for *leisure* and *tourism*. Concern over the harmful effects of increasing numbers of visitors has led to the designation of 32 per cent of the coastline of England and Wales as Heritage Coast. A programme of work, partly funded by the *Countryside Agency*, to ensure that the Coasts remain in good heart includes creating and repairing footpaths, cleaning up beaches and stabilising sand dunes. Stretches of coastline are also protected by the *National Trust* under its *Enterprise Neptune* project. The Coastal Heritage Forum, supported by the Countryside Agency, now represents the interest of rural coastlines. Weblink: www.countryside.gov.uk/heritagecoasts

Heritage Lottery Fund: a body that has been set up to distribute funds from the *National Lottery* to projects which safeguard land, buildings, objects and collections of outstanding interest to the nation's heritage. Projects eligible for financial help could include work on ancient monuments, special library collections, manuscripts, archives and collections held by *museums* and galleries. Weblink: www.hlf.org.uk

Herzberg: an American psychologist who is best known for his two-factor theory of *staff motivation* in the workplace. Herzberg identified a series of positive motivational factors, which he called 'satisfiers', and negative motivational factors termed 'dissatisfiers'. 'Satisfiers' included recognition, sense of achievement, responsibility and personal development. Negative factors were salary, job security, working conditions, level and quality of supervision and interpersonal relations. Herzberg's theory has been implemented in many large corporations, but is sometimes criticised for taking little account of the benefits of *group motivation*.

HETB: see *Heart of England Tourist Board*

HHA: see *Historic Houses Association*

HIE: see *Highlands and Islands Enterprise*

hierarchical organisation: a type of *organisational structure* that is characterised by a small number of senior decision makers at the top of the organisation who control its activities and resources. Sometimes called pyramid structures, hierarchical organisations are often very *centralised structures*, with power and *responsibility* resting with a very small number of senior staff. Decisions flow downwards from the top, affecting a succession of layers of employees lower down. Hierarchical organisations are often criticised for being too bureaucratic. Depending on the degree of centralisation, they are sometimes referred to as *steep pyramids* or *flat pyramids*.

hierarchy of needs: see *Maslow's hierarchy of needs*

high season: see *peak season*

Highlands and Islands Enterprise (HIE): the government funded *quango* that promotes inward investment to the north of Scotland and carries out measures to help the social and economic well-being of those living there. HIE's activities include the provision of business support services, delivery of training programmes and measures for environmental renewal. HIE works with *VisitScotland* to improve the quality of tourism in its area and its *promotion* to as wide an audience as possible. HIE used to be known as the Highlands and Islands Development Board. (See also *Welsh Development Agency*.) Weblink: www.hie.co.uk

hire purchase is a method of providing medium-term finance for a business or an individual. Hire purchase is commonly used by organisations to buy *fixed assets* such as equipment, vehicles and machinery, allowing repayments to be spread over an extended period of time, rather than a large cash payment having to be made at the outset. Ownership of the property being bought on hire purchase remains with the finance company until all payments, including interest, have been made.

histogram: a diagram used to gain a quick visual impression of data. Unlike a *bar chart*, the bars used in a histogram are usually connected (see figure below).

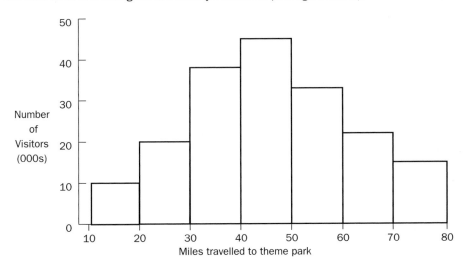

Historic Houses Association (HHA): an independent body representing the interests of private owners of historic houses and gardens in the UK. It advises members on the commercial, legal and financial aspects of running a *tourism* and *leisure* business, and plays an active role in lobbying national and local government on matters of concern to private owners, e.g. inheritance tax legislation. Weblink: www.hha.org.uk

Historic Royal Palaces Agency (HRPA): originally a directorate within the former *Department of National Heritage*, HRPA was created in 1989 to manage the unoccupied royal palaces. In April 1998 all the activities of the Agency were transferred to a Royal Charter Body with charitable status. The Agency is contracted by the *Department for Culture, Media and Sport* for the care, conservation and presentation to the public of the Tower of London, Hampton Court Palace, Kensington Palace State Apartments and the Royal Ceremonial Dress Collection, the Banqueting House, Whitehall and Kew Palace with Queen Charlotte's Cottage. Weblink: www.hrp.org.uk

historic monuments play an important role in leisure and tourism in the UK. Most are under public ownership or management, with *English Heritage* and *CADW* in Wales as the lead bodies. The *National Trust* also plays a very important role in preserving and presenting many historic monuments in the UK.

historical destination: see *cultural destination*

holiday: a period of time when work is officially suspended. For statistical purposes, UK *tourist boards* define a holiday as a stay of four nights or more away from home, although this is sometimes relaxed for overseas holidays. Holidays are sometimes divided into *package holidays* and independent holidays. (See also *Bank Holidays, independent travel*.)

holiday camp: a purpose-built complex providing family *accommodation* and a range of entertainment facilities on one site for a low, all-inclusive price. Now more commonly referred to as holiday centres, the concept of the holiday camp was pioneered in the 1930s by Billy *Butlin*, who opened his first camp at Skegness in 1936. Holiday camps worked on the principle that if the children were happy on holiday, then the parents would be as well. To this end, today's camps still offer a child-minding service to allow parents to enjoy themselves. *Butlin's*, Pontin's and Warner's became market leaders in this type of holiday which is still popular today, albeit in a modified form.

Holiday Care Service: a national registered charity, set up in 1981 with *sponsorship* from the then *English Tourist Board* and the full support of the UK *travel industry*, including the *Regional Tourist Boards*. It is a free service to those who are elderly, disabled or with special family circumstances and who are looking for budget holidays or holidays suitable for single parents or unaccompanied children. Now branded as Holiday Care, it handles more than 50,000 enquiries per year from people in the UK and overseas. The Holiday Care Service provides information and offers a reservations service to individuals, their families or friends, or those who care for them. Weblink: www.holidaycare.org.uk

holiday centre: see *holiday camp*

Holiday Which?: a magazine produced by the *Consumers' Association* that includes features on *destinations* and resorts, as well as articles on issues of concern to the travelling public, e.g. ferry safety and *overbooking*. The magazine claims to provide unbiased opinions and independent research to help readers choose their holidays and travel arrangements with confidence. Weblink: www.which.net

Holidays with Pay Act 1938: government *legislation* that encouraged voluntary agreements on paid holidays for employees and began the notion of a two-week paid holiday for all staff in British companies.

home-based leisure is any leisure activity that takes place in the home and includes such activities as watching television, listening to the radio, reading books, gardening, DIY, dressmaking and visiting or entertaining friends and relatives. Watching television is the most popular home-based leisure activity; 99 per cent of all people interviewed as part of a *Social Trends* survey in 1997 had watched TV at some time in the month leading up to their interview. Industry analysts predict that home-based leisure will grow significantly in the early years of the twenty-first century. In particular, the development of new technology equipment, including DVDs, Internet-based systems, computers, multimedia, digital television and *virtual reality*, will open up a huge array of home entertainment possibilities.

'honey pot': the term given to an area or destination that attracts large numbers of visitors, often to the detriment of the natural environment and *host communities*. Sensitive *visitor management* is often needed to ensure that honey pot areas, which include many *National Parks* and historic cities in the UK, do not become congested.

horizontal integration: unlike *vertical integration*, which links companies at different levels in the distribution chain, horizontal integration refers to mergers between organisations at the same level in the distribution chain, e.g. a large hotel company taking over a small independent hotel or the takeover of go by easyJet. Firms integrate horizontally to gain *competitive advantage*.

hospitality: a general term to describe the *hotel* and *catering* sectors of the leisure and tourism industries. Hospitality is a major source of *employment in leisure and tourism*.

Hospitality Training Foundation (HTF): an independent organisation representing hospitality employers on all aspects of education, training and qualifications. Formerly known as the Hotel and Catering Training Company, HTF became the *National Training Organisation* for the hospitality sector in 1997 and is aiming to become the *Sector Skills Council* when it is established in 2003. HTF's funding comes from a combination of commercial activities, government-funded projects and sponsorship. Weblink: www.htf.org.uk

host community: a term used in the debate on *sustainable tourism* to denote a place where people go for holidays and, more especially, the people who live there. There is a growing acceptance that the wishes of host communities in relation to *tourism development* need to be given a higher priority, to allow minimum disruption to their lives, while at the same time offering the economic and social benefits that tourism can bring.

hotel: defined in the UK as 'an establishment having five or more letting bedrooms, not calling itself a guesthouse or boarding house, and not being listed as providing bed and breakfast accommodation'. On the basis of this definition, the *BTA* estimates that there are in the region of 27,000 hotels in England, Wales, Scotland and Northern Ireland. The majority are operated by owner-proprietors who usually live on the premises. Many of the larger establishments are run by hotel groups, such as Marriott, Hilton and Swallow Hotels, which benefit from *economies of scale* in terms of purchasing, recruitment and marketing. To ensure consistency of standards, there are a number of voluntary *accommodation grading schemes* in operation in Britain.

A B C D E F G H I J K L M N O P Q R S T U V W X Y Z

Hotel and Catering International Management Association (HCIMA): established in 1971 as the Hotel, Catering and Institutional Management Association, HCIMA is an independent professional body representing public and private sector organisations involved with providing food and accommodation services. It undertakes a wide-ranging programme of activities, including running professional qualification courses, assisting with management development, keeping members informed of developments in the industry, *lobbying* government and organising conferences. Membership in 2002 stood at 18,000 within 27 UK regional branches and 17 international groups. Weblink: www.hcima.org.uk

Hotel and Catering Training Company (HCTC): the former company now known as the *Hospitality Training Foundation (HTF)*.

Hotel, Catering and Institutional Management Association: see *Hotel and Catering International Management Association*

hotel grading: see *accommodation grading schemes*

HRM: see *human resource management*

HSC: see *Health and Safety Commission*

HSE: see *Health and Safety Executive*

HTF: see *Hospitality Training Foundation*

hub and spoke system: a *transportation* arrangement, most often associated with air transport, where a central airport acts as a 'hub' for feeder services from other outlying destinations (the 'spokes'). Birmingham Airport, for example, acts as a hub for many of *British Airway's* European flights. Operating a hub and spoke system leads to increased airline efficiency and reduced operating costs.

human resource management (HRM) is the activity that deals with all aspects of an organisation's staff, their deployment, *training*, development, support and relationships with their employer. More than merely the mechanistic approach of personnel management, HRM is a more all-embracing concept to signal that an organisation is taking a more long-term view of all aspects of employing, empowering, supporting and rewarding its employees. HRM is concerned with achieving a balance between the ambitions of the individual and the returns to the organisation. It is crucial that the right balance is achieved, particularly since staff costs typically make up more than three-quarters of all the costs for many leisure and tourism businesses.

hypothesis: a theory or research question that can be tested analytically using a range of statistical techniques.

IATA: see *International Air Transport Association*

IATA agent: a *travel agent* who has been accepted into membership of the *International Air Transport Association (IATA)* and, as such, can sell tickets of IATA member airlines and offer a full service of worldwide air travel. To gain acceptance as an IATA agent, the organisation must first meet a number of strict criteria, including staff *training* requirements, security of premises and financial security of the business. The majority of multiple travel agencies and larger independent agents hold IATA licences.

IBRM: see *Institute of Sport and Recreation Management*

ICAO: see *International Civil Aviation Organisation*

ICT: see *information and communications technology*

IFTO: see *International Federation of Tour Operators*

IIP: see *Investors in People*

ILAM: see *Institute of Leisure and Amenity Management*

ILB: see *Industry Lead Body*

ILG: see *International Leisure Group*

image: the impression that a *product*, organisation or destination makes on the outside world. Image is very important in leisure and tourism, particularly in relation to *destination marketing*. The good or bad image portrayed by a holiday destination will materially affect its popularity. Images that people have of destinations and products are gained from a number of information sources, including *brochures*, television, the Internet, radio programmes, newspaper articles, first-hand experience and 'word of mouth'. Organisations try to portray a consistent, positive image to the outside world, by means of a clear *corporate identity* and effective *advertising* and *public relations* campaigns. *Branding* is sometimes used as a way of standardising an image of an organisation.

impacts of leisure, travel and tourism: these are generally categorised into:

- *environmental impacts* – e.g. pollution, erosion, etc.
- *socio-cultural impacts* – e.g. loss of traditional crafts, overcrowding, etc.
- *economic impacts* – e.g. job creation, income generation.

Impacts may be positive or negative, with environmental and socio-cultural impacts generally being seen as negative, while economic impacts are invariably portrayed as positive. *Planning* can help to reduce the negative impacts on a nation or local community.

improvement notice: one of the options open to a health and safety inspector if he or she discovers that an organisation is contravening the *Health and Safety at Work, etc. Act*; the other option is the issuing of a *prohibition notice*. The improvement notice is, in effect, a written warning to the organisation, indicating what must be done to comply with the requirements of the Act and the time limit within which the action must be completed.

imports are goods and services brought into a country from overseas. They may be either *visible* or *invisible* items and the flow of currency associated with imports is shown in a country's *balance of payments*. The expenditure by British people on holidays and travel abroad is considered to be an import, since money is flowing out of the country, in the same way that it does when a manufacturing company pays an overseas company for imported goods.

inbound tourism: see *incoming tourism*

incentives are payments and other inducements made to:

● employees, to encourage them to work more effectively

● customers, to persuade them to buy a particular product or service.

Examples of incentives include free gifts, special offers, discounts, store vouchers, *bonuses* (for staff) and free use of facilities.

incentive travel is a type of *business tourism* concerned with offering *holidays* and *leisure* products as incentives for staff. These sort of incentives are not only on offer to employees in leisure and tourism, but are a common reward system in many industry sectors, e.g. banking, insurance, financial services, retail. An example would be a weekend break at Gleneagles for achieving top monthly sales for a company, or a two-week holiday in Florida for clinching a new multi-million pound deal.

inclusive tour (IT): another name for a *package holiday*.

inclusive tour by charter (ITC) is a package holiday where the travel component is made up of a *charter flight*, as opposed to a *scheduled flight*. The vast majority of package holidays sold in the UK use this arrangement. (See also *inclusive tour by excursion*.)

inclusive tour by excursion (ITX) is a package holiday where the travel component consists of a *scheduled flight*, rather than a *charter flight*. In the UK this arrangement is less common and more expensive than an *inclusive tour by charter*.

income: all sources of monetary gain applicable to an individual or organisation.

income multiplier: see *multiplier effect*

income tax: a *direct tax* paid by individuals on their earnings and investments. The basic rate of income tax in the UK for 2002–2003 is 22 per cent for people earning up to £29,900 and 40 per cent above that salary level. Income tax is payable on a person's taxable income, i.e. that which is left after certain tax allowances are taken into account, such as the personal allowance and any allowances for expenses. Weblink: www.inlandrevenue.gov.uk

incoming tour operator: a company that specialises in meeting the needs of visitors from overseas who wish to stay in its country. In the case of Britain, incoming tour operators develop products and market themselves to the increasing numbers of *overseas visitors* who visit this country. There are some 300 such operators based in the UK. Some are little more than handling agents, offering a transfer or 'meet and greet' service on behalf of an agent or operator. Others, such as Frames Rickards and British Heritage Tours, offer complete *package tours* of the UK, including visits based on gardens, castles or theatres. Many UK incoming tour operators are members of *BITOA*.

incoming tourism is a form of international tourism which deals with people entering another country from their own country of origin or another country which is not their home. For example, an Italian couple flying from Rome to Heathrow Airport and a Spanish family arriving by ferry at Newcastle from Scandinavia are both types of incoming tourism to the UK. The *British Tourist Authority* estimates that there were 22.8 million overseas visitors to Britain in 2001, spending a total of £11.3 billion, although incoming tourism to the UK was severely affected by both *foot and mouth disease* and the events surrounding *September 11*. Incoming tourism is sometimes referred to as inbound tourism. (See also *outbound tourism*.)

independent travel is generally considered to be any form of travel which is not part of a *package holiday*. Independent travellers prefer to put their own itinerary together by purchasing *accommodation* and *transportation* directly from suppliers or via *travel agents*. Independent travel from the UK to overseas destinations has grown at a faster rate than the sales of package holidays since the mid-1970s, indicating that tourists like the flexibility that this travel arrangement can offer. The growth of the *Internet* and *low-cost airlines* has contributed greatly to the rise in the number of independent travellers. (See also *'new tourist'*.)

independent travel agent: a travel retailer who is not part of a *travel agency* chain. Independent agents offer as wide a range of holiday and travel products as the multiple travel agents (some would say more!), and may be members of the *National Association of Independent Travel Agents (NAITA)* or the *Campaign for Real Travel Agents (CARTA)*.

indexing: the practice of linking a value to a defined index of numbers, such as the *retail price index (RPI)*, in order to preserve its real value. In the UK, rises in *pensions* and wages are sometimes linked to the RPI.

indirect costs: see *overheads*

indirect tax: tax which is levied by *central government* on goods and services that people buy, as opposed to *direct taxes*, which are paid on income and profits. Examples of indirect taxes are *value added tax (VAT)* and duty on alcohol and petrol. Governments often try to shift the burden of taxation away from direct to indirect taxation on the grounds that taxes on income are a disincentive to hard work and enterprise.

induction is an important part of the *recruitment and selection process* in leisure and tourism, concerned with providing a new member of staff with a structured introduction to their new organisation and its employees. An induction programme should be designed to help new members of staff familiarise themselves with their new work environment, to settle easily into their new jobs and to establish good working relationships with other members of staff (see figure on page 122). Some organisations ask a member of the existing workforce to take care of a new employee until he or she is settled; this member of staff is known as a *mentor*.

induction booklet: a document given to all new members of staff outlining the structure of their new organisation and including a number of important points of information, including health and safety, *first aid* and *disciplinary procedures*, as well as details about social clubs, *pension* arrangements and *trade union* membership.

INDUCTION CHECKLIST

Your Manager will tick the tasks that have been completed during your induction.

1 **Show the Starter:**
a) Main areas of the Club
b) Position of the clocking-in machine / signing in book
c) Position of Fire-fighting equipment
d) Staff room
e) Emergency exits
f) Video
g) Pensions Video

2 **Introduce Starter to:**
a) Management Team
b) Appropriate Supervisor
c) Staff Representative
d) Departmental Colleagues

3 **Issue to all new Starters:**
a) Conditions of Employment Agreement
b) Statement of Hours
c) Uniform Receipt
d) Wishes Letter (all employees)
e) Disciplinary Rules & Procedures booklet
f) Health and safety at Work Policy booklet
g) Fire Information & Procedures booklet
h) Legal requirements form
   (to be signed on engagement and thereafter every 12 months)
i) Cinema Discount Card (after 6 months)
j) Pensions
   * Gatefold leaflet "Your Pension Choice"
   * Pension Plan application card
   * Money Purchase Scheme application card
   * Disclaimer card
   * Pension booklet (as appropriate)

4 **Explain to all Starters:**
a) Conditions of Employment (show "Employees Guide")
b) Job Description
c) Fire Drill & Evacuation Procedure
d) Benefits
e) Legal Requirements
   - Main provisions of the Gaming Act
   - Health & Safety Policy
   - Hygiene Regulations
f) Company Pension Arrangements

An induction checklist (courtesy of Top Rank Ltd)

industrial heritage: the term used to describe *visitor attractions* which depict the workings of a bygone age. Parts of Britain that were once dependent on primary and secondary industries, for example coal mining in South Wales, shipbuilding on Tyneside and textile manufacturing in Lancashire, have developed industrial museums and centres to attract *tourists*, thereby contributing to their local economies. Various industrial processes are explained to visitors with the help of guides, audio-visual aids and other types of *interpretation*. Examples in the UK include Beamish Museum, Ironbridge Gorge Museum and Big Pit Mining Museum. (See also *factory tourism.*)

industrial relations is a broad term covering all aspects of the relationship between employers and employees and their representatives, including works councils and *trade unions*. The government also has an influence on industrial relations through its employment *legislation*. In the 1980s, a series of Acts of Parliament were aimed at reducing the perceived power of trade unions. In the workplace, harmonious industrial relations make for a contented workforce and an efficient organisation. If things go wrong, it may be necessary to call on the services of arbitrators, who may be attached to the *Advisory Conciliation and Arbitration Service*.

Industrial Revolution: a period in eighteenth- and nineteenth-century Britain characterised by rapid urbanisation in response to greater mechanisation and mass production techniques. The often overcrowded housing conditions, with long working hours and low wages, gave few opportunities for travel and leisure activities to the majority of the population. The privileged 'middle classes', however, had the means to indulge in a variety of recreational pursuits, ranging from horse racing to prize fighting. As the Industrial Revolution progressed, working people began to demand greater freedom from work and time for *leisure*. Many of the sporting associations still surviving today were formed during the Industrial Revolution, including the Football Association and the Rugby Union. The development of the railways from 1830 onwards was to give working people greater *access* to the countryside and coast. Today, we have entered the realms of the post-industrial society, with a shift from a manufacturing economy to one based on service industries.

industrial tribunal: a court at which cases arising out of employment *legislation* are dealt with. Industrial tribunals were set up by the government in 1964 and commonly deal with cases of *unfair dismissal* and discrimination in the workplace. They aim to try and obtain an agreement between the employer and the aggrieved employee and have the power to demand reinstatement of the employee or to award financial compensation if the former is not practicable.

Industry Lead Body (ILB): an organisation, working under the direction of the *Department for Employment and Skills* and *Qualifications and Curriculum Authority*, given the responsibility of developing *occupational standards* for its own industry. Since the late 1990s, ILBs have been more commonly known as *National Training Organisations* and these will become Sector Skills Councils from 2003 onwards. Within leisure and tourism, there are a number of NTOs representing different industry sectors, e.g. the *Travel, Tourism and Events National Training Organisation (TTENTO)*, *National Training Organisation for Sport, Recreation and Allied Occupations (SPRITO)* and *Metier*, the NTO for the arts and entertainment sector.

inflation: the process of sustained rises in the price of goods and services in an economy. Rising inflation is considered to be undesirable because it leads to an overall reduction in buying power and increases the price of unfinished capital projects, such as major *leisure* developments and *hotel* construction. Travel to countries with spiralling inflation and generally unstable economies becomes unappealing, leading to reductions in revenue from *incoming tourism*.

in-flight catering: food and drink provided as part of a flight on an aircraft, sometimes free of charge. The service is often provided on a contract basis by large catering firms such as Gardner Merchant, now part of the Sodexho Group.

in-flight entertainment: services such as videos and magazines provided as part of a flight on an aircraft. Increasing competition between major airlines has led to the provision of in-flight entertainment services becoming an important factor in attracting business, although the policy of *low-cost airlines* is to offer a 'no frills' service with few in-flight services.

informal communication: unlike *formal communication*, which takes place as a result of a pre-planned course of action, informal communication is a more spontaneous activity, e.g. a chance conversation with a colleague in another department or a favourable comment by a client to a travel agency manager. Although informal communication can sometimes lead to problems at work (e.g. gossip and the spreading of rumours) it is nonetheless an important and common way of passing information and instructions between staff.

information and communications technology (ICT): see *information technology (IT)*

information overload occurs when a person is given so much information from a variety of sources that he or she cannot cope and, to relieve the stress of the situation, chooses to ignore much of what is received.

information processing is the collection, storage, retrieval, distribution and analysis of information, and its presentation in a form that is readily usable for *management* purposes. Systems for processing information have existed since the beginning of human enterprise, but the advent of the *computer* has revolutionised information processing, with many mundane tasks previously carried out manually being transferred to automated systems. Information processing is sometimes divided into *word processing* and data processing, each with its own dedicated computer software.

information superhighway: see *Internet*

information technology (IT): a term that is used to describe the systems that collect, interpret, store, analyse and distribute data, using *computers* and telecommunications equipment. Sometimes referred to as ICT (information and communications technology), IT is giving all leisure, travel and tourism enterprises, regardless of their size, the opportunity of communicating and conducting business on a global scale, using *global distribution systems (GDS)* and access to the *Internet*. In domestic tourism, IT is increasingly being used by *tourist information centres (TICs)* to offer booking and information services. In the home, IT forms the basis of much *home-based leisure* and entertainment, with computer games and DVD technology becoming commonplace.

infrastructure refers to items such as airports, communications, roads, railways, water supply and sewage services, i.e. all those services that need to be in place before *development* of any kind, including *leisure* and *tourism* projects, can go ahead. A country's infrastructure is generally financed and built by the public sector, with private sector operators developing the *superstructure*. There are, however, an increasing number of private/public sector *partnerships* to provide infrastructure improvements.

injection: an economics term used to describe payments into a national or local economy. In the case of tourism, injections would include payments for *accommodation, transportation* and other services, *tourist taxes* and duty on goods sold in retail outlets. (See also *multiplier effect*, *leakage*.)

Institute of Groundsmanship (IoG) aims to promote the profession of groundsmanship and the *management*, maintenance and improvement of playing surfaces, sports stadia, recreation grounds, golf courses, playing fields and amenity areas. Established in 1934, the IoG is Europe's largest association of turf care professionals, who benefit from a range of services, including lectures and exhibitions, Institute examinations and proficiency tests, legal advice and information booklets. Weblink: www.iog.org

Institute of Leisure and Amenity Management (ILAM) is a *professional body* formed in 1983 to represent the interests of leisure professionals involved in the management of parks and open spaces, *recreation, tourism,* the arts and *sport*. With a membership of over 6000, ILAM recognises the need for all leisure managers to develop a wide range of professional expertise in order to fulfil their personal potential and that of the industry. ILAM has its own professional development programme and liaises with educational establishments in the development of courses in leisure management. ILAM is headed by a National Council which oversees the work of its 12 UK regions. The Institute has specialist panels, covering interests such as *arts and entertainments*, leisure education *sports development* and *tourism*. Weblink: www.ilam.co.uk

Institute of Sport and Recreation Management (ISRM): a voluntary membership organisation that aims to improve the management of swimming pools and other indoor leisure and recreation facilities. Formerly known as the Institute of Baths and Recreation Management, ISRM organises a programme of training events, regional seminars, lectures and short courses for its members, as well as an annual conference. In 2002, it had a membership of 1700 professionals employed at all levels in the sport and recreation industry. Weblink: www.isrm.co.uk

Institute of Sports Sponsorship (ISS) was founded in 1985, with HRH The Duke of Edinburgh as its president, to be the representative voice of the UK sports *sponsorship* sector. ISS promotes *best practice* in sponsorship, works closely with sports bodies, government and the media to improve understanding of the subject. It also lobbies government on behalf of its members, which include many major sporting companies, *consultancies* and research agencies. Weblink: www.sports-sponsorship.co.uk

Institute of Tourist Guiding (ITG): see *Blue Badge guides*

Institute of Travel and Tourism (ITT): a *professional body* established in 1956 with the aim of developing the professionalism of its members within the industry. Unlike the *Tourism Society* and *Tourism Management Institute*, which attract their membership mainly from public sector tourism, the ITT was originally set up to promote the interests of *travel agents* and *tour operators*, and today still draws its membership primarily from these sectors. The Institute accredits college courses throughout the UK and organises seminars on subjects as diverse as travel law, technology, brochure production and selling skills. Weblink: www.itt.co.uk

insurance represents a payment to cover the consequences of a specific eventuality, which may be an illness while on holiday abroad, an injury while playing sport or the loss of business income as a result of a fire on the premises. *Travel agents* can earn substantial *commission* payments from selling holiday and travel insurance alongside their more conventional products.

intangibility is a characteristic of leisure and tourism *products*, in that a customer cannot actually touch and examine many products before they agree to a sale. We are all accustomed to examining, for example, *sporting goods* or luggage, before we buy, but with many leisure and tourism products we are buying the expectation of an experience.

integrated quality management (IQM): a structured process that aims to improve the quality of tourism products and services in an area, by careful attention to detail in such matters as visitor satisfaction, *customer service*, *marketing*, the provision of facilities, *interpretation*, signage and training. The *European Commission* published a series of reports on IQM in the late 1990s focusing on *rural tourism*, *urban tourism* and coastal tourism. An important aspect of IQM is that any tourism developments must take into account social, community, cultural and environmental factors in order to develop *sustainable tourism* projects and communities. Weblink: www.iqmwales.co.uk

integrated services digital network (ISDN): a sophisticated electronic system, developed by British Telecom, that makes use of cable technology to transfer signals, allowing services such as *Internet* access, *video conferencing*, *desktop conferencing* and data transfer to take place at high speeds.

integration: see *horizontal integration* and *vertical integration*

intelligent tourism: see *green tourism*

interest rate: the cost of borrowing money, paid by both individuals and organisations. Interest rates in the UK economy are set by the Bank of England. From these figures, banks and other lending institutions set their own interest rates for the *overdrafts* and *loans* to their own *customers*. If interest rates are increased, there is a general 'knock-on' effect, with banks increasing their rates in similar proportions. This has the result of reducing the general level of spending in the economy, and at the same time making it more expensive for businesses to finance their operations and expansion plans. When interest rates rise, leisure and tourism tend to suffer, given that they are discretionary purchases.

interlining: the reciprocal facility offered by airlines of issuing tickets and accepting bookings for airline companies other than their own.

intermediary: a person or organisation that comes between two parties, perhaps providing a service or offering *conciliation* and advice. In the travel industry, the best known intermediaries are *travel agents*, who provide the link between customers and principals, such as airlines, tour operators and hotel companies (see figure on next page). For their services, agents earn a *commission*, usually a percentage of the value of what they sell. In industrial relations, intermediaries are sometimes needed to resolve conflicts between workers and their employers. In such circumstance, officers of the *Advisory Conciliation and Arbitration Service* are sometimes called upon to mediate.

internal communication is liaison within an organisation, perhaps between staff in different departments or in different branches of the same company. Organisations use a range of different *communication systems* to distribute information throughout their organisation. (See also *external communication*.)

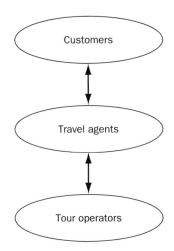

The travel agent as intermediary

internal constraint: something within an organisation that limits its ability to achieve its full potential or *objectives*. Internal constraints are usually factors over which the organisation has some degree of control, e.g. staff, *management style, suppliers*, finance, *marketing strategy*, buildings and facilities. A common internal constraint in leisure and tourism organisations is that there is insufficient investment in *staff training*, either through lack of funds or poor *management*. (See also *external constraint*.)

internal costs: expenditure that affects an organisation's own accounts directly, as opposed to *external costs*, which are outside of its immediate sphere of activity and are borne by the community and society in general.

internal customer: a colleague working in the same organisation who you come across in the course of normal day-to-day work activities and on whom you rely for services and support. Examples of internal customers are maintenance staff, receptionists, clerical and administrative staff, canteen staff and computer support staff. Good customer service requires a team approach within an organisation and a recognition that it is not just the customers 'on the other side of the counter' who need respect and consideration, but colleagues working in the same organisation as well.

internal environment: see *micro environment*

internal recruitment: the process of identifying and employing the most suitable person to fill a job vacancy from an organisation's existing staff members.

International Air Transport Association (IATA): a voluntary international trade body representing the interests of more than 80 per cent of the world's major airlines. IATA's principal aim is to promote safe, regular and economic air travel. It offers a clearing house system, which organises financial settlements between members, and promotes standardised procedures for the issuing of tickets and appointment of *IATA agents* worldwide. It is influential in determining price structures for some airline routes, although the final approval lies with national governments, operating through its three *Traffic Conference Areas* of the world. Weblink: www.iata.org

International Bank for Reconstruction and Development: see *World Bank*

International Civil Aviation Organisation (ICAO): established in 1944 under the *Chicago Convention on Civil Aviation*, ICAO is a specialist agency of the *United Nations,* which works with national aviation authorities, including the *Civil Aviation Authority* to ensure safe and efficient practices in air travel around the world. Weblink: www.icao.int

International Date Line: an artificial time boundary broadly corresponding to 180° from the *Greenwich Meridian*. The Date Line represents the point at which calendar days change, so that countries on the western side of the Line are one day ahead of those on the eastern side, resulting in travellers across the Date Line either 'gaining' or 'losing' a day depending on their direction of travel. (See also *time zones*.)

International Federation of Tour Operators (IFTO) is a European network of leading, mass market *tour operators*. Established as an independent membership organisation, IFTO lobbies on behalf of its members at European level in the same way that the *Federation of Tour Operators (FTO)* does for UK operators at national level.

International Leisure Group (ILG): a major leisure and tourism company which expanded rapidly in the 1980s, only to collapse dramatically in 1991. Perhaps best known for its Intasun holidays brand, the majority of ILG's holiday clients were transferred to its rivals, principally *Thomson* and Airtours (now My Travel).

International Olympic Committee (IOC): a body founded in 1894, in advance of the first Modern *Olympic Games* held in 1896 in Athens. The IOC enlisted the help of sports organisations and individuals to draw up a policy for the modern games. The aims of the IOC are the promotion of those physical and moral qualities which are the basis of sport, education through sport towards understanding and friendship, the spread of the Olympic principles, creating goodwill and the bringing together of athletes from all over the world in a festival of sport. With its headquarters in Switzerland, the IOC currently recognises the work of 199 national Olympic committees across five continents, including the *British Olympic Association*. Members of the IOC are responsible for choosing the sites for the winter and summer Olympic Games. Athens and Bejing will host the Games in 2004 and 2008 respectively. Weblink: www.olympic.org

International Passenger Survey (IPS) is a large, multi-purpose survey which collects information from passengers as they enter or leave the UK. It is carried out by the *Office for National Statistics* for a range of *public* and *private sector organisations*, including the *British Tourist Authority*. In particular, the survey provides figures used for the travel account of the UK *balance of payments*, international migration statistics and for informing decisions on tourism policy in the UK. The IPS is based on *face-to-face interviews* with a *sample* of passengers travelling via the principal airports, sea routes and the *Channel Tunnel*. The number of interviews in 2000 was 261,000, which represented about 0.2 per cent of all travellers. Results are published regularly on a monthly, quarterly and annual basis. (See also *United Kingdom Tourism Survey*.)

international sports federation (ISF): a body of elected individuals which represents the interests of a particular sport at international level; its work may involve formulating the rules of the sport, arranging *sponsorship*, negotiating television rights and organising international events. Two of the best-known ISFs are FIFA, the sports federation for international football, and the FIA, which represents the interests of Formula 1 motor racing.

International Standards Organisation (ISO): an independent body that lays down minimum *quality* standards across a wide range of industry sectors and production processes. Of particular interest to leisure and tourism organisations is *ISO 9000*, the standard incorporating *BS 5750* and focusing on consistent levels of service delivery. Weblink: www.iso.ch

international tourism: travel by residents of one country to another country, as distinct from *domestic tourism*.

international visitor: see *visitor*

Internet: sometimes called the 'information superhighway' or simply 'the net', the Internet is a non-centralised, interactive system of networked computer databases, which offers households and businesses a wide range of on-line services. The use of the Internet has grown dramatically in recent years; the United Nations estimated that there were 655 million Internet users across the world in 2002, with the single most popular country being the USA with 143 million users. Many people regard the Internet as the biggest development in global electronic technology since the introduction of the *personal computer*. (See also *World Wide Web*.)

Internet service provider (ISP): a company that provides a link to the Internet on payment of a one-off fee or regular payment. Successful ISPs used in the UK include BT Openworld, AoL and Claranet.

interpersonal skills: a variety of skills that are useful not only in the workplace, but throughout life in general. They include negotiation, *communication*, listening, decision-making, problem solving, working collaboratively, and many more. Training in these skills can be carried out 'in house' or with the help of a specialist training *consultancy*. A popular way of developing interpersonal skills is for members of staff to spend time at *outdoor activity centres*, where they are given practical and mental challenges in group situations.

interpretation is defined by the *Centre for Environmental Interpretation* as 'the art of explaining the meaning of sites visited by the public'. It is concerned with offering visitors more than just an enjoyable experience, but one that will help them better understand the place they are visiting. Sites as varied as farms, ancient buildings, archaeological excavations, coasts, wildlife reserves, landscape features and urban areas, can all be interpreted using a range of different techniques, including leaflets, signposting, *self-guided trails*, audio-visual aids, *guided walks* and demonstrations. Interpretation is also an important tool in the *management* of sites, helping to reduce conflict and physical *erosion*.

interview: an important part of the *recruitment and selection* process in leisure, travel and tourism. An interview gives the organisation offering a job the opportunity to meet candidates face-to-face and discover more about their qualifications, experience and *personality*, while at the same time giving candidates the chance to formulate their assessment of what the job entails and to meet their prospective work colleagues.

interview survey: see *face-to-face interview*

interviewer: the name given to an individual who asks questions of another person, either as part of a *face-to-face interview* survey, a *staff appraisal* or as part of the *recruitment and selection* process for a job. To be a good interviewer takes a great deal of *training* and commitment. (See also *respondent*.)

interviewing has a number of meanings in leisure and tourism, including that part of the *recruitment and selection* process at which a candidate is asked to attend a formal meeting, where he or she is asked questions and given the opportunity of learning about the post on offer. Another meaning of interviewing is carrying out a *face-to-face interview* survey or *telephone survey* as part of a *market research* exercise.

investment appraisal: an in-depth financial analysis of a potential capital project to investigate if there are sufficient grounds for it to go ahead. A range of techniques can facilitate the appraisal, such as *discounted cash-flow*. Investment appraisal is common for large leisure and tourism projects such as airports and *tourist attractions*.

Investors in People (IIP) is the national quality standard in the UK for effective investment in the training and development of people to achieve organisational objectives. Developed in 1990 as a government initiative, IIP has been administered since 1993 by a private company. IIP provides a framework for improving business performance, through a planned approach to offering employees training and development opportunities to help an organisation survive and flourish. In other words, what people can do and are motivated to do in an organisation, matches what the organisation needs them to do for it to be successful. Many *leisure* and *tourism* organisations, large and small, have achieved or are working towards achieving IIP (see figure below) . Weblink: www.iipuk.co.uk

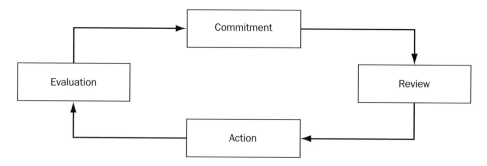

Key principles of IIP

invisibles are services whose value is shown on a country's balance of payments, i.e. those items that cannot be seen or touched, for example banking, financial services, shipping and *tourism*. Such services brought into a country are known as imports, while those sent abroad are exports. Historically, Britain's balance of payments has enjoyed a surplus on invisible items, which has helped to offset the deficits on *visible* items.

invoice: a document which is provided by a supplier to a customer as a request for payment. The invoice shows details of the goods or services supplied, their costs, any credit period offered and the total cost payable by the buyer.

IOC: see *International Olympic Committee*

IPS: see *International Passenger Survey*

IQM: see *integrated quality management*

Iron Curtain: a phrase first coined by Winston Churchill to denote the divide between East and West Europe. The momentous events that began in 1989 with the fall of the Berlin Wall, have opened up the former Eastern bloc countries to the West, allowing people to move freely and enjoy each others' cultures and scenery. To all intents and purposes, the term 'Iron Curtain' is now obsolete, although much still needs to be accomplished to raise living standards in many of the former Eastern bloc countries.

ISDN: see *integrated services digital network*

ISF: see *international sports federation*

ISO: see *International Standards Organisation*

ISO 9000: see *BS EN ISO 9000*

ISP: see *Internet service provider*

ISRM: see *Institute of Sport and Recreation Management*

ISS: see *Institute of Sports Sponsorship*

Istel: a *viewdata system* used in travel agencies to access *principal's computerised reservation systems* using a *VDU* plus either a telephone line or cable connection.

IT: see *information technology, inclusive tour*

ITC: see *inclusive tour by charter*

ITG: see *Institute of Tourist Guiding*

ITT: see *Institute of Travel and Tourism*

ITX: see *inclusive tour by excursion*

Do you know we also have A–Zs for:

- Geography
- Business Studies
- ICT and Computing
- Geography Coursework?

Ask for them in your local bookshop or see the inside back cover for ordering details.

JES: see *job evaluation study*

jet aircraft: a method of *transportation* that was instrumental in developing *mass tourism* in the latter half of the twentieth century. Technological advances in jet aircraft design resulting from the Second World War led to air travel becoming a reality for an increasing proportion of the population from the 1950s onwards. The Boeing 707 was introduced in 1958 and led to a surge in *scheduled* and *charter flights*, the latter becoming the basis for the *package holidays* so familiar to us all today.

JICNARS: see *socio-economic classification*

job analysis: the starting point in the *recruitment and selection* process, concerned with identifying what a particular post entails, before setting about finding a suitable person for the job. Information to be included in a job analysis can be obtained from the existing postholder, previous records, other members of staff and by direct observation. The job analysis should form the basis for writing a *job description*.

job description: a document outlining the nature of a particular job and the duties and responsibilities involved. A typical job description includes details such as the title of the job, the key *objectives* of the post, to whom responsible and for whom responsible, detailed duties and general *conditions of employment*, which are likely to form part of an employee's *contract of employment*.

job enlargement: the practice of increasing the scope and variety of a job and the range of tasks that a person is responsible for carrying out. A public relations assistant for a large tour operator, for example, whose job usually consists of writing *press releases*, may be given the responsibility of organising a *familiarisation visit* for a group of journalists. While job enlargement can be useful for a person's career development, it must not be seen as a form of 'cheap labour', i.e. getting junior staff to carry out jobs that are usually done by more senior, and higher paid, employees. If managed as part of an individual's *career development*, however, job enlargement can give added *job satisfaction*.

job enrichment is a human resources process that aims to give a person greater responsibility in their work, more opportunities for achievement and recognition, and a greater involvement in their own personal development, so as to achieve more *job satisfaction* and become a more motivated individual. Job enrichment can be achieved in many different ways, e.g. by giving workers greater freedom in the scheduling of their work tasks, reducing the level of direct supervision over employees and providing opportunities for more direct contact with customers.

job evaluation study (JES): an exercise that compares the relative demands of different jobs, so as to help with the setting of pay scales and grading of employees. Under the terms of the *Equal Pay Acts*, a JES may need to be undertaken before similar jobs can be said to be of equal value, thereby resulting in equal pay for the workers involved. The study will look at factors such as skills needed, degrees of *responsibility*, levels of decision making and effort required to carry out the job.

job opportunities in leisure and recreation: see careers in *leisure, travel and tourism*

job opportunities in travel and tourism: see careers in *leisure, travel and tourism*

job role: the expected pattern of behaviour of an employee occupying a specific position in an organisation. The particular roles associated with a post are normally set out in a *job description* and form part of a *contract of employment*.

job rotation is a type of *job enlargement*, with an employee's work tasks being alternated over a period of time, so as to relieve the monotony of mundane tasks and to expose employees to the work of other departments or individuals in their organisation. Job rotation should be seen as a form of staff training and development, allowing employees to gain useful, transferable skills. It needs to be well planned and managed in order to give staff sufficient time to master the changed *job roles* that they are expected to fill.

job satisfaction reflects the degree to which a person feels fulfilled and motivated in his or her work environment. Time and money spent by an organisation on measures to increase employees' job satisfaction can pay dividends in the long run, with reduced absenteeism and staff turnover, enhanced *customer service* standards and greater staff productivity. Introducing *job enrichment* schemes, such as *job rotation* and *job enlargement*, can lead to greater job satisfaction for employees.

job specification: a written document, often used in conjunction with a *job description*, listing the skills and characteristics needed to do a particular job successfully. Sometimes called a 'person specification', it acts as a blueprint of the 'ideal' person for the job, in terms of qualifications, experience, skills, character and achievements, and is a helpful tool in an organisation's *recruitment and selection* process. Some job specifications divide the qualities, experience and skills sought into those that are essential and those which are desirable.

jobs in leisure and recreation: see *careers in leisure, travel and tourism, employment in leisure, travel and tourism*

jobs in travel and tourism: see *careers in leisure, travel and tourism, employment in leisure, travel and tourism*

joint marketing: see *co-operative marketing*

joint use is the shared use of a facility so as to maximise revenue or use. Sometimes referred to as 'dual use', it is common for *local authority* leisure facilities to be operated on a joint use basis, e.g. a school having exclusive use of a sports centre between 9 am and 4 pm, with the local community able to use it at all other times.

k: a shorthand way of writing thousand, e.g. a salary of £13k would mean £13,000 or a computer with 120 kbytes of memory would mean 120,000 bytes.

Key Classification Scheme: a voluntary grading scheme for *self-catering accommodation* introduced in Britain in the 1980s. Operated on similar lines to the *Crown Classification Scheme* for serviced accommodation, the Key scheme was designed to help people choose the type of self-catering accommodation which best suits their requirements and expectations. It covered both the level of facilities provided and an objective measure of quality, from 'approved' to 'de luxe'. Self-catering establishments were awarded from one to five Keys, depending on the level of facilities provided. The scheme has since been replaced by the 'Star' accommodation grading scheme.

kitemark: a seal of approval awarded by the *British Standards Institution (BSI)* to organisations whose products and services meet certain minimum *quality* or safety standards.

LAI: see *Local Area Initiative*

LAN: see *local area network*

Landmark Trust: a charitable trust that preserves unusual historic buildings in the UK and lets them out for holidays. Included in their directory are castles, follies, cottages and light-houses. Most Landmark properties are let on a *self-catering* basis. Weblink: www.landmarktrust.co.uk

land transport includes travel by private car, coach, bus, train, motor cycle and pedal cycle. (See also *transportation*.)

Lantra: formerly *ATB Landbase*, Lantra is the *National Training Organisation (NTO)* for the environmental and land-based sector. It is licensed by the government to drive forward a new skills, training and business development agenda for the sector. Lantra represents a variety of industries, including landscaping, floristry, game conservation and equine. It works with *Learning and Skills Councils* to support the needs of the 400,000 employers and their 1 million employees in the sector. Weblink: www.lantra.co.uk

laptop computer: a portable *personal computer (PC)* that allows its user to carry out a range of computing functions while on the move. Laptops do not need a fixed power supply, so can be used in aircraft, trains, cars and even in the great outdoors! The latest laptop computers are as powerful as many PCs found in offices, with the ability to run sophisti-cated communications, *wordprocessing*, database and *spreadsheet software*.

latent demand: see *deferred demand*

laws: see *legislation*

leadership style: see *management style*

leading question: a question that invites a pre-determined response, e.g. 'don't you agree that the accommodation is comfortable?' suggests that the person being asked the question should agree with the questioner. This question would be better if written as follows; 'What are your views on the level of comfort in the accommodation?' When designing *questionnaires*, it is important not to introduce bias by including leading questions.

leakage: the loss of money from a local or national economy as a result of, for example, fluctuations in exchange rates, payments to *shareholders*, *taxation* or purchases of goods and services from national distributors. (See also *multiplier effect*, *injection*.)

Learning and Skills Council (LSC): government-funded organisation responsible for funding and planning education and training for over 16-year-olds in England. Its *mission* is to raise participation and attainment through high quality education and training which puts learners first. With a budget in 2002 of £7.3 billion, the LSC operates through 47 local offices and a national headquarters in Coventry. The LSC took over the work of the *Training and Enterprise Councils (TECs)* in 2001. (See also *ELWA – Education and Learning Wales*.) Weblink: www.lsc.gov.uk

leaseback: see *sale and leaseback*

leasing is the practice of acquiring specific *fixed assets* from a leasing company in return for the payment of an agreed, regular sum. Leasing is a common method of providing vehicles, office equipment and fixtures and fittings. The main advantage of leasing is that an organisation avoids the need for a large initial payment. It is particularly suitable for equipment that quickly goes out of date, such as *computers* and telephone systems. At the end of the leasing period, the equipment or vehicle is returned to the leasing company, or it may be purchased on favourable terms.

legal requirement: any procedure or practice that has to be carried out by law, e.g. completing *value added tax (VAT)* documentation for HM Customs and Excise.

legislation: refers to Acts of Parliament passed by *central government*, e.g. *Health and Safety at Work, etc. Act 1974* and *Development of Tourism Act 1969.*

leisure: a complex issue which most people associate with *leisure time* or *leisure activities,* choosing to spend their spare time in ways which give them the most satisfaction. Some people regard leisure as time when they are not at work, while others think of leisure in terms of the recreational activities they carry out in their leisure time, such as gardening, watching television, reading books or knitting. Treating leisure as time away from paid employment does not give a complete picture of the nature of leisure, since it fails to take into account the many necessary duties and functions that we all have to perform in our daily lives, such as eating, sleeping and carrying out domestic chores. Unemployed people don't fit into such a notion of leisure either, with most agreeing that they have more leisure time than they want.

Given that it is a difficult concept to fully understand, any definition of leisure would nevertheless conclude that it is:

- time outside of a formal employment situation
- time over and above that devoted to household chores
- time outside sleeping, eating and personal hygiene functions
- time at the disposal of the individual
- time when a person has the freedom to do as they please.

The last two points concerning an individual's freedom of choice are perhaps getting closer to the true meaning of leisure, in that it is a creative period during which a person can strive to reach his or her potential as a human being and productive member of society.

leisure activities are normally divided into those that are *home-based,* including reading books, listening to the radio and hi-fi, gardening, dressmaking, needlework, watching television and do-it-yourself, and those that take place away from the home, such as going to the cinema, visiting *tourist attractions,* taking part in *sport, sports spectating,* taking holidays and day trips. Leisure activities can also be classified as either *passive* or *active,* with *adventure activities* such as mountain climbing, trekking, quad biking, gliding and paint balling growing in popularity. Research data in *Social Trends* shows that British people spend more on leisure activities than any other item of household expenditure, including food, housing and travel. Total spending on leisure and recreation by the British in 2001 amounted to £77 billion, according to information from the *Office for National Statistics*. (See also *consumer spending*.)

leisure and recreation industry: a diverse part of the UK economy, spanning the public, private and voluntary sectors, and made up of a number of interrelated components, including:

- *sport* and *physical recreation*
- *arts and entertainment*
- *countryside recreation*
- *community recreation*
- *outdoor activities*
- *home-based leisure*
- *play*
- *heritage*
- *leisure shopping.*

The leisure and recreation industry is one of the fastest growing sectors of the UK economy.

leisure and recreation products and services: all facilities provided by individuals and organisations that are part of the *leisure and recreation industry*, e.g. dance classes, *sporting goods* and *leisure centres*.

leisure away from home: see *leisure activities*

leisure centre: a purpose-built facility providing a variety of indoor and outdoor *sport* and *recreation* activities. The introduction of *compulsory competitive tendering* dramatically changed the management of local leisure centres, in an attempt to make them compete more effectively with commercial facilities.

leisure in the home: see *home-based leisure*

leisure participation: a person's ability to take part in leisure. It is affected by many factors, some within the control of individuals, some not, including:

- availability of leisure time – no leisure time equals no leisure activity
- income level – people with higher *disposable incomes* are more likely to take part in leisure activities
- *personal mobility* – access to a car greatly increases the opportunities for leisure activities
- culture and demography (age, gender, cultural background, etc.) – studies have shown that leisure participation is lower among certain minority groups in society
- level of provision of facilities – if there are few facilities available, participation rates will be lower
- long-term changes in society – factors such as the *ageing population*, increasing rates of divorce, technological advances and changing patterns of employment, all affect participation rates for *leisure activities*.

leisure shopping refers to the growing trend for shopping centres, particularly those in out-of-town locations, to become the focus of a new type of leisure activity, often combining a number of elements, e.g. shopping plus a visit to the cinema or shopping plus a meal out. The growth in out-of-town retail centres, such as Meadowhall near Sheffield and Lakeside in Essex, coupled with the relaxation of Sunday trading legislation, have given a boost to trading and further developed the concept of leisure shopping, particularly with families.

Leisure Studies Association: a body established in 1975, in response to the (then) little known and little researched concept of leisure. Today, the Association represents researchers, planners, policy makers, administrators and practitioners in a wide range of leisure areas. LSA's objectives include stimulating an exchange of ideas on contemporary leisure issues, dis-seminating knowledge of leisure studies to create the conditions for informed decision making, encouraging leisure *research* and promoting discussion through its publications and conferences. Weblink: www.leisure-studies-association/LSAWEB/index.html

leisure time is time outside of paid employment, at the disposal of the individual and during which he or she has the freedom to choose what to do. Not surprisingly, statistics in *Social Trends* show that in the UK retired people have the most leisure time in a typical week, retired men enjoying 90 hours and retired women 71 hours of leisure time. Women in full-time employment have less leisure time than their male counterparts, the result of spending more time on household chores and childcare.

leisure travel: see *leisure tourism*

leisure tourism is the category of the *travel and tourism industry* concerned with travel for leisure purposes, rather than travel for business purposes (*business tourism*). Leisure tourism includes taking holidays at home and abroad, *visiting friends and relatives (VFR)* and travel for a variety of purposes, such as for health and fitness, *sport*, education, culture, religious and spiritual reasons.

le Shuttle is the vehicle-carrying rail shuttle system that operates through the *Channel Tunnel* (the passenger train service is known as *Eurostar*). At peak times in the summer months, le Shuttle operates four services per hour, on a turn-up-and-go basis, linking Folkestone and Calais. Freight and passenger vehicles are driven onto specially constructed shuttle carriages for the 30 minute journey through the Channel Tunnel. The introduction of the service has led to fierce competition with the Channel ferry operators, particularly those on the Dover–Calais route.

lessee: the party in a *leasing* agreement to whom equipment is provided by the leasing company, in return for regular payments.

lessor is another name for the *leasing* company in a leasing agreement, which provides equipment to the *lessee* in return for regular payments. The lessor generally retains ownership of the property when the leasing agreement expires.

LGA: see *Local Government Association*

liabilities are what an organisation or individual owes to another party. Liabilities are of two types. *Current liabilities* are those that will be converted into cash within a short period of time, such as taxation and short-term bank loans. Long-term liabilities are those that are due to be repaid in a period of longer than one year, such as *commercial mortgages* and *debentures*.

liberalisation: see *deregulation*

licensing: the regulation of certain activities by *central* and *local government*, and other regulatory authorities. In leisure and tourism, this includes the regulation of those providing public facilities in order to ensure the moral and physical protection of the general public. The main licences that a leisure or tourism operator needs to consider include the *Public Entertainments' Licence*, Indoor Sports' Licence, Cinema Licence, *Liquor Licence* and Theatre Licence.

life cycle: see *product life cycle*

life cycle classification: a type of *market segmentation* when marketers classify people according to where they are in their life cycle, rather than according to their social status or occupation as with the *socio-economic classification*. The stages are as follows:

- bachelor
- newly-wed/living together
- full nest (couples with children)
- empty nest (children have left home)
- solitary survivor.

By placing people in one of the categories, marketers are able to determine their likes and dislikes, even down to what newspaper they are likely to read and what type of *holidays* and *leisure* products will appeal to them.

life style classification: a technique used in *marketing* to classify people according to their lifestyle, rather than their social status or occupation, as with the *socio-economic classification*. Lifestyle classifications are increasingly being seen as the most effective way of classifying people and thereby segmenting the market. One such classification is the 4Cs, developed by advertising agency Young and Rubicam, which labels people as either mainstreamers, aspirers, succeeders or reformers, each with quite distinct work, leisure and holiday habits.

limited company: a commercial organisation whose owners enjoy the benefit of *limited liability*, thereby limiting their risk to the amount they have invested in the company. A limited company, denoted by the words 'limited' or 'ltd.' after its name, is a separate entity in law, capable of suing and being sued in its own right. Limited companies fall into one of two categories:

- company limited by shares – by far the most common and further sub-divided into two types, *public limited company* and *private limited company*
- company limited by guarantee – when company documents show that an individual (known as a guarantor) will contribute a specified sum of money in the event of the company being wound up.

All limited companies are regulated by the *Companies Acts* of 1985 and 1989, which state that they must produce a *Memorandum of Association* and *Articles of Association*.

limited liability: a benefit enjoyed by investors in *limited companies*, meaning that they are only liable, in the event of company failure, to the amount they have actually invested in the business, rather than risking seizure of their personal wealth and possessions.

line manager: an individual who is given the *authority* to make executive decisions and is responsible for the performance of one or more members of staff. Line managers have an agreed place in a *hierarchical organisation*, where they report to a senior manager and employees report to them.

linear park: a recreational space that follows a number of linear features, such as railway lines, bridleways, footpaths, cycle tracks or canal towpaths. Often developed in urban areas, they provide opportunities for passive *recreation* and nature *conservation*.

liquidity is a measure of whether an organisation has sufficient funds to pay its debts when they fall due. Comparisons can be made between years to see whether liquidity is improving or declining and whether the organisation is remaining in a solvent state when comparing actual with forecast results. Liquidity can be estimated from a company's published accounts using the *liquidity ratio*.

liquidity ratio: this tells us the ratio between a company's readily available cash or near-cash assets and its *current liabilities*. It is calculated by dividing a company's current liabilities into its liquid assets (current assets less stock). It is sometimes called the acid-test ratio or current ratio.

liquor licence: a licence needed by the operators of all establishments where alcohol is sold or consumed. Liquor licences range from a full on-licence, where the licence holder can sell alcohol for consumption on the premises, to a seasonal licence, which allows the establishment to sell alcohol only at certain times of the year, normally the main holiday periods. In deciding whether or not to grant a liquor licence, a magistrates' court will consider a number of factors, including the character of the applicant, the suitability of the premises, previous applications for licences and the views of official agencies, including the police and the *local authority*.

load factor: the number of airline seats sold as a percentage of the total number available, i.e. if 125 seats are sold for a flight on an aircraft that hold 250 passengers, the load factor would be 50 per cent. Load factor, like the *occupancy rate* in hotels, is a performance measure that companies use to determine their profitability and plan their operations. (See also *break-even load factor*.)

loan: a source of medium- or long-term *capital* for a business to allow expansion and *development*. Most leisure and tourism organisations will approach banks to obtain a loan at some stage in their development. A bank usually requires *security* before it agrees to a loan, in case the lender should default on repayments. Interest is charged, the rate depending on the term of the loan, the amount being borrowed, the degree of risk involved and the track record of the applicant. In leisure and tourism, medium-term loans are typically used to finance new plant and equipment, while long-term loans are used for new building work or for extending premises.

loan capital: that part of a company's *capital* made available from *loans*.

lobbying is the practice of informing key decision makers about specific concerns, opinions and issues, in the hope of gaining their support for change. Lobbying takes place at a variety of levels, e.g. *pressure groups* let local councillors know their views on an issue or large commercial organisations may inform central government of its concerns over proposed legislation at home or in Europe. Lobbying is seen as a legitimate part of any country's democratic processes, but is sometimes misused by those in positions of power and influence.

Local Agenda 21: see *Earth Summit*

local area initiative (LAI): see *Tourism Development Action Programmes*

local area network (LAN): see *network*

local authority is the name given to the elected body responsible for providing a range of facilities and services in a locality. The policies of a local authority are determined by elected representatives of the local people (councillors) and put into operation by council employees and officers. For example, spending and priorities on *leisure* and sports facilities will be agreed by a committee of the council, who will expect the staff in the leisure services department to carry out or oversee the day-to-day operation of facilities. Local authorities, sometimes known as local government, play an important role in the local provision of leisure and tourism facilities, both for residents and visitors. All local authorities in England and Wales are members of the *Local Government Association*.

local government: see *local authority*

Local Government Association (LGA): established in 1997, the LGA builds on the strengths of the three previous local authority associations – the *Association of County Councils, Association of District Councils* and *Association of Metropolitan Authorities*. It was formed from the belief that one strong voice could present the case for local government better than three separate organisations. LGA represents the interests of all the local authorities in England and Wales, a total of just under 500 authorities (34 county councils, 36 metropolitan district councils, 47 English unitary authorities, 33 London authorities, 238 shire district councils and 22 Welsh unitary authorities). Weblink: www.lga.gov.uk

Local Plan: a document produced by a district or borough council indicating its priorities for the future development of the area. A Local Plan will implement many of the recommendations of a county council's *Structure Plan*, giving detailed plans for housing, leisure services, refuse collection and environmental improvements. *Local authorities* are obliged to consult local residents as part of the process of drawing up their Local Plans.

location can be an important factor in many aspects of leisure, travel and tourism, e.g. a hotel or travel agency located on a busy high street will benefit from passing trade, whereas the remoteness of a country house hotel or activity centre may discourage visitors or at least involve the operators in a lot of marketing activity. (See also *catchment area*.)

logo: a symbol used by an organisation as part of its *corporate identity*. Effective logos in leisure, travel and tourism include the *ABTA* logo and the Nike 'tick'.

London Eye is the largest observation wheel ever built and the fourth tallest structure in London, giving a bird's eye view of the capital. In its first year of operation, 3.5 million people visited the London Eye, making it one of the most popular paid tourist attractions in the UK in 2000. British Airways have championed the idea of the attraction since 1996 and the *Tussauds Group* is responsible for its day-to-day management. Weblink: www.londoneye.com

London Marathon: an annual race around the streets of London, with around 35,000 competitors, most running to raise money for charity. One of the main objectives of the event is to generate a surplus of funds, which can be used to improve recreation and leisure facilities in the London Boroughs. The marathon also aims to help British marathon running in general and to give competitors the opportunity to enjoy themselves. The field is made up of club runners, ordinary members of the general public and a small number of elite runners. The event relies heavily on the *sponsorship* of large and small organisations; past race sponsors have included Gillette, Mars, ADT, NutraSweet and Flora. Weblink: www.london-marathon.co.uk

London Tourist Board is the official *Regional Tourist Board* serving the Greater London area. Weblink: www.londontouristboard.com

London Transport (LT) is the former statutory corporation established in 1984, with a remit to plan, provide or procure services to meet the present and future public transport needs of London. In so doing, LT had a responsibility to ensure that the operation of its services were safe, efficient, economic and made provision for all passengers, including those with disabilities. With the establishment of the Greater London Authority (GLA) in July 2000, London Transport became part of *Transport for London (TfL)*.

long distance footpath: see *National Trails*

long haul destinations are generally considered to be those beyond Europe, for example Australia, the Far East, USA and India. Advances in aircraft technology, coupled with low prices offered by some mass market *tour operators*, have opened up many new long haul destinations for package holidays, e.g. Goa, the Gambia and the Caribbean. While this trend has provided much-needed foreign currency in the short-term for the destinations concerned, there are fears for the long-term *socio-cultural impacts* of such developments.

loss leader: see *penetration pricing*

Lottery Sports Fund (LSF) is the body set up in 1994 by the *Sports Council* (now *UK Sport*) to make decisions on which sporting projects should receive funds from the *National Lottery*. The range of projects eligible to apply for finance from the Fund is very wide, but most projects are of a capital nature, i.e. construction, buying land, upgrading facilities. Typical examples include the building or refurbishment of sports pitches, sports halls, swimming pools, jetties. Some revenue funding is available to elite level sports people to assist with training, coaching, travelling, etc. Funds are distributed by the Sports Councils for England (Sport England), Wales, Northern Ireland and the Scottish Sports Council. Between 1994 and September 2002 the Sport England Lottery Fund distributed £1.35 billion to more than 3500 projects across all English counties covering 63 different sports.

low-cost airline: a company that offers low fares to travellers in return for a service with few 'extras'. Low-cost airlines sell direct to the public, using the *Internet* and call centres, and often use airports just outside main cities in order to keep fares low. They have been extremely popular in recent years in the UK and are serious competitors for established airlines on many routes, particularly to *short haul* destinations. Examples of low-cost airlines in the UK include easyJet, Ryanair and bmibaby.

low season: the period when there is least *demand* for a product or service, e.g. the winter months for destinations that offer summer package holidays. Many tourism businesses close down altogether in the low season, making many resort areas feel rather 'dead' out of season. The low season, on the other hand, can be a good time to pick up a bargain holiday, since those establishments that do remain open will offer discounted rates for *accommodation* and other facilities in order to attract some custom.

LSA: see *Leisure Studies Association*

LSC: see *Learning and Skills Council*

LSF: see *Lottery Sports Fund*

LTB: see *London Tourist Board*

macro environment: a term used to denote certain factors 'in the wider world' which may have an effect on an organisation and its operation and *profitability*. Sometimes referred to as the external environment, they are often factors over which the organisation will have little control, such as the state of the national economy, the level of unemployment, changes in the social structure, government *legislation* and technological advances. The acronym *PEST* is sometimes used to classify these factors, standing for political, economic, social and technological. (See also *micro environment*.)

MAFF: see *Ministry of Agriculture, Fisheries and Food*

mail merge: a facility available on many *wordprocessing* packages that allows the creation of personalised documents from the merging of a standard letter and a list of names and addresses. A mail merge facility is very useful for producing promotional letters as part of a *direct mail* campaign.

mailing house: a specialist firm that handles all aspects of the distribution of items that form part of *direct mail* campaigns. A large *tour operator*, for example, may use the services of a mailing house to co-ordinate the distribution of its *brochures*, either to travel agents or direct to the public. The services offered by the mailing house will include folding items, filling and closing envelopes, franking and onward distribution.

mailing list: a list of names and addresses used as part of a *direct mail* campaign. Lists can be assembled from internal records or bought from specialist suppliers, grouped according to interests, geographical location, gender, etc.

maintenance is any work undertaken to keep an asset at an acceptably safe standard; by assets, we mean buildings, machinery, plant, accommodation, equipment, vehicles, communication systems, etc. Failure on the part of a leisure or tourism organisation to effectively maintain its assets may have serious repercussions, including:

- poor safety standards
- poor *image* to the outside world
- customer dissatisfaction
- loss of service as a result of breakdowns and closures
- loss of *revenue* and possible legal proceedings.

Maintenance can be either *planned* or *corrective*; planned maintenance is programmed and scheduled in advance, whereas corrective maintenance is carried out in response to an emergency or failure of equipment. It is good *management* practice to adopt a policy of planned maintenance in order to reduce the probability of the failure of systems or equipment and so avoid the need for expensive corrective maintenance.

management is a structured process involving *planning*, organising, directing, co-ordinating and controlling a range of *resources*, to achieve pre-determined *objectives*. (See also *management style, management by objectives*.)

management accounting: whereas *financial accounting* focuses on the preparation of statutory accounts, management accounting is concerned with the provision of financial information to help with business decision making and for control purposes. Management accounts are used purely within an organisation and there is no statutory requirement for them to be published. Management accounts provide an organisation with information on such matters as the costs of the operation, total sales, performance of individual *profit centres* and the profit for the organisation as a whole.

management buy-out: the process of former employees, directors or senior managers of an organisation, taking over its *management* and operation by acquiring a substantial *equity* stake in the business. Examples of management buy-outs in leisure and tourism include the acquisition of *National Express* by its former managers in 1988 and the purchase of Wookey Hole Caves in Somerset from its former owners the *Tussauds Group*. The winning of a contract by the management of a former local authority *leisure centre* is also a form of management buy-out. (See also *direct services organisation*.)

management by objectives (MBO) is a formal approach to the management of an organisation, which has four identifiable steps:

- the establishment of clear *objectives*
- the agreement of targets and time limits for action
- monitoring to see that action is taken
- review of the process and amendment of objectives as necessary.

MBO operates best within a clearly identified management structure, where each manager and member of staff is aware of his or her responsibilities and duties. Advocates of MBO argue that it offers many benefits to an organisation, such as clear lines of communication and the encouragement of *motivation*. Others believe that it is too rigid a structure, not allowing individual managers the flexibility needed to operate effectively in a dynamic environment.

Management Charter Initiative (MCI): a government and industry sponsored attempt to introduce a range of competence-based qualifications for working managers in all industries. The Initiative is linked to the *National Vocational Qualifications (NVQ)* system, and offers three levels of achievement at Certificate, Diploma and Masters levels. The aim of the MCI is to identify the core skills and competences needed by managers in industry and the public sector, and to help organisations fill any skills gaps they detect, through a programme of *staff training* and development.

management information system (MIS): a mixture of manual and automated resources, concerned with the collection, collation, storage, retrieval, communication and use of data for purposes of an organisation's sound *management* and forward *planning*. A MIS used in a leisure or tourism facility will focus on three distinct types of information: financial data, operational information and customer details.

management style: the manner in which a senior member of an organisation deals with his or her subordinates in the workplace. Management styles vary enormously, but can be categorised as follows:

- Motivational management – a leader who is supportive and who consults widely with staff.
- Aggressive management – a manager who is generally not a good listener and prefers not to enter into discussion on decisions.
- Administrative management – a manager who 'does everything by the book', but lacks a motivational spark.
- Committee management – a manager who always steers a middle course and is afraid to make decisions.
- Passive management – a leader who does the bare minimum and will resist change.

A motivational manager is one who will have the best chance of achieving success in an organisation; displaying a management style that is 'open' rather than defensive, is assertive rather than aggressive and praises rather than undermines staff achievement, is far more likely to achieve results.

manager: a person who takes responsibility for *planning*, organising, directing and controlling specified elements of an organisation's business, to help achieve its *objectives*. Managers have to marshal their *resources*, be they staff, plant, finance, machinery or facilities, determine priorities and work within *budgets* to achieve their aims. Managers often have leadership roles and must be able to communicate with their employees and motivate them to achieve overall success.

managing director: an individual responsible for executing an organisation's *strategy* and running its day-to-day affairs, in conjunction with other directors and staff. The managing director is the most senior of the board of directors and, in some cases, he or she may also be its *chairman*. The managing director is chosen by the other board members, who will be looking for an individual who has the ability to work under pressure, is a good communicator and leader, has wide experience of business and excellent management skills.

manifest: an official list of the names of the passengers carried on an airline, vessel or vehicle.

man-made attractions, or built attractions, are purpose-built tourist facilities designed to give enjoyment, education and entertainment. Popular man-made attractions in the UK include *theme parks* such as Alton Towers and Chessington World of Adventures, historic sites including Stonehenge and Windsor Castle, and *museums* such as the British Museum and the Museum of Science and Industry in Manchester. (See also *natural attractions*.)

manpower planning gives an organisation the opportunity to look at its existing staffing levels and to forecast the mix of *human resources* it will need to meet its future objectives. The stages in developing an organisation's manpower plan will include:

- an examination of its strategic plan
- analysis of the existing staff resources in the context of the strategic plan
- an estimate of any likely future changes in the supply of staff
- the likely demand for staff in the future
- development of the future human resource 'mix'.

The dynamic nature of the *leisure* and *tourism* industries makes manpower planning an essential *management* exercise in order to keep costs to a minimum, thereby maintaining *profitability*. At a national level, governments undertake manpower planning as a way of determining future training and employment needs.

manual handling of loads: the Manual Handling Operations Regulations came into force on January 1 1993 as a direct result of the *EU Directives on health and safety*. They apply to any manual handling operations that may cause injury at work, for example loading bulk supplies of brochures into a travel agency or moving sports equipment in a *leisure centre*. Under the regulations, employers must avoid hazardous manual handling operations whenever possible, assess any operations that cannot be avoided and reduce the risk of any injury as far as is reasonably practicable.

MAP: see *Modified American Plan*

marginal costing is another name for *contribution pricing*.

market: the total number of people who buy (existing market), or may buy (potential market), a *product* or *service*. It is generally expressed in monetary terms, e.g. the total market for spending on leisure products in the UK is estimated to be more than £100 billion. Organisations need to have reliable data on the characteristics of the market for their products and services, most often obtained by undertaking a *market research* exercise. The size of the market for overseas *package holidays* bought by British people is currently in the region of 14 million holidays per year. *Tour operators* compete to get as big a share of this market as possible by constant *product development* and market analysis.

market analysis: examination of the customers (existing and potential) for a product or service, their characteristics and preferences. Market analysis is carried out by leisure, travel and tourism companies to retain or improve *market share*. (See also *market research*.)

market-led pricing is a pricing *policy* that takes market factors and conditions, rather than costs of production, as the basis on which prices are determined. A market-led approach to pricing is common in leisure and tourism, given the highly competitive nature of the industries. Two of the most widely used market-led methods are *competitive pricing* and *penetration pricing*. (See also *cost-based pricing*.)

Market Opinion and Research International (MORI): a commercial organisation that specialises in commissioning and conducting *market research*. Perhaps best known for the polls that it carries out on behalf of political parties, MORI undertakes surveys of a wide range of national and international topics, including attitudes to new technology, use of *leisure time* and holiday taking. Weblink: www.mori.com

market orientation is concerned with spending time and money on researching the *needs* of the *market* and providing products and services that *customers* will want to buy. It is a *management* practice that is more concerned with giving customers complete satisfaction than purely concentrating on the features of products and services that are supplied (*product orientation*).

market penetration: the technique of attempting to increase *market share* by offering customers a range of promotional incentives, such as discounts, free gifts and *extra product*.

market research is the process of gathering information on existing and potential *customers* and its use for *management purposes*. It is an essential first step in an organisation's *marketing* activity, since without reliable data on customers' attitudes and desires, any leisure or tourism organisation will have difficulty in providing appropriate products and services. Research may be needed at any stage in the marketing process and can help an organisation plan for the future, identify new market opportunities or sales outlets, identify problems and suggest solutions, monitor the reaction of customers, reduce costs and monitor general trends in the leisure and tourism industries. Market research involves the collection of both *secondary data*, i.e. information that is already published, and *primary data*, which is new data collected for a specific purpose, often involving *observation*, a *focus group* or a *survey*.

Market Research Society (MRS): an independent membership organisation that oversees the work of the major *market research* companies operating in the UK. It has introduced a strict *code of practice* for its members, in order to increase the professionalism of the industry and improve the image of market research generally. Weblink: www.mrs.org.uk

market segment: see *market segmentation*

market segmentation is the process of sub-dividing the total *market* for a product or service into different groups, each with similar characteristics. Market segmentation enables an organisation to target a particular group, whose members become the focus of all its marketing efforts, with the introduction and *promotion* of products and services designed to meet the individual's needs. Markets can be segmented in a number of ways, including:

- by region – e.g. all the people living in a particular postcode area of a city
- by age – e.g. designing products for senior citizens
- by social class – e.g. targeting all the people in a town in the C2 socio-economic group
- by gender – e.g. developing courses for women
- by lifestyle – e.g. introducing new holidays for young people who live adventurous lifestyles.

Mass market *tour operators* are constantly looking to develop new products to meet the needs of particular market segments as a way of maintaining their *market share* and improving profitability.

market share is the proportion of a *market* that is held by an organisation, in relation to its main competitors, e.g. Eurotunnel's share of the cross-Channel market is approximately 50 per cent. In leisure and tourism, market share is usually measured either by volume, for example the number of holidays sold to a particular *destination*, or by value, for example the revenue generated by sales of *sporting goods*. Organisations are constantly monitoring and refining their range of products and services, to maintain or increase market share.

market size: the total sales of all the producers in a particular market, e.g. the total market for overseas *package holidays* in the UK is around 14 million each year. It is important for an organisation to know the precise volume or value of the market in which it operates, or hopes to operate, in order to identify whether it is an expanding or contracting market. Knowing the total market size will also enable an organisation to calculate its own *market share*, and if that too is growing or shrinking.

market trends: the way in which the *demand* for, and supply of, particular goods and services fluctuates over time. The market for UK holidays, for example, has remained fairly static since the beginning of the 1990s, while the demand for overseas package holidays taken by British people has increased sharply. The study of market trends, and the analysis of the reasons for their fluctuations, is a key factor in helping organisations survive and grow, giving them the opportunity to forecast the likely demand for their products and services. Analysing market trends requires an organisation to have access to comprehensive *market research* data.

marketing is the process concerned with identifying *customers' needs* and supplying products and services in the right place, at the right time and at the right price. It is defined by the *Chartered Institute of Marketing* as 'the management process for identifying and satisfying customer needs profitably'. Being a management process means that marketing ranks alongside personnel, finance and other management functions in terms of the structure of an organisation. The importance given to marketing will depend in part on the nature of the business and the attitude of management. *Market research* plays a fundamental role in any marketing process, in helping to discover customer likes and dislikes. Satisfying customer needs is all about developing products and services that customers will want to use or buy, as well as the various techniques that can be used to promote their sale or use, e.g. *advertising*, *direct mail*, *public relations*, *direct marketing* and *personal selling*. Marketing must be undertaken with the aims of the organisation in mind, since not all leisure and tourism organisations put profit maximisation as their main *objective*.

marketing budget: the sum of money that a leisure or tourism organisation has at its disposal to carry out its *marketing* plans. It is important to remember that the marketing budget will not only be spent on advertising (*above-the-line promotion*), but also on *below-the-line* activities such as *direct marketing, sales promotion, merchandising* and *public relations* work. The cost of producing brochures and other promotional items will also fall within this budget. An organisation's marketing budget changes from year to year, in response to factors in both the *internal* and *external environment.*

marketing communications: the term used to identify the techniques and channels that an organisation uses to inform and influence its *customers*. In leisure and tourism, the most important marketing communications techniques are *advertising, public relations* activity, *sales promotion, direct marketing* and *personal selling*. The range of techniques used is chosen to help the organisation best achieve its *marketing objectives*. Whichever techniques are chosen, each is likely to follow the *AIDA* principle (attention, interest, desire, action).

marketing concept: see *marketing*

marketing environment: see *business environment*

marketing mix: commonly referred to as the 4 Ps (*product, price, place* and *promotion*), the marketing mix is one of the most important concepts in *marketing* today. In attempting to achieve its *marketing objectives*, an organisation must decide what emphasis is put on each element of the mix. A newly opened *leisure centre*, for example, will spend more on promotion in order to attract new customers; a major *tour operator* may be forced to change its pricing structures when it discovers that a competitor has undercut its prices; a *visitor attraction* will need to review its product from time to time in response to changing market expectations; and a major travel company may decide to close down its regional sales offices, thereby altering the 'place' component of the marketing mix. These examples show that the emphasis on the different components of the marketing mix will vary over time, as well as between the different sectors of the industry.

marketing objectives: the specific aims or goals that an organisation has in mind when devising its *marketing* activity. Examples of marketing objectives could be:

- to maximise income
- to manage the effects of change
- to expand the customer base
- to analyse *competitor activity*
- to identify *customer needs*.

Marketing objectives, which must be clear, measurable and realistic (see *SMART objectives*), will vary between different sectors of the leisure and tourism industries. Private sector operators, for example, gear their marketing towards achieving maximum sales, while the public and voluntary sectors will seek to fulfil their wider community and social aims, perhaps by targeting under-represented and disadvantaged groups in society.

marketing plan: a written document giving details of what action an organisation will take to achieve its overall *marketing strategy* and thereby fulfil its *marketing objectives*. The plan should consider what the organisation wants to achieve, where it sees itself now (*situation analysis*), where it wants to be in the future and how it reaches that point, by careful attention to the different elements in the *marketing mix*. The plan should give a timescale and include details of *budgets*.

marketing principles: the underlying practices and processes that guide all marketing activity, for example the *marketing mix, market segmentation, customer needs, target marketing*. It is the job of the marketer to apply these principles to best effect, given the nature of the *business environment*.

marketing process: see *marketing*

marketing research is the term used to describe the process of gathering and analysing data that affects a wide range of factors that influence the marketing process of an organisation. Unlike *market research*, which is concerned specifically with customers and their attitudes to products and services, marketing research is a more all-embracing activity, involving, for example, product research, promotion research and price research.

marketing strategy: this refers to the overall means by which an organisation hopes to meet its *marketing objectives*. In deciding on its marketing strategy, an organisation has a number of different options, including:

- Undifferentiated marketing – when a single marketing mix is offered to the whole market. This is unlikely to succeed, since markets are made up of many types of buyers, all with different characteristics.
- Differentiated marketing – when different marketing approaches are tailored to different sectors of the market. A leisure centre, for example, will have different ideas for promoting itself to families and senior citizens.
- Concentrated marketing – when an organisation chooses to compete in only one sector of the market, developing the most effective marketing mix for that sector. Eurocamp is a good example of a company that concentrates on one sector of the market, those wanting continental camping holidays.

In addition to deciding which type of strategy to adopt, any *leisure* or *tourism* organisation can implement the strategy in a different way. It may, for example, adopt a defensive

149

strategy, which is designed to hold on to its existing customers. It could opt for a developing strategy, designed to offer existing customers a wider range of products or services. Another option would be to implement an attacking strategy, with the aim of generating extra business through new customers. Having decided on its overall marketing strategy, its next step is to draw up a *marketing plan*.

mark-up is the amount by which retailers increase the price of an article, to cover their *costs* and produce a profit margin.

Maslow's hierarchy of needs is a theory of individual development and *motivation*, based on the principle that all human beings have *needs*, and that these needs vary between people and over time. Maslow developed different needs into a hierarchy as shown in the figure below.

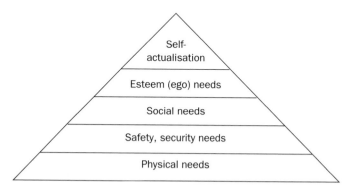

Maslow's concept can be related to the demand for leisure and tourism products and services, in terms of demand *motivators*. Taking the example of a holiday:

- physical needs – food, sleep and drink. etc.
- safety and security needs – safe means of transportation, safe destination, etc.;
- social needs – meeting new people, socialising, etc.
- esteem/ego needs – going to a fashionable resort, travelling in style on Concorde, etc.
- self-actualisation – learning a new skill on holiday, becoming spiritually enlightened, etc.

It should be remembered that Maslow's model relates to individual development and motivation in life and not just to motivation in the workplace.

mass media: channels of *communication* that are accessible to the majority of the population, such as *television* and daily newspapers. The *mass media* can exert a great influence over people's lives, by promoting particular ideas, beliefs, products and fashions. Advertisers regard the mass media as their most powerful promotional channels, especially television, which is why the mass media are able to command the highest prices for advertising.

mass tourism: the term used to describe the movement of people in large numbers for leisure and business purposes, a characteristic of the latter half of the twentieth century in Western developed countries. Mass tourism became a reality as a result of developments in *jet aircraft* technology, increased personal mobility, higher *disposable incomes* and the development of *package holidays*. Although it has brought economic and political benefits to many countries, mass tourism does have its disadvantages, including harmful *environmental* and *socio-cultural* *impacts*. These problems have given rise to pressure for tourism that is more *sustainable*.

MASTA: see *Medical Advisory Service for Travellers Abroad*

matrix organisation: a type of organisational structure combining the roles of *line managers* with a range of *'staff' functions*, including personnel, administration and finance. Matrix organisations evolved to try and create more effective work teams, where employees could cross divisional boundaries and the organisation benefit from decentralisation. There may, however, be difficulties with this type of structure, since the lines of *responsibility* and *accountability* can become blurred leading to lengthy decision-making processes.

MBO: see *management by objectives*

McGregor: an American psychologist who is credited with extending *Maslow's hierarchy of needs* and applying it to the real world. McGregor devised the two opposing styles of management, which he called Theory X and Theory Y. In Theory X, managers believed that human beings were born lazy and would do as little as possible at work, shunning *responsibility* and showing no ambition. Theory Y, on the other hand, proposed that employees were more than willing to work hard, accept *responsibility* and be involved in making decisions. McGregor's work has encouraged managers to take a more positive view of their workforce and adopt a more open style of management.

MCI: see *Management Charter Initiative*

MCO: see *miscellaneous charges order*

mean: the most common way of calculating the arithmetic average of a set of data. It is found by adding all the values together and dividing by the total number of values. As an example, the results of a visitor survey conducted at a zoo concerning how far people had travelled were as follows:

20, 30, 30, 25, 15, 20, 40, 25, 20, 25

In this example the mean is 25 (250 divided by 10). One disadvantage of using the mean is that extreme results can distort the situation, giving misleading results. (See also *mode, median*.)

media: a term used to denote the various channels of communication available, including those that an organisation can use to advertise its *products* and services (a single channel is known as a medium). Types of advertising media include:

- *consumer press*
- *trade press*
- television
- cinema advertising
- commercial radio
- outdoor advertising
- transport advertising.

The types of media selected will depend on the size of advertising budget and target market. *Advertising agencies* specialise in helping organisations plan and execute *advertising campaigns* in a variety of media. Details of the costs of advertising in the various media can be found in the publication *British Rate and Data*. (See also *broadcast media*, *printed media*.)

media buyer: a specialist working in an *advertising agency* whose role is to liaise with the various *printed media* (newspapers, magazines, journals, etc.) and *broadcast media* (TV, cinema, cable TV, commercial radio, etc.) to place advertisements on behalf of the agency's clients. The agency earns a *commission* from the media company, which may be passed on to the client in the form of a reduced fee for services provided.

media coverage refers to exposure in either *printed* or *broadcast media*. Planned media coverage is a type of *public relations* activity and can be very beneficial to the individual, company or organisation concerned, resulting in greater exposure and an enhanced public *image*.

media planner: usually one of a team of people working in an *advertising agency*, responsible for deciding when and where particular *advertisements* will be placed for a particular client's *advertising campaign*. The media planner will often decide on a mixture of *above-the-line* and *below-the-line* promotional activities, e.g. a newspaper advertising campaign linked to a discount coupon promotion on breakfast cereal packets. Once the schedules have been agreed, a *media buyer* will liaise with the chosen *media* to confirm arrangements.

median: a value calculated from a set of data so as to show a typical value for the set. A *mean* (commonly called an average) is more usually used, but in certain circumstances the median may provide a more useful, or typical result. It is less influenced by 'rogue' values that are very high or low. The median is calculated by listing all the data in order of size, and taking the middle value (or *mean* of the middle two if an even number of data values is listed). So for the following data: 45, 37, 29, 25, 47, 46, 26, 25, 14, 36, 26, the median is 29:

(listed in order of size) 14, 25, 25, 26, 26, **29**, 36, 37, 45, 46, 47.

(See also *mode*.)

mediation: another name for *arbitration*.

Medical Advisory Service for Travellers Abroad (MASTA): a commercial organisation that was set up in 1984 at the London School of Hygiene and Tropical Medicine with the aim of raising the awareness of health issues associated with international travel. Today, MASTA offers a service to the public, General Practitioners, hospitals and others with a specialist need. It has grown into an organisation with an international presence, whose services range from the supply of vaccines and travel medicines to research on important travel issues and the development of unique products for travellers. Weblink: www.masta.org

Meetings Industry Association (MIA): a professional trade organisation for the conference industry in the UK. Founded in 1990, MIA encourages the maintenance of the highest professional standards within the meetings industry. It maintains a regular dialogue with government, the *media*, buyers and industry colleagues, in order to strengthen the position of its members' businesses and raise the profile of the United Kingdom as an international conference destination.

memorandum: a type of *written communication* commonly used in organisations in place of a formal letter or *report*. Usually shortened to memo, it can be used for a number of reasons, such as to confirm a verbal agreement or message, to ask for information, to remind a colleague of something or to pass on information or instructions. In organisations that use *electronic communications*, e-mail is often used in place of written memos.

Memorandum of Association: one of two formal documents that must be produced by a *limited company*, under the terms of the *Companies Acts* of 1985 and 1989, the other being the *Articles of Association*. The Memorandum of Association is concerned with a company's relationship with the outside world and contains the company name, its address, the purpose for which the company is formed, the liability and voting rights of the *shareholders* and the amount of *share capital*.

mentor: an individual who volunteers, or is chosen, to look after a new member of staff in an organisation and make him or her settle into the new surroundings as easily as possible. The mentor will be able to advise the new recruit on *organisational structures* and operational practices.

MEP stands for Member of the *European Parliament*, a person directly elected to represent their country's interests in the *EU* Parliament.

merchandising: a range of methods adopted by retailers to stimulate customers to purchase at the *point-of-sale*. This may include brochure racks, posters, hanging cards, displays and signs. Merchandising opportunities are often linked to a popular media personality or current fashion, e.g. T-shirts, mugs, calendars, books, etc. with the name and photograph of a pop group or Disney cartoon hero.

Metier: the *National Training Organisation* for the *arts and entertainment* sector, with responsibility for all aspects of training, education, qualifications and labour market data. Weblink: www.metier.org.uk

MIA: see *Meetings Industry Association*

micro business: any enterprise employing less than 10 full-time employees, as defined by the *European Commission (EC)*. The great majority of leisure, travel and tourism businesses in the EC fall into this category.

micro environment: a term used to denote those influences and factors that are close to an organisation and over which it has some degree of control. Sometimes called the internal environment, these include staff, facilities and *suppliers*. Prudent control within an organisation should ensure that these internal elements are effectively managed, but an organisation will be affected by a number of factors in the *macro (external) environment* over which it has little control.

microcomputer: see *personal computer*

mid-centric: one of a number of descriptions of tourist behaviour developed by Plog in 1977 as part of a research study for airline companies. Mid-centrics made up the bulk of tourists to a particular destination, i.e. the mass market. They tend to move in after resorts have been discovered by the more adventurous *allocentrics*, who are then forced to move on to discover another area. (See also *psychocentric*.)

Mid-Wales Festival of the Countryside: a series of events which take place in the towns, countryside and villages of mid-Wales each year from June to December. Its aim is to show that informed concern and respect for the environment can go hand-in-hand with *economic development*. Launched in 1985 as a contribution to the World Conservation Strategy, the Festival of the Countryside has grown into a pioneering model of *sustainable tourism* in a rural environment. Weblink: www.foc.org.uk

milk run: the name given to the network of UK regions and cities most frequented by *overseas visitors* to Britain. It is made up of London, Oxford, Bath, Cardiff, Chester, the Lake District, Edinburgh, York, Cambridge and returning to London. The round trip is most commonly undertaken by visitors on their first visit to Britain.

Millennium Fund: administered by the *Millennium Commission* under the direction of the *Department for Culture, Media and Sport*, these were the proceeds from the *National Lottery* that were used to fund projects celebrating the start of the twenty-first century. The Fund was used to support around a dozen large scale projects throughout the UK, a larger number of smaller projects of local significance, the Millennium Festival and a bursary scheme.

Millennium Commission: this was one of the five 'good causes', financed from *National Lottery* proceeds, set up to help communities mark the start of the new millennium. It used money raised by the *National Lottery* to support projects throughout the *United Kingdom* which will be lasting monuments to the achievements of the nation. Financial support was given to a range of projects to appeal to all ages and interests, and which will contribute to the local, regional and national *heritage*. The Commission made its first allocation of funds in August 1995, granting £66.5 million to 27 projects, with £42.5 million going to *Sustrans,* to help set up a national network of cycleways. The Millennium Commission ceased to exist on December 31 2000 and its allocation of National Lottery funding was transferred to the *New Opportunities Fund*.

miniple travel agent: a travel company that has a number of branches located in a particular part of the country, meeting a regional demand, e.g. Woodcock Travel, with branches mainly in Yorkshire. Miniples do not benefit from 'economies of scale' to the same extent as *multiple travel agents*, but they are able to build close ties with business and leisure travellers in their region and operate very successful businesses. Their success, however, often makes them prime targets for takeovers or *mergers*.

Ministry of Agriculture, Fisheries and Food (MAFF): the former government department responsible for the nation's agricultural policy, but with interests and responsibilities in other countryside matters, such as set-aside, *Environmentally Sensitive Areas* and rural business advisory services. MAFF ceased to exist in 2001 and was superseded by the *Department for Environment, Food and Rural Affairs (DEFRA)*.

minority groups: see *disadvantaged groups*

minutes: a written record of a meeting, usually written down by a secretary, including details of who was in attendance and what was decided. The minutes of a meeting are often agreed to be an accurate record of what happened before the start of a future meeting.

MIS: see *management information system*

miscellaneous charges order (MCO): a voucher issued by an airline and exchangeable for a specified service in connection with the *transportation* covered by the airline ticket, e.g. car hire, accommodation, excursions or meals.

mission: the principal purpose of an individual or organisation, often described in its *mission statement*.

mission statement: a brief explanation of an organisation's fundamental purpose. Its aim is to convey to all those with an interest in the organisation, be they staff, *shareholders* or the public in general, what business it is in, where it sees itself going and how it will relate to its environment and other organisations. Some mission statements also introduce an element of an organisation's philosophy and values. Some individuals are very sceptical about the value of mission statements, considering them nothing more than a *public relations* exercise. What a mission statement can do is set out the general direction in which an organisation is hoping to progress and provide a framework for the development of more specific *objectives*.

MMC: see *Monopolies and Mergers Commission*

mobility: see *personal mobility*

mode: an arithmetic term which denotes the number that occurs most frequently in a given set of data, e.g. a visitor survey gives the following results for the amount spent by children to a theme park:

3, 5, 6, 2, 5, 3, 7, 4, 2, 5

The mode in this example is 5, since it appears more frequently than any other number. It is a rather crude method of choosing a typical figure to describe a set of data, so statisticians usually prefer to use the *mean* or *median*, but in some circumstances the mode can be useful.

models are representations of reality that are used to give an understanding of past developments and/or a forecast of future occurrences. Often constructed in graphical form, a model can be used to help management decision making and the wise use of an organisation's *resources*. The *destination life cycle* is a common model used in leisure and *tourism development*.

modem: an electronic device that connects a *personal computer* to a telephone line, allowing the transmission of *data* and the establishment of a communications network. A modem is necessary for gaining access to the *Internet* and other on-line databases.

Modified American Plan: an *accommodation* arrangement based on half board, with a room and breakfast plus one other meal per day, either at midday or in the evening. (See also *American Plan, Continental Plan, European Plan*.)

Monopolies and Mergers Commission (MMC): the former government-funded body set up to monitor trading activity to make sure that the public's interest is safeguarded. The MMC was superseded by the *Competition Commission* on April 1 1999.

monopoly: an economics term to denote many purchasers but only one supplier of a product or service. In reality, monopoly suppliers rarely exist, since there are many competing suppliers for the vast majority of goods and services. Even the former state-controlled monopolies supplying the nation's utilities and energy resources (water, electricity and gas) are now subject to competitive pressures. Monopoly situations generally act against the public interest, since it is thought that a single supplier will exploit customers by charging higher prices. It is for this reason that the government established the *Competition Commission* to safeguard the public interest.

MORI: see *Market Opinion and Research International*

Mosaic: a *database marketing* system that allows potential *customers* to be targeted according to their lifestyles and residential neighbourhoods. Mosaic is a computer-based system that works in a similar way to *ACORN* and allows leisure and tourism organisations to market their products and services effectively.

motel: an *accommodation* establishment providing rooms and eating facilities for passing motorists, who often stay for just one night. The concept originated in the USA, but has now spread to all parts of the world, although the term 'lodge' is preferred in some European countries. (See also *budget hotel*.)

motivation: see *staff motivation, group motivation*

motivational management: a supportive *leadership style* that seeks to cement a *partner-ship* between a *manager* and his or her staff, thereby empowering individuals and inspiring them to work more effectively. A manager adopting this style will agree goals and targets with members of staff, let them know clearly what is expected of them and monitor their progress regularly. Motivational management contrasts starkly with an aggressive manage-ment style, where there is little consultation between manager and staff.

motivators are factors within the psychological make-up of an individual that help influence his or her patterns of behaviour. In leisure and tourism, motivators are an important con-sideration when it comes to examining the present and future *demand* for products and services. Typical motivators of concern to the leisure and tourism professional include:

- status, social and ego needs (as shown in *Maslow's hierarchy of needs*)
- education levels
- income levels
- employment status
- state of health
- amount of *leisure time*.

A study of motivators helps to show why, for example, one person's ideal holiday is sailing in the Mediterranean, while another's is bird-watching in Suffolk. Motivators are usually studied alongside *determinants*, to give marketers a full picture of the pattern of demand and, as a result, a guide as to which products and services to develop.

In a work situation, motivators are those factors that give a person a degree of job satis-faction, e.g. tangible recognition for good work, *staff training* and development opportunities, and a supportive environment.

MRS: see *Market Research Society*

MTI: see *Museum Training Institute*

multinational corporation: a *company* that operates across international frontiers, with its headquarters in one country and operating interests in a number of others. In leisure and tourism, multinationals (sometimes called transnationals) are involved in the produc-tion of both goods and services. Many household names are multinationals, including Dunlop, Marriott, Reebok, Nike, Avis, Sheraton, Holiday Inn and *British Airways*. *Developing countries* are often happy to welcome multinational corporations who may wish to build hotels and leisure resorts, but they are sometimes criticised for exploiting virgin areas, providing only poorly paid jobs and taking their profits away from the developing nations.

multiple travel agency: a travel *company* that has many branches located throughout the UK. Many are household names in the travel industry, such as Thomas Cook, Lunn Poly and Going Places (now My Travel). They are sometimes part of large parent organisations; Lunn Poly, for example, is owned by *Thomson*, while Going Places is owned by the My Travel group. Multiple travel agents benefit from *'economies of scale'* and can negotiate the best prices on holidays that they sell. They are not always able, however, to match the level of personal service and range of products offered by independent agents. (See also *miniple travel agent*.)

multiplex: a cinema complex offering the choice of a number of screens and films, often coupled with other leisure facilities, such as fast-food outlets, bowling and roller skating.

multiplier effect: an economic concept which, when applied to tourism, shows that the money spent by visitors to an area is re-spent in the local economy and is actually worth more than its face value. The factor by which the final sum is greater than the original spent is known as the multiplier, or income multiplier. For example, £200 spent by a family on a short break in a guesthouse, could be worth, say, £200 x 1.5 (the multiplier), i.e. a total of £300 to the local economy. The actual value of the multiplier will vary, depending on which area of the country is concerned and the type of accommodation used. A farm guesthouse, for example, will have a higher multiplier than a city centre hotel that is part of a *multinational* chain. This is because the guesthouse is more likely to buy its goods and services locally, thereby retaining money in the local economy, whereas the city centre hotel will have bulk purchasing contracts with national distributors, with payments being made outside of the local economy. This loss to the local economy is known as a *leakage*.

museums have long been an important part of the *tourism* industry, with more than 2000 in the UK alone, according to *Museums and Galleries Commission*. Museums are popular with UK and overseas visitors, both for their entertainment and educational value. Museums of national significance in Britain are not only located in London, but are also to be found in places as diverse as Bradford (the National Museum of Photography, Film and Television), St Ives in Cornwall (the Tate Gallery) and Cardiff (the National Museum of Wales). Local museums and galleries also play an important role in meeting the needs of visitors to both town and country, helping to sustain local economies and services. In recent years there have been moves to try and change the sometimes 'stuffy' image of museums with the introduction of more 'hands on' exhibits, e.g. Eureka! the Museum for Children in Halifax. (See also *Resource*.)

Museums and Galleries Commission (MGC): originally formed in 1931, the MGC took on a range of new functions in 1982 on all matters relating to museums. Its objectives were to encourage better standards in museums, provide advice to the government and work directly with museums. It established a museums' registration scheme, created a series of standards and guidelines for the profession, provided grant aid for a number of *museums* and galleries, and developed a conservation unit to support the highest standards of work in maintaining the nation's *heritage*. In April 2000, the Commission merged with the Library and Information Commission to form a new body known simply as *Resource*.

Museums Association is a non-governmental national organisation established in 1888 to represent the interest of museum and gallery employees, museums and galleries as institutions, and their collections. It aims to maintain and improve professional standards through information and advice, and to raise awareness of the key issues affecting museums. One of its main functions is to promote and protect the development of museum services and to advance the cause of museums at all levels of government through *lobbying* and consultation. The Association has a membership of over 5000 drawn from all sections of the museum community. Weblink: www.museumsassociation.org

'mystery shopper' is the term given to somebody who anonymously visits a *leisure* or *tourism* facility, or uses a product or service, and reports back to the management on his or her experiences. The technique can be used to gain valuable information on, for example, the performance and attitude of staff to customers, or even the level of service offered by competitor organisations. 'Mystery shoppers' are widely used in the commercial sectors of leisure, travel and tourism, especially in airlines and travel agencies to help gain a *competitive advantage*.

NAITA: see *National Association of Independent Travel Agents*

National Assembly for Wales (NAW): established under the Government of Wales Act 1998 and launched on July 1 1999, the National Assembly is a devolved body with a range of governmental powers affecting the people of Wales. The Assembly decides its own priorities, and allocates funds made available to it from the Treasury, in a number of areas, including agriculture, heritage, culture, *sport* and *leisure*, *economic development*, transport and *tourism*. Weblink: www.wales.gov.uk

National Association of Independent Travel Agents (NAITA): a grouping of independent *travel agents* in the UK, set up to act in a similar way to *ABTA*. Representing more than 860 independent branch outlets in the UK, NAITA has been able to negotiate favourable trading terms for its members with a number of *principals* and has established a free legal advisory service. NAITA membership criteria includes the holding of an *IATA* licence and membership of ABTA. Weblink: www.advantage4travel.com

National Coaching Foundation (NCF): an independent organisation established in 1983 and funded primarily by the then *Sports Council*. Known as Sports Coach UK since 2001, the overall aim of the NCF is to work with partners to develop more and better coaches in as wide a range of sports as possible, for people of all levels of experience. The NCF provides a comprehensive range of services, available regionally via a network of Coaching Development Officers, including:

- a general enquiry service for coaches, including a selection of basic factsheets
- an in-depth information search service for coaches
- a current awareness service for coaches to help keep them up to date with current issues.

NCF's in-house database on coaching and performance contains over 5000 records of books and articles. In 2001, its membership rose to 12,000, while 30,000 coaches and teachers attended training programmes across the UK. (See also *Champion Coaching*.) Weblink: www.sportscoachuk.org

National Council for Vocational Qualifications (NCVQ): a government funded body that was established in 1986 to develop a new system of *vocational qualifications* for all occupations. Working with *Industry Lead Bodies*, NCVQ oversaw the development of occupational standards and subsequent qualifications at levels 1 to 5. NCVQ was also responsible for the introduction of *General National Vocational Qualifications (GNVQs)* in conjunction with a number of *awarding bodies*. NCVQ's work is now carried out by the *Qualifications and Curriculum Authority*.

National Council for Voluntary Organisations (NCVO): established in 1919, NCVO seeks to be the voice of voluntary organisations in all sectors, including *leisure* and *tourism*. It aims to extend the involvement of voluntary bodies in responding to social issues of the day, to be a resource centre and to protect the interests and independence of voluntary organisations. Weblink: www.ncvo-vol.org.uk

National Cycle Network: a 5000-mile network of traffic-free paths through urban and country areas, protected on-road sections and minor roads, which, when fully completed will make a safe route for cyclists throughout Britain. Launched by *Sustrans* in 1994, the Network will stretch from Inverness to Penzance, passing through the centre of each town and city along its way, linking schools, houses, shops and workplaces with each other and with the countryside. Sustrans received a grant of £42.5 million from the *Millennium Commission* to help fund the building of 2000 miles of the network.

National Exhibition Centre (NEC): a purpose-built facility located close to the motorway network near to the city of Birmingham and its international airport. The NEC stages business events, such as conferences and exhibitions, as well as a wide range of sporting and entertainment events, including concerts by world famous artists. It is currently home to the annual *British Travel Trade Fair*. Weblink: www.necgroup.co.uk

National Express is best-known as Britain's only national, scheduled coach service, serving more than 1200 destinations every day, from Penzance in Cornwall to Thurso in the north of Scotland. National Express tickets are available through over 2000 agents nation-wide, ranging from newsagents to large coach stations such as London Victoria. The former state-run enterprise, which was bought by its management in 1988, offers a range of con-cessionary fares via a number of discount offers, targeted particularly at students, young people and senior citizens. National Express's sister company, Eurolines, offers European coach travel to more than 270 destinations, while Scottish Citylink provides Scotland with a networked coach service. The National Express coach division is part of the National Express Group, which also offers rail services in the UK. It has interests in Eurostar, the Gatwick Express, Scot Rail and Central Trains (as a *train operating company*). Weblink: www.gobycoach.com, www.nationalexpressgroup.com

national government: see *central government*

national identity: the mixture of a variety of real and perceived symbols and traditions that give a country its unique identity, and often make it an attraction as a *tourist destination*. Ireland, for example, is viewed as an easy-going, friendly and scenic country to visit, with a rich musical and cultural heritage. Marketers often use the positive aspects of a country's national identity in their *advertising campaigns*. Effective t*ourism management* is concerned with ensuring that destinations do not lose their national identities when developed for *tourism*, but rather rejoice in the traditions that make them unique.

National Liaison Group for Higher Education in Tourism in the UK (NLG) an indepen-dent membership organisation established in 1993 to provide a focus for the development of *tourism* in higher education in the UK. Initially developed under the auspices of the *Tourism Society*, NLG encouraged high standards in course provision, developed and promoted links between education and industry, communicated *good practice* and liaised with other bodies concerned with higher education in tourism. The work of the NLG was taken over by the *Association of Tourism in Higher Education* in 2000.

National Lottery: launched in the UK in November 1994, with the principal aim of providing extra funds for a range of 'good causes', the National Lottery has come as a welcome boost to the *leisure* and *tourism* industries. Five specific areas were identified in the National Lottery Act 1993 to receive Lottery funding:

- *sport*
- the arts
- *heritage*
- charities
- projects to mark the start of the new millennium.

In 1998, the *New Opportunities Fund* was added as a sixth good cause, covering health, education and environmental projects. *Camelot*, a private company, operates the National Lottery on behalf of the *Department for Culture, Media and Sport (DCMS)*. Proceeds from the Lottery go into the National Lottery Distribution Fund, which is divided between the six good causes listed above. There are 12 distributing bodies responsible to the DCMS for giving *grants* to projects within the good causes. They are:

- The Sports Councils of England, Wales, Scotland and Northern Ireland (together, 16.66 per cent)
- The Arts Councils of England, Wales, Scotland and Northern Ireland (together, 16.66 per cent)
- The National Lottery Charities Board (16.66 per cent)
- The National Heritage Memorial Fund (16.66 per cent)
- The Millennium Commission
- The New Opportunities Fund (33.33 per cent).

Out of every pound spent on the National Lottery, around 28 pence goes to the good causes, in the proportions shown above. The Millennium Commission ceased to exist on December 31 2000 (it had previously been allocated 20 per cent), when the allocation to the New Opportunities Fund was increased from 13.33 per cent to 33.33 per cent. At the beginning of May 2000 the total donations to good causes stood at £9.3 billion.

Camelot's activities are closely regulated by the National Lottery Commission, whose duties are to safeguard the integrity of the Lottery, to protect players and, subject to these, to maximise the income to the National Lottery Distribution Fund.

A number of tourism projects, large and small, have benefited from National Lottery funding particularly visitor attractions, e.g. the Dome in Greenwich and the Earth Centre in Yorkshire. (See also *OFLOT, Millennium Commission, Lottery Sports Fund and Heritage Lottery Fund*.)

National Lottery Commission: see *Office of the National Lottery (OFLOT)*

National Nature Reserve (NNR): there are some 130 of these reserves in England, covering around 43,000 hectares. They represent the best examples of different kinds of countryside or contain unusual communities of plants or animals, or important natural features such as rock exposures or gorges. Most NNRs are either owned or controlled by *English Nature* and all of them are specifically managed for nature *conservation*.

National Parks: the 1949 National Parks and Access to the Countryside Act led to the formation of 10 National Parks in England and Wales, each administered by a National Park Authority (see figure below). In addition, the Norfolk Broads enjoys similar status as the other National Parks and in October 1999, the *Countryside Agency* began the process of designating the New Forest as a National Park. The South Downs is also presently being considered for designation as a National Park. Following on from the American idea, with the establishment of the first US National Park at Yellowstone in 1872, the National Parks in England and Wales were established with two prime objectives in mind; the preservation and enhancement of their natural beauty and amenity, and their promotion for *leisure* and *recreation*. Today, the *Countryside Agency* in England and the *Countryside Council for Wales*, as the bodies charged with overseeing the *management* of the Parks, are faced with trying to maintain a delicate balance between the recreational needs of the visitors and the *conservation* of the natural environment. Concern is also expressed about potential conflicts between those visiting for enjoyment and the needs of the people who live and work in the National Parks all year round. Increasing *car ownership* has opened up the countryside to urban dwellers and poses a particular threat to the National Parks. Weblink: www.countryside.gov.uk/nationalparks

National Play Information Centre: this was set up in 1988 with the aim of developing a national library on children's *play*, available on a variety of different *media*. It provides an extensive collection of information for people in a wide range of professions. Researchers and historians are able to use its archives and there is up-to-date information for all those interested in play issues. The Centre's library material now amounts to the largest specialist collection on play in the world. Weblink: www.playwork.org.uk

National Playing Fields Association (NPFA) was established in 1925 to mount a *campaign* to ensure that everyone had *access* to recreational and play space within easy reach of their homes. It is the only national organisation which has specific responsibility for acquiring, protecting and improving playing fields, playgrounds and other *public open spaces*. It does not generally receive funding from *central* or *local government*, but raises funds through membership, public subscription, fund raising, the sale of its expertise and publications. In recent years, the role of the NPFA has changed significantly, with more emphasis being placed on the provision of *play* space for disabled people. Weblink: www.npfa.co.uk

National Rivers Authority (NRA): a former government agency established under the Water Act 1989. The NRA operated in ten regions based upon the river catchment areas of England and Wales. As well as responsibilities for pollution control, environmental protection, water resources and flood defence, it was also responsible for the *promotion* of *leisure* and *recreation*, such as fishing and boating. NRA officials regularly sampled the bathing water around our coasts in accordance with the *EU Bathing Water Directive*. The NRA's activities are now carried out by the Environment Agency.

National Sports Centres are purpose-built facilities aimed at raising the standards of performance of *sport* in England and Wales. Funded primarily from resources provided by *Sport England* and the *Sports Council for Wales*, the six 'centres of excellence' currently operating are at Crystal Palace, Bisham Abbey, Lilleshall, Holme Pierrepont (water-based activities), Plas y Brenin (mountain activities) and the National Cycling Centre near Manchester. Managed by Leisure Connection PLC, the centres are home to a number of *governing bodies of sport* and form the key hub sites for the *English Institute of Sport*. Weblink: www.nationalsportscentres.co.uk

national tourism organisation (NTO): an official body concerned with the *planning*, *development* and *promotion* of *tourism* within its own country, e.g. the Spanish National Tourism Organisation, French Government Tourist Office and *British Tourist Authority*. NTOs may be full departments of government or independent agencies financed wholly or partly from governments funds. Sometimes also known as National Tourist Offices, NTOs establish information offices in the main countries from which their visitors originate, e.g. the *British Tourist Authority* has a network of offices in major cities around the world, including New York, Paris, Tokyo and Rome.

national tourism strategy: a long-term plan for the future development of tourism in a country, listing priority areas and action plans. The UK government published its national tourism strategy 'Tomorrow's Tourism' in 1999 and 'Achieving Our Potential', the tourism strategy for Wales was completed in 2000.

National Tourist Office: see *National Tourism Organisation (NTO)*

National Trails: some of the most challenging public footpaths and bridleways designated in coastal and countryside areas of England and Wales. To date, 13 long distance footpaths have been designated as National Trails, 10 of which are fully developed with three in the process of completion. The first to be designated was the 412km Pennine Way opened in 1965. The longest is the 982km South West Coast Path which meanders through Somerset, Devon, Cornwall and Dorset. The latest is the Thames Path (288km) following the course of the River Thames from its source in Gloucestershire to the Thames Barrier.

National Training Organisation (NTO): a body selected by government to represent the training and employment needs of a particular industry, occupational or service sector. NTOs are central to the government's learning and skills agenda across the UK, and are committed to ensuring that the UK workforce has the necessary skills to compete in the global market. NTOs are owned and led by groups of employers from within each industry sector and are concerned with a range of activities, including *National Vocational Qualifications (NVQs)*, promoting careers and collating labour market information. Within leisure and tourism, there are a number of NTOs representing different industry sectors, e.g. the *Travel, Tourism and Events National Training Organisation*, the *National Training Organisation for Sport, Recreation and Allied Occupations*, the *Cultural Heritage National Training Organisation* and *Metier*, the NTO for the arts and entertainment sector.

National Training Organisation for Sport, Recreation and Allied Occupations (SPRITO): an employer-led membership organisation responsible for all education and training matters relating to UK sport, recreation, playwork, outdoor education, fitness, exercise, caravan and leisure parks. SPRITO serves the needs of over 608,000 employees, 2 million volunteers and their estimated 178,000 employers. It advises on the development of *vocational qualifications* in these areas, reporting to the *Qualifications and Curriculum Authority*. Weblink: www.sprito.org.uk

National Trust: one of Europe's leading *conservation* charities, which celebrated its centenary in 1995. It is independent of government and relies on its voluntary supporters, including more than 3 million members, for most of its income. The Trust is one of the largest private landowners in the country, protecting more than 248,000 hectares of land in England, Wales and Northern Ireland (there is a separate National Trust for Scotland), as well as 600 miles of coastline and more than 200 buildings and gardens of outstanding interest and importance. Each year, some 11 million people visit its facilities for which there is a charge, while untold millions freely enjoy the coastline, hills and woodlands that the Trust preserves. The Trust is at present running several special appeals including *Enterprise Neptune*, launched in 1965. Weblink: www.nationaltrust.org.uk

National Vocational Qualifications (NVQs): a range of qualifications introduced by the government in the 1990s to raise standards in the workplace by creating a highly skilled, flexible and qualified workforce. NVQs (Scottish Vocational Qualifications/SVQs in Scotland) are designed to test skills and competence in the workplace, rather than knowledge, in a particular industry sector. NVQs/SVQs are based on *occupational standards* developed by *Industry Lead Bodies* and *National Training Organisations*, which have documented appropriate tasks and skills for employees at different levels of experience. NVQs/SVQs are available in specific sectors of the leisure and tourism industries, including travel services, sport and recreation, cultural heritage, hotel and catering, and management. They are offered at five levels, from basic skills at level 1 to professional skills at level 5. The development of NVQs is overseen by the *Qualifications and Curriculum Authority*. (See also *General National Vocational Qualifications*, *Advanced Vocational Certificate in Vocational Education*.)

natural attractions are an important element of the *attractions* sector of the *tourism* industry. Unlike *man-made attractions*, which are purpose-built facilities, natural attractions include the *National Parks*, *Areas of Outstanding Natural Beauty* and *Heritage Coasts* in England and Wales. Britain has an abundance of natural attractions, in its fine landscapes, rugged mountains, beautiful coastline, inland waterways and picturesque dales. They are magnets for UK residents and *overseas visitors*.

natural disasters can have dramatic consequences on a country's tourism industry. Events such as flooding, hurricanes, forest fires and earthquakes can literally wipe out a nation's tourism revenue overnight, which can take many years to recover to its former levels.

Nature Conservancy Council (NCC): see *English Nature*

NAW: see *National Assembly for Wales*

NCC: see *Nature Conservancy Council*

NCF: see *National Coaching Foundation*

NCVO: see *National Council for Voluntary Organisations*

NCVQ: see *National Council for Vocational Qualifications*

NEC: see *National Exhibition Centre*

needs are an important consideration for all producers of leisure and tourism facilities and services, since they have a direct bearing on *demand*. *Maslow's hierarchy of needs* shows us that all human beings have needs in their lives, for example self-expression, ego and security. *Leisure* can help an individual fulfil his or her needs and contribute to a sense of well being. A person's needs will vary with age and family circumstances and will affect demand for leisure, travel and tourism products and services.

negative impacts of tourism can be:

- economic, e.g. the rise in house prices in popular tourist areas

- environmental, e.g. *erosion* of footpaths in 'honey pot' areas

- socio-cultural, e.g. the loss of language and cultural traditions in *developing countries*.

Organisations such as *Tourism Concern* campaign to minimise tourism's negative impacts. (See also *economic impacts of leisure, travel and tourism; environmental impacts of leisure, travel and tourism; socio-cultural impacts of leisure, travel and tourism.*)

Neptune Coastline Campaign: see *Enterprise Neptune*

net current assets: see *working capital*

net profit is the difference between a company's *sales* revenue and its total *costs*. Sometimes called operating profit, it can be expressed either before or after deducting items such as taxation, *depreciation* and finance charges.

net profit/sales ratio is an important measure of an organisation's financial performance, giving a figure for profit (or loss) made per £ of income. It is calculated as follows:

$$\frac{\text{net profit (before tax)}}{\text{sales}} \times 100$$

The percentage profit on sales varies between different sectors, so it is essential to compare the ratio with similar businesses and also to make allowance for prevailing economic conditions.

network: a group of computers each with a cable connecting it to a central *computer* (the file server), allowing the simultaneous use of computer applications on a number of different machines. The file server is able to send and receive signals over these cables and store information on its large fixed disk. Computers linked in this way in a single facility are sometimes said to be part of a local area network (LAN).

Network Rail: an engineering company that took over the work begun by *Railtrack*. Network Rail is responsible for improving and upgrading every aspect of the UK rail infrastructure, including the track, signalling systems, bridges, viaducts, tunnels, level crossings and stations. Weblink: www.railtrack.co.uk

networking is liaising with business contacts to create new opportunities for business activities. On a worldwide basis, networking can be carried out electronically using *e-mail* and *video conferencing*, but it is most often associated with face-to-face meetings at, for example, conferences, exhibitions and seminars.

New Opportunities Fund (NOF): a sixth 'good cause' added to the list of distributors of *National Lottery* funds in 1998. NOF awards grants to education, health and environment projects throughout the UK. Many of its grant programmes focus particularly on those in society who are most disadvantaged, for whatever reason. NOF has funded projects such as healthy living centres, out of school clubs for children, childcare schemes, computers in public libraries and improving local green spaces. Weblink: www.nof.org.uk

new tourist: an emerging term used to identify a particular type of tourist who displays a number of characteristics, including:

- a wish to be more independent in their holiday habits
- greater travel experience
- more environmental awareness
- computer literacy
- greater flexibility in travel arrangements
- more health conscious
- more conscious of *quality*.

Travel companies have identified these 'new tourists' as a *niche market* that is looking for more than a conventional two-week *package holiday* in the sun. Analysts believe that this segment of the market will grow in size in years to come, particularly as a result of the growth of the *Internet*.

news release: see *press release*

NGO: see *non-governmental organisation*

niche marketing is the process of targeting small, readily identifiable sections of a *market*, each with clearly defined characteristics, rather than trying to cover it all. By their very nature, specialist *tour operators* develop products for niche markets, whether they are wine lovers, collectors of antiques or white water rafters. In leisure and tourism, niche marketing can be a very effective *strategy*, since consumers are often willing to pay a premium for a more exclusive product, e.g. a flight on Concorde or a trip on the Venice-Simplon Orient Express.

NITB: see *Northern Ireland Tourist Board*

NLG: see *National Liaison Group for Higher Education in Tourism in the UK*

NNR: see *National Nature Reserve*

no-frills airline: see *low-cost airline*

no show: the term used to denote a hotel guest or traveller with a reservation who fails to turn up without any prior notification. In some circumstances, a deposit may be forfeited or the individual may be liable for the full value of the reservation. Operators sometimes *overbook* in order to compensate for anticipated no shows.

NOF: see *New Opportunities Fund*

Noise at Work Regulations 1989: a set of very technical regulations, which came into force on January 1 1990, requiring managers and operators of facilities to monitor noise levels and take appropriate action to control any adverse effects. This may result in the wearing of ear defenders by staff or the reduction in the volume of music at *events*.

non-commercial organisations are *public* and *voluntary sector organisations* that are seeking to achieve non-commercial *objectives* and that do not have profit maximisation as their prime aim. In leisure, travel and tourism, organisations such as the *National Trust* and *Youth Hostels Association* are non-commercial, but nonetheless are accountable for the wise use of their financial resources. (See also *commercial organisations*.)

non-executive director: a part-time employee of a *company* appointed to its board of directors because of his or her broad knowledge of industry or because they have political influence. Their knowledge and contacts may prove useful in determining *policy* or securing funding or contracts. Non-executive directors may be the representatives of large *shareholders* who are keen to see that their interests are safeguarded.

non-governmental organisation (NGO): an independent international body, free from government influence, established by individuals, charities or other organisations, to pursue a specific aim. The NGO creates its own organisational structure and is normally subject to the law of the nation in which its headquarters are located. NGOs often assume the role of *pressure groups*, for example Greenpeace, *World Wide Fund for Nature* and *Tourism Concern*.

non-verbal communication (NVC) is the process by which we send and receive messages without the use of spoken or written words. We all use our eyes, hands and facial expressions to emphasise points and to confirm information we have received. These are all examples of *body language*, the most common type of NVC. In the leisure and tourism industries, it is important to develop listening and observation skills, so as to be able to operate as an effective individual or member of a team.

non-user survey: a type of *research* activity concerned with discovering why people are not using or buying a particular product, service or facility. In leisure, travel and tourism, it is often very useful to have this sort of information in order to be able to make changes in the light of the research findings.

norming: the stage of team development that is concerned with setting guidelines and standards of acceptable behaviour under which the team will operate. The *storming* stage should have united the group, while the norming stage sets the parameters within which all *team members* will seek to achieve their *objectives*. (See also *forming, performing*.)

North West Tourist Board is the official *Regional Tourist Board* covering the counties of Cheshire, Merseyside, Greater Manchester, Lancashire and the High Peak District of Derbyshire. Weblink: www.visitnorthwest.com

Northern Ireland Sports Council: a government-funded body established as the lead facilitator in the development of *sport* in Northern Ireland. It works with a range of partners to increase and sustain participation in sport (particularly by young people) and raise standards of sporting excellence. The Council is also responsible for distributing *Lottery Sports Fund* awards to worthy projects, such as improvements to sports facilities, supporting elite athletes and hosting major international sporting events. Weblink: www.sportni.org

Northern Ireland Tourist Board (NITB) is the official *tourist board* responsible for tourism *promotion* and *development* in Northern Ireland. Established under the Development of Tourist Traffic Act (N Ireland) in 1948, the NITB is funded primarily by grant-in-aid from the Northern Ireland Assembly. The aims of the NITB are to encourage UK residents and *overseas visitors* to visit the province, by providing advice to tourism businesses, funding tourism projects, co-ordinating the *tourist information centre network* in Northern Ireland, running *marketing campaigns* and advising *central* and *local governments*. With the recent moves towards permanent peace in Northern Ireland, the NITB has joined forces with the Irish Tourist Board south of the border on major national and international promotional campaigns to attract tourists to the whole of the island of Ireland. Weblink: www.discovernorthernireland.com

Northumbria Tourist Board is the official *Regional Tourist Board* covering the counties of Northumberland, Tyne and Wear, Durham and the Tees valley area. Weblink: www.ntb.org.uk

not-for-profit: a term which is increasingly being used to denote an organisation whose prime *objective* is not profit maximisation. Examples include voluntary societies, local clubs, charities and national organisations such as the *National Trust*. Although not primarily concerned with making a profit, these organisations must, nevertheless, be seen to be making the best use of their resources at all times.

NPFA: see *National Playing Fields Association*

NRA: see *National Rivers Authority*

NTB: see *Northumbria Tourist Board*

NTO: see *National Tourism Organisation, National Training Organisation*

NVC: see *non-verbal communication*

NVQs: see *National Vocational Qualifications*

NWTB: see *North West Tourist Board*

Do you need revision help and advice?

Go to pages 265–75 for a range of revision appendices that include plenty of exam advice and tips.

OAG: stands for Overseas Airways Guides, one of the leading companies supplying flight schedule information and publications relating to hotels and tourism destinations. Customers of OAG include airlines, airports, business travellers, travel agents and travel organisers. Weblink: www.oag.com

objectives are *aims* or *goals* that individuals and organisations set themselves, and which determine the *strategies* they undertake and the best use of their *resources*. Objectives may be short-term, e.g. an airline achieving a *load factor* of 95 per cent for its coming winter flight programme, or long-term, e.g. to be the number one *tour operator* from the UK to South America. Long-term objectives are usually contained in an organisation's *policy* and may be reflected in its *mission statement*. To be useful for management purposes, objectives must be clear, realistic, achievable and set within a stated time scale (see *SMART objectives*). The principal objective of a commercial organisation will be profit maximisation, whereas non-commercial bodies will have wider *social objectives*, such as promoting *community recreation*. An organisation's objectives will be determined by those who have an interest in its affairs, sometimes referred to as *stakeholders*.

objectives of tourism development: as the figure below shows these can be economic, environmental, political or socio-cultural. Many governments and *local authorities* often cite economic objectives, such as creating jobs and earning foreign currency, as the prime motivation for developing tourism. (See also *tourism development*.)

The objectives of tourism development

observation is the process of gathering *market research* information by direct observation of *customers* and their movements. Often carried out with the help of sophisticated electronic techniques such as *closed-circuit TV* and *tally counters*, observation is used by management as a way of making alterations to systems and equipment, e.g. observation of the traffic flow at a major *theme park* may highlight the need for the separation of people from vehicles for safety reasons. On occasions, staff may be asked to 'mingle' anonymously with visitors and to eavesdrop on their conversations; people are often far more honest about their true feelings when talking in private, than when asked questions as part of a *survey*.

occupancy rate: a measure of how successful a *hotel* or other *accommodation* provider is at filling available bedspaces over a given period of time. It is calculation of the number of rooms occupied as a proportion of total rooms available, expressed on a percentage basis. Sometimes referred to as room occupancy, it is a similar performance measure to the *load factors* used by airlines.

occupational standards are standards of performance recognised by an industry sector as being necessary for the satisfactory completion of work tasks. A travel clerk, for example, is likely to need skills and competence in selling, using *IT* systems, fare calculations, knowledge of overseas resorts and *customer care*, to name but a few. As part of the government initiative to introduce *National Vocational Qualifications (NVQs), Industry Lead Bodies* and *National Training Organisations* have been given the task of identifying occupational standards for their particular sector. The standards, sometimes called workplace standards, are ultimately endorsed by the *Qualifications and Curriculum Authority* and form the basis for the development of the NVQs.

Occupiers' Liability Act 1984: *legislation* stating that the operator of a leisure and tourism facility owes a legal duty to all the people who use it, including visitors, contract workers, full-time staff and spectators, to ensure that it is reasonably safe for its intended purpose. This would include, for example, making sure that seating for spectators is safe. As well as a duty to those on the premises, occupiers also have a duty to their neighbours and others living nearby. For example, a golf ball striking a pedestrian walking on a *public right of way* alongside the 18th fairway of a golf course, is likely to result in a successful claim for negligence against the golf course owner, if the incident could reasonably have been foreseen.

OCR: an independent examinations and awarding body that offers a range of educational qualifications, including *vocational qualifications* in leisure, travel and tourism. It was formed in 1998 from the merger of the University of Cambridge Local Examinations Syndicate and the Royal Society for the Arts. OCR is accountable to the *Qualifications and Curriculum Authority*. (See also *Edexcel, AQA*.) Weblink: www.ocr.org.uk

OECD: see *Organisation for Economic Co-operation and Development*

off-the-job training is *training* that takes place away from a person's normal place of work. Some leisure and tourism organisations make use of 'day release' courses at local colleges, sometimes leading to *National Vocational Qualifications*. Evening classes are also popular in sectors such as travel and leisure centre management, while *distance learning* is increasingly used for *management* and supervisory training. Many organisations have found that *customer care* and foreign language training are particularly beneficial for staff working in leisure and tourism. (See also *on-the-job training*.)

Office for National Statistics (ONS): a government agency responsible to the Chancellor of the Exchequer for providing up-to-date, comprehensive and meaningful data on the UK's economy and society. ONS provides a great deal of information of use to the leisure, travel and tourism industries in the UK, gathered in surveys such as the census, *International Passenger Survey* and *General Household Survey*. Much of the data is made available to the general public in a range of publications, including *Social Trends*. Launched in 2001, ONS replaced the *Office of Population, Censuses and Surveys*. Weblink: www.statistics.gov.uk

Office of Fair Trading (OFT): established under the Fair Trading Act 1973, the OFT is the main government body responsible for monitoring and controlling trading activities in the interests of the general public. The increasing trend in the *travel industry* of tour operators owning travel agency chains and even their own airlines (*vertical integration*), has led the OFT to consider if such activity is against the public interest. The OFT also considers whether takeover bids should be investigated by the *Competition Commission* (formerly the *Monopolies and Mergers Commission*). The OFT also advises industry bodies on the content and wording of *codes of conduct*. Weblink: www.oft.gov.uk

Office of the National Lottery (OFLOT) is the government agency responsible, through the *Department for Culture, Media and Sport*, for the smooth running of the *National Lottery*. Established under the 1993 National Lottery Act, OFLOT has a duty to ensure that the Lottery is run with 'due propriety', that the interests of all participants in the Lottery are protected and that the maximum amount possible is raised for the good causes. From 1999, the Office became part of the National Lottery Commission. Weblink: www.natlotcomm.gov.uk

Office of Population Censuses and Surveys (OPCS): a former government department that commissioned and co-ordinated a number of important statistical surveys, including the *General Household Survey* and the *Census*. This type of work is now the responsibility of the *Office for National Statistics*.

off-line: a term meaning that a *computer* is being operated without a cable or telephone connection to another computer or central *database*. Although a computer may well have such a connection, it saves money if it can be used for some of the time 'off-line', thereby saving on telephone rental or cable usage charges.

off-peak refers to the time outside of the most popular dates and times for holidays (known as the *peak season*). For overseas *package holidays* from the UK, this tends to be any time outside of the school holidays, the period of peak demand. Tourists gain by travelling off-peak, with reduced prices and other *incentives* and offers. The operators of leisure and tourism facilities are keen to extend the peak season into off-peak periods so as to increase their *revenue*, while tourist boards promote off-peak travel as a way of providing year-round employment in the industry and reducing the harmful impacts of tourism. (See also *shoulder period*.)

OFLOT: see *Office of the National Lottery*

OFT: see *Office of Fair Trading*

Olympic Games: an international athletic event held in a different host city every four years and attracting competitors from the majority of countries of the world. Divided into summer and winter events, the first modern Olympic Games was held in 1896 in Athens, based on the original Games first held in 776 BC. The Games have come to signify the pinnacle of human sporting achievement. Athens is to host the Olympic Games again in 2004. (See also International *Olympic Committee, British Olympic Association*.)

OMR: see *optical mark reading*

on-line: a term indicating that a *computer* is linked in some way to another terminal or a central *database*, either by a fixed cable of via a telephone line. A number of global communications companies offer a range of 'on-line' services to computer users, such as access to the *Internet*, financial *data* and travel information.

on-the-job training is any form of *training* that occurs in the workplace. Many jobs in *leisure* and *tourism* are ideally suited to this type of 'hands on' training, e.g. learning to operate a *VDU* in a travel agency, working in a plant room at a *leisure centre* or training to be a chef in a restaurant or hotel. On-the-job training often gives employees the opportunity of gaining *National Vocational Qualifications*, giving staff credit for competence-based training related to the world of work. (See also *off-the-job training*.)

one-way communication: the process of passing a message or conveying information without receiving a response from the recipient. Examples of one-way communication methods in leisure, travel and tourism include notices, newsletters, signs, memoranda, reports and letters. One-way communication is an effective medium if no *feedback* is required from individuals or groups, but is ineffective if a response is needed. In such circumstances, *two-way communication* is preferable.

ONS: see *Office for National Statistics*

OPCS: see *Office of Population Censuses and Surveys*

open-jaw is a travel arrangement consisting of a different departure and arrival point for a return journey, e.g. a train journey from Manchester to Leeds and then on to Sheffield.

open question: one that allows a *respondent* to give an expanded reply to a question, rather than inviting a specific response from within a small selection of replies, as is the case with a *closed question*. Examples of open questions are 'which company have you travelled with in the past?' and 'which country are you thinking of visiting?' Open questions allow sales staff to quickly establish a rapport with a *customer*. They are also useful for survey work, when in-depth analysis is required, e.g. in a *focus group*.

operating profit: see *net profit*

operations management is concerned with the *planning* and use of an organisation's *resources* in order to meet its customers' needs. It is both a strategic process, focusing on the overall allocation of human, financial and physical resources to meet an organisation's *objectives*, and the operation of a company or facility on a day-to-day basis. It is the job of the operations manager to link the resources of an organisation to actual *demand* for its products and services, ensuring satisfied customers and an acceptable rate of return on investment.

opportunities: see *SWOT analysis*

opportunities to see (OTS) is a term used in the *advertising* industry to denote the number of occasions an advertisement could feasibly be seen by its intended audience, e.g. an advertisement placed for three consecutive days in a newspaper with a circulation of 1.5 million per day would equate to an OTS of 4.5 million.

opportunity cost is a term used by economists to indicate the monetary cost or other advantage that is lost when a particular course of action is taken. For example, a *local authority* which decides to use its capital resources to build an ice rink rather than a swimming pool could evaluate the opportunity cost of its decision, including the fact that local swimmers are denied a *leisure* opportunity.

optical mark reading (OMR) is a technique used in the analysis of *questionnaires* and other survey documents, to speed up the process and reduce error. OMR equipment automatically 'reads' the written responses marked on a questionnaire by an interviewer or respondent and transmits the data to an automated system, usually linked to appropriate computer software. OMR is particularly useful when a large number of responses is being analysed.

option is a term used in the travel business to describe a booking for a holiday or flight that has been reserved for a client pending his or her final confirmation. The option is held for a specific period of time to give the customer time to consider the purchase and pay the deposit.

ordinary shares are certificates which give their owners (*shareholders*) the right to a share of the profits of a *company*. The annual payment that an ordinary shareholder receives is known as a *dividend*, and will vary from one year to another depending on the profits earned by the company. *Dividends* are only paid to ordinary *shareholders* once all other calls on a company's profits have been met. (See also *preference shares*, *debentures*.)

organisation chart: a diagram showing, at a given moment in time, patterns of *authority*, lines of *communication*, division of *responsibilities* and work relationships, within an organisation. Organisation charts vary greatly, some being very rigid, others more fluid and responsive to change. It is important to remember that leisure and tourism organisations operate in a very dynamic and competitive environment and that any organisation chart should be seen as temporary and liable to change in response to *opportunities* and *threats*. (See also *organisational structures*.)

Organisation for Economic Co-operation and Development (OECD): an alliance established in 1961 of countries drawn from the developed world to act as a forum for discussion on global economic and trade issues. In the field of *tourism*, the OECD has an input into *tourism planning* in individual countries, particularly in developing countries, and regularly produces statistical data and reports on global travel and *tourism development*. Weblink: www.oecd.org

organisation of sport occurs at many levels. Bodies such as the *International Olympic Committee* and *International Sports Federations* have global remits in respect of sport. At national level in the UK, the *Department for Culture, Media and Sport* oversees the work of *Sport England* (the English Sports Council) and *UK Sport*, and provides funding for their activities. *Governing bodies and local authorities* also have important roles to play in the organisation of sport. (See also *Northern Ireland Sports Council, Scottish Sports Council, Sports Council for Wales*.)

organisational structures: the systems for allocating tasks and responsibilities within an organisation to aid decision making and the ultimate achievement of its goals. All but the smallest of leisure or tourism enterprises will need a clearly defined organisational structure, so that day-to-day operations and longer term *planning* are effective. A clear organisational structure will help to:

- define lines of *communication*
- identify sources of authority and *responsibility*

- clarify relationships between individual workers or departments
- identify the pattern of control for external and internal parties.

In small enterprises the organisational structure is likely to be simple, with relationships between staff roles developing on an informal basis. Larger organisations require a more complex *hierarchical* organisational structure, with more formal lines of *communication* and interaction between staff and departments. The nature of organisational structures varies greatly between one enterprise and another, depending on a range of external and internal factors. Some will be *centralised*, bureaucratic structures, while others will opt for *decentralisation*, where decision making is devolved down from senior management. (See also *'steep' pyramid*, *'flat' pyramid*.)

OTS: see *opportunities to view*

outbound tourism is a form of *international tourism* which concerns people travelling away from their main country of residence for leisure or business purposes. Examples of outbound tourism would be a couple travelling from London to Brussels on the *Eurostar* train service or a businesswoman flying from Birmingham to Paris for a sales conference. The number of overseas holidays taken by British people has risen steadily in recent years, from 15.5 million in 1984, to 26.25 million in 1994 and 38 million in 2002, of which 21 million were *package holidays*. This growing trend is at the expense of holidays taken at home which have fallen over the same period of time. Indeed, in 1998 for the first time ever the number of long (4+ nights) holidays taken by the British abroad exceeded the number taken in the UK.

outdoor activities: a wide-ranging term that can include any physical activity carried out in the open air, but which is most often associated with organised group activities held in outdoor facilities, e.g. canoeing, camping, orienteering, abseiling and rock climbing. Outdoor activity centres in the UK are operated in the public, private and voluntary sectors of the *leisure and recreation industry*, with many urban local authorities owning centres in the countryside for school children to use. The safety of outdoor centres was the subject of much debate in the 1990s, following the Lyme Bay canoeing tragedy in 1993 when four teenagers died. Incidents such as this led to the establishment of the *Adventure Activities Licensing Authority* to regulate outdoor activity centres. (See also *adventure activities*.)

outgoing tourism: see *outbound tourism*

outreach is the name given to work undertaken away from a leisure facility to help determine local needs and particularly to encourage participation by under-represented groups and individuals. *Local authorities* can sometimes secure funding to appoint officers to undertake specific projects in their local communities with, for example, *ethnic minorities* and disabled people.

Outward Bound is the trading name of the Outward Bound Trust Limited, an organisation that organises courses for anybody between the ages of 14 and 50 plus. As well as outdoor activity programmes, Outward Bound run a series of personal development events, specialist training courses and events that contribute towards gaining the *Duke of Edinburgh's Award*, at its centres in Wales, the Lake District and Scotland. Weblink: www.outwardbound-uk.org

overbooking is the practice of selling more seats on an aircraft, or other form of transport, or rooms in *accommodation*, than are actually available. This is sometimes merely a mistake on the part of the provider, but more often than not it is designed to compensate for the failure of people to turn up (*no shows*). It is common practice for airlines to overbook, offering generous compensation or *upgrades* on future flights if the plane becomes full.

over-commercialisation is a term that is sometimes used to describe large *tourist destinations* and facilities that have grown too quickly and with little prior *planning* or effective *tourism management*, often causing environmental and socio-cultural problems for *host communities*.

overdraft: a type of borrowing available to both individuals and organisations used primarily to finance short-term cash deficiencies. Overdrafts are provided by banks for a fixed period of time and up to an agreed maximum limit. Overdrafts are usually offered to a borrower at a lower rate of interest than a *loan*, and may not require *security*. They are a very flexible way of meeting temporary *cash-flow* problems, often important given the peaks and troughs of activity experienced by many *leisure* and *tourism* operators.

overheads are *costs* associated with a business that tend to be *fixed* and which are not readily allocated to a particular activity. Typical overheads (sometimes referred to as indirect costs) in leisure and tourism include energy costs, rent, *Uniform Business Rates*, insurance, salaries and equipment *leasing* costs. (See also *fixed costs, direct costs*.)

override commission is a payment made over and above any existing *commission* earned by an agent. This may be as an incentive to boost sales or where a travel agent acts on a sole agency basis in a town for, say, the supply of foreign currency.

overseas representative: see *courier*

Overseas Visitor Survey (OVS): a former annual *survey* of the behavioural patterns and opinions of visitors to Britain, conducted on behalf of the *British Tourist Authority*. OVS has been superseded by the *International Passenger Survey*.

overseas visitors are a very important part of any country's *tourism* industry, helping to create and sustain jobs, provide income to businesses, improve local environments, contribute to tax revenues, and support music and the arts. Spending by the 22.8 million overseas visitors to Britain in 2001 amounted to more than £11 billion. Tourists are attracted to Britain's culture, heritage and history, as well as its countryside, cities and coastline.

OVS: see *Overseas Visitor Survey*

What other subjects are you studying?

A–Zs cover 18 different subjects. See the inside back cover for a list of all the titles in the series and how to order.

PA: see *public address, personal assistant*

Pacific Asia Travel Association (PATA): a *marketing* body, responsible for the Pacific Asia region, whose aim is to foster co-operation between the various private and public *tourism* concerns in the area and to promote its destinations direct to tourists and through the *travel trade*. PATA fulfils a similar role to the *European Travel Commission* in Europe. Weblink: www.pata.org

package holiday: an all-inclusive holiday, sometimes referred to as a package tour or inclusive tour, which normally consists of three components:

- *accommodation*
- *transportation*
- other services, e.g. *courier* support, excursions, etc.

Package holidays are put together by *tour operators* and offered for sale by *travel agents*, although it is possible to book direct with some package holiday companies. The popularity of package holidays has grown dramatically since they were first introduced in the UK in the early 1960s. In 1991 10.6 million overseas package holidays were sold in the UK, to destinations such as Majorca, mainland Spain, Greece, Turkey and Cyprus. By 2002, this figure had risen to 21 million, according to data from the *Association of British Travel Agents* (ABTA). The economic well-being of many Mediterranean countries rests heavily on their tourism industries and, in particular, the package tourists from the UK and other Western European countries. There is some evidence to suggest that the growth in package holidays has reached its peak and that what will change in the future is not the total number of packages sold, but the countries on offer, with *long haul destinations* set for continued growth.

package tour: see *package holiday*

Package Travel Directive: this *EU Directive* (full title the Package Travel, Package Holidays and Package Tours Directive) came into operation on January 1 1993 in the 12 member states of the *European Union* (now 15, soon to be 25). Its main aim is to give people buying package holidays greater protection in law and access to compensation when things go wrong. The Directive places a number of duties on the organisers of *package holidays*, including providing clear contract terms, giving emergency telephone numbers, providing a variety of compensation options if the agreed services are not supplied, producing accurate promotional materials including brochures and providing proof of the organiser's security against *insolvency*. The Package Travel Directive has come as something of a shock to the UK tourist industry, since the Directive covers *domestic tourism* as well as holidays taken abroad. This means that hotels, tourist information centres, resort offices, conference organisers, coach operators and even school trip organisers have discovered that they may well fall within the scope of the Directive.

parador: a type of *serviced accommodation* available in Spain, often using converted buildings of historic interest, such as castles and abbeys. Paradors are controlled by the Spanish National Tourist Office and can be found all over Spain, particularly in country districts off the beaten track. Tour operators use paradors as the basis for *fly-drive* and other touring packages. (See also *pousada*.)

Pareto principle: the rule stating that 80 per cent of the benefits in a *company* tend to come from 20 per cent of the items sold. Conversely, 80 per cent of breakdowns will come from 20 per cent of the machines. In *travel and tourism*, it is a well known fact that around 80 per cent of *package holidays* are sold through 20 per cent of the retail agents. The clear message from the Pareto principle, also known as the eighty/twenty rule, is that managers should concentrate their efforts on the key 20 per cent rather than spread their *resources* too thinly.

parish council: see *community council*

park and ride: a scheme to help ease traffic congestion in city centres and other popular tourist resorts. *Visitors* are encouraged to leave their cars at a point outside the town and travel instead by public transport, which may be a bus, tram or train. Popular UK tourist cities, including Cambridge, York and Oxford, operate such schemes in order to provide a more pleasant experience for visitors.

participation in sport: see *sports participation*

partnership: a form of business unit composed of between two and 20 people working in common with a view to making a profit. Partnerships are common in the *accommodation* sector of leisure and tourism, for example hotels and guesthouses. Although partnerships have some advantages over *sole traders* (such as shared risks and access to extra funds for expansion) each partner is still liable for all trading debts; in other words, they do not enjoy the benefit of *limited liability* as is the case with a limited company. Also, the decision of any one partner is binding on the others, which may cause problems if an individual proves to be unreliable or untrustworthy. Not all those involved in a partnership will neces- sarily be concerned with the day-to-day management of the enterprise; firms sometimes have 'sleeping partners' who merely invest money in the partnership in the hope of a healthy return.

Passenger Shipping Association (PSA): an independent body representing the interests of UK-based ferry companies and cruise ship operators. Originally established in 1958 as the Ocean Travel Development, the PSA liaises with government and the *travel trade* to raise the profile of shipping and lobbies on behalf of its members on such matters as *duty-free* sales and safety issues. In recent years, the PSA has initiated an extensive educational campaign, known as *PSARA*, aimed at *travel agency* staff to encourage the sales of shipping products to the public. Weblink: www.psa.org

passive leisure activity: any activity carried out in a person's *leisure time* that requires little active commitment, e.g. watching television, reading, knitting, listening to music, etc. Many passive leisure activities form part of *home-based leisure*. (See also *active leisure activity*.)

passport: an official document which confirms the nationality of an individual when travel- ling between countries. The move towards greater integration in the *European Union* has resulted in an easing of border controls and less inspection of passports by some member states.

PATA: see *Pacific Asia Travel Association*

payroll is the department within an organisation that deals with all matters relating to the payment of wages and salaries, including tax deductions, superannuation payments, *trade union* subscriptions, National Insurance payments and other regular deductions. The term is also used to indicate the total salary and wages bill of an organisation and the number of people it employs.

PC: see *personal computer*

peak season refers to the time of greatest *demand* for holidays and other travel products, e.g. the winter months for skiing holidays and the summer months for overseas *package holidays* to the Mediterranean. Holidaymakers will pay the highest prices in peak season, so it makes sense for those people who can travel *off-peak* to do so. The times either side of the peak season are known as *shoulder periods*.

peer appraisal involves the evaluation of the performance of members of staff by the other people in their peer group, e.g. their work colleagues. Formal peer appraisal is more constructive than informal peer appraisal, since it can prevent the exercise becoming too personalised. If managed effectively peer appraisal can be very enlightening and help to identify any strengths and weaknesses present in members of staff, who can use the outcomes to identify any remedial measures that may be necessary as part of their *career development*.

peer group: the people that an individual works or socialises with on a regular basis, whose opinions and attitudes may be highly influential, e.g. the peer group of a recreation assistant at a *leisure centre* will be the other staff that he or she works with on a day-to-day basis.

peer pressure: the influence that others from within the same *peer group* can have on an individual and his or her actions and experiences. In a work situation, this pressure can be both beneficial, in that it may motivate an individual to work harder, and harmful, in creating undue stress and anxiety, thereby affecting work performance.

PEL: see *Public Entertainments Licence*

penetration pricing: a pricing method that is used by organisations wanting to break into a new *market*, where suppliers of the same product or service already exist. Prices are set sufficiently low to persuade *customers* to switch their allegiance. A new health and fitness club, for example, opening in a city where other clubs already exist, may offer reduced membership fees to entice people away from their current clubs. Sometimes referred to as a 'loss leader', it is important that penetration pricing is seen as a medium to long term *strategy,* since customers will resent an early increase in prices. (See also *contribution pricing*.)

pension: a payment, which may be a lump sum or an amount paid regularly, made to an individual once he or she has retired from work. All UK citizens are entitled to receive a state pension when they reach retirement age. Nowadays, many people are part of company pension schemes or take out personal pensions in order to supplement their state pension. Company schemes are either contributory, where a member of staff pays a certain amount towards the pension, or non-contributory, when all pension payments are made by the employer. It is usual for both employers and employees to pay into a pension fund. Some people make extra payments, known as *additional voluntary contributions*, to top up a pension and give themselves a bigger pension on retirement. Many experts believe that there will be problems in the future with pensions in the UK, given that people are living longer and there is a general trend towards taking early retirement.

perceptual capacity: see *carrying capacity*

performance indicator (PI) is a management device used to evaluate the *efficiency* and *effectiveness* of an organisation or individual. At senior *management* level, the most important PIs are those that help with the evaluation of financial and operational performance, for example the income per visitor to a *theme park* or the number of staff employed per 1000 seats sold in an arena. The *hospitality* sector of leisure and tourism has long used PIs to evaluate performance and, as such, there is a wealth of information available that can facilitate performance evaluation both within a particular hotel and even between hotels with similar characteristics. In the leisure and recreation sector, the *Chartered Institute of Public Finance and Accountancy* publishes comprehensive data on the finances and operation of *leisure centres*, which is useful for comparative purposes. (See also *financial ratios*.)

performance-related pay (PRP): remuneration that is linked to an employee's performance in the workplace, e.g. a *travel agent* being paid a bonus for every 10 holidays sold with a particular *tour operator*. PRP can act as an incentive for staff to work harder and thereby increase an organisation's *profitability*.

performance standards are targets against which the performance of an individual or organisation can be measured. These could be concerned with financial performance, *market share*, levels of *customer service*, operational efficiency, etc. In leisure and tourism, much work is currently in progress to devise *occupational standards* in particular sectors of the industries, as a way of establishing minimum criteria for particular tasks and to act as a starting point for the development of *National Vocational Qualifications*.

performing is the final stage in team development, when its members have moved through the *forming*, *storming* and *norming* stages, and are in a position to perform their roles and achieve the team's *objectives*, under the direction of the *team leader*.

perishability is a feature of leisure and tourism *products*, since an airline seat, theatre ticket or coach seat for use today cannot be resold tomorrow. Perishability makes leisure and tourism operators introduce techniques to maximise current sales, such as *standby* fares and late availability discounts.

perks is shorthand for perquisites, meaning any benefits that an employee receives over and above his or her salary or wages. Perks, also called fringe benefits, are common in leisure and tourism, and are seen as a way of supplementing sometimes low basic pay. One of the most widespread perks is the right to buy or use facilities and services either free or at discounted prices, for example discounted flights for *travel agents*, free use of leisure facilities for *recreation* workers and discounted rates at hotels for employees and their friends. Perks are an important way of rewarding loyalty and helping reduce staff turnover.

person specification: see *job specification*

personal assistant (PA): an employee who works closely with a senior member of staff and assumes a high degree of *responsibility,* particularly in his or her absence. PAs perform a range of secretarial and administrative functions, and are chosen for their integrity, *responsibility*, reliability and ability to work under pressure.

personal computer (PC): powerful machines which, since their introduction, have revolutionised the way that individuals and organisations manage their affairs, offering greater speed and capacity than many manual systems. PCs (sometimes called microcomputers) are found extensively in the *leisure* and *tourism* industries, from travel agencies to the desks of managers in *multinational corporations*. PCs are able to run a wide range of *software*, including *wordprocessing, spreadsheets, databases* and communications packages, allowing access to global information systems such as the *Internet*. PCs can be 'stand alone' or 'networked', i.e. joined to other computers and/or a central processor.

personal fitness trainer: a specialist who provides health and fitness training to individuals on a one-to-one basis. The numbers of trainers has grown rapidly in recent years in response to a raised awareness of the importance of fitness and maintaining a healthy lifestyle.

personal hygiene is a vital, if not always mentioned, aspect of employment in leisure, travel and tourism. All staff must pay careful attention to their personal hygiene while on duty so as not to offend or embarrass customers.

personal identification number (PIN): a unique number issued to an individual, often associated with *credit* and *debit cards*, or security codes for gaining entry to restricted areas in a building. PIN numbers, once memorised, should not be divulged to a third party in case of improper use.

personal mobility refers to a person's capacity to move around freely. *Access* to *public transport* and/or *car ownership* gives people greater freedom to take part in a range of leisure, travel and tourism opportunities. Legislation such as the *Disability Discrimination Act 1995* aims to give people with limited mobility greater access to a range of facilities, including those offered by leisure, travel and tourism organisations.

personal presentation is an essential aspect of employment in leisure, travel and tourism. The way that staff present themselves to customers has a direct bearing on the customers' enjoyment, the member of staff's job satisfaction and the future success of the organisation. Employees need to pay careful attention to a number of matters, including appropriate dress, *personal hygiene, personality* and *attitude*.

personal protective equipment (PPE): the Personal Protective Equipment at Work Regulations 1992 were developed as a direct result of the *EU Directives on health and safety*, replacing parts of more than 20 pieces of old law. PPE includes most types of protective clothing and equipment such as eye, foot and head protection, safety harnesses, life jackets and high visibility clothing. Employers must supply PPE free of charge to their employees and have a duty to ensure that it is properly used, stored and maintained.

personal qualities: see *personal skills and qualities*

personal selling: see *selling*

personal skills and qualities can play an important part in *employment in leisure, travel and tourism*. The ability to listen, empathise, take responsibility, communicate and provide leadership can all help staff to offer high standards of *customer care* and assist them in their *career development*.

personal trainer: see *personal fitness trainer*

personality can play an important part in *employment in leisure, travel and tourism*. Some jobs, especially those where dealing with the public is commonplace, require staff with lively, friendly and engaging personalities.

personnel management: see *human resource management (HRM)*

personnel records: see *staff records*

PERT: see *programme evaluation and review technique*

PEST analysis: a technique used by an organisation to investigate the *business environment* in which it operates, with a view to helping determine its future strategies. PEST stands for 'political, economic, social, technological', which are the main factors that influence organisations. The PEST (or STEP – social, technological, economic and political) analysis will vary between different leisure and tourism organisations, but is likely to include reference to:

- political – taxation, government policy, *EU policy*, local government policies
- economic – levels of *disposable income*, exchange rates, unemployment, *inflation*
- social – demographic trends, lifestyle changes, education, changing work practices
- technological – global communications, home leisure, reservation systems, transport developments.

The carrying out of a PEST analysis involves an organisation in an extensive *data* collection exercise, from both internal and external sources.

PEX: see *public excursion fare*

physical recreation: a *leisure* activity that involves some degree of physical effort, as opposed to passive leisure activities such as watching television, knitting and reading. Participation in *sport* is one of the most common types of physical recreation, with over half of the adult population in the UK taking part in sport of some kind on a regular basis. (See also *sports participation*.)

physiotherapist: a specialist trained in the treatment of injuries and strains of the body. It is increasingly common for physiotherapists to treat sports injuries of all kinds. Many professional sports clubs employ full-time physiotherapy staff.

PI: see *performance indicator*

pictogram: a *bar chart* in which the bars are presented in pictorial form. A chart showing levels of *car ownership*, for example, may use symbols of cars to represent the bars, the greater the number of cars the higher the value (see figure on next page).

pie chart: a way of presenting data in which a circle is divided into segments, with each segment representing a share of the total value. Pie charts are particularly useful for giving an approximate idea of different proportions or values, e.g. the number of *overseas visitors* to Britain from each of a range of different countries.

pilot survey: a preliminary *survey* involving a small number of *interviews*, carried out in advance of a main survey, to test whether the *questionnaire* is understood by the *respondents* and the whole of the survey process runs smoothly. The results of the pilot survey are integrated into the main survey to improve the *data* collection process.

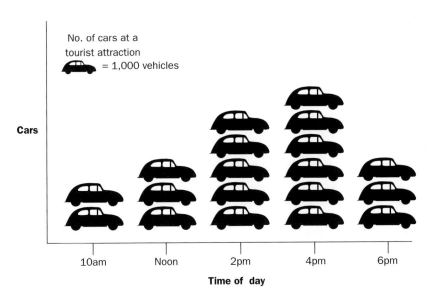

No. of cars at a tourist attraction
= 1,000 vehicles

Cars

10am   Noon   2pm   4pm   6pm

Time of day

An example of a pictogram

PIN: see *personal identification number*

place is one of the four key elements of the *marketing mix* in leisure and tourism, along with *price, promotion* and *product*. Place is concerned with both the location of facilities and the way in which products and services are made available to customers (*distribution channels*). Location can be crucial to the success of an organisation; a farm guesthouse, for example, which is deep in the countryside and well off the beaten track is unlikely to benefit from passing trade, whereas a high street travel agency in a busy location should attract a constant stream of clients. For a leisure company looking for a suitable site for a new *visitor attraction*, the prime location is likely to be close to major centres of population. Location, therefore, is closely linked to accessibility, at the local, regional and national level.

planned maintenance: see *maintenance*

planning: a structured, dynamic process that seeks to provide the right *leisure* and *tourism* facilities, in the best location, at the right time and at the right price, to meet current and future *demand*. In the public sector, planning takes place at a number of levels; at national and regional levels, planning tries to ensure the best mix and geographical spread of facilities in a country or region. Locally, planning is about meeting the needs of communities within the limited resources available. Private sector enterprises also have to plan their future *strategies*, to ensure long-term viability in changing market conditions. It is also the function of planners to ensure that resources are not abused and to promote development that is *sustainable* in the long-term.

planning control: the system implemented by *central* and *local government* to regulate the development of land, buildings and associated *infrastructure*. Sometimes referred to as 'development control', planning control exists to safeguard the environment and protect local communities from unregulated development.

planning permission is required for the construction and alteration of buildings above a certain size, and for change of use of existing buildings. In leisure and tourism, this would include major construction projects, such as the building of a *leisure centre* or an extension to a *hotel*. The conversion of a house into a hotel would also need planning approval, granted by the local district council, under the change of use rules. The need to apply for planning permission exists to protect the environment and local people from unsuitable development. (See also *planning control*.)

planning regulations are the rules and conditions that apply when an individual or organisation seeks *planning permission*. They are contained in Acts of Parliament but are enforced by local councils, sometimes leading to different interpretations in different parts of the country. Planning regulations are particularly strict in the *National Parks* and other protected areas, such as *Sites of Special Scientific Interest* and *Areas of Outstanding Natural Beauty*.

play is an activity carried out in people's *leisure time*, designed to give them pleasure and satisfaction, as well as allowing a degree of self-expression. Play has no age barriers, although it is most usually associated with children's activities; a pre-school child may play in a sand pit, teenagers play musical instruments, middle-age people play sports such as tennis and bowls, while retired couples may play dominoes or cards. Play can be spontaneous, such as children throwing snowballs, or it may be more organised and formal, such as a football match or a tennis tournament. Indeed many games have specific rules associated with them, often regulated by their *governing bodies*. (See also *National Play Information Centre*.)

PLC: see *public limited company*

point-of-sale (POS): usually refers to promotional materials that are displayed at the point where a *customer* makes a sale, e.g. a counter in a *travel agency*, a box office in a theatre or a desk at an airport. In the case of a retail travel agency, typical point-of-sale materials would include posters, hanging cards and window displays.

policy: a statement of the overall *objectives* of an organisation and its *strategies* for achieving these objectives. Larger organisations produce policy documents, which set out clearly what they hope to achieve. (See also *mission statement*.)

political benefits of tourism development could include enhancing the *image* of a country, region or tourist area and helping to create a *regional* or *national identity*.

political instability and unrest can have disastrous impacts on a country's *travel and tourism industry*. The recent examples of war in the Balkans, terrorism in Egypt and the Middle East, and instability in some African states, all highlight the problem.

political unrest: see *political instability*

politics is the term used to describe the affairs of government, at international, national and local level. Politics affect everybody's daily lives; effects include the rate of tax paid on earnings, the state of the roads, what happens in schools, the quality of housing and the defence of the country, to name but a few. To many people, politics equates to power and control of *resources*. We live in a democracy in the UK, meaning that our political representatives are elected to represent the views of the majority of the population. Governments can have a considerable effect on *leisure* and *tourism* in their countries, taking either a positive or negative attitude to the industries. Most countries view tourism positively, as a way of generating foreign exchange, creating jobs and promoting their countries to the outside world. Local politicians devise leisure and tourism policies that should reflect the needs of local communities.

poll tax: see *Community Charge*

pollution is an unfortunate consequence of much *leisure* and *tourism* activity, e.g. noise pollution from events, contamination of waterways by motor craft and pollution of the air from car exhausts and aircraft emissions. Increasing concern for environmental issues has forced organisations to take seriously the impacts they have on the environment. Many developers of leisure and tourism facilities are required to carry out *environmental impact assessments* as part of the *planning* process.

portfolio analysis: the process of examining the current range of products and services offered by an organisation, *forecasting* future needs and putting measures in place to make changes to what is offered to the *customer*. This is most commonly undertaken with the help of the *Ansoff's matrix* model, the *Boston Consulting Group matrix* or a *SWOT analysis*.

portion control is a method of *stock control* used extensively in all sectors of the catering trade to reduce waste, produce consistency and help cost control. Under a system of portion control, the ingredients needed for a complete meal or a particular dish are calculated and agreed in advance. Portions must be constantly monitored and adjusted as necessary, depending on *customer needs*.

POS: see *point-of-sale*

positive action: see *positive discrimination*

positive discrimination: the practice of giving preferential treatment to a section of the community that is currently under-represented. Sometimes referred to as 'positive action', an example in *leisure* and *tourism* would be providing extra facilities and events for *ethnic minority* groups in a community. Positive discrimination may also be possible in recruitment, when it is considered ethical to appoint a person from a particular ethnic background because of the nature of a particular job.

positive impacts of tourism: can be economic, e.g. the creation of jobs in popular tourist areas, environmental, e.g. the improvement of derelict land and waterways, or socio-cultural, e.g. greater understanding between cultures and communities. (See also *economic impacts of leisure, travel and tourism; environmental impacts of leisure, travel and tourism; socio-cultural impacts of leisure, travel and tourism*.)

postal survey: a type of *primary research* that involves mailing a *questionnaire* to a random sample of *respondents* who complete and return the questionnaires by post. Postal surveys are a relatively cheap method of data collection, since there is no need to recruit and train *interviewers*. It is not possible, however, to obtain the same depth of response as in a *face-to-face interview* or *focus group*. *Response rates* can also be relatively low, but may be improved by sending a reminder to the respondents to return their questionnaires.

post-industrial society: the term used to describe the stage reached by many formerly-industrial societies in the latter half of the twentieth century. It is characterised by a decline in traditional primary and secondary industries, such as coal mining, shipbuilding and engineering, in favour of the *service sector* of the economy. The growth of service industries such as banking, information technology, *leisure* and *tourism,* is an important part of the post-industrial society, which is also a period of rapid social changes, e.g. more single parents, improved health care and an *ageing population*.

post-modernism is a philosophy that looks beyond the mass consumption of the post-industrial society and at the underlying social, cultural and political factors that shape late twentieth and early twenty-first century 'Western' society. *Tourism* and *leisure* are essential features of a post-modern culture.

potential demand consists of those people who are not currently using or buying a particular product or service because of a problem on the *demand* side. Such people are likely to buy in the future when their circumstances change, i.e. potential demand will become *effective demand*. The circumstances in question may be that they have a low *disposable income*, no *access* to private transport or a health problem.

potential market: see *market*

pousada: a type of *serviced accommodation* found in Portugal, often made available in converted buildings of historic interest, such as castles, stately homes or abbeys. Pousadas are controlled by the Portuguese Government Tourist Office and can be found all over Portugal, particularly in country districts off the beaten track. *Tour operators* use pousadas as the basis for *fly-drive* and other touring packages. (See also *parador*.)

PPE: see *personal protective equipment*

PR: see *public relations*

PR agency: a firm that works with an organisation to handle some, or all, of its *public relations* work. Larger leisure and tourism organisations regularly use a PR agency to handle all of their links with the *media,* while smaller enterprises may contract with an agency for a specific task or event, for example the launch of a new product or staging an *event*. While some PR agencies are free-standing, many have links with *advertising agencies*.

pre-feasibility study: a brief analysis of a potential project to ascertain whether an organisation should invest further *resources* in having a fully-costed *feasibility study* carried out. A pre-feasibility study concentrates on estimated *revenue* and expenditure, as well as the expected level of *demand*.

preference shares are certificates which give their owners (*shareholders*) the right to a proportion of the profits of a *company*. Preference shares pay a fixed *dividend*, unlike ordinary shares whose return will vary from year to year. In the event of a company going into liquidation, preference shareholders receive priority over ordinary shareholders in terms of dividend payments. (See also *debentures*.)

press conference: a type of *public relations* activity where representatives of the various news *media* are invited to attend a staged event, such as the launch of a major leisure company's annual report or the opening of a new *tourist attraction* by a celebrity, in the hope that the organiser will gain valuable *media coverage* in the press or on television or radio.

press day: an invitation to the *media* to attend an event or facility before it is open to the public, for example a new 'ride' at a *theme park*, or the trade, e.g. the *World Travel Market*. The expectation is that the journalists will include information on the event of facility in their articles and programmes, thereby gaining valuable publicity for the operators. (See also *familiarisation trip*.)

press release: a written document circulated by an organisation to newspapers, magazines, radio, TV stations and other media outlets to keep them informed of current events, with the hope of gaining extra publicity. The issuing of press releases, sometimes called news releases, is an important *public relations* activity, which can form an important part of an overall *promotional strategy*. The disadvantage of press releases is that the originator has no control over what an editor may choose to include or exclude, sometimes leading to a mixed message being given or a remark being taken out of context. Advances in electronic communication mean that press releases are increasingly being sent via *electronic mail*.

pressure group: an organisation that uses the collective talents and beliefs of its members to *campaign* for a particular issue or against a specific proposal. Organisations such as the *Ramblers' Association* and the *Campaign for the Protection of Rural Wales* are actively involved in campaigning on countryside issues and *lobbying* central, local and European politicians to further their cause. Pressure groups sometimes form for a short period of time to fight specific developments, e.g. plans for the expansion of an airport terminal.

Prestel: a *viewdata* system developed by British Telecom and used in travel agencies to access *principal's computerised reservation systems* using a *VDU* plus a telephone line.

price is a crucial element in an organisation's *marketing mix*. Price is influenced by many factors including *demand*, the state of the economy, competitor products and services, the *objectives* of the organisation and the costs of providing a product or service. In leisure and tourism, it is customary to charge different amounts for the same product at different times of the year and even different times of the day, reflecting changes in demand and *seasonality*. A *package holiday* to Spain, for example, will cost more in August than in January, while a round of golf at a local municipal course may well cost more on a Sunday morning than on a Wednesday afternoon. (See also *pricing policy*.)

price determination: the techniques used to arrive at a final price for a product or service. (See also *pricing policy*.)

price research: see *marketing research*

price war: this occurs when one or more competitors decide to reduce their prices for a product or service in the hope of gaining market share. For example, when the *Channel Tunnel* first opened there was a price war between *Le Shuttle* and the ferry operators on the Dover–Calais route. If a price war continues over a long period of time, it is likely that one of the competing companies will be forced out of business, since it will be unable to stand the losses. This has, indeed, happened on cross-Channel routes with a reduction in the number of companies offering services. (See also *competitor activity*.)

pricing policy: the practice of determining the price for a *product* or range of products, within an organisation's overall *objectives*. Setting a pricing policy is notoriously difficult with leisure and tourism products given the volatility of the industry and its *customers,* the perishable nature of the products on offer, the influence of *seasonality* and high levels of *competition*. An organisation's pricing policy should be developed from its *marketing plan* and will reflect the market segment(s) being targeted and the *image* that it wants to portray. The most common pricing policies adopted by leisure and tourism organisations include *skimming, cost-plus pricing, penetration pricing* and *competitive pricing*.

primary data is *data* that is collected for the first time, usually as part of a *market research* study. Unlike *secondary data*, which refers to already-published information, primary data involves the use of *surveys, observation* and *focus groups* to collect new facts and figures. Although there is a good supply of statistical information relating to the leisure and tourism industries, it is highly likely that an organisation, at some stage in its development, will need to collect primary data that is specific to its own operations, e.g. a *leisure centre* carrying out a visitor survey or a *visitor attraction* observing and recording the flow of vehicles and people.

primary ratio: see *return on capital employed (ROCE)*

primary research is the process of collecting and analysing *primary data*, from a range of different sources. It is sometimes known as *field research*.

primary research source refers to any organisation or individual that is consulted as part of a study involving *primary research*, e.g. visitors to a tourist destination, colleagues or experts in particular subject areas (using the *Delphi technique*).

primary sector: the part of a nation's economy concerned with the extraction of raw materials, e.g. farming, mining and fishing. (See also *service sector*, *secondary sector*.)

prime costs: see *direct costs*

Prince's Trust: an organisation, founded by the Prince of Wales in 1976, that helps young, disadvantaged people and organisations that work with them or on their behalf. It awards grants to young people between the ages of 14 and 25, who may be unemployed, homeless or lacking in confidence, and who would benefit from some financial help to accomplish something positive. Eligible projects include owning and learning to play a musical instrument, finding and holding down a job, becoming a *personal fitness trainer* or nature conservation work. The Trust's sister organisation, The Prince's Youth Business Trust, helps young unemployed people to become self-employed through practical support, *loans* and bursaries to set up their own businesses. Weblink: www.princes-trust.org.uk

principal: the name given to a company that a *travel agent* does business with and whose products and services it sells. For example, if a branch of *Thomas Cook* sells a *Thomson's* holiday, the agent in the deal is Thomas Cook and the principal is Thomson. The most common principals that a high street travel agency will deal with are tour operators, rail companies, airlines, ferry companies, car hire companies and hotel groups. For selling the principal's products, the agent receives a *commission*.

printed media: refers to newspapers, magazines and journals, aimed at either consumer or trade buyers.

private limited company: a firm whose owners benefit from *limited liability*, but which cannot advertise the sale of its shares nor obtain a listing on the *Stock Exchange*, as is the case with a *public limited company (PLC)*. Many commercial leisure and tourism enterprises in the UK are private limited companies, with examples as diverse as country house hotels, *tourist attractions* and leisure clubs. Although trading as a private limited company does have certain advantages over *sole traders* and *partnerships*, there are disadvantages, such as the need to publish annual accounts and complete complex administrative and legal requirements.

private sector enterprises: see *private sector leisure, travel and tourism*

private sector leisure, travel and tourism: the sector of the industries that is concerned principally with commercial activities and maximising profits. The majority of leisure and tourism organisations are private sector enterprises, e.g. *hotels,* airlines, travel agencies, *tour operators*, car hire firms, *tourist attractions* and transport operators. Private sector enterprises range in size from large *multinational corporations* and *public limited companies,* such as Hertz and *British Airways* PLC, to small one-person operations providing support services to leisure and tourism, e.g. *couriers*, guides and *personal fitness trainers*. (See also *public sector leisure and tourism*.)

private sector organisations: see *private sector leisure, travel and tourism*

privatisation: the transfer of former public sector bodies and services to private sector enterprises, e.g. British Telecom, *British Airways* and the *British Airports Authority* were all previously public corporations, but are now private sector organisations. Supporters of privatisation argue that the competitive nature of the private sector leads to better *products* and standards of service than was the case under state control. Opponents suggest that private sector operators will only be concerned with profit maximisation, with no concern for wider *social objectives* and community benefits. *British Rail* is the former public corporation that used to own the UK rail network and was responsible for providing passenger and freight services nationwide. It was privatised in the mid-1990s, with the establishment of *Railtrack* and a number of *train operating companies*.

PRO: see *public relations officer*

product is one of the four key elements of an organisation's *marketing mix*, along with *place, price* and *promotion*. Leisure and tourism products are very different from many other everyday products we buy and use, since it is often not possible to see or touch the product, e.g. a package holiday or a 30-minute session in a swimming pool; this is known as *intangibility*. Leisure and tourism products also demonstrate *perishability* and are very often non-standardised, i.e. the experience that a person gets on the same holiday from one year to another could be very different. Some leisure and tourism products can also be unpredictable and fragile, since customers who feel unhappy with a product or standard of service may take their custom elsewhere.

product development: the techniques and processes that an organisation undertakes to make its *product portfolio* as appealing as possible to existing and potential customers. Product development is often founded on extensive *market research* and may be supported by techniques such as the *Boston Consulting Group Matrix* and *Ansoff's Matrix*.

product endorsement is when a personality lends his or her name to a *product* or service to stimulate sales or build an *image*. The use of a personality gives an organisation, destination or product, added credibility.

product knowledge is an essential requirement of a successful *sales process*. Staff working in leisure and tourism must have regular *training* to help them learn about the features and benefits of the *products* they are selling. Good product knowledge creates the impression of a professional organisation, since staff can suggest alternatives if a customer's first choice of product is not available, or provide in-depth information on the range of products available. In the leisure and tourism industries, product knowledge is sometimes gained by staff experiencing the products and services first-hand, e.g. *familiarisation trips* for travel agency staff.

product life cycle: a concept which suggests that all products and services follow the same pattern of growth during their lifespan (see figure on following page). The five stages in the product life cycle are:

- launch – when a product or service is introduced, with heavy promotional effort
- growth – sales grow steadily with increasing profits

- maturity – sales begin to slow down, perhaps because competitors are offering products with greater benefits
- saturation – sales have reached a plateau
- decline – sales drop off quickly.

The concept can be useful to an organisation in developing its *marketing strategy*, since it can show past peaks and troughs in sales performance, thereby giving pointers to possible new *product development* and promotional opportunities. Critics of the product life cycle concept argue, however, that it cannot be used to effectively forecast future developments since it is a retrospective model. (See also *destination life cycle*.)

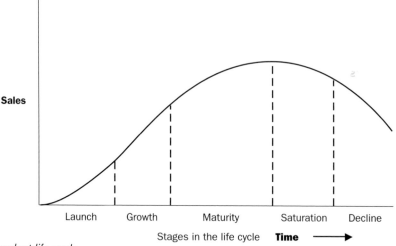

The product life cycle

product orientation: a business philosophy and *management style* that focuses on the details of *products* and services supplied rather than the *needs* of *customers* (known as *market* or *customer orientation*), e.g. a hotelier may invest in a new health and fitness suite only to find that his customers are more interested in drinking in the bar and watching television.

product portfolio is the mix of products and services offered by an organisation to its *customers.* If it wishes to survive in the longer term, it must constantly monitor customer reactions and make alterations to its portfolio on the basis of its findings. Large leisure and tourism organisations have extensive product ranges aimed at different *market segments.*

product research: see *marketing research*

professional body: an organisation set up by, and representing the interests of, professional people in certain industry sectors. There are many professional bodies in leisure and tourism, including the *Tourism Society*, the *Institute of Leisure and Amenity Management*, the *Tourism Management Institute* and the *Hotel and Catering International Management Association*. Professional bodies keep members up to date with what is happening in their particular sector by organising regular meetings, disseminating information and running training events. Most professional bodies control membership by applying certain criteria, such as the holding of particular qualifications or periods of employment in the industry.

professional sport is an avenue open to the most talented in their particular sporting activity, whether male or female. Successful basketball, baseball and American football stars earn vast salaries on the professional circuit in the USA. Although the rewards may not be so high in the UK, Premier League footballers are among the highest paid individuals in sport, along with top golfers, athletes, snooker players, jockeys, tennis stars, rugby players and Formula 1 racing drivers. In the UK, talented sports people may be helped financially in their development activities by grants from the *Lottery Sports Fund* or by using the facilities offered by the *English Institute of Sport*.

profit is the amount by which an organisation's total *turnover* exceeds its total *costs*. Gross *profit* is the difference between sales revenue and the cost of sales, while *net profit* is usually calculated by deducting payroll, *direct costs*, *indirect costs*, and financing costs from the gross profit figure, before tax. The profit after tax is the net profit attributable to *shareholders* after taxes have been paid. The different types of profit are shown in a company's *profit and loss account*.

profit and loss account: a financial statement that shows an organisation's income and expenditure over a given period of time, generally twelve months, resulting from its normal trading activities. A company's profit and loss account shows whether it is carrying forward a deficit or surplus into the next accounting period and is a useful tool for comparing *financial performance* over different time periods. It also indicates, if read in conjunction with the *balance sheet*, the success or failure of *management* policies in deploying its resources to generate profits. An example of the structure of a profit and loss account is given in the accompanying figure.

Manor Country House Hotel
Profit and loss account for the year ending 31/3/03

	£000
SALES	
Rooms	140
Food and beverage	150
Other	20
TOTAL	310
Cost of sales	70
GROSS PROFIT	240
Expenses	160
OPERATING PROFIT	80
Interest	40
NET PROFIT	40

profit centre: a clearly identifiable aspect of an organisation's work that generates revenue, thereby contributing to overall *profitability*. Sometimes called revenue centres, the profit centres for a typical hotel, for example, are likely to include:

- rooms
- valet services
- food and beverage

- conference and banqueting
- telephone and business services
- special events.

The managers of profit centres are allocated specific *budgets* and performance criteria against which their performance can be measured. (See also *cost centres*.)

profitability: a measure of the size of *profit* an organisation has earned compared with previous years or throughout the year, when comparing actual with budgeted results. It is measured in terms of total *assets* employed, long-term capital or number of employees.

profit-sharing scheme: a type of remuneration where an employee receives an extra payment, in addition to his or her basic pay, which is directly related to the overall *profitability* of the organisation. For example, a 10 per cent increase in the profits of an international airline over a 12 month period may result in its employees receiving a bonus equivalent to 10 per cent of their annual salary. Such schemes are offered in many of the larger leisure, travel and tourism companies, as an *incentive* for staff to work more efficiently and increase the organisation's *profitability* and their own pay levels.

programme evaluation and review technique (PERT) is a *management* technique used in major construction projects, such as *tourist attractions*, leisure complexes and hotel developments, to make sure that projects are completed at the least expense and in the shortest possible time.

programming: a way of making sure that a leisure or tourism facility is used to its full capacity at all times. Programming is most commonly associated with *leisure* and sports centres, but is equally applicable to theatres, local community centres, concert halls and a number of other facilities. In the public sector, programming aims to ensure that facilities are used by as wide a cross-section of the local community as possible, i.e. meeting the *social objectives* of the *local authority*. Programming must not only take account of the needs of customers but also the availability and expertise of staff, as well as the physical *resources* at the organisation's disposal.

prohibition notice: a written order, served by a health and safety inspector, when he or she discovers a serious contravention of the *Health and Safety at Work, etc. Act,* which could result in serious personal injury. The notice, which can be served on either the person undertaking the activity or the person in control of it, effectively stops the activity in question until such time as the specified action to render the situation safe has been completed to the satisfaction of the inspector.

project management: an important part of *operations management* that covers *planning*, scheduling, controlling, implementation and *evaluation*. The building or extension of facilities, or the staging of events, all require a degree of project management regardless of the scale of the project. Project managers sometimes use techniques such as *PERT* and *cost-benefit analysis* to help their decision making.

promotion is one of the four key elements of an organisation's *marketing mix*, along with *place, price* and *product*. Promotion is used to:

- inform *customers* of product benefits
- make customers aware of particular products and services
- stimulate *demand*

- provide *incentives* to purchase
- remind customers of the existence of a product or service.

Leisure, travel and tourism organisations use a variety of promotional techniques, referred to as the *promotional mix*. These include *advertising, direct marketing, public relations, personal selling* and *sales promotion* techniques.

promotion research: see *marketing research*

promotional materials: posters, brochures, leaflets, T-shirts, balloons, pens and any other items that are used for *sales promotion* purposes.

promotional mix: the different promotional techniques that an organisation uses to raise awareness of its products and services, thereby stimulating sales. These could include *advertising, direct marketing, sales promotion* and *public relations* activities.

promotional strategy is the way in which an organisation implements its *promotional mix* in order to achieve its *marketing objectives*. This could be through a strategy that concentrates solely on one type of promotional technique, e.g. *direct mail*.

Protestant work ethic: a movement that developed in Europe in the fifteenth and sixteenth centuries and which attacked the excesses and corruption of the pleasure-seeking nobility, leading to a sharp decline in the availability and respectability of *leisure* and *recreation*.

PRP: see *performance-related pay*

PSA: see *Passenger Shipping Association*

PSARA stands for Passenger Shipping Association Retail Agents' Scheme, a training initiative developed by the *Passenger Shipping Association* as a way of increasing the *product knowledge* and understanding of shipping and cruising among *travel agency* staff. Weblink: www.psa-psara.org

psychocentric: one of a number of types of tourist behaviour developed by Plog in 1977 as part of a research study for airline companies. Psychocentrics tended to be mainstream in their behaviour, rather unadventurous when it came to travelling, preferred familiar surroundings and had below average income levels. (See also *allocentric, mid-centric*.)

psychological carrying capacity: see *carrying capacity*

psychometric testing: a technique sometimes used by organisations when selecting and recruiting staff. It usually takes the form of a multiple choice test, designed to discover an applicant's *personality* type and to answer such questions as whether he or she will be a good team member, or work well under pressure.

public address (PA): an amplification system used in a wide variety of situations in leisure and tourism, for example at *events*, concerts, in leisure centres and at sports matches. From a health and safety point of view, it is important to make sure that a PA system is audible to all, particularly in the event of an accident or other incident. An alternative system should be available as a back-up should there be a power failure.

public corporation: a state-owned organisation established to provide a service to the public. Many former public corporations in the UK have been *privatised* under the conservative government, e.g. British Steel, British Telecom and *British Airways*, which are all now commercial concerns operating as *public limited companies (PLCs)*. *British Rail* was formerly a public corporation, but was privatised at the beginning of 1996.

Public Entertainments' Licence (PEL): a licence that is needed by any leisure or entertainment facility that provides dancing, indoor sports, music or other public entertainment of a like kind in any of its buildings to which the public are invited. Application for a PEL is made to the local council, who may, in some areas, insist that a licence is issued for open-air entertainment. As is the case with the granting of most licences, the decision as to whether a PEL application is successful or not will depend on a number of factors, including the nature of the event, the suitability of the premises, the impact of the event on the surrounding area and the character of the applicant.

public excursion fare (PEX): a special discounted fare offered by an airline to those booking and travelling on the same day on certain specified routes. (See also *standby*, *APEX*.)

public image: see *image*

public limited company (PLC): a large organisation with a minimum *share capital* of £50,000, which finances its expansion by offering shares to the public on the *Stock Exchange*. Some of the best-known leisure and tourism organisations in the UK are PLCs, including My Travel PLC, *British Airways* PLC and *Virgin* PLC. Investors in public limited companies have the benefit of *limited liability*, limiting their liability in the event of failure, to the amount they have invested in the company. PLCs often have a parent company acting as the head of a group with a number of subsidiary companies working beneath it, e.g. Mecca Bingo, Grosvenor Casinos and Hard Rock Café International are all subsidiaries of the Rank Group.

public open space: an area of land to which the public has free *access* for enjoyment and *recreation*. Public open space includes parks, gardens, commons, sports grounds, bowling greens and public golf courses. Bodies such as the *National Playing Fields' Association* campaign for tracts of public open space to remain accessible to all.

Public Order Act 1986: government *legislation* that seeks to protect the general public by providing legal restraints against private or public nuisance. Aggrieved neighbours, for example, may decide to pursue an action in the courts against a rock concert or a noisy speedway event. For the action to have any chance of success, there must be continuity of nuisance, i.e. it must occur more than once over a reasonable period of time. In reality, individuals may get a faster result by complaining to their local environmental health department.

public relations (PR) is an important part of the *promotion* element of the *marketing mix* in leisure and tourism. It is defined by the Institute of Public Relations as 'the planned and sustained effort to establish and maintain goodwill and mutual understanding between an organisation and its publics'. The last word in the definition is deliberately used in the plural, since an organisation has to deal with a wide range of people while carrying out its business, including customers, suppliers, trade unions, the press, councillors (in the public sector), *shareholders* (in the private sector), tax inspectors, members, neighbours, voluntary helpers and many more. PR is most often associated with press or media relations, when an organisation builds a relationship with journalists, radio reporters and television stations, in order to gain publicity. This is most often achieved through issuing *press releases* and organising *familiarisation trips*. Good PR can also help when a tragedy strikes an organisation or unfavourable stories begin to circulate.

public relations officer (PRO): a person given the *responsibility* for carrying out an organisation's *public relations* function. He or she handles all relationships with the press, including creating news stories and hosting press visits and familiarisation trips. The job of the PRO is to maintain the 'external face' of an organisation and they may occasionally be called upon to react quickly to a potential problem linked to the organisation. The PRO may write *press releases* or liaise with an *advertising agency* to handle this work.

public right of way: a route over which members of the public have freedom to travel, usually only on foot, but in certain circumstances also on horseback or bicycle. Some rights of way have been created under government *legislation,* while others have developed through continuous use over a long period of time. *Local authorities* are responsible for ensuring that rights of way are adequately maintained. (See also *bridleway.*)

public sector leisure, travel and tourism is the sector of the industries concerned with providing a service to a local community or society in general, rather than having profit max-imisation as a prime *objective.* This does not mean that public sector operators are not concerned with giving value-for-money in the facilities and services they provide. Increasing *competition* from the rival facilities in the private sector has forced public sector managers to adopt many commercial practices in order to survive and expand their operations. Leisure and tourism facilities provided by the public sector include:

- libraries and *museums*
- sports and *leisure centres*
- *visitor attractions*
- arts centres and galleries
- *tourist information centres*
- swimming pools
- parks and play areas
- community centres.

Public sector provision operates at both local and national level. *Local authorities* play a vital role in providing *leisure* and *recreation* facilities for local communities, while organisa-tions such as *UK Sport* and the *English Tourism Council* co-ordinate and sponsor national initiatives.

public sector organisation: see *public sector leisure, travel and tourism*

public transport refers to a range of services made available to members of the public and funded by *local* or *national government*. Public transport provides a valuable means of *access* to leisure, travel and tourism products and services for those people who do not own a car. It also plays an important part in helping to achieve *sustainability* by reducing car dependency.

purchase ledger: a record of an organisation's purchases over a given period of time, listing *creditors* by name and also recording any payments made to them.

purpose-built resort: a centre built exclusively as a holiday or leisure destination, e.g. Disneyland Paris or *Center Parcs*. (See also *tourist enclave.*)

pyramid structure: see *hierarchical organisation*

QA: see *quality assurance*

QCA: see *Qualifications and Curriculum Authority*

Qualifications and Curriculum Authority (QCA) is the guardian of standards in education and training in England (ACAC has the same responsibilities in Wales). It works with a range of partners to maintain and develop the school curriculum and associated assessments, as well accrediting and monitoring qualifications in schools, colleges and at work. Its work is designed to give pupils, students, trainees, parents, teachers, further and higher education tutors and employers increased confidence in the standards that underpin the curriculum and national qualification systems. It oversees *National Vocational Qualifications (NVQs)* and the *Advanced Vocational Certificate in Education (AVCE)*. Weblink: www.qca.org.uk

qualitative data is information, often gathered as part of a *market research* process, that is concerned with an organisation's standing in the marketplace, rather than an exact measurement of its performance. It may be data that reflects an individual's opinion or attitude, e.g. whether the holidaymakers on a *package holiday* were happy with their *accommodation* in the resort or the opinions of a family on the facilities on offer in a tourist attraction. Qualitative data can be collected in a number of ways, including *surveys* and *focus groups*. (See also *quantitative data*.)

quality is one of the 'buzzwords' in the leisure, travel and tourism industries in the new millennium. A whole host of organisations, in the public, private and voluntary sectors, have pledged their commitment to improving the quality of the products, services and facilities they offer their customers. Quality is synonymous with satisfying customer *needs,* i.e. the introduction of any quality system or set of quality standards must place the customer as the focus of all activity. This is borne out by the *International Standards Organisation*, which defines quality as 'the totality of features and characteristics of a product or service that bear on its ability to satisfy stated or implied needs'. Some leisure and tourism organisations have sought external recognition of their quality initiatives, either by gaining certification under *BS 5750* or the *Investors in People* scheme. (See also *integrated quality management*.)

quality assurance (QA) is the process of attempting to make sure that the standards of product and service quality are right first time, every time, to achieve complete customer satisfaction. In a leisure or tourism organisation, QA will involve attention to such factors as the *products* on offer, levels of *customer service*, assessment of performance standards and *after-sales service*. (See also *quality control*.)

quality circle is a practice used in *operations management* to improve an organisation's *efficiency* and *effectiveness*. Found commonly in Japanese firms, quality circles involve regular meetings between employees and management/supervisory staff to discuss work methods, problems and solutions, with a view to deciding how best to achieve quality targets. Quality circles help reinforce the notion that quality is a shared responsibility and that everyone should strive to ensure quality in their individual efforts.

quality control: unlike *quality assurance*, which aims to make sure that quality standards are met from the outset, quality control is concerned with monitoring product and service quality by identifying and addressing quality problems, through checking and inspection.

quality criteria: see *quality standards*

quality press: generally considered to be newspapers, such as The Times, The Guardian, The Daily Telegraph, The Independent and The Observer, that are non-tabloid in format and offer a balance of news, comment and *advertising*. Such 'quality' newspapers are generally, but not exclusively, read by people in the higher *socio-economic* groups.

quality standards are levels of performance and product quality which organisations seek to achieve in order to satisfy customer *needs* and thereby remain competitive. Some organisations seek external recognition of their work performance, e.g. by gaining a quality standard such as *BS EN ISO 9000* or by implementing *Investors in People*. Others operate very well without the need to formally register for recognition, based on the fact that management and staff have practised a customer-focused approach for many years.

quango stands for 'quasi-autonomous non-governmental organisation'. Although usually linked to a government department and primarily funded from public money, quangos enjoy greater freedom than bodies under direct government control, with board members appointed rather than elected. Examples of quangos in leisure and tourism include *Sport England*, the *British Tourist Authority* and the *Wales Tourist Board*. Opponents of quangos argue that the non-elected status of their members may lead to political bias, while those in favour say that the freedom from *red tape* means that quangos can work speedily in reaching their *objectives*.

quantitative data is factual information that can be measured and analysed, often gathered as part of a *market research* process, e.g. the number of visitors to a theme park, the stock of accommodation in a holiday resort or the country of origin of visitors to Britain. Such data is invaluable for *management* decision making and may influence, for example, an organisation's marketing strategy or range of available products. Quantitative data is available from a number of *secondary* and *primary research* sources, including *surveys, observation* and sales figures. (See also *qualitative data*.)

questionnaire: a document containing a series of questions designed to help an organisation gain valuable data to help with its forward *planning* and decision making. Specialists in the design of questionnaires suggest that there are a number of important steps to go through before finalising the questionnaire, including making a list of expected 'outcomes', formulating the questions that will achieve these, carrying out a *pilot survey* with the first draft of the questionnaire, amending as necessary and lastly producing sufficient quantities of the final version for the main survey. Questionnaires are one of the most common methods used by leisure and tourism organisations to gain their *market research* information. (See also *questionnaire design*.)

questionnaire design is the process of developing a questionnaire so that it fully meets the *objectives* of the *survey* in which it is being used. Questionnaire design is a skilled and time-consuming procedure, often best left to professionals in *advertising agencies* and *market research* bureaux. There are many guidelines that should be followed when attempting to design an effective questionnaire, including:

- always put sensitive questions, e.g. concerning age, occupation, marital status, etc. at the end of the questionnaire
- avoid ambiguous questions
- avoid using jargon
- don't be tempted to include superfluous questions
- keep questions simple
- avoid *'leading questions'*
- use appropriate language.

quorum refers to the minimum number of people at a meeting to allow the decisions made at the meeting to be valid. Under the constitution of a Leisure Services Committee of 24 members, for example, it may have been decided that there must be a minimum of 12 people in attendance for a quorum to exist and for the Committee to be able to make binding decisions. Any less than 12 members would make the Committee meeting 'inquorate'.

quota sample: one of the most common types of *sampling* used in *research* studies. When using a quota sampling method for a *market research* survey, *interviewers* are given instructions as to the number of respondents in certain categories that they must interview, e.g. defined by age, gender or social class. For example, interviewers may be asked to select only women over the age of 50 for a particular survey. (See also *random sample*.)

Do you know we also have A–Zs for:

- **Geography**
- **Business Studies**
- **ICT and Computing**
- **Geography Coursework?**

Ask for them in your local bookshop or see the inside back cover for ordering details.

RABs: see *Regional Arts Boards*

Race Relations Act 1976: government *legislation* making it unlawful to discriminate on the grounds of colour, race, nationality or ethnic origin. Under the terms of the Act, employers must not discriminate in matters relating to staff recruitment, training and promotion. The Act established the *Commission for Racial Equality*, with powers to issue non-discrimination notices to employers and trade unions found to be infringing its requirements.

racism in sport is a major issue for the twenty-first century. It is clear that racism in sport reflects racism in society in general. In the UK, issues concerned with racism in sport have been most evident in professional football. The Professional Footballers' Association (PFA) worked with the *Commission for Racial Equality* to develop 'let's kick racism out of football', a campaign aimed at eradicating the problem from the sport. Other sports, including tennis, golf and cricket have been criticised for their small numbers of top-level black performers.

rack rate refers to the full, published price at which a hotel room is sold. Depending on levels of *demand*, it is likely that the rack rate will be discounted for particular *customers*, at specific times of the week or year, and for special events. Most hotels offer particularly high discounts at weekends, when they are not being used by business travellers.

racking policy refers to the *tour operators' brochures* that a *travel agent* will have on display in the agency. Independent agents carry a wide range of brochures from both specialist and mass market operators, whereas the multiple agents have clearly defined policies as to which particular brochures they are allowed to stock. This will be determined by, among other things, levels of *commission* on offer and whether the agent has a trading link with the operator, e.g. *Thomson* owns Lunn Poly and JMC Holidays is part of the Thomas Cook Group.

RADAR: see *Royal Association for Disability and Rehabilitation*

Railtrack: the publicly-subsidised, private operator that owned and operated the national rail infrastructure in the UK until late 2002. Responsibility for track, signalling, etc. and direct management of 14 major stations has now passed to *Network Rail*. *Train operating companies (TOCs)* are awarded franchises to run passenger rail services on the rail network. Weblink: www.railtrack.co.uk

rail travel is an element of the UK *transportation* scene, made up of a network of public services provided by *train operating companies (TOCs)* and a small number of private rail operators catering for tourists from the UK and overseas, e.g. the North York Moors Railway and the Ffestiniog Railway, one of the 'Great Little Trains in Wales'.

Ramblers' Association: a registered charity working to defend the beauty and diversity of the British countryside for the benefit of walkers of all ages. Founded in 1935, the Association has been active in lobbying central and local governments on issues relating to *access in the countryside*, particularly the introduction of the *Countryside and Rights of Way Act (CROW)*. It campaigns to keep Britain's thousands of miles of rights of way open, to ensure that public woodlands remain accessible, to protect Britain's *National Parks* and to make the countryside available to the whole community. The Ramblers' Association currently has more than 137,000 members and nearly 450 local groups throughout England, Scotland and Wales. Weblink: www.ramblers.org.uk

random sample: when every member of a 'population' has an equal chance of being selected in a research study. For a survey based on a random sample, which is considered to be the most accurate type of sample, individuals are normally pre-selected from a sampling frame, such as the electoral register. *Interviewers* are then asked to carry out interviews at the selected households chosen at random. Many government *surveys* operate in this way. (See also *sampling, quota sample*.)

Rank Group PLC was founded in 1937, when Odeon Cinemas, the forerunner to the Rank Organisation, was formed. Rank is now one of the world's leading *leisure* and entertainment companies, and an international provider of services to the film industry. The Group employs over 20,000 people worldwide and in its UK gaming businesses it has memberships in excess of 3 million people. The Group includes Mecca Bingo, Grosvenor Casinos and Hard Rock Café International. Weblink: www.rank.com

rate of exchange refers to the price at which one *currency* is exchanged for another. The world's various currencies are allowed to fluctuate in line with demand and supply, an effect that has been eliminated between the *EU* countries that have adopted the *Euro*. Adverse changes in exchange rates can have serious consequences on the demand for holidays in a particular country.

rate of return: a measure of the *profits* of a business, expressed as a percentage of the total *capital* employed in the venture.

ratio analysis: the development of performance measures from financial and operational information and their use in management decision making. Ratios such as the *return on capital employed (ROCE)* and *occupancy rates* can be used to compare the internal performance of an organisation and how it compares with its competitors.

RCI stands for Resort Condominiums International, the world's leading *timeshare* exchange company. RCI operates a 'clearing house' for the owners of timeshare properties worldwide, who want to exchange use of their property for one in a different country or a different time of year. As an example, the owner of a week's timeshare in a lodge at Loch Rannoch in Scotland could deposit his or her time period into the RCI 'bank' and select, say, a week in a timeshare apartment in Florida. RCI was founded in 1974 and is now a global business, serving more than 3700 resorts in over 90 countries. Weblink: www.rci.com

RDAs: see *Regional Development Agencies*

receiving country: see *tourist receiving country*

recreation: the activities that people carry out in their *leisure time*, which may be active or passive, and take place inside or outside the home. The term comes from the Latin word 'recreatio', meaning that which refreshes or restores. *Countryside recreation* and *community recreation* are particular elements of the total recreation sector, the former concentrating on pursuits such as rambling or mountain biking, while the latter is concerned with providing recreational facilities for all sectors of a community, irrespective of their social status, race or gender.

recreational activities: see *recreation*

Recreational Managers Association of Great Britain (RMA): formed in 1956, RMA is one of the leading private leisure associations in the UK and is affiliated to many organisations, such as *Sport England* and the *Central Council for Physical Recreation*. The RMA aims to promote the interests of individuals associated with the *management* of sports clubs, leisure centres, health clubs, ice rinks, bowling centres and hotel leisure centres. RMA's stated *objectives* include providing members with a forum for the exchange of ideas and information, preserving and enhancing the standards of recreation management in the UK and fostering an appreciation by both management and club members of the importance of the association's work. Members of RMA manage recreation and leisure facilities for more than 3 million people in the UK.

recruitment agency: a firm specialising in finding suitable applicants for jobs. Leisure and tourism organisations sometimes use the services of a recruitment agency to fill senior appointments, such as a Director of Marketing or a Head of Leisure Services. The agency advertises the post and selects suitable applicants for *interview*. Agencies are also used in situations where posts are difficult to fill, e.g. some manual jobs in the hotel and catering sector. Agencies specialising in leisure, travel and tourism posts advertise their services in the relevant trade newspapers and journals.

recruitment and selection: a structured process that aims to identify and employ the most suitable person for a job vacancy. It has five clearly-defined stages:

- job analysis – identification of what the job entails
- finding suitable applicants – by *advertising*, through agencies, internal candidates, etc.
- selection – drawing up a short list and interviewing candidates
- appointment – making a formal offer of employment
- induction – ensuring that the new member understands the working of the organisation.

Recruitment and selection can be carried out 'in house' or left to a *recruitment agency* to organise.

red tape: the term given to unnecessary paperwork and procedures, most often associated with public bodies. The government has made a pledge to reduce red tape wherever possible, although many people would say that further moves to privatise services and facilities is likely to lead to more, not less, unnecessary paperwork.

redundancy: the *dismissal* of an employee on the grounds that their job has ceased to exist, rather than because of anything to do with their conduct or work performance. Redundancy may be voluntary or compulsory, with redundant staff being eligible for certain redundancy payments, depending on how long they were employed with the organisation and how many hours they worked per week.

redundant building grants: sums of money, administered by the *Rural Development Commission,* made available to the owners of derelict buildings in the countryside to return them to productive use. Eligible uses for the buildings would include tourist *accommodation*, craft workshops and *telecottages*.

Regional Arts Boards (RABs): ten autonomous, strategic bodies that work in partnership with *local authorities* and a wide range of other public, private and voluntary sector bodies to promote the arts within their particular region of England. They are concerned with all arts and crafts, including visual, performing, media and published; they work at regional level as partners of the three national agencies which provide most of their funding, the *Arts Council of England*, *British Film Institute* and the *Crafts Council*. On April 1 2002, the *RABs* and the Arts Council of England joined together to form a single development organisation for the arts.

Regional Development Agencies (RDAs) were formally launched in eight English regions on April 1 1999. The ninth, in London, was established on July 3 2000 following the creation of the Greater London Authority (GLA). They aim to co-ordinate regional *economic development* and *regeneration*, promote employment, enhance the development and appli-cation of *skills* relevant to employment, and contribute to *sustainable development*. RDAs work with their respective *Regional Tourist Boards* in carrying out their work.

regional identity: the mixture of a variety of real and perceived symbols and traditions that give a region its unique identity, and often make it attractive as a *tourist destination*. In the UK, *Regional Tourist Boards* and *Regional Development Agencies* use positive aspects of regional identity to stimulate *economic development*.

Regional Tourist Board (RTB): an official organisation that works in tandem with a *National Tourism Organisation* on matters of interest in a particular region. In the case of England, there are 10 RTBs (see figure on next page) working under the auspices of the *English Tourism Council (ETC)*. The English RTBs operate on a more commercial basis than the ETC, earning revenue from commercial membership subscriptions, *advertising* sales and other commercial ventures. A typical English RTB will have a diverse range of members, including:

- *local authorities*
- hoteliers
- regional airports
- *bed and breakfast* establishments
- caravan parks
- operators of *tourist attractions*.

Regional Tourist Boards seek to co-ordinate tourism initiatives in their regions, particularly *marketing* and publicity, as well as providing a service to both members and the general public. In Wales, there are four Regional Tourism Partnerships which report to the *Wales Tourist Board*.

relaunch: the need to make a *product* or service available for a second or subsequent time, usually in modified form. A leisure facility, for example, may install new *virtual reality* amusements or update its decor in order to retain its *customers* or appeal to a new *market*. *Tour operators* are sometimes forced to withdraw brochure stocks from travel agencies and relaunch their holiday products, often in response to price reductions by competitors.

Regional Tourist Boards in England

remuneration is the tangible reward that employees receive in return for giving their time, commitment and expertise to an employer. The remuneration for the majority of staff working in leisure and tourism will consist of a weekly wage or monthly salary. To this may be added *commission* or *incentive* payments, based on sales achieved. Many workers in leisure and tourism will be offered a range of *perks*, such as free or discounted use of facilities or subsidised travel, as a form of remuneration. *Profit-sharing schemes* also operate in larger leisure and tourism companies.

repeat business is crucial to the success of any leisure, travel or tourism organisation, since existing *customers* generate a higher profit contribution than new clients and provide a much firmer base from which to develop new business. Indeed, research from the US

Office of Consumer Affairs shows us that it takes five times as much effort, time and money to attract a new customer as it does to keep an existing customer. Companies use a number of techniques to encourage repeat business, and thereby promote *customer loyalty*, such as special offers and *incentives*, e.g. *frequent flyer programmes*.

report: a type of *written communication* used extensively in leisure and tourism in a variety of situations, including:

- presenting statistical information
- investigating the feasibility of a new development
- recommending changes to a *management* or staff structure
- meeting legal requirements
- investigating a disciplinary matter involving members of staff.

A report should follow a logical sequence and structure, beginning with its *terms of reference*, followed by procedure, findings, conclusions and recommendations. Depending on the type of report, it may also be useful to include a bibliography and a section detailing sources of information.

research: the collection, collation and analysis of data in response to a specific enquiry. (See also *primary research, secondary research*.)

research objectives vary according to the nature of the research study, but must be carefully agreed in advance to ensure success in the research process. The objective of a research study in travel and tourism could be 'to discover the reasons why travellers choose to fly with airline A rather than airline B'. (See also *SMART objectives*.)

research skills include all the techniques and processes involved with undertaking a research study, including interviewing, data collection, *questionnaire design*, data analysis, report writing.

research sources: see *primary research source, secondary research source*

research strategy: an agreed plan of action for a research study that seeks to answer a range of questions, (what?, where?, why?, when? and how?) in respect of the research in question.

reservation systems: procedures and equipment that leisure and tourism organisations use to sell products such as *package holidays,* airline flights, hotel accommodation, car hire, theatre tickets and leisure facilities. They work on the basis that there is a known stock of product to be sold and an up-to-date count of what is still on offer is always easily obtainable. Reservation systems can be either manual or computer-based, the latter providing greater storage capacity, flexibility and speed of operation. The development of new technology, particularly in the travel sector, has led to the widespread use of *computerised reservation systems (CRSs)*, particularly in the airline and tour operating sectors.

resort: the name given to a holiday destination, which may be a village, town or city, e.g. Palma or Rome, or a purpose-built complex, such as Disneyland Paris. Resorts are the focus for many elements of the *leisure* and *tourism* industries, including *accommodation*, catering, *arts and entertainment, transportation* and leisure facilities. The popularity of resorts is constantly changing, as people's fashions, tastes and preferences change, as shown in the *destination life cycle* concept. (See also *seaside resorts*.)

resort representative: see *courier*

Resource was launched in April 2000 as the strategic body working with and for museums, archives and libraries, tapping the potential for collaboration between them. The new organisation replaced the *Museums and Galleries Commission* and the Library and Information Commission. With the full title 'Resource: the Council for Museums, Archives and Libraries', it has a number of core roles, which include providing strategic leadership, acting as a powerful advocate, developing capacity within the sector and promoting innovation and change. Weblink: www.resource.gov.uk

resources: a general term used to identify the tools that a manager has at his or her disposal to achieve an organisation's *objectives*. Resources may be financial, human, operational or physical. It is the job of a manager to marshal his or her resources, gaining the best possible outcomes. The term can also be used to denote the *natural attractions* of a tourist area, e.g. lakes, mountains, streams and beaches.

respondent: the name given to the person in an interview survey who answers the questions asked by an *interviewer*.

response rate is a measure of the number of replies to a survey as a proportion of the total number of *questionnaires* distributed or *respondents* questioned. In general, *self-completed questionnaire* surveys have a lower response rate than *face-to-face interviews*. If a response rate is too low, bias may be introduced into the survey and its subsequent analysis. Response rates can sometimes be improved by sending reminders to respondents by post or *e-mail*.

responsibility: an obligation on a subordinate member of staff to carry out certain tasks or make particular decisions. An employee is held responsible for his or her performance at work, measured against targets and *performance criteria*. Failure to achieve targets, or poor performance in the workplace, may result in a reprimand from a line manager. (See also *authority, accountability, delegation*.)

responsible tourism: see *'green' tourism*

retail price index (RPI) is the main method of measuring *inflation* in the UK economy. It is based on the weighted average of the prices of a standard range of household products, calculated on a monthly basis. The RPI is also used as a broad indicator of wage rises in the economy.

return on capital employed (ROCE) is the most widely used indicator of the *profitability* of an organisation, since it is meaningless to look at profitability without also analysing the *resources* used to generate the profits. Sometimes called the primary ratio, ROCE is calculated as follows:

$$\text{return on capital employed} = \frac{\text{net profit}}{\text{capital employed}}$$

The calculation of ROCE has many variations, which leads to inconsistency and sometimes distortion. The ratio can be used to compare the amount of profit made per £100 invested in an organisation, which will be useful to potential investors and business operators.

return on investment: a term which is sometimes used to mean *return on capital employed (ROCE)*.

revenue is another name for *turnover*. It is sometimes referred to as 'sales revenue'.

revenue centre: see *profit centre*

revenue costs: see *revenue expenditure*

revenue expenditure: all costs to an enterprise other than expenditure on capital items; it will fluctuate in response to sales volumes. Examples include expenses, salary costs and postage. (See also *capital expenditure*.)

revenue generation: any activity that produces income for an enterprise or organisation, e.g. sales, returns on investment, taxation, etc.

RIDDOR stands for the Reporting of Injuries, Diseases and Dangerous Occurrences Regulations 1995, which contain the obligations relating to the reporting of accidents and incidents in the workplace. Under the Regulations, any employer has a duty to inform the relevant authorities of any fatal or serious injuries to employees or other people in an accident connected with any business. In the case of leisure and tourism organisations, the incidents should be reported to the local Environmental Health Department. Weblink: www.riddor.gov.uk

risk assessment: a systematic investigation of the potential risks to the health and safety of employees and anybody else who may be affected by an organisation's work activities, e.g. spectators, *visitors* and contractors. All employers with five or more employees must formally carry out risk assessments under the regulations of the *EU Directives on health and safety*.

risks: see *hazards*

RLSS: see *Royal Life Saving Society UK*

RMA: see *Recreational Managers Association of Great Britain*

ROCE: see *return on capital employed*

roll-on/roll-off (RORO): a type of ferry onto which vehicles are loaded and unloaded by means of ramps. Past tragedies, such as happened with the Estonia and Herald of Free Enterprise ferries, have led to calls for greater safety on RORO vessels.

room occupancy: see *occupancy rate*

RORO: see *roll-on/roll-off*

Royal Association for Disability and Rehabilitation (RADAR): a national voluntary organisation working with and for people with physical disabilities. RADAR acts as a *pressure group* to improve the environment for disabled people, in areas such as health, education, social services, employment, housing, mobility, *leisure* and *tourism*. RADAR played an active role in the development of the *Disability Discrimination Act 1995*. Weblink: www.radar.org.uk

Royal Life Saving Society UK (RLSS) is the leading drowning-prevention organisation in the UK, and the governing body for lifesaving and lifeguarding. Founded in 1891, the Society has more than 13,000 members in 50 branches, plus 2000 active lifesaving and lifeguarding clubs throughout the UK. It has devised the *'Water Safety Code'* to help prevent accidents to children in or near water. Weblink: www.lifesavers.org.uk

Royal Life Saving Society UK's 'Water Safety Code': a voluntary *code of conduct* devised by the *RLSS* to help ensure safety for children in or near water. The code has five key points:

1 spot the dangers

2 take safety advice

3 don't go alone

4 learn how to help

5 get involved with the RLSS.

Royal Society for the Protection of Birds (RSPB): founded in 1889, the RSPB is Europe's largest wildlife *conservation* charity taking action for birds and their environment. It has more than 1 million members in the UK, who enjoy free *access* to over 100 nature reserves and have access to a network of local members' groups. The RSPB leads action for bird conservation by promoting conservation of birds and their habitats, carrying out research, working with central and *local government* to find solutions to conservation problems, and buying and managing land as nature reserves. The RSPB has a junior section, known as the Young Ornithologists' Club, to encourage bird conservation from an early age. Weblink: www.rspb.org.uk

RPI: see *retail price index*

RSPB: see *Royal Society for the Protection of Birds*

RTB: see *Regional Tourist Board*

Rural Development Commission: the former government agency concerned with the wellbeing of the 10 million people who live and work in England's rural areas. Before its merger with the *Countryside Agency* it had the statutory duty to advise government on all matters relating to the economic and social development of rural England. It supported projects concerned with training, tourism and environmental improvement. It saw its priorities as stemming unemployment in rural areas, addressing the shortage of affordable housing and halting the decline in village services.

rural tourism: any type of tourist activity that takes place in the countryside, including *farm tourism*, countryside events, nature trails and rural attractions. Rural tourism is seen as a way of maintaining the social, cultural and economic viability of country areas, by creating employment, generating income and giving farmers the opportunity to diversify into different leisure and tourism enterprises. The growth in rural tourism in recent years has gone hand-in-hand with greater concern for the environment and countryside generally.

Do you need revision help and advice?

Go to pages 265–75 for a range of revision appendices that include plenty of exam advice and tips.

Sabre: a *computerised reservation system (CRS)* developed by American Airlines and made available to *travel agents* worldwide.

SAF: see *Sports Aid Foundation*

safe working practices are crucial in the leisure, travel and tourism industries, whether it is a ferry company taking passengers across the English Channel or a leisure centre offering a wide range of activities, the same requirement of providing a safe and secure environment for customers must be adhered to. There is a great deal of UK *legislation* concerning health and safety, the most notable being the *Health and Safety at Work Act 1974*. *Risk assessments* form the basis of many safe working practices in the leisure, travel and tourism industries.

safety audit: a systematic investigation of a facility aimed at identifying potential safety risks and *hazards*, with a view to reducing the risk potential and minimising the likelihood of personal injury. A safety audit will include investigations of similar factors to those contained in a *risk assessment*.

safety officer: a member of staff given the responsibility of implementing health and safety procedures and monitoring their effectiveness. Depending on the size of the organisation, the post of safety officer may be a full-time appointment or carried out on a part-time basis by an employee with other responsibilities.

Safety of Sports Grounds Act 1975: government *legislation* aimed at ensuring a safe environment at spectator sports' facilities, including rugby and football grounds. (See also *Taylor Report*.)

sale and leaseback is a way for an individual or organisation to raise *capital* by selling a *fixed asset,* such as land or a building, and immediately taking out a long-term lease with the new owner to carry on using the asset for business purposes. It is a technique often used by companies that are experiencing financial difficulties, e.g. a hotelier who has cash flow problems may enter into a sale and leaseback agreement as a way of surviving in business.

Sale of Goods Act 1979 states that all goods sold or hired must be 'fit for the purpose' for which they were bought or hired, of 'merchantable quality' and must match their description, whether verbal or written. Under the Act, *tour operators*, for example, should not be found liable if they have exercised due care when selecting the different elements of their packages. Under the *Package Travel Directive*, however, operators cannot disclaim responsibility for poor products and services supplied by third parties, e.g. hoteliers and airlines. The Sale of Goods Act 1979 was amended by two pieces of legislation in the 1990s – the Sale and Supply of Goods Act 1994 and the Sale of Goods (Amendment) Act 1995.

sales administration systems: procedures and techniques for recording sales data, issuing tickets and other documentation, updating customer databases, processing orders and tracking sales progress. Such administrative systems are invariably computerised, with the benefits of speed, accuracy and large storage capacities.

sales budget: a chart that shows the predicted level of sales over a given time period. It is often the starting point of an organisation's financial planning process, since the *demand* for products and services is often the overriding factor in determining success or failure. In *forecasting* its likely sales, a company takes into account many factors, including past sales figures, existing and potential *competition*, the state of the *market* and the results of any *market research* work. Sales budgets are often constructed so as to allow actual figures achieved to be entered alongside the budgeted sales. (See also *expenditure budget*.)

sales invoice: see *invoice*

sales ledger: a chronological record of an organisation's *debtors* by company account, with details of sales made on *credit*, any sales returns and payments made to debtors.

sales objectives: apart from the obvious objective of making a sale, other objectives of the sales process could include generating repeat business, meeting planned increases in sales volumes, increasing customer satisfaction levels or securing *competitive advantage*.

sales process: a sequence of six key stages, which every sales person should undertake to achieve a successful sale of a product or service. The stages are:

- raising customer awareness
- establishing rapport with the customer
- investigating customer *needs*
- presenting the product or service
- *closing the sale*
- providing an *after-sales service*.

Identifying and following these six stages indicates that selling is a structured activity that can be learned and is not just for those who are 'born sales people'.

sales promotion: one of the key aspects of *promotion* within a leisure and tourism organisation, along with *advertising, direct marketing, public relations* and *personal selling*. Some of the most common sales promotion techniques are competitions, discount vouchers, free demonstrations, *brochures, extra product*, 'giveaways' and exhibitions. The main features of sales promotion techniques are that they are temporary and aim to stimulate demand in the short-term. The dynamic nature of the leisure and tourism industries means that organisations are having to respond constantly to fluctuations in demand. Sales promotion offers the flexibility needed to respond quickly to these changes.

sales revenue: see *revenue*

sales staff are people involved in all aspects of an organisation's *sales process*, from establishing rapport with a customer, to *closing a sale* and providing an *after-sales service*. Sales staff need a wide range of skills and qualities, including a friendly *personality*, good *communication skills*, a determination to succeed, consistency, enthusiasm, *product knowledge* and self-motivation. Most sales staff are involved in far more than the actual selling activity, either face-to-face or over the telephone; a sales person's job may also entail liaison with other work colleagues, travelling, entertaining, networking with external organisations and individuals, gaining *product knowledge* and servicing distribution channels.

sales turnover: see *turnover*

sampling is the practice of selecting the proportion of a total 'population' to be included in a research study, as opposed to a *census*, when the whole 'population' is surveyed. If the selection of the sample is fair, accurate and based on proven statistical methods, the responses of the people surveyed should mirror those of the total 'population', within known limits of accuracy. (See also *random sample, quota sample*.)

SASH: see *Standardised Approach to Sports Halls*

scheduled air services: flights that operate to a published timetable on specific routes. Unlike *charter flights*, scheduled services are committed to operate even if the *load factor* is very low. Scheduled services are particularly appropriate for business travel, although some package holidays do use scheduled services (known as *inclusive tours by excursion*).

scheduled flight: see *scheduled air services*

Scottish Arts Council: one of the main channels for government funding for the arts in Scotland, receiving *grant aid* from the Scottish Executive. It also distributes *National Lottery* funds received from the *Department for Culture, Media and Sport*. The Council supports a range of arts organisations in Scotland for their annual programmes of work and makes grants to individual artists and arts organisations. Weblink: www.sac.org.uk

Scottish Natural Heritage (SNH) is the key statutory agency in Scotland for advising government and for acting as its agent in the delivery of conservation designations. Its task is to secure the conservation and enhancement of Scotland's natural heritage – the wildlife, habitats and landscapes that have evolved through the long partnership between people and nature. SNH designates 'protected areas', which account for approximately 20 per cent of the land area. The main protected area designations are *National Nature Reserves (NNRs), Sites of Special Scientific Interest (SSSIs)*, RAMSAR Sites, Special Protection Areas (SPAs), proposed Special Areas of Conservation (SACs) and National Scenic Areas (NSAs). Weblink: www.snh.org.uk

Scottish Sports Council: the national agency dedicated to promoting sporting opportunities for all Scots at all levels, whatever their interest and ability. The Council, also known as Sport Scotland, provides advice on sport-related matters to the Scottish Executive, *local authorities, governing bodies* and others involved in sport. It also distributes approximately £40 million per year to help deliver a wide range of sports facilities and *sports development* programmes; in 2002, £12 million of this came from the Scottish Executive and £28 million from *National Lottery* funds. Weblink: www.sportscotland.org.uk

Scottish Tourist Board (STB) is the official *tourist board* responsible for tourism *promotion* and development in Scotland. Established under the *1969 Development of Tourism Act,* the STB is funded primarily by *grant-in-aid* from the Scottish Executive. The aims of the STB are to encourage UK residents and *overseas visitors* to visit the country, by providing advice to tourism businesses, funding tourism projects, co-ordinating the *tourist information centre* network in Scotland, running *marketing* campaigns and advising central and local governments. The Scottish Tourist Board is also known as VisitScotland for *marketing* purposes. Weblink: www.visitscotland.com

Scottish Vocational Qualifications (SVQs): see *National Vocational Qualifications*

SDO: see *Sports Development Officer*

sea transport: see *sea travel*

sea travel is the category of *transportation* that includes ferries, cruise liners, hovercraft and hydrofoils.

search engine: a facility that allows an individual to locate a *website* on the *Internet*. Popular search engines include Google, MSN Search, Alta Vista and Yahoo.

seasonality: variations in the *demand* for *products* and services at different times of the year. The demand for package holidays, for example, is very seasonal, with periods of high demand corresponding to school holidays in the UK. Many holiday regions in Britain also experience seasonal fluctuations, with high demand in peak periods followed by troughs in the winter, when the facilities in many resorts close altogether. Public agencies and private companies try to extend the season whenever possible, by targeting people who can take holidays outside of the main peaks and offering discounted rates at these times. Extending the season makes economic sense, since it allows hoteliers and other tourist businesses to offer year-round employment.

Seaside Award: a scheme introduced in 1992 to provide information about a wide range of beaches in the UK. Co-ordinated by ENCAMs, a body concerned with environmental campaigns, Seaside Awards are given to beaches which are clean, well managed and display information about current and previous water quality. There are two categories of beaches, resort and rural, which are assessed for a variety of criteria, including safety, *management,* cleanliness and information. A Seaside Award resort beach is one which actively encourages visitors and has developed its facilities to provide varied recreational opportunities. A rural beach is one which has limited facilities and is visited and enjoyed for its less developed, more natural characteristics. (See also *Blue Flag Campaign*.) Weblink: www.seasideawards.org.uk

seaside resorts in the UK have experienced a hard time in recent years in terms of numbers of *visitors*. Although there are examples of UK resorts that have prospered, many have seen their tourist numbers drop since the mid-1980s, due in part to the availability and low prices of overseas *package holidays*, but also to the fact that the seaside product no longer meets the needs of a more discerning public. Many of the resorts were developed to cater for the needs of a type of tourist who has all but disappeared; one who travelled by train, stayed in a boarding house and was content to walk along the promenade, play in the sand and spend money on the amusements.

seat only sales: the name given to purchases of flight tickets without any *accommodation*. These sales are an important part of the *travel industry*, with tourists prepared to find their own accommodation, or use the facility to fly to their *second home* or *timeshare* accommodation abroad. Business travellers on a budget also make use of seat only sales from time to time. *Low-cost airlines* are a recent example of this type of travel and tourism product.

second home: a property bought especially for use as a holiday home at certain times of the year and sometimes let to friends and other holidaymakers on an infrequent basis. Too many second homes in a single location can sometimes force up the prices of property and cause problems for local people, who may not be able to afford to buy. Second homes can also change the social fabric of certain rural areas, especially when their owners retire and come to live on a permanent basis.

secondary data is information available from existing sources, usually in written form, but increasingly now available from electronic sources such as *CD-ROMs* and the *Internet*. Secondary data is available from both internal sources, such as an organisation's address lists, sales figures and results of visitor *surveys*, as well as from external sources, including company reports, government data, *professional bodies* and independent consultants.

secondary research: sometimes referred to as *field research*, this is the process of collecting and analysing *secondary data*, from a range of different sources, internal and external to an organisation.

secondary research source refers to previously published information that is consulted as part of a study involving *secondary research*, e.g. gazetteers, academic journals, textbooks, the *Internet*, newspapers, etc.

secondary sector: the part of a nation's economy concerned with producing manufactured items from raw materials, e.g. engineering, construction and electronics. (See also *service sector*, *primary sector*.)

secondary spend is the money spent by *customers* over and above the cost of the primary reason for their visit to a leisure or tourism facility, e.g. money spent in the café at a *visitor attraction*, drinks bought from a vending machine at a *leisure centre* or money spent on goods on a cross-Channel ferry. Many organisations devote a great deal of attention to providing secondary spend opportunities, which may yield a higher profit margin than their primary activities.

secret ballot: a vote held in secret so as not to pressurise individuals into voting in a particular way. Under the *Trade Union Act 1984*, the government has made it a requirement that trade unions hold secret ballots of their members before authorising strike action. A vote held in secret, as opposed to a show of hands, is likely to give a better indication of an individual's true feelings.

section 4 grants were made available to *tourism* businesses under the *1969 Development of Tourism Act* to encourage new tourism projects. Although initially available in England, Scotland and Wales, the *English Tourism Council* no longer has powers to distribute section 4 grants, although they remain available in Wales and Scotland. The grants have been used mainly for improvements to hotel accommodation, but areas such as marina developments, *tourist attractions* and *farm tourism* have also benefited.

Sector Skills Councils (SSCs): organisations that will replace *National Training Organisations* in the UK from 2003 onwards.

secure environment: see *security*

security has two meanings in leisure and tourism. The first is to do with *loans*, where some form of security is often required by a lender in case a borrower should default on repayments. Security in this case could include the deeds to property or an insurance policy.

The other meaning of security is more general and relates to the security of people, property, staff and information, at tourism facilities. Organisations have a duty to provide a secure environment; staff must be trained in safe and secure procedures in the workplace, and to be on their guard against suspicious characters and circumstances.

security hazards: a variety of existing and potential problems that a leisure and tourism organisation may need to be aware of and possibly insure against, e.g. violence to staff, theft of information, valuables, cash and other property, fraud, sabotage and accidental damage.

security measures: procedures that organisations put in place to ensure the provision of a *secure environment*, e.g. CCTV, security guards, lockers, safes, lockable fire-proof filing cabinets.

SEETB: see *South East England Tourist Board*

segmentation: see *market segmentation*

selection: see *recruitment and selection process*

self-appraisal: see *self-evaluation*

self-catering accommodation is regarded as any type of *accommodation* where guests take care of themselves and where, unlike *serviced accommodation*, there are no, or very few, services provided for them during their stay. It can take many forms, including:

- chalets in holiday camps
- cottages and apartments
- converted farm buildings
- forest lodges
- villas
- *timeshare*
- camping and caravanning.

In 1999, £1.3 billion was spent on 6.4 million self-catering holidays in England, the most popular regions being the West Country, East of England and Cumbria. Holidaymakers like the freedom and value-for-money that all forms of self-catering accommodation offer, particularly families with young children. Self-catering units may be part of an accommodation complex which provides a range of central services, such as restaurants, swimming pools and games facilities. (See also *serviced accommodation*.)

self-completed survey: a survey that requires the person answering the questions (the *respondent*) to fill in a *questionnaire* themselves, rather than giving answers to an interviewer, as is the case with a *face-to-face interview*. Self-completed surveys have the advantage of being cheaper than interview surveys, since there is no need to recruit and train *interviewers*. They do, however, have their drawbacks, such as lower response rates, which can be improved by sending a reminder to the respondent. Also, if a respondent does not fully understand a question, there is no interviewer to ask for clarification.

self-evaluation is the term used when a person reviews his or her progress in a given situation against pre-determined *objectives* and *performance criteria*. Sometimes called self-appraisal, it takes place most commonly in work situations, particularly for individual members of a team. Self-evaluation can produce useful *feedback* both for the individual member of staff and his or her line manager. Such an appraisal can be fed into any wider *staff development* review that the organisation may undertake.

self-guided trail: a route used by walkers, cyclists and/or car drivers, who follow a series of signs and/or a route map, to learn about places and people featured on the trail. Most self-guided trails are provided for walkers and are found in woodland and other country areas, marked with numbered or colour-coded signs, which are cross-referenced to an explanatory leaflet. Self-guided trails are a common type of *interpretation*, aiming to enhance a person's experience of the place they are visiting.

selling is a structured activity involving *communication* between a buyer and a seller, which is designed to inform the *customer* and persuade him or her to purchase the products or services on offer. Although the obvious objective of any selling activity is to ultimately achieve a sale, it should be seen as a continuous process that can help cement customer relationships, build customer loyalty and provide lasting benefits in an enhanced level of *customer service*. All staff in leisure and tourism are likely to be involved in some form of 'selling' in the course of their work. Selling in private sector organisations is geared towards meeting commercial *objectives*, while public and voluntary sector bodies use selling to help achieve wider social and community aims. (See also *sales process*.)

selling skills: techniques that enable staff to make a successful sale, by identifying *customer needs*, presenting products in the correct manner, *closing a sale* and offering *after-sales service*. Effective selling demands a high level of *interpersonal* and *communication skills* on the part of the sales person.

semi-variable costs: expenditure that is made up of a fixed element, that remains the same irrespective of an organisation's level of business activity, and an element that fluctuates in line with its output. Examples of semi-variable costs in leisure and tourism include telephone, *fax* and *telex* charges, all of which have a constant rental element plus added charges related to the level of use.

sensitivity analysis: a technique used in *forecasting* to measure the overall effect on a *business plan* of any changes in the elements that go to make up the plan. A *theme park*, for example, may base its financial projections on an annual attendance figure of 150,000; with the aid of a computer spreadsheet, the effect of, say, a ten per cent reduction or increase in visitor numbers on the overall financial position can be quickly calculated.

September 11th: the date of the devastating terrorist attack in 2001 on the World Trade Centre in New York. As well as the long-term effects of the catastrophic loss of life, it has also had a dramatic impact on international travel. Many countries saw their tourist activity drop very quickly after the attack and many commentators suggest that it will take many years for the travel and tourism industry to regain the business lost. In the six-month period immediately following September 11, the *British Tourist Authority* estimates that overseas visitors to Britain fell by 12 per cent, which equated to 1.3 million visits. Spending also fell by some 19 per cent in the same period, down from £5.3 million in 2000 to £4.3 million in 2001. The events of September 11 came as a severe blow to the UK tourism industry that had already been ravaged by the outbreak of *foot and mouth disease* in February 2001.

service charge: an additional amount, usually expressed as a percentage, added to the selling price of a meal to cover service costs. Some menus indicate that service is included in the cost of the meal, so that no extra gratuity is expected; in this case, the French term 'service compris' is sometimes used.

service sector: the part of a nation's economy that is made up of *tertiary industries*, i.e. those concerned with providing a service rather than extracting raw materials (*primary sector*) or producing manufactured goods (*secondary sector*). The service sector includes retailing, banking, insurance, financial services, information technology, shipping, leisure, travel and tourism. Like many industrialised societies, the UK is moving away from an economy based on primary and secondary industries towards one that is dominated by the service sector. It is estimated that more than half of the country's *gross national product* currently comes from service sector industries and that three out of every four jobs in Britain are in service industries. The service sector makes an important contribution to Britain's *balance of payments*.

serviced accommodation refers to *hotels*, guesthouses and any other type of *accommodation* where guests are offered a range of different services during their stay, such as food, portering, valet services and possibly entertainment. *BTA* statistics show that there are in the region of 27,000 hotels in the UK, to which can be added an estimated 20,000 *bed and breakfast* establishments, guesthouses and providers of farmhouse accommodation. (See also *self-catering accommodation*.)

Seven Wonders of the World: works of art and architecture regarded by Ancient Greek and Roman observers as worthy of exceptional note. The Seven Wonders were:

- the pyramids of Egypt
- the hanging gardens of Babylon
- the statue of Zeus at Olympia
- the Temple of Artemis at Ephesus
- the Mausoleum of Halicarnassus
- the Colossus of Rhodes
- the Pharos of Alexandria.

Sex Discrimination Act 1975: *legislation* introduced to outlaw discrimination on the grounds of gender. The Act states that employers must not treat people of a particular gender any less favourably when it comes to recruitment, *training* and promotion. There are certain circumstances when the employment of staff of a particular sex is allowable, e.g. an advertisement for an attendant to work in the female changing rooms at a sports centre could legally ask for female candidates only to apply.

sex tourism: the practice of attracting tourists with the offer of sexual encounters. Countries such as Thailand and the Philippines are often associated with sex tourism, which is increasingly being condemned by many Western states, religious leaders and the countries themselves.

SGITs is an acronym for special group inclusive tour rates, which are discounted *scheduled airline* fares offered to *tour operators* who sell *inclusive tours by excursion*.

share capital: that part of a company's *capital* made available from *shareholders*.

shareholder: an individual or institution that holds *shares* in a *company* or number of companies. The shareholder buys shares as an investment and hopes that, in the long term, the return on investment (known as the *dividend*) will be greater than that available from other sources. Depending on the type of shares held, the shareholder enjoys a number of other rights, including the right to attend the *annual general meeting* and vote on the election of new directors.

shares are certificates giving their holders part ownership of a *company* and the right to receive a proportion of its profits by way of a *dividend*. There are different types of shares, such as *ordinary shares*, *debentures* and *preference shares*, each giving different shareholder rights. Companies issue shares as a way of raising *capital* for business expansion.

shell leaflet: a promotional leaflet which contains colour pictures and images, but no written text. Organisations add their own text, thereby generating a colour *brochure* at a reduced cost.

shift work: a work pattern which is implemented when employees are needed to cover more than a standard eight-hour day. A *leisure centre*, for example, that is open from 7am to 11pm is likely to have two eight-hour shifts, one from 7am until 3pm and a second from 3pm until 11pm. Staff are rotated, sometimes working the early shift and sometimes the late shift. In certain circumstances staff will be paid extra for working *unsocial hours*.

shopping: see *leisure shopping*

short break: a short duration trip in the UK or abroad as a main holiday or second, additional vacation. Although the traditional British two-week holiday is in something of a decline, short breaks have been a resounding success story since the early 1980s. Their popularity lies in the changing leisure habits of much of the population, linked to changes in working practices, making the two-week break unpopular with a large section of the travelling public, many of whom have sufficient *disposable income* to be able to enjoy more than one holiday each year. Figures from *Star UK* website show that UK residents took 63.8 million short holidays of 1–3 nights duration in 2001, spending £8.1 billion. Developments in *transportation*, such as the growth of *low-cost airlines*, the success of the *Channel Tunnel* travel services and cheaper ferry fares, have boosted the market for short breaks to the continent. According to figures from *ABTA*, 5.6 million short break overseas holidays were taken by the British in 2002 and the market share of short breaks taken abroad increased from 11.7 per cent of all holidays in 1997 to 15 per cent in 2002.

short haul: the name given to *destinations* on the near continent, such as Holland, France, Belgium, parts of Germany and the Scandinavian countries. (See also *long haul.*) Short haul destinations have benefited considerably from extra visitors as a result of the growth of *low-cost airlines*.

short take-off and landing (STOL): a type of aircraft technology that allows an aeroplane to operate on a reduced length runway. STOL aircraft, such as the Dash 7 and British Aerospace 146, have influenced airport developments, particularly serving the needs of business travellers, by allowing development close to the heart of cities and business districts. London City Airport in Docklands was developed on the basis of accepting STOL aircraft.

shoulder period refers to the times either side of *peak season*. In the case of overseas *package holidays*, shoulder periods are either side of July and August, and the time just before and just after Easter. The term 'shoulder' comes from the shape of the demand graph for the holidays, which resembles the shoulders on a body (see figure on next page).

Since there is less demand during the shoulder periods, prices for leisure and tourism products and services are generally lower than for *peak season*.

shuttle service: a type of frequent *transportation* that carries passengers on popular routes with a minimum of check-in procedures, e.g. airline shuttle services between London and Manchester, and Glasgow and Aberdeen.

SIBH: see *Society for the Interpretation of Britain's Heritage*

SIC: see *Standard Industrial Classification*

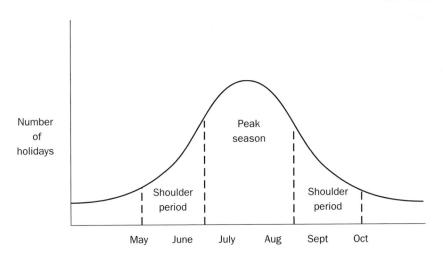

Example of shoulder periods

significance of UK tourism: see *UK tourism*

single currency: the final stage of *Economic and Monetary Union* for the member states of the *European Union (EU)*, when there was to be a single currency operating across all EU countries. In 2002, 12 EU member states adopted the *Euro* as their national currency.

Single Market: the agreement that was to allow, by the end of 1992, the free movement of goods, services, people and capital between the member states of the *European Community* (now *European Union*). The aims of the creation of the Single Market were to reduce *red tape* by removing trade barriers, create more competition between companies, make travel between member countries easier and create more jobs. Despite the optimism of the early 1990s, much still has to be done to complete the process, although some measures are in place, e.g. reduction in frontier controls.

single supplement: an extra payment for *accommodation* or other travel services paid by a person travelling alone. A hotel, for example, may feel justified in making an additional charge for single occupancy of a double room, since it is losing potential revenue. Single supplements for hotel accommodation are often resented by tourists and are now not universally levied.

Site of Special Scientific Interest (SSSI) is an area designated by *English Nature, Scottish Natural Heritage* or the *Countryside Council for Wales* because it has special examples of mammals, birds, insects, plants or geological features. Most SSSIs are in private ownership, with around 40 per cent owned or managed by public bodies such as the Ministry of Defence or the *Forestry Commission.* English Nature provides advice to the owners of SSSIs on protecting the nature conservation value of their land. Designation of a piece of land as an SSSI may mean that its owners are barred from undertaking certain activities, such as ploughing.

situation analysis: see *SWOT analysis*

Skal Clubs are international groups of senior *travel trade* employees who meet regularly to socialise and promote mutual understanding. There are more then 500 Skal Clubs throughout the world, which arrange luncheons and dinners for members and guests. Membership is restricted to those who have held a position of responsibility in the *travel and tourism industry* for at least five years. Weblink: www.skaluk.org

skills: see *personal skills and qualities, interpersonal skills, business skills, communication skills, research skills, selling skills*

skimming is when a high *price* is charged initially for a new *product* or service that is unique and that attracts *customers* who are willing to pay a high price for status reasons (see figure below). Creating an artificially high price for a product can help to give it an up-market image. Examples of skimming in leisure and tourism include flights on Concorde, trips on the Venice-Simplon Orient Express and exclusive cruises. Adopting a skimming policy may lead to problems in the long run when competitors enter the *market* with similar products offered at lower prices.

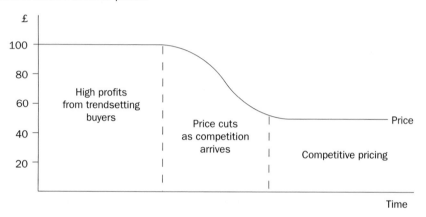

Skimming the market

Sky Television is part of the British Sky Broadcasting Group (BSkyB), the operator of the UK's largest digital television platform and a leading broadcaster of sport, movies, entertainment and news. More than 15 million viewers in 6.1 million homes in the UK are subscribers to more than 200 channels offered by Sky, plus its range of interactive services. BskyB's own channels, such as Sky News and Sky Sports, are available in a further 4.1 million cable homes in the UK and Ireland. Sky owns the *television rights* to a number of popular sports in the UK, including Premiership football, cricket and golf. Weblink: www.sky.com

sleeping partner: an individual who enters into a *partnership* agreement and contributes finance, but takes no part in the day-to-day running of the business. This may be for purely investment purposes or for tax reasons. It is important to remember that the decisions of a sleeping partner are nevertheless binding on all other partners.

smart card: a further development of the *credit* or *debit card* that stores an individual's personal and financial information on a microchip within a plastic card. Some people believe that smart cards will soon become commonplace in society, while others point to the possible loss of liberty if the information contained on the card is misused.

small and medium-sized enterprises (SMEs) are classified as those that employ less than 250 employees. Nearly all (99 per cent) of the *tourism* enterprises in Europe fall within this category, with 94 per cent employing less than 10 people (classified as *micro enterprises*).

SMART objectives refers to *objectives* that are **s**pecific, **m**easurable **a**chievable, **r**ealistic and **t**imed.

SMEs: see *small and medium-sized enterprises*

SNH: see *Scottish Natural Heritage*

SNVQs: see *Scottish National Vocational Qualifications*

social class: see *socio-economic classification*

social costs: unlike economic costs, which are relatively easy to quantify, social costs are the social, environmental and operational effects of a particular project or decision, which are borne by a local community or by society in general. An analysis of the social costs of a project are an essential part of a *cost-benefit analysis*, i.e. the widening of a road may result in the loss of trees and amenity land, extra pollution, more noise, loss of housing and may lead to more vehicle accidents. All of these social costs (sometimes called external costs), need to be quantified and considered against the economic costs of the proposal. It is often left to *pressure groups* and public sector bodies to make developers aware of the social costs of their actions.

social impacts of tourism: see *socio-cultural impacts of leisure, travel and tourism*

social objectives: whereas private sector organisations set themselves commercial *objectives*, such as increasing *market share* or maximising revenue, *non-commercial organisations* have wider social objectives, which can include:

- increasing participation in leisure activities in an inner city area
- providing facilities for disabled visitors at a *theme park*
- running courses for disadvantaged children at an outdoor activity centre
- gaining support for an environmental cause
- protecting country areas from further *development*.

Although social objectives are not always easy to measure, the introduction of *compulsory competitive tendering* and other efficiency initiatives has forced local authorities to put a value on them, so that social aims can be measured along with the more conventional financial and operational objectives.

social tourism is the name given to the development and encouragement of tourist facilities and services for disadvantaged members of society, e.g. those on low incomes, disabled people, single parent families, the elderly and other deprived minorities. This can be achieved through voluntary measures, such as fund raising by charities for holidays and day trips, or by local and central government initiatives such as *grants* and low-interest loans. The tourism policy of the *European Union* includes the encouragement of social tourism as one of its priority areas. In the UK, the work of the *Holiday Care Service* has helped many individuals find suitable *accommodation* for their needs.

Social Trends is a government publication that provides national data about a wide range of topics, including many allied to the leisure, travel and tourism industries. It is published by the *Office for National Statistics (ONS)* and contains data about, for example, how people use their leisure time, how many are members of particular societies, how many attend football matches and what proportion of the population owns or has access to a car. Much of the data is taken from government departments and other ONS sources, including the

General Household Survey, as well as surveys sponsored by the tourist boards, e.g. the *International Passenger Survey*. Weblink: www.statistics.gov.uk

Society for the Interpretation of Britain's Heritage (SIBH) a former independent membership organisation that focused on issues concerned with the *interpretation* of Britain's *heritage*. Its work is now carried on by the *Association for Heritage Interpretation*.

Society of London Theatre (SOLT) is a trade association which represents theatre managers, owners and producers of the 50 major commercial and grant-aided theatres in central London. With annual West End theatre attendances of nearly 12 million, the Society encourages and promotes theatre-going to the domestic, overseas, group and corporate markets through a variety of promotions and events. Founded in 1908, it plays a major role in *industrial relations* with the main unions serving the needs of employees in music and the arts. Members of SOLT benefit from a range of services, including legal advice, promotional work and *lobbying* on matters of concern. Weblink: www.solt.co.uk

socio-cultural impacts of leisure, travel and tourism include both positive and negative outcomes. Socio-cultural problems include:

* overcrowding
* loss of traditional industries and crafts
* distortion of local customs
* alteration of religious practices
* loss of languages
* loss of authenticity.

On the positive side, leisure and tourism can contribute to the revitalisation of neglected regions and customs, the rebirth of local arts and crafts, and greater understanding between different cultures. Many people consider that the negative socio-cultural impacts of leisure and tourism are far more harmful than harmful *environmental impacts*, since they may take generations to eradicate.

socio-economic classification: an attempt to classify individuals into one of six 'social class' groups on the basis of their occupation (see figure on next page). Developed originally by the Joint Industry Committee for National Readership Surveys (JICNARS), the classification has been used by marketers to develop products and market them to specific groups, based on the notion that all people in a particular social class grouping will have similar patterns of buyer behaviour. The classification has been criticised by marketing professionals for being too general. Today, classifications based on *life style* and *life cycle* are favoured by marketers.

socio-economic groupings: see *socio-economic classification*

soft tourism: see *'green' tourism*

software: the programs and other applications that operate on computer *hardware*. *Personal computers (PCs)* can be loaded with a wide range of software packages for business, domestic and leisure uses. Some of the most common packages used by businesses are *databases, spreadsheets, desktop publishing (DTP)*, communications and *word processing* software. Software programs are either pre-installed on a computer's internal memory or downloaded from floppy disks or CDs. Today, most software runs on 'Windows'-based systems, developed by the Microsoft Corporation.

Social grade	Social class	Typical occupations
A	Upper middle	Higher managerial, admin. and professional (e.g. judges, surgeons)
B	Middle	Intermediate managerial and admin. (e.g. lawyers, teachers, doctors)
C1	Lower middle	Supervisory, clerical, junior management (e.g. bank clerk, estate agent)
C2	Skilled working	Skilled manual workers (e.g. joiner, welder)
D	Working	Semi- and unskilled manual workers (e.g. driver, postman, porter)
E	Those at lowest level of subsistence	Pensioners, widows, casual workers, students, unemployed people

Socio-economic classification

sole trader: the simplest form of business unit in which an individual has full ownership and control of an enterprise, with the advantage of swift decision making and lack of bureaucracy. Many leisure and tourism businesses start as sole traders, perhaps converting to *partnerships* or *limited companies* as they expand their operations. Disadvantages of operating as a sole trader include the fact that the owner is personally liable for all the debts of the business, there may be limited capital available for expansion and, often overlooked in leisure and tourism, the long hours the sole trader often has to work to make a success of his or her venture.

SOLT: see *Society of London Theatre*

solvency: see *liquidity*

South East England Tourist Board is the official *Regional Tourist Board* covering the counties of Kent, Surrey, East Sussex and West Sussex. Weblink: www.seetb.org.uk

Southern Tourist Board is the official *Regional Tourist Board* covering the counties of Oxfordshire, Buckinghamshire, Berkshire, East and North Dorset, Hampshire and the Isle of Wight. Weblink: www.southerntb.co.uk

spa: a natural attraction that many towns have exploited for *tourism* purposes. Spa towns in the UK, such as Cheltenham, Buxton and Llandrindod Wells, have used the healing powers of spa waters as a way of attracting tourists since the early seventeenth century. In recent years, there has been something of a revival in the promotion of UK spa towns, under the direction of the *British Spas Federation*.

special needs: the general term given to those people who have extra requirements or who demand special care and attention. In leisure and tourism, these may be children, older people or those with physical disabilities.

specific needs: see *special needs*

spectator safety has become an important issue since the tragic fire at Bradford City Football Club in 1985 when 56 people died and the Hillsborough Stadium disaster in 1989 when 96 football fans were killed. Early legislation to improve matters included the *Safety of Sports Grounds Act 1975*, which gave the operators of grounds certain responsibilities in relation to health and safety. The Hillsborough disaster led to the publication of the *Taylor Report* into safety at football stadia.

spectator sports: see *sports spectating*

sponsor: an individual, company or organisation that agrees to provide services or funding to another party, usually in return for media coverage.

sponsorship is an important, if uncertain, source of extra income for certain sectors of the UK leisure and tourism industries, particularly *spectator sports* and the arts. It varies enormously in scale, from the Barclaycard company's sponsorship of soccer's Premiership to a local builder providing the cost of the kit for a local junior hockey team. Either way, the principle is the same, with both the builder and Barclaycard expecting a return on their investment, in the form of wider publicity in the *media* leading to increased levels of business. Sponsorship of the arts at local, regional and national levels is encouraged by organisations such as Arts and Business, while a group of commercial and public sector bodies known as the *Institute of Sports Sponsorship (ISS)* meets regularly to promote sponsorship in sport. The ISS estimates that sponsors in the UK invest more than £1 billion annually in sport in the UK.

sport is a major component of the UK *leisure and recreation industry*, playing an important part in most people's lives. Some 36 million people take part in sport or physical recreation at least once a month in the UK (*sports participation*). Millions more watch or follow sport on a regular basis (*sports spectating*). In attempting to define sport, there are a number of characteristics; sport usually involves some type of physical activity, it often requires an element of skill, contains rules and regulations, and usually involves a competitive element or at least a challenge to the individual.

Sport brings with it a number of economic and social benefits, including:

- a contribution to better health and a sense of personal well-being
- playing a vital role in children's education
- generating nearly £10 billion of financial expenditure for the UK economy
- providing around 414,000 jobs
- the promotion and enhancement of Britain on the international scene.

Public sector sport is administered by *UK Sport*, which is funded by the *Department for Culture, Media and Sport*, and the Sports Councils representing England, Wales, Scotland and Northern Ireland. *Local authorities* in England and Wales spend approximately £1.5 billion on sports and leisure facilities and services, contributing to the quality of life and prosperity of their areas.

Sport and Recreation Information Group (SPRIG) is a non-profit making organisation made up of individuals and organisations working in a number of *sport* and *leisure* information fields, with representatives from the various sports councils, *ILAM*, *local authorities*, universities, colleges and various other interested bodies. SPRIG aims to encourage collaboration throughout the information profession, with a view to raising the profile of sport and recreation documentation. It publishes a twice-yearly bulletin, which includes articles on information services, notification of meetings, book reviews and conference reports. Weblink: www.sprig.org.uk

Sport England: a *quango* established in 1997 (formerly known as the *English Sports Council*) with the primary role of developing and maintaining the infrastructure of *sport* in England. It is also responsible for distributing *National Lottery* funds to sport in England via the *National Lottery Sports Fund*. Sport England is accountable to government through the *Department for Culture, Media and Sport*, which is also its principal funding source. It has three main policy areas:

1   development of excellence in sport through support for *governing bodies* and *National Sports Centres*

2   support for youth sport in schools and support for other bodies such as the *Youth Sports Trust*

3   distribution of grants from the *National Lottery Sports Fund*.

Within these three policy areas it promotes causes such as women in sport and sport for people with disabilities. Sport England's ten regional offices co-ordinate its activities, provide information services, administrative support and sports science support. (See also *UK Sport*). Weblink: www.sportengland.org

Sport for All was originally a campaign started by the *Sports Council* in 1972. It has since become a generic term associated with all aspects of encouraging people from all sections of the community to participate in sport in the UK, regardless of race, creed, colour, ability, social status, mobility, income, age, location or gender. Studies conducted from the 1970s onwards into the use of leisure and recreation facilities in the UK have invariably concluded that the majority of users of such facilities were white, male, car-borne and middle class. *UK Sport* sees *sports equity* as one of its major priorities for the new millennium. (See also *sports participation*.)

Sport Scotland: see *Scottish Sports Council*

sporting goods are any items that are needed for playing sports, e.g. football kit, golf clubs, a snooker table.

sports academy: a purpose-built facility whose purpose is to raise the standards of performance in a particular sport or in sports people generally. Staffed by experts in their particular field, sports academies select and train those individuals who show the greatest potential of making an impact in sport at the highest level. Academies are found across the UK, often linked to professional sports teams such as Premiership football clubs. (See also *UK Sports Institute, English Institute of Sport*.)

Sports Aid Foundation (SAF) was established in 1976 to raise funds to help British sports people compete in major international events. *Grants* are awarded to individual competitors to assist with preparation and training expenses, travel and subsistence while away from home, special diets and equipment. The SAF is an independent body funded by joint promotions with commercial sponsors, national and regional events and individual donations. With the advent of the *National Lottery*, and particularly the *Lottery Sports Fund*, the Foundation has begun to change its role, concentrating more on providing support and assistance to young people to develop their talents and to sports people with disabilities. Weblink: www.sportsaid.org.uk

Sports Coach UK: see *National Coaching Foundation*

sports coaching: the practice of training individuals to improve their performance in a particular sport. Coaching takes place at a variety of levels, from school PE lessons, through amateur sports clubs, to the work of *Sports Development Officers* and elite sports people working professionally. (See also *National Coaching Foundation*.)

Sports Council: an independent body, established in 1972 by Royal Charter, and financed largely through funds from the *Department of National Heritage*. The Sports Council was the first body to take on the role of co-ordinating sport in the UK and was given specific responsibilities for:

- increasing participation in sport and physical recreation
- increasing the quality and quantity of sports facilities
- raising standards of performance in sport
- providing information for and about sport.

The Sports Council was replaced in 1996 by a new, streamlined structure made up of two bodies, the *UK Sports Council* (now called *UK Sport*) and the *English Sports Council* (now called *Sport England*). (See also *Sports Council for Wales, Scottish Sports Council, Northern Ireland Sports Council*.)

Sports Council for Wales: the national organisation responsible for developing and promoting *sport* and *recreation* in Wales. Its aims are to provide opportunities for everyone to participate and enjoy the benefits of sport, develop those individuals with potential into competitors who generate national pride, and to gain international recognition for Wales as a nation with a sporting culture. Established in 1972, it is the main adviser to the *National Assembly for Wales* on all sporting matters. It is also a distributor of *National Lottery* funds for capital and revenue purposes under its SPORTLOT initiative. Weblink: www.sports-council-wales.co.uk

sports development is an educational process championed by *UK Sport* and the Sports Councils representing England, Wales, Scotland and Northern Ireland, and put into practice by *Sports Development Officers* throughout the UK. It is about making sure that adequate structures are in place to allow people, regardless of their starting point or ability, the opportunity to learn basic skills in the sport of their choice. It represents an awareness that the notion of *Sport for All* requires an investment in people as well as facilities. (See also *Champion Coaching*.)

Sports Development Officer (SDO): an individual whose role is to encourage sports participation among a range of different groups of all ages, abilities and standards. SDOs may be employed in a specific sport, for example a tennis development officer or a football development officer, or may take on a more general sports development role. SDOs are usually employed by local authorities, with funding from a wide range of sources including the *National Lottery* and *governing bodies of sport*. There are more than 1000 SDOs in the UK working with community groups, coaches and local authority officials to help improve sports performance.

sports equity seeks to ensure fairness at all levels of *sport*, to recognise that there are inequalities in the ways in which sports are organised, and takes steps to eradicate the unfairness for the mutual benefit of all sports people. *UK Sport* regards the promotion of sports equity as one of its major objectives. (See also *sports development*.)

sports injury clinic: a specialist facility used to treat a range of injuries to sports people and staffed by trained personnel including *physiotherapists*.

sports medicine: the science underpinning *sports development*, nutrition and individual performance. We see the darker side of sports medicine when considering *drugs in sport*.

sports participation is an important aspect of the nation's use of its *leisure time*, with nearly two-thirds of the adult population of Britain taking part in sport and physical recreation at least once a month. Figures for 1997 from *Social Trends* indicate that, after walking (44 per cent), swimming is the most popular sporting activity in the UK, with 15 per cent of all adults participating. Other popular sports activities include keep fit/yoga (12 per cent), snooker/pool (11 per cent), cycling (11 per cent), weight training (5 per cent), football (5 per cent), golf (5 per cent) and running (5 per cent). The top sports participated in by young people outside school lessons are football (boys) and swimming (girls). Although there has been a gradual increase in sports participation in recent years, there is some concern about the low participation rates in some sections of society, notably women, people from ethnic minorities and those on low incomes. These concerns have led organisations such as the sports councils representing the home countries and local authorities to introduce campaigns such as *Sport for All* to address this problem of *sports equity*.

sports-related gambling is a term that covers many activities, including betting on horse racing, dog racing, football and a variety of other sports. Almost three-quarters of the population took part in some gambling activity in 1999. There has been a change in the nature of gambling since the introduction of the *National Lottery* in 1994. The British Gambling Preference Survey found that two-thirds of the population had bought at least one National Lottery ticket in 1999. The popularity of the Lottery has drawn money away from sports-related gambling, although the sector is fighting back with innovations such as Internet-based betting services.

sports spectating is an important *leisure time* activity in the UK, with football being the most popular spectator sport, although attendances fell during the 1980s and 1990s. Spectator sports, including rugby, hockey, cricket, bowls, darts and tennis operate under the auspices of their relevant *governing body*, which sets the rules and determines policies. Commercial involvement, however, is never far away, although its scale varies from one spectator sport to another. *Sponsorship* is big business in some sports and large football clubs, such as Manchester United and Tottenham Hotspur, both of which are *public limited companies*.

sports tourism: any tourist activity that has sport as a major component or theme, e.g. travelling to Monte Carlo to watch the Monaco Grand Prix, watching the British Open golf tournament at the Belfry or travelling to a football match in Germany. Sports tourism is one of the fastest-growing sectors of the industry.

spreadsheet: a powerful *computer* application that can be used to perform a range of numerical and financial calculations, so as to aid *management* decision making. Spreadsheet packages are used extensively in both large and small leisure and tourism organisations to provide financial information, such *cash-flow forecasts*, budget predictions and tax returns. In its simplest form, a spreadsheet is little more than a grid consisting of horizontal rows and vertical columns, into which data is written. Spreadsheets are particularly useful for a process known as *'sensitivity analysis'*, when the outcome of alterations to one or more elements of a speadsheet will automatically be calculated by the programme.

SPRIG: see *Sport and Recreation Information Group*

Springboard UK is an organisation that promotes careers in hospitality, leisure, tourism and travel to a range of potential recruits and influencers through a network of centres across the UK. It also runs the *Travel and Tourism Programme*, which is designed to help teachers in schools and colleges deliver travel, tourism, leisure and hospitality courses more effectively with the direct support of the Programme's sponsors. Weblink: www.springboarduk.org.uk

SPRITO: see *National Training Organisation for Sport, Recreation and Allied Occupations*

SSCs: see *Sector Skills Councils*

SSSI: see *Site of Special Scientific Interest*

Stabiliser is the name given to a type of 'closed shop' arrangement legally operated by *ABTA* up until the end of 1993. Under a process known as Operation Stabiliser, ABTA *travel agents* could only sell package holidays from tour operators who were themselves members of ABTA, and the holidays of ABTA *tour operators* could only be sold through ABTA travel agents. The Stabiliser was introduced in the mid-1960s to safeguard the public interest, and that of ABTA members, against unscrupulous agents and operators. The arrangement was dismantled in 1993, since it was considered to be against the public interest and also because the introduction of the *EU Package Travel Directive* rendered it obsolete.

staff appraisal: a formal system for reviewing an employee's performance at work and agreeing targets and support for the future. The appraisal (sometimes called a staff development review) normally takes the form of an interview between a member of staff and his or her line manager, at which each party looks back on past achievements and identifies areas for further development. The outcome of the appraisal, which may be part of a wider remuneration exercise linking pay to performance, should be a written *staff development* plan agreed by the member of staff and the person carrying out the appraisal, listing personal development objectives and the activities needed to achieve them.

staff development: all aspects of an individual's career and personal development that contribute towards the ability to perform to the maximum in the workplace. This could include, for example, *staff appraisal, staff training, job enlargement, job rotation* or *job enrichment*. It is in the interest of employers to invest time and money in their employees in order to produce excellent members of staff and reduce staff turnover. (See also *career development*.)

staff development review: see *staff appraisal*

'staff' functions are carried out by specialists within an organisation in support of *line managers*, who are given the *responsibility* for achieving specific business objectives ('line' functions). Typical 'staff' functions include personnel, accounting and finance, *research* and development, *marketing* and administration. Many large leisure and tourism organisations operate a *matrix organisation*, combining both 'line' and 'staff' functions.

staff motivation is concerned with encouraging, enabling and empowering employees to enjoy their work and contribute effectively to an organisation's activities. Motivation is closely related to *job satisfaction*, a complex issue that depends on many interlinking factors, such as the quality of the working environment, the attitude of senior management, co-operation with colleagues, pay and reward systems, terms of employment, status and recognition of achievements. Motivated staff bring benefits to an organisation, such as reduced absenteeism, better standards of customer service and greater productivity. (See also *Herzberg*.)

staff records are held by *leisure* and *tourism* organisations, with details of past employees and current staff. The records contain a range of information, including personal details, job title and grade, accident and sickness records, absenteeism, *payroll* information, references and records of any *staff appraisal* interviews. The records may be held on a manual or computerised system.

staff training: any learning activity that enables a member of staff to gain knowledge, learn new skills or update existing skills relating to their work situation. Staff training is sometimes divided into those activities that take place at work (*on-the-job training*) and activities carried out away from work (*off-the-job training*). A structured programme of staff training can increase staff morale, boost productivity, improve levels of *customer service*, reduce costs, increase flexibility and trigger new ideas.

stakeholder is a term used to describe all those who have an interest in the affairs of an organisation or activity and who have an influence on its *management*. In *private sector organisations*, stakeholders include owners, *managers, shareholders,* staff, *customers,* banks and statutory agencies (e.g. Inland Revenue, *Health and Safety Executive*) Stakeholders in *public sector organisations* include local councillors, council officials, local communities and society in general. Stakeholders have an important role to play in helping to determine *objectives* and in setting *policy*.

Standardised Approach to Sports Halls (SASH): an initiative promoted by the *Sports Council* in the 1980s to stimulate the provision of a greater number of local sports halls by offering a building of standard design that could be constructed in any region. The original design incorporated four badminton courts with ancillary services. The adoption of a standard design reduced both capital and operating costs, thereby offering local communities a value-for-money solution to widening community involvement in *sport* and *recreation*.

Standard Industrial Classification (SIC): a system that places jobs in various employment categories in order to analyse movements in particular occupations and provide indicators of trends in employment generally. Co-ordinated by the *Department for Education and Skills,* the SIC includes a number of categories of interest to leisure and tourism, including jobs in hotels, restaurants, transport services and libraries. There is not, however, a single category for either 'tourism' or 'leisure', making estimates of employment in these industries an inexact science. Figures for employment in various industry sectors are published regularly in the *Employment Gazette*.

standby: the name given to a discounted fare offered by airlines and other travel companies to travellers who are prepared to turn up without booking in advance, in the hope of securing a vacant seat.

'Star' accommodation grading scheme: an *accommodating grading scheme* adopted by the four national tourist boards representing England, Wales, Scotland and Northern Ireland.

Star UK: a website resource providing up-to-date statistics and information on *UK tourism*. Weblink: www.staruk.org.uk

'stars': see *Boston Consulting Group matrix*

start-up costs are the costs that an enterprise will face when first starting to trade. These could include *capital costs*, such as the purchase or *leasing* of premises, vehicles and equipment, or *revenue costs*, including salaries, postage and Internet charges. Start-up costs can be financed through a bank *loan* or *overdraft*.

stately homes are an important part of the *UK tourism* scene, enjoyed by both *overseas visitors* and British people alike. Many stately homes are in the ownership of the National Trust, while others are privately owned. The high costs of maintaining stately homes has led many owners to open their doors to the public, Beaulieu, Longleat and Chatsworth, to name but a few. The income from day visitors, overnight guests, special events and *corporate hospitality*, has been ploughed back into the running of the houses and their grounds for the benefit of generations to come.

Statistical Office of the European Communities: see *Eurostat*

Stats MR is a commercial organisation that provides *market research* services to major *travel and tourism* companies on a subscription basis. Mass market tour operators, such as JMC Holidays, *Thomson* and First Choice Holidays, use the data supplied by Stats MR to forecast future market trends and refine their *product portfolios* and *marketing strategies* accordingly.

statutory refers to any regulation which has the backing of government *legislation*, e.g. an Act of Parliament such as the *Development of Tourism Act 1969*.

STB: see *Scottish Tourist Board*

steamships were introduced in Britain soon after the development of the railways in 1830. The Peninsular and Oriental Steam Navigation Company (P&O) was one of the first companies to harness the power of steam for passenger travel, running the first regular long-distance services to India and the Far East in 1838. The Cunard Steamship Company started services between Europe and North America in 1840. The development of jet aircraft during and after the Second World War led to the introduction of trans-Atlantic passenger aircraft travel, which was to have a devastating effect on the *demand* for passenger shipping, although in recent years cruising has been enjoying something of a revival in fortunes.

'steep' pyramid: a type of *hierarchical* structure in which there is a very narrow span of control, i.e. power and *responsibility* within an organisation rest with a small number of senior managers, below which there are many tiers of *management* (see figure on next page). 'Steep' pyramid structures (sometimes called tall hierarchies) tend to be very centralised and bureaucratic, with decisions having to pass through many channels for confirmation. (See also *'flat' pyramid*.)

steering group: a group of people given the task of overseeing or implementing an initiative or project through to its completion, providing guidance and advice throughout. (See also *committee*.)

STEP analysis: see *PEST analysis*

stock control is the practice of *managing* stocks of goods to ensure a continuous supply. It is a broad term covering the storage of stock, recording of stock levels, stocktaking and withdrawing items from stock. The development of automated systems such as *EPOS* has greatly simplified and speeded up an organisation's stock control function. In leisure and tourism, stock control is necessary for items such as drinks, food, souvenirs, *sporting goods*, equipment and clothing.

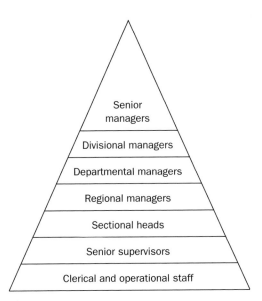

The 'steep' pyramid structure

Stock Exchange: the place where stocks and *shares* are bought and sold. Britain's principal Stock Exchange is located in the heart of the City of London, although there are exchanges at a number of regional centres, including Birmingham and Glasgow. The London Stock Exchange is one of the busiest in the world, along with the New York and Tokyo Exchanges. Weblink: www.londonstockexchange.com

STOL: see *short take-off and landing*

storming refers to the stage of team development immediately following *forming*, when team members have got to know each other and are more willing to challenge others' views and opinions, thereby leading to a group with a clarified purpose. (See also *norming, performing*.)

strap line is a term used in *advertising* to denote a phrase or saying that is used regularly to accompany a promotional campaign. Examples of strap lines used in leisure and tourism are 'the world's favourite airline' (*British Airways*), 'we try harder' (Avis) and 'we're getting there' *(British Rail)*. Strap lines are a type of *branding* that is used to create an *image* and ultimately generate extra business.

strategic alliance: this is formed when a company or organisation joins forces with another for mutual benefit. There have been a number of strategic alliances formed in the travel and tourism industry, principally in the airline sector, e.g. the Star Alliance and One World, where airlines have co-operated with each other as a way of increasing their global influence and *market share*. (See also *takeover*.)

strategic marketing: the medium- to long-term process of determining how best an organisation can achieve its *marketing objectives*. A tour operator, for example, may have set itself a *marketing objective* of capturing 50 per cent of the total market for *package tours* from the UK to Greece. Its strategic *marketing plan* will indicate how it intends to achieve this, giving details of levels of *advertising* and other promotional work, costs of the marketing activities, the timescale within which it is operating, its range of products, etc.

Within its overall marketing strategy the company will develop specific *marketing plans*, giving greater detail and costings.

strategic planning is the process of determining the methods that an organisation will implement in order to meet its *objectives*. A strategic plan tries to answer the following questions:

- what do we want to achieve?
- where are we now?
- where do we want to be in *x* years' time?
- what do we have to do to get there?
- how do we know when we've arrived?

In seeking to answer these questions, the organisation needs to adopt a strategic *planning* process that includes the following stages:

1 clarification of the organisation's aims and *objectives*

2 analysis of its current financial and *market* position

3 the development of action plans to achieve the desired aims

4 implementation of the action plans

5 monitoring and evaluation of the plans.

Given that the strategic planning process aims to achieve the best use of an organisation's *resources*, it is equally applicable to public, private and voluntary sector leisure, travel and tourism organisations.

strategy: the techniques, practices and methods that an organisation uses to help achieve its *aims* and *objectives*. (See also *strategic planning*.)

strengths: see *SWOT analysis*

structure of sport: see *sport*

structure of the travel and tourism industry: see *travel and tourism industry*

Structure Plan: a document, produced by a local planning authority under the 1968 Town and Country Planning Act, setting out the future strategy for the area. Structure plans include detailed plans relating to a number of *local authority* responsibilities, such as housing, transportation, social services, education and *leisure* and *tourism*. Structure Plans are a useful starting point for an organisation wishing to establish or expand their operation, since they give broad indications of what the authority will look favourably upon and what it is trying to discourage, e.g. in terms of tourism, they may welcome new businesses that focus on activity centres but discourage more caravan sites on environmental grounds. Structure Plans are generally prepared by *county councils,* with *district councils* producing their own *Local Plans*.

suggestion box: a type of *feedback* that encourages customers and users to write down their comments and suggestions on a facility and post them in a strategically placed box.

suggestion scheme: a device that encourages staff to make suggestions for improvements to the product or service they are supplying, the environment in which they are working, ways of reducing costs or the *management style* within the organisation. The suggestion scheme is often linked to a series of incentives for staff, such as cash bonuses or gifts.

superstructure is generally accepted to mean any construction that takes place above ground and which uses a pre-existing *infrastructure*. In the case of leisure and tourism, superstructure projects include *hotels* and *tourist attractions*. The majority of superstructure developments in leisure, travel and tourism are financed from private sector sources.

supervisor: an employee who is given *responsibility* for the well-being and work perfor-mance of other members of staff in an organisation, e.g. a travel supervisor overseeing the work of three travel clerks in a *travel agency*. Supervisors are sometimes given the task of convening groups of staff to discuss work methods and productivity. (*See quality circles.*)

supplement: an extra payment, sometimes called a surcharge, levied for the provision of a particular benefit, e.g. an additional payment for occupying a *hotel* room with a sea view, an extra payment for travelling from a regional airport or an extra charge for travelling in business class rather than economy class on an airline.

suppliers are individuals and organisations that provide goods and services in support of an enterprise. The range of suppliers to leisure, travel and tourism organisations is vast, including equipment suppliers, food companies, vehicle suppliers and clothing manufacturers. In terms of *customer service*, it is essential for organisations to make suppliers aware that the suppliers' contribution to the firm's business activities is just as important as their own.

suppressed demand consists of those people who are not currently using or buying a par-ticular *product* or service, because of a problem on either the *demand* side (*potential demand*) or the supply side (*deferred demand*).

summary accounts: the term used to describe financial statements that summarise a series of transactions over a given period of time, e.g. a company's *profit and loss account* and *balance sheet*.

surcharge: see *supplement*

surface travel: see *land transport*

surveys are by far the most common method used by leisure and tourism organisations to collect *primary data*. A survey involves the collection of data from a proportion of a total 'population', which researchers refer to as the 'sample'; in this context, 'population' means the total number of people who could be interviewed. For example, the owner of a *tourist attraction* may decide to interview a 10 per cent sample of visitors on a particular day. If the total number of visitors is 2000 (the 'population'), 200 interviews (the 'sample') will need to be carried out. The most common surveys used by leisure and tourism organisations are *face-to-face interviews*, *self-completed surveys* and *telephone surveys*, although surveys using *e-mail* are gaining in popularity.

sustainable development: see *Brundtland Report*

sustainable tourism: an emerging concept that seeks to address the long-term environ-mental and socio-cultural issues surrounding uncontrolled *tourism development* worldwide. An extension of *'green' tourism*, it is part of a much wider global debate on sustainable development, highlighted by the *Brundtland Report* in 1987 and the *Earth Summits* in Rio in 1992 and Johannesburg in 2002. Various bodies concerned with travel and tourism have issued policy statements and guidelines for sustainable tourism, including the *Association of Independent Tour Operators, World Tourism Organisation, World Travel and Tourism Council, Tourism Concern* and the *English Tourism Council*. The challenge facing the industry, espe-cially the mass market operators, is to implement these guidelines for the benefit of present and future *host communities*.

sustainability: see *Brundtland Report, sustainable tourism*

Sustrans is a registered charity which designs and builds routes for cyclists, walkers and those in wheelchairs. It aims to encourage sustainable transport *policies*, so as to lessen dependence on the motor car. Sustrans employs practical engineers and designers, aiming to create at least one traffic-free route into every urban area in Britain, and to link these to form a *National Cycle Network*. Sustrans was one of the first beneficiaries of *National Lottery* funds, receiving £42.5 million to further its work. Weblink: www.sustrans.org.uk

SVQs: see *Scottish Vocational Qualifications*

SWOT analysis: one of the most commonly used techniques that an organisation can undertake to try and establish where it stands in the marketplace and what it needs to do to maintain or improve its competitive position. SWOT stands for **s**trengths, **w**eaknesses, **o**pportunities and **t**hreats, which for a local authority *leisure centre* could include the factors shown in the following figure:

Strengths	Weaknesses
• Commitment and enthusiasm from staff • Excellent pool facility with high usage • Established balanced pool programme • Lack of immediate competition	• Staffing problems/turnover/commitment to customer care • Ageing dryside environment • Unco-ordinated and restrictive marketing • Limited market research achieved
Opportunities	**Threats**
• Growing market • Press attention and interest • Corporate business market • Re-launch of facilities potential	• New competition • Decrease in disposable incomes • Local management of schools • Changing demographic patterns

Example of a SWOT analysis for a local authority leisure centre

A SWOT analysis, sometimes called a situation analysis, can form the basis for a re-assessment of *products* and *marketing strategies,* leading to improved organisational performance.

synergy: a term used to describe the positive relationship between individuals, products or organisations, which results in 'the whole being better than the sum of its parts'. By way of example, two organisations that decide to merge as a way of increasing sales would expect the sum of their individual turnovers of, say, £2 million and £3 million respectively, to be greater than £5 million.

synthetic surface: artificial playing surfaces that allow sports to take place in adverse weather conditions. They are found in sports stadia, athletics grounds and *leisure centres,* sometimes referred to as 'Astroturf' after the *brand name* of one of the leading manufacturers.

table d'hôte refers to a menu with a fixed price for a specified combination of courses. A table d'hôte menu is sometimes known as a 'fixed menu' or may be given a particular name such as 'chef's special'.

tactical marketing is a short-term *marketing* activity carried out in response to unforeseen or unplanned occurrences in the marketplace, e.g. the introduction by a nearby competitor hotel or a series of themed events may lead a hotelier to reduce his prices or increase his publicity. Tactical marketing is quite different to *strategic marketing*, which is planned and costed well in advance.

tactical pricing: the practice of altering the prices of products and services, often in response to competitors' price changes, with the aim of maintaining *market share.* Tactical pricing is a short-term activity within an organisation's overall *pricing policy* and is often carried out in the highly competitive tour operations and airline sectors of the *travel and tourism industry*.

tactics: short-term measures that an organisation carries out in response to a *threat* or business *opportunity.* Tactics are temporary measures that tend to be superimposed on its overall business *strategy*.

takeover: the *acquisition* of one company by another, through purchasing more than 50 per cent of its *share capital* and thereby gaining full management control.

TALC: see *tourist area lifecycle*

tall hierarchy: see *'steep' pyramid*

tally counter: a device used to count the number of people or vehicles using, for example, a *tourist information centre, leisure centre,* event or *theme park.* Some tally counters are operated manually, while automatic counters work electronically.

Target Group Index (TGI) is a national survey of consumers and their purchasing habits funded by the British Market Research Bureau. TGI is an annual survey covering nearly 5000 brands regularly bought from shops in the UK. It includes some questions on people's use of their *leisure time,* which are of a rather general nature.

target market: the *customers* an organisation considers will be most likely to buy its products and services, and at whom all marketing activity is targeted. The target market for a newly-opened *theme park,* for example, may be families living within a 20-mile radius of the attraction. With the help of computer-based systems such as *ACORN,* it is possible to estimate the size of the total market for a product or service and undertake an effective *target marketing* exercise.

target marketing is the practice of selecting particular groups or individuals (known as the *target market*), and using the different components of the *marketing mix* to encourage them to buy or use products or services. To be able to carry out effective target marketing, an organisation needs detailed *market research* data and will have undertaken a *market segmentation* exercise.

taxation: payments to *local* and *central government* for the provision of a range of local and national services, including leisure and tourism facilities. Taxes are levied on individuals and organisations, and may take the form of *direct* or *indirect taxation*. Local taxes include the *Council Tax* and *Uniform Business Rate*. (See also *income tax*.)

Taylor Report: a report into the safety of football grounds, undertaken by the Right Honourable Lord Justice Taylor in response to the Hillsborough disaster of 1989, which resulted in the death of 96 football supporters. The Taylor Report, published in January 1990, made 76 recommendations, the most significant of which were:

- the formation of a Stadia Advisory Design Council
- the establishment of the *Football Licensing Authority*
- the elimination of standing accommodation at grounds by August 1994 for the top two divisions in England and Wales, and the top division in Scotland.

In addition, the recommendations of the Taylor Report have resulted in perimeter fences being taken down, better trained stewards, the employment of safety officers by clubs and improved internal and external ground *communication* systems.

TCA: see *Traffic Conference Area*

TDA: see *Timeshare Developers' Association*

TDAPs: see *Tourism Development Action Programmes*

team: a group of people working collectively towards a clearly defined goal. In order to be totally effective, a team must be given the necessary *authority* and *resources* to carry out its task. The team should be made up of individuals committed to the task and operate in an 'open' fashion, with team members sharing their concerns and ideas. Teams may develop formally or informally. Teams created in a work environment often operate on a formal basis, with a leader, clear channels of *communication* and defined lines of authority and responsibility. Informal teams tend to develop organically rather than through an organisational structure and may form for social or work-related reasons. (See also *teamwork*.)

team building is the process of creating and developing a group of people so that they operate in an effective and efficient fashion, thereby achieving their goals. Building an effective team follows six main stages:

- giving the team clear *objectives*
- selecting appropriate team members
- providing the team with other necessary resources
- developing a team approach to operations
- encouraging the development of individual team members
- evaluating the performance of the team and its individual members.

Team building should focus on the improvement of *interpersonal skills*, decision making and *communication skills*.

team evaluation: the process when members of a team take time to reflect on their individual and collective performances and achievements. This usually takes place soon after the finish of an event, when details are fresh in their minds, and will include consideration of both formal and informal *feedback*, from a variety of sources, including:

- customer *surveys*
- attendance figures
- sales returns
- views of observers.

The overall aim of the process is to evaluate whether the event was successful in meetings its *objectives*.

team leader: an individual who takes on the *responsibility* of guiding the development and operation of a group of people, to help achieve the team's *objectives*. In leisure and tourism, the team leader must be more than just a figurehead, but an effective *manager* as well. Whenever possible, a team leader should be involved at the team building stage when team members are being selected. The leader will act as a facilitator when the real teamwork is underway, helping to support team members and letting them know exactly what is expected of them. To be most effective, a team leader needs a mixture of essential characteristics, including:

- enthusiasm
- effective *communication skills*
- good *planning* skills
- excellent negotiating skills
- a supportive manner
- an action-orientated approach.

It is important for *management* to realise that a *team leader* must be given the *resources* and authority to enable the team to achieve its objectives.

team objectives: the targets that a *team leader* and team members are expected to achieve. Team objectives may be set by the team itself, by management or by an external agency, and must be realistic, achievable, measurable and set within a timescale (see *SMART objectives*). The objectives help determine the team's working methods, assist in *planning tasks*, and are an essential guide when team performance is being evaluated.

team rationale: an important first stage in building an effective team It is important all those concerned with the operation of the team are informed exactly why it has been set up and what it is expected to achieve, that is, the team rationale.

team structure: the precise arrangement of staff in a team situation, designed to use team members as effectively as possible and best achieve the team's aims and *objectives*. The structure may be formal, with clearly defined lines of authority and responsibility, or informal, with growth occurring organically. Informal teams develop for both social and work-related reasons, giving people the chance to have their say in a less confrontational setting than that offered by a formal team set-up.

team training refers to any formal or informal activities that team members undertake to improve their knowledge and skill levels, thereby helping the team to achieve its objectives.

This could include training in *interpersonal skills*, administrative procedures, *technical skills* (such as using computer *software*) or *management* skills. All team members, whether full-time, part-time or volunteers, should be included in any team training programmes.

teamwork: individuals working together in a cohesive manner to achieve a common goal. Teamwork is an essential part of the *leisure, travel* and *tourism* industries, and is common in all sectors, including conference organisation, hotel management, *leisure centre* operation and retail travel (see figure below). Teamwork brings benefits to both individuals and the organisations they work for; individuals may enjoy greater *job satisfaction*, an enhanced sense of their worth to their employer, the chance to be innovative and creative and gain increased rewards for their efforts. Organisations are likely to benefit from increased efficiency, a higher level of sales, reduced staff conflict and a happier workforce. Above all, management should be keen to see that by developing teamwork within an organisation, it is getting more than just 'the sum of the parts'.

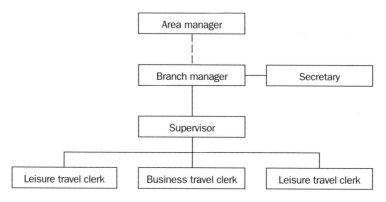

A formal team structure in a travel agency

technological developments, such as the growth of the *Internet*, advances in sports equipment and clothing and the development of *transportation*, have long been important in the leisure, travel and tourism industries and will continue to influence developments in the future. (See also *PEST analysis*.)

technology: equipment and systems that facilitate *communication*, decision making, *marketing* and *management*, within and between organisations. Leisure, travel and tourism are industries that have always made extensive use of new technology equipment and systems. *Computerised reservation systems*, the use of the *Internet*, computers in leisure centres and sophisticated *database marketing* systems, are all examples of this trend. Increasing competition within the industries will force organisations to use new technology to the full, for example in the fields of *transportation*, global communications and *home-based leisure*.

TECs: see *Training and Enterprise Councils*

teleconferencing: a technique that allows a number of people to hold a round table meeting over the telephone, where each person can hear, and be heard by, the other members of the group. Teleconferencing reduces the need for people to travel long distances merely to attend meetings. Unlike *video conferencing*, however, people taking part in a teleconference cannot see each other.

telecottage: an establishment in a rural area that provides a range of *computers* and communications equipment for use by teleworkers in the local area. Telecottages are often subsidised by *local authorities*, enterprise agencies or *Learning and Skills Councils* as a way of contributing to the creation of jobs and *economic development* in country districts.

telemarketing is a type of direct selling over the telephone, when a representative of a *company* contacts a member of the public or an organisation with the intention of making a sale. This kind of selling, sometimes known as telephone marketing, is common in the USA, but its use in UK leisure and tourism is limited to business-to-business sales and selling products such as *timeshare* and membership of certain clubs.

telephone marketing: see *telemarketing*

telephone survey: a technique used to gain both *qualitative* and *quantitative data* to help with an organisation's decision making. Telephone surveys are gaining in popularity in leisure and tourism, as a way of getting a quick response to an event, facility or service. They are used widely in the USA, but are largely restricted in UK leisure, travel and tourism to business-to-business activities, such as following up enquiries after trade shows and selling business services. Companies specialising in selling *timeshare* also use telephone surveys to target potential customers.

telephone technique is the style and tone that a person adopts when making a telephone call. Many leisure, travel and tourism organisations spend time and money developing the telephone technique of key members of staff, such as sales teams and *customer service* staff. An efficient and friendly manner on the telephone can create a good impression of an organisation and is part of a wider *public relations* strategy. Many trainers suggest that staff should always smile when talking on the telephone, since this automatically makes the speaker sound more pleasant.

Teletext: a company specialising in broadcasting pages of information and *advertising* on adapted television sets. Teletext is also the generic term applied to any such system, e.g. BBC TV's Ceefax is an example of a teletext system currently operating in the UK. Teletext is becoming an increasingly popular way of getting information on *holidays,* flights and other travel products, since it is regularly updated by the service providers. Weblink: www.teletext.co.uk

telex: communications equipment which links machines via telephone lines and allows messages to be sent and received instantaneously. A message is typed on machine A and sent to machine B, which automatically prints it out. Telexes are used in travel and tourism to confirm arrangements and send passenger *manifests.* The introduction of low cost *fax machines* and growth in *e-mail* messaging has considerably reduced the use of telex machines in recent years.

television: one of the most powerful *media* in society today, with the ability to influence people's lifestyles, their purchasing habits and fashion trends. Watching television is also an important leisure activity in its own right, with 99 per cent of households owning a television set and viewing figures in excess of 20 million for some of the most popular UK programmes. With the development of satellite technology, worldwide audiences of hundreds of millions are easily achievable. The growth of cable and digital television has led to an explosion in the number of channels available to subscribers, covering everything from gardening and travel to films and history.

television rights: permission to televise and broadcast an event in return for a negotiated payment to the event organiser. The issue of television rights has become most controversial in the context of sport. Companies such as *Sky Television*, the BBC, ITV, Channel 4 and Channel 5, negotiate very competitively with sports bodies for the rights to televise popular sporting events, e.g. football matches, golf tournaments, etc. Individual sports clubs and their *governing bodies* are keen to have their sports televised, both to provide a welcome source of income and to raise the profile of the sport concerned. Without the proceeds from television rights many small sports clubs would find it hard to survive.

teleworking is the practice of working from home but maintaining a link with an organisation, by the use of *computers* and communications equipment, such as *fax machines* and *electronic mail*. Teleworking is a growing trend in the UK, since it offers workers more flexibility and reduces an organisation's *overheads*. (See also *telecottage*.)

tender: a document outlining a bid for the provision of a product or service, with the lowest bid usually winning the contract. The privatisation of many *local authority* services, including the management of leisure and recreation facilities, has meant that many councils now put jobs out to tender, whereas formerly the tasks would have been given to staff on the *payroll*. (See also *compulsory competitive tendering*.)

terminal has two meanings in leisure, travel and tourism. The first is a building at an airport or ferry port which houses all the facilities for departing and arriving passengers, including check-in, immigration and catering facilities.

The second meaning is a *computer* that is part of a network, operating either within an organisation or linked to the outside world.

terms of reference: the first part of a written *report* giving the reason why the report has been written, for whom it has been undertaken, what it hopes to achieve and the date by which it is to be completed.

tertiary industry: an industry located within the *service sector* of the economy, e.g. banking, insurance, leisure, travel or tourism.

test market: the practice of testing a new product or service in a tightly controlled geographical area, prior to a full nationwide launch, so as to measure sales activity. The test market area might be as small as a town or as large as a region, e.g. the south-west of England. Test marketing is a cost-effective way of ensuring that all the *advertising* and promotional work associated with a new *product* or service has not been wasted.

TfL: see *Transport for London*

TGI: see *Target Group Index*

TGV stands for 'train à grande vitesse', the name given to the high speed rail network operated by SNCF, the French railway organisation. France has adopted a policy of publicly-funded rail transport that has resulted in one of the most comprehensive and efficient operations in Europe.

Thatcher years: the period between 1979 and 1990 when Margaret Thatcher was UK Prime Minister. It was a time when policies were put in place to advance *privatisation*, reduce the influence of trade unions and promote free market operations, in the hope of creating a more efficient economy for Britain. Many regard the Thatcher years as a time when the gap between rich and poor widened. The terms *'yuppie'* and *'dinky'* were coined, denoting individuals who were driven by money and status symbols and who often took part in high-risk activities in their *leisure time.*

theatres are an important component of the UK *arts and entertainments* sector. There are approximately 130 professional theatres in Britain, half operated by private sector companies, with the majority of the theatres being in the West End of London. In recent years, the popularity of traditional musicals, comedy shows and shows for children has fallen at the expense of a rise in the popularity of modern musicals such as Grease, Fame and Chicago. (See also *Society of London Theatre.*)

Theatrical Management Association (TMA) is a trade association representing theatre owners, grant-aided theatres, local authority controlled venues, commercial producers, opera and ballet companies, children's theatre companies and community theatres in England, Scotland, Wales and Northern Ireland. Founded by Sir Henry Irving in 1894, the TMA now has some 400 members, who have access to a range of services, including negotiation expertise, industrial relations advice, campaigning, *training* and legal advice. Weblink: www.tmauk.org

theme park: a purpose-built attraction offering a wide range of facilities, including *white knuckle rides*, live entertainment, *events*, catering, shops and amusements. The bigger British theme parks have been modelled on North American examples, particularly the popular *Disney* complexes in Florida and California. Theme parks are particularly aimed at families and young people, who pay an all-inclusive entrance charge, which permits an unlimited number of rides. Examples of successful theme parks in the UK are *Alton Towers* and Chessington World of Adventures.

Theory X: see *McGregor*

Theory Y: see *McGregor*

third world countries: see *developing countries*

Thomas Cook: an *entrepreneur*, who was destined to have a far-reaching impact on the early development and future of travel. He organised his first excursion by rail in 1841 from Leicester to Loughborough for his local Temperance Association. Within 15 years, spurred on by the success of his first trip, Cook was running a fully commercial travel company, which, along with *American Express,* has survived to become one of the founding companies of today's travel trade. Today, Thomas Cook employs some 16,000 staff , is a leading travel organisation and one of the best-known travel *brands* in the world. The company is wholly owned by Thomas Cook AG (formerly C & N Touristic AG), which acquired it from the German *tour operator* LTU in December 2000. Thomas Cook AG is the second largest travel group in Europe and the third largest in the world, operating through a network of 1050 locations in the UK and overseas. It is an example of *vertical integration*, having interests in both retail travel agencies and tour operations. Weblink: www.thomascook.com

Thomson On-line Program (TOP) was the first attempt by a *tour operator* to allow *travel agents* to directly access its main reservations computer, to check availability of holidays and make bookings, without the need to talk to Thomson sales staff on the telephone. First developed in 1986, the TOP system soon became the 'industry standard', imitated by all major mass market tour operators. Today all Thomson holiday bookings by agents must be made through TOP. Access is via the agent's *viewdata* terminal or *VDU* and a suitable *'gateway'* facility.

Thomson Tour Operations is the number one UK outbound *tour operator* in terms of package holidays sold. Formerly part of the multinational Thomson Corporation with its headquarters in Canada, Thomson is now part of the German company World of TUI, a global partnership of 200 leading travel companies across 16 countries. Thomson is an example of *vertical integration*, owning both the Lunn Poly travel agency chain and Britannia Airways. Thomson offers a full range of holiday products, sold under a variety of *brand names*, including Thomson Cities and Thomson Small and Friendly. Thomson was a pioneer in terms of *viewdata systems*, introducing its *Thomson On-line Program* system in 1986. Weblink: www.thomson-holidays.com

threats: see *SWOT analysis*

TIC: see *tourist information centre*

Tidy Britain Group: a national litter abatement agency that works closely with local communities, central and local government, for improved local environments. It used to co-ordinate a number of environmental improvement schemes in the UK, including *Britain in Bloom* (now operated by the Royal Horticultural Society), the *Seaside Award* and the *Blue Flag Campaign*, both now the responsibility of ENCAMs, a body concerned with environmental campaigns.

time series charter: a *charter flight* arrangement where a *tour operator* contracts with an airline for the use of an aircraft for a specific period of time, normally the duration of the season or a whole year. (See also *flight series charter*.)

time zones are artificial divisions of the world's surface into 24 time bands. All time zones are based on the *Greenwich Meridian*, which is 0° longitude. Travelling west from the Greenwich Meridian gives us time zones that are behind *Greenwich Mean Time (GMT)*, while time zones east of Greenwich are ahead of GMT. For example, New York time is five hours behind GMT whereas that of South Africa is two hours ahead of GMT. It is important to remember that many countries in the world, including the UK, operate some form of daylight saving time, with clocks altered to make maximum use of daylight.

timeshare: the practice of buying a period of time (usually in blocks of weeks) in an *accommodation facility*, rather than owning the accommodation outright. The advantage to the customer is that he or she does not have to worry about the maintenance and security of the property for most of the year, although an annual maintenance charge is usually levied. The disadvantage is that the owner has the same property for the same period of time each year. This can be overcome by letting the property independently or through a timeshare exchange company such as *RCI*, giving the chance to stay in a range of properties around the world. Timeshare is most commonly associated with self-catering apartments and villas, although it is possible to find timeshares in hotels and even on yachts! The selling of timeshare apartments in Europe has something of an image problem, with a small number of companies using sometimes questionable sales techniques.

Timeshare Developers' Association (TDA): an independent trade association representing UK *timeshare* operators. Membership of TDA is confined to companies that follow a strict *code of conduct*, concerning selling methods, promotion techniques and property specifications. The TDA hopes that by promoting a professional image of the industry among its members and the public in general, 'cowboy' operators will be driven out of business.

TLC: see *Tourism and Leisure Consortium*

TMA: see *Theatrical Management Association*

TMI: *see Tourism Management Institute*

TNA: see *training needs analysis*

TOCs: see *train operating companies*

toll: a charge levied on travellers for using a road or a canal, crossing a bridge or going through a tunnel. A proportion of the tolls collected is used for maintenance and repair, or to pay off interest charges incurred as a result of construction costs.

'Tomorrow's Tourism': see *national tourism strategy*

TOP: see *Thomson On-line Program*

TOP Programmes: see *Youth Sport Trust*

topography: the variety of natural features that go to make up a landscape, such as mountain ranges, valleys and hilltops. The varied landscapes found in Britain today are the result of human activities over thousands of years, coupled with the effects of climate and the underlying geological formations. The topography of an area determines which *leisure* pursuits can be carried out, e.g. orienteering in woodlands, rock climbing in mountain areas and fishing in rivers.

TOSG: see *Federation of Tour Operators*

total quality management (TQM) is a *management* philosophy which recognises that customer *needs* and organisational objectives are inseparable. Rather than merely a well-documented set of procedures, as is the case with *BS EN ISO 9000*, TQM is an all-embracing concept, taking *quality assurance* a stage further, and is designed to permeate throughout an organisation, from the top to bottom. Creating a TQM culture in an organisation should be seen as a long term aim, based on encouraging staff enthusiasm and ownership of services, with a view to meeting or exceeding the expectations of *customers*. (See also *integrated quality management*.)

tour operator: an individual or organisation that organises *inclusive tours* to a variety of domestic and international destinations. In the *travel industry*, they take on the role of a wholesaler, since they buy their 'raw materials' in bulk (aircraft seats and hotel bedspaces) and break the bulk into manageable products, that is the package holidays themselves. These are then sold to customers by *travel agents*, the retail outlets. Some operators, known as *direct sell*, do not make their products available through travel agents, but prefer to sell direct to the public. The main types of tour operators found in the UK are:

● mass market operators – e.g. *Thomson*, First Choice, My Travel (formerly Airtours)

● specialist operators – e.g. Vacances Franco-Britannique (VFB), Himalayan Kingdoms

● domestic operators – companies that specialise in tours in Britain, e.g. Superbreak, *YHA*

● *incoming tour operators* – companies that specialise in tours of Britain for overseas visitors, e.g. Evan Evans, British Heritage Tours.

Many UK tour operators are members of trade associations, including the *Association of British Travel Agents (ABTA), Association of Independent Tour Operators (AITO)* or the *British Incoming Tour Operators' Association (BITOA)*.

Tour Operators' Code of Conduct is one of the codes of conduct operated by *ABTA* and drawn up in conjunction with the *Office of Fair Trading*. It lays down the minimum standards of tour operators' brochures, requiring that they contain clear, comprehensive and accurate descriptions of facilities and services offered. The Code details rules which govern booking conditions in brochures as they relate, for example, to the cancellation or alteration of tours, holidays or other travel arrangements by the *tour operator*. The Code also contains strict rules concerning the prompt handling of *complaints* and regulations relating to the conduct between travel agents and tour operators (See also *Package Travel Directive, Travel Agents' Code of Conduct.*)

Tour Operators' Study Group: see *Federation of Tour Operators*

tourism is destined to become the world's biggest industry in the early years of the twenty-first century, forecast to double its output between 1990 and 2005, according to the *World Travel and Tourism Council*. It is defined by the *World Tourism Organisation* as '..the activities of persons travelling to and staying in places outside their usual environment for not more than one consecutive year for leisure, business and other purposes'. Another definition from the *Tourism Society* is that tourism is '..the temporary, short-term movement of people to destinations outside the places where they normally live and work, and their activities during the stay at these destinations..'. Both definitions reinforce a number of key points about tourism, namely that it is concerned with people who are:

- away from their normal place of residence
- on a visit that is temporary and short-term
- engaged in activities that would normally be associated with leisure and tourism
- not necessarily staying away from home overnight
- not always away from home for holiday purposes, but may be on business.

When it comes to the location of tourist activity, there are three principal strands within the industry:

domestic tourism – people taking holidays and trips in their own country

inbound tourism – people entering a country other than their own for holidays and trips

outbound tourism – people leaving their own country to take a holiday or trip abroad.

Tourism has considerable *economic, environmental* and *socio-cultural impacts* on destinations, some negative and some positive. The negative environmental and socio-cultural impacts of tourism have become the subject of considerable debate since the mid-1980s, leading to calls for types of tourism that are less environmentally and culturally damaging. Terms such as *green tourism*, responsible tourism and *sustainable tourism* are now common within the study of tourism. (See also *UK tourism.*)

Tourism Alliance: a consortium of leading UK travel and tourism trade associations and other bodies formed to provide a 'single voice' for UK tourism, partly as a result of the impact of foot and mouth disease on the industry in 2001. Its mission is to '...seek to establish and maintain a favourable operating environment for all businesses involved in the delivery of tourism, particularly in England' (Wales has its own organisation with a similar purpose). Spearheaded by an Executive Group chaired by the Director General of the *Confederation of British Industry*, the Alliance provides a forum for discussion, as well as lobbying on issues of competitiveness, quality and *best practice*. Membership on April 1

2002 stood at 60 and included the *Association of British Travel Agents, the Tourism Society, National Trust* and the *Local Government Association*. Weblink: www.cbi.org.uk

tourism balance: see *travel balance*

Tourism Concern is a membership organisation set up in 1989 to bring together British people with an active concern for tourism's impact on community and environment, both in the UK and worldwide. Tourism Concern advocates tourism that is just, participatory and *sustainable*, and aims to look past the cosmetic 'green issues', such as recycling and energy conservation, to the way that tourism affects the people living in destination areas. Tourism Concern seeks to achieve its aims by campaigning, networking, lobbying, informing, educating and developing a resource base. Weblink: www.tourismconcern.org.uk

tourism destinations: see *destinations*

tourism development: the process by which a destination area provides facilities and services for visitors, whether on business or at leisure, as a way of securing economic and social benefits. Tourism development has a number of identifiable characteristics, which can be summarised as follows:

- It takes many forms – everything from the building of a resort complex, construction of an airport, hotel developments to the provision of *tourist attractions*, are different types of tourism development.

- It has associated *infrastructure* – tourism development can only take place where there is existing or planned infrastructure, i.e. roads, railways, airports, telecommunications, power supplies and other utilities. Commercial developers often rely on the public sector to provide these facilities and services.

- It occurs on differing scales – tourism development can be as small as a local village hall committee organising an exhibition for day visitors or as big as a major tourist attraction such as Disneyland Paris.

- It occurs at different rates – advances in travel and communications technology mean that some tourism development can take place very quickly, e.g. the growth in the development of *long haul destinations* has been very rapid in recent years since the introduction of aircraft that can travel greater distances without stopping. Other developments occur at a much slower rate, with more planning and a greater concern for the negative impacts of tourism development, e.g. the controlled tourism policies of countries bordering the Himalayas.

- It occurs in all countries – whether a developed, *developing* or under-developed country, all regions of the world now recognise the important economic benefits that tourism can generate.

- It takes place in a variety of environments – from virgin South American rain forests to the hustle and bustle of cities such as Bangkok, New York and Sydney.

- It has both negative and positive impacts – tourism development can add significantly to the economic wellbeing of regions, but it can also have negative impacts on the people, environment and culture in destination areas.

(See also *objectives of tourism development*.)

Tourism Development Action Programmes (TDAPs): a series of initaitives co-ordinated and part-funded by the *English Tourist Board* in the late 1980s. TDAPs were partnerships between the public and private sector, typically involving district councils, county councils, attraction operators, hoteliers and other accommodation providers. They aimed to develop a planned approach to *tourism development* each in a particular region of England. The first TDAPs covered 20 areas including Bristol, Torbay, North Pennines, Shropshire, Cornwall and Bradford. TDAPs have more recently come to be known as Local Area Initiatives (LAIs).

tourism education: all aspects of the way that tourism is taught as an academic and vocational subject. In the UK, tourism education occurs at a variety of levels, from school-based and college vocational qualifications to undergraduate and postgraduate courses in universities. (See also *Association for Tourism in Higher Education*, *Advanced Vocational Certificate in Education, General National Vocational Qualifications*.)

Tourism Intelligence Quarterly: an information resource provided by the *BTA/ETC* which collates and interprets current statistical information relating to international tourism, as well as tourism into, within and out of Britain.

tourism management is defined by the *Tourism Management Institute* as 'the activity of managing *tourism* in specific geographical locations for the economic, social and environmental benefit of the recipient business and residential communities'.

Tourism Management Institute (TMI): established in 1997 as the successor to the *British Association of Tourism Officers*, TMI is a *professional body* with a number of objectives, including furthering the education of people associated with the *tourism management* profession, devising and imposing standards of knowledge and skill for those seeking corporate membership of the Institute and furthering *research* into all aspects of tourism management. Weblink: www.tmi.org.uk

tourism planning: a dynamic process that aims to make best use of available resources to provide the correct range of tourism facilities in an area, without causing long-term negative effects to local people, their culture or environment. Tourism planning is normally co-ordinated by public sector agencies, such as *National Tourism Organisations* and *local authority* tourism and planning departments, working in partnership with commercial companies. The tourism planning process includes an element of regulation, in order to conserve natural and built resources for future generations and control undesirable developments. (See also *planning control*.)

Tourism (Sleeping Price Display Order) 1977: a law introduced in Britain in February 1978 that requires *hotels, motels*, guesthouses, inns and *self-catering* establishments with four or more letting bedrooms to display in their entrance halls the maximum and minimum prices charged for each category of room.

Tourism Society: the *professional body* representing the interests of individuals making a career in the tourism industry. Founded in 1977, the Society is managed by a council elected by the membership, and is funded by subscriptions, *sponsorship* and other income-generating activities. Within the Society there are two specialist groups, the *Association of Teachers and Trainers in Tourism* and the Consultants' Group. The Society's objectives include improving industry-wide recognition of members' professionalism, linking the mutual interests of individuals in the many sectors of tourism and communicating information and knowledge through meetings, seminars and publications. Weblink: www.tourismsociety.org

tourist: defined by the *World Tourism Organisation* as 'a visitor whose visit is for at least one night and whose main purpose of visit may be classified under one of the following three groups: (a) leisure and holidays; (b) business and professional; (c) other tourism purposes'. Tourists may be divided into those who travel in their own country (domestic tourists) and those who travel between countries (international tourists).

tourist area life cycle (TALC): see *destination life cycle*

tourist attraction: see *attractions*

tourist board: a generic term to describe an official body that has certain responsibilities for tourism at international, national, regional or local level. The structure of tourist boards in the UK is as follows:

- *British Tourist Authority* (the *National Tourism Organisation*) – responsible for promoting the whole of Britain abroad
- National Tourist Boards of the four home countries (*Wales, England, Scotland* and *Northern Ireland*) – responsible for tourism planning, development and marketing in their own countries
- *Regional Tourist Boards* – responsible for co-ordination of development and promotion in their own regions
- Local tourist boards/tourism associations – members of the industry working in partnership to promote their facilities to tourists.

Tourist boards obtain their funding from a number of sources, including *grant-in-aid* from *central government*, *local authority* funding, *sponsorship*, commercial membership subscriptions, other commercial activities and European funding.

tourist destinations: see *destinations*

tourist enclave: an enclosed area within which *tourists* are isolated from the residents of a destination (the *host community*) often for security reasons. Tourist police are sometimes deployed in the zoned area to give further protection to tourists. Enclaves occur particularly in developing nations, where the gap between rich visitors and the poor residents is most marked. (See also *demonstration effect*.)

tourist generating country is the country of origin of travellers, as opposed to the *tourist receiving country,* which is their destination country. Current figures from the *World Tourism Organisation* show that the USA is the number one generating country for international travel in terms of expenditure.

tourist information refers to any information relating to tourism in a country or destination, either received in advance of a trip or picked up in the destination, perhaps from a tourist information centre. Increasingly, prospective travellers are gaining valuable tourist information and advice from the *Internet*.

tourist information centre (TIC): a purpose-built facility offering information on a range of local, and sometimes national, *tourist attractions, events, transportation* and accommodation. In Britain, the National Tourist Boards co-ordinate a network of over 800 TICs, although the great majority are funded by their *district* or *county councils.* TICs play a vital role in marketing their local areas and providing up-to-date information and a warm welcome. Some larger centres offer a selection of extra services, such as an accommodation booking facility, a *book-a-bed-ahead service*, local guides or computerised information. With reductions in funding from local and national sources, TICs are looking to become more commercial in their operations, by charging for their services and selling a range of *products.*

tourist receiving country is the *destination* country that travellers arrive at, as opposed to a *tourist generating country*, which is where their journey originates. Current figures from the *World Tourism Organisation* show that France is the most popular tourist receiving country for international travel in terms of number of arrivals, welcoming 76.5 million overseas visitors in 2001.

tourist tax: a levy imposed on tourists and collected by either *central* or *local government*. It may take the form of a hotel levy, visitor tax, airport tax or charge for other tourist services. Tourist taxes are an important source of revenue for countries whose economies rely heavily on tourism, particularly the developing countries of the world. However, they are sometimes resented by tourists, as was the case when an 'eco tax' of 1 Euro per person per day was imposed by the tourist authorities in the Balearic Islands from January 1 2002.

trade directory: an information source compiled exclusively for the use of organisations in a particular industry sector, rather than being generally available to the public. The Travel Trade Directory and UK Leisure Centre Directory are examples in the leisure and tourism industries. Trade directories are often updated annually and include contact points for a range of *suppliers* and *public sector organisations*.

trade discount: a reduction in the price of goods and services offered by one business to another and not normally available to the general public.

trade exhibition: an event, open exclusively to industry representatives, which gives the buyers of *products* and services the opportunity to meet with *suppliers*, to conduct business deals and discuss new business opportunities. Some of the best-known trade exhibitions, also known as trade fairs, in the leisure, travel and tourism industries are the *World Travel Market,* Leisure Industry Week and the *British Travel Trade Fair*.

trade fair: see *trade exhibition*

trade journals: see *trade press*

trade press: magazines, newspapers and journals that are aimed specifically at industry and business people, rather than consumers. In leisure and tourism, this would include publications such as Caterer and Hotelkeeper, Travel Trade Gazette and Leisure Management. The trade press seeks to keep people working in industry up to date with developments in their sector and includes relevant articles and paid *advertising*.

trade union: a association formed to protect the interests of working people. Since the Trade Union Act of 1871, the trade union movement has used its influence and collective power, latterly through the work of the *Trades Union Congress (TUC)*, to grow into an important industrial and political force, that has influenced government policy and provided support for workers. Trade unions negotiate with management on behalf of their members on such matters as pay, working conditions, *pension* rights and *contracts of employment*. Recent legislation, including the *Trade Union Act 1984* and the *Trade Union Reform and Employment Rights Act 1993*, have sought to regulate the workings of trade unions and improve competitiveness.

Trade Union Act 1984: government legislation which obliged *trade unions* to hold a *secret ballot* of members before authorising a strike and to ensure that executive committee members are elected by the union's membership and offer themselves for re-election every five years.

Trade Union Reform and Employment Rights Act 1993: *legislation* which critics say was enacted to weaken the power of *trade unions*, while those in favour considered it to be a further step towards making trade unions more accountable to their membership. The Act included provisions to abolish the remaining wages councils, require unions to give employers at least seven days' notice of industrial action and to oblige union members to be given periodic written agreement to the deduction of union subscriptions from their pay.

Trades Description Act 1968 is a key piece of *consumer protection* legislation that aims to protect customers against false descriptions, either verbally or in writing, by those who are providing goods or services. Any description of, for example, a hotel or leisure club, must be truthful at the time it was written (if circumstances subsequently change, the operator must inform the customer of the changes). The Act places a duty on the owners and managers of leisure and tourism facilities to produce *brochures* and other *promotional materials* that are not intended to deceive the *customer*.

Trades Union Congress (TUC) is the national organisation representing British *trade unions*. Formed in 1868, the TUC aims to promote the interests of the trade union movement as a whole, act as a voice for organised labour at national level, settle inter-union disputes and promote international labour solidarity, particularly within Europe.

Trading Standards Officer (TSO): an official employed by a local authority with the general task of 'policing' traders to ensure that consumers are being given a fair deal and that *consumer protection* legislation is being implemented in their locality. It is common for TSOs to advise on problems relating to holidays, where, for example, the product sold was below standard or did not match descriptions given in promotional materials. In this regard the TSOs will apply the conditions contained in the *Package Travel Directive*.

Traffic Conference Area (TCA): a zonal classification of the world's major airline routes into three areas:

- TCA1 comprises North and South America
- TCA2 includes Europe and Africa
- TCA3 is Asia.

The TCAs were devised by *IATA* and are used as the basis for the settlement of air fares and timetabling.

train operating companies (TOCs) are state-funded, private companies that are awarded franchises to operate passenger rail services on the UK rail network. TOCs pay Network Rail for the use of tracks, some stations and associated infrastructure. Current examples of TOCs include Central Trains, Virgin Trains, GNER and Connex.

training: see *staff training*

Training and Enterprise Councils (TECs) are former government funded *quangos* established in 1990 to provide Britain with a skilled workforce, through the local and regional co-ordination of *training* and vocational education. Managed primarily by local business people, the TECs did not themselves provide training, but contracted training providers to deliver schemes in their area. TECs were also responsible for promoting the *Investors in People* initiative. The work of the TECs was taken over in 2001 by the *Learning and Skills Council* in England and *ELWA – Education and Learning Wales*.

training needs analysis (TNA): an auditing process that aims to identify the current level of technical and *management* skills within an organisation, the required level of skills needed to be wholly effective and highlight any shortfall or surplus in skill levels. If a shortfall is identified, which is often the case in the leisure and tourism industries, the TNA should make recommendations on the action necessary to bridge the training gap, which may be by a mixture of *off-the-job* and *on-the-job training*.

transnational corporation: see *multinational corporation*

transport: see *transportation*

Transport for London (TfL) is an executive agency of the Greater London Authority responsible for the capital's transport system. Its role is to implement the Mayor's Transport Strategy for London and manage the transport services across the capital for which the Mayor has responsibility, which include London's buses, the Docklands Light Railway and Croydon Tramlink, London River Services, Victoria Coach Station and the London Transport Museum. When private-public partnership contracts are signed, London Underground will become part of TfL as well. TfL also manages a 550km network of main roads, all of London's 4600 traffic lights and it regulates taxis and the private hire trade. TfL is responsible for regulating new congestion charges on private vehicles coming into London introduced in February 2003. TfL is directed by a management board whose members are chosen for their understanding of transport matters and appointed by the Mayor of London (currently Ken Livingstone). Weblink: www.londontransport.co.uk

transportation is one of the three key elements of the *travel and tourism industry*, along with *accommodation* and *attractions/entertainment*. The *British Tourist Authority (BTA)* estimates that in 2001, UK residents and overseas visitors spent £5.8 billion on transportation within the UK, accounting for 16 per cent of all spending by domestic and overseas visitors. Transportation can be sub-divided into *surface, sea* and *air travel*, each with its own distinct characteristics, products and markets. The rapid rise in transport networks and demand for new services and facilities, has led to severe pressures on many aspects of the UK transportation scene since the early 1960s, giving rise to a number of important issues and considerations, including:

- congestion and overcrowding in urban areas
- the impact of the Channel Tunnel
- privatisation of the rail network
- airport expansion and congestion
- loss of land for new developments.

The move towards *deregulation* of travel has led to increased competition between operators and, in some cases, cheaper fares for the travelling public.

travel: the movement of people from one place to another using a variety of modes of *transport*. Travel may be for any one of a variety of purposes, classified as *leisure tourism*, *business tourism* or *visiting friends and relatives*, as shown in the figure on the next page.

travel account: a statement of a country's earnings from *inbound tourism* and the expenditure by its residents on overseas travel. The travel account is also known as the *travel* (or *tourism) balance*.

Tourism		
Leisure and tourism	**Visiting friends and relatives (VFR)**	**Business tourism**
• Holidays • Health and fitness • Sport • Education • Cultural and religion • Social and spiritual		• Business meetings • Exhibitions and trade fairs • Conferences and conventions • Incentive travel

Why people travel

travel agent: a company or individual that sells a range of holidays and other travel products to the general public and may offer *business travel* services as well. Travel agents are acting on behalf of two parties when they undertake their work. They act for the *customer,* referred to as the client, on whose behalf they are making the travel arrangements. They are also agents for the company that is supplying the product; this is sometimes referred to as the *principal* and may include a *tour operator*, airline, car hire company, ferry operator, rail company, cruise line, theatre, hotel, etc. Travel agents earn *commission* from the principals whose products they sell. As well as selling package holidays, travel agents, who may be part of a multiple chain or independent, also offer a variety of other products and services, including UK *short breaks, travel insurance*, foreign exchange, rail tickets, care hire and ferry bookings. Travel agents may be members of a number of trade associations, including the *Association of British Travel Agents (ABTA)*, the *National Association of Independent Travel Agents (NAITA)* or the *Campaign for Real Travel Agents (CARTA)*.

Travel Agents' Code of Conduct is one of the *codes of conduct* operated by *ABTA* and drawn up in conjunction with the *Office of Fair Trading*. The Code regulates all aspects of travel agents' relationships with their customers, covering their responsibility with regard to the standard of service they provide and the information they give to clients. It also lays down rules governing travel agents' trading relationships with *tour operators.* (See also *Tour Operators' Code of Conduct*.)

travel and tourism industry: an all-embracing term used to describe the many private, public and voluntary sector organisations that provide services for the travelling public and work together to promote the economic and social benefits of the industry worldwide. It includes the commercial *travel industry*, e.g. *travel agents* and *tour operators*, plus public agencies, such as the *tourist boards* and *National Tourism Organisations*, and the many companies and individuals that provide *accommodation, transportation* and *attractions/entertainment* services to customers. Travel and tourism is set to become the world's biggest industry in the early years of the twenty-firt century. (See also *tourism*.)

Travel and Tourism Programme (TTP): this is an industry/education initiative working in partnership to improve the knowledge and appreciation of the *tourism* industry and the service sector in general. Managed by *Springboard UK*, current sponsors of the Programme are *American Express, British Tourist Authority, English Tourist Board (ETB)* and *Thomas Cook*. Weblink: www.springboarduk.org.uk

travel balance: sometimes called the tourism balance or travel account, this is the difference between the value of a country's earnings from *inbound tourism* and the expenditure by its residents on overseas tourism. In Britain, the travel balance was in a surplus (positive) position until the beginning of the 1980s, i.e. the revenue from overseas tourism was greater than the expenditure on overseas tourism by British people. Since that time, however, the travel balance has been in deficit, due mainly to increased demand for overseas *package holidays*.

travel destinations: see *destinations*

travel industry: considered to be a specialist sector within *tourism*, existing to serve people's holiday and business travel requirements. It ranges from high street *travel agencies,* which sell a variety of leisure travel products and services, to the tour operators which assemble the various components of *package holidays*. It also encompasses *business travel*, sometimes through specialist business house agencies. Specifically, the UK travel industry comprises:

- leisure travel services
- business travel services
- tour operators
- ground arrangements
- escorting tours
- tour management
- guiding services.

The travel industry employs around 140,000 people in the UK in a wide variety of jobs, such as travel consultants, *couriers*, marketing executives, business travel clerks and tour managers.

travel motivators: see *motivators*

travel propensity refers to the proportion of a population who are actively involved in travel, whether for business or leisure purposes. Travel propensity is higher in Western, developed countries than in the *developing nations* of the world.

Travel, Tourism and Events National Training Organisation (TTENTO): one of a number of *National Tourism Organisations* covering sectors of the leisure, travel and tourism industries, TTENTO's remit covers travel, tourism and events.

travel trade: the term used to describe all commercial sectors within the *travel and tourism industry*, including *travel agents, tour operators*, coach operators, car hire firms, airlines, ferry companies and providers of specialist support services.

Travel Training Company (TTC): at one time a subsidiary of the *Association of British Travel Agents (ABTA)* and formerly known as ABTA National Training Board, the TTC offers a range of in-house training courses for travel industry staff, as well as the *ABTAC* qualification and air travel courses. The company delivers training and other services to around 5000 students in the UK and Ireland. It was also instrumental in the establishment of the *Travel, Tourism and Events National Training Organisation (TTENTO)*. Weblink: www.ttctraining.co.uk

traveller's cheque: a *cheque* issued in one country that can be exchanged for cash in the local *currency* of another country, e.g. a £10 traveller's cheque could be exchanged for, say,

US Dollars or *Euros*. Traveller's cheques are a convenient way of carrying money and offer travellers the security of knowing that if they are stolen, the issuing company will normally replace them immediately, free of charge.

Travicom: an early type of airline *computerised reservation system* introduced in the UK in 1977. Travicom became part of the *Galileo* network in 1987.

TSO: see *Trading Standards Officer*

TTENTO: see *Travel, Tourism and Events National Training Organisation*

TTC: see *Travel Training Company*

TTP: see *Travel and Tourism Programme*

TQM: see *total quality management*

TUC: see *Trades Union Congress*

Tuckman's stages of team development: see *forming, storming, norming, performing*

turnover is the total sales of an organisation over a given time period. Sometimes called sales revenue, revenue or sales turnover, it is calculated by multiplying the quantity of goods and services sold by the price of the goods and services, e.g. the turnover of a coach company may be made up as follows:

total coach tours sold (1500) × price of each tour (£750) = turnover of £1,125,000

It is important to remember that turnover is not the same as *profit,* which is what remains when all *costs* have been deducted from the turnover.

Tussauds Group: reputed to be Europe's number one *attractions* business and one of the leading leisure and entertainment companies. Its facilities (including the *London Eye*, Warwick Castle, *Alton Towers*, Thorpe Park and Chessington World of Adventures) attract around 15 million visitors per year. Weblink: www.tussauds.com

TV: see *television*

TV rights: see *television rights*

two-way communication involves the sending of information and a response from the person receiving the message. It is generally preferable to *one-way communication*, where information passes in one direction only, since it enables a discussion to take place and any misunderstandings between the parties to be cleared up. Examples of two-way communication methods used in leisure, travel and tourism include telephone conversations, face-to-face conversations, meetings and *video conferencing*. Although initially more time-consuming than one-way communication, two-way communication has many advantages and should be used whenever possible.

What other subjects are you studying?

A–Zs cover 18 different subjects. See the inside back cover for a list of all the titles in the series and how to order.

UBR: see *Uniform Business Rate*

UDCs: see *Urban Development Corporations*

UK: see *United Kingdom*

UK Sport: formerly known as the UK Sports Council, this is one of the bodies that replaced the *Sports Council* on April 1 1996 (the other being the *English Sports Council*). UK Sport's purpose is to lead the UK to sporting excellence by supporting:

1   winning athletes

2   world class events

3   ethically fair and drug-free sport.

Its aim is that the UK will be in the world's top five sporting nations by the year 2012, measured by athletes' performances at World Championships, Olympic and Paralympic Games. UK Sport also acts as a co-ordinating body for the sports councils of England, Wales, Scotland and Northern Ireland. (See also *Sport England, Sport Scotland, Sports Council for Wales, Northern Ireland Sports Council*). Weblink: www.uk.sport.gov.uk

UK Sports Council: see *UK Sport*

UK Sports Institute (UKSI): the name given to a network of centres and a central team of experts that supports the UK's top sports people. Launched in November 2000, the UKSI is made up of four home country sports institutes in England, Wales, Scotland and Northern Ireland, known respectively as the *English Institute of Sport (EIS),* UKSI Cymru, Scottish Institute of Sport and the Sports Institute Northern Ireland. UKSI co-ordinates a range of programmes and services for the sports people themselves and their coaches, including the latest developments in *sports medicine* and sports science.

UK tourism is an expanding industry that makes a significant contribution to the national economy. The total value of *tourism* to the UK economy in 2001 was £74 billion, equivalent to 4.5 per cent of *gross domestic product*. UK residents made 163 million trips in 2001 within the UK spending more than £26 billion. There were 22.8 million trips made by overseas visitors in the same year, spending more than £11 billion. In September 2001, there were an estimated 2.12 million employees in tourism-related industries in the UK, including those in self-employment, representing some 7 per cent of all people employed in Great Britain. The structure of the UK tourism industry is complex, covering a range of sectors, including the travel industry, accommodation, catering, transportation and visitor attractions. Public sector involvement comes at national level with co-ordination by the Department for Culture, Media and Sport and *National Tourist Boards* of the four home nations, plus the *British Tourist Authority*. Local authorities also play a vital role in providing facilities for tourists.

UKOS: see *United Kingdom Occupancy Survey*

UKSC: see *United Kingdom Sports Council*

UKSI: see *UK Sports Institute*

UKTS: see *United Kingdom Tourism Survey*

UN: see *United Nations*

undifferentiated marketing is a type of *marketing strategy* when the same marketing approach is offered to all those who go to make up a total *market*.

unfair dismissal: a claim by an employee that he or she has been unfairly treated in having their employment terminated. An *industrial tribunal* would regard any cause other than *gross misconduct*, inability to carry out a job properly, absenteeism, *redundancy*, ill health or a legal restriction on a person's employment, as possible grounds for a claim of unfair dismissal. Any such claim must be made to the tribunal within three months of the employment termination date.

Uniform Business Rate (UBR): a tax levied by a *local authority* on businesses in its area. UBR is payable for the provision of services such as street lighting and refuse collection and is the business equivalent of the *Council Tax*. It is levied on both manufacturing and service sector companies, including hotels, restaurants and cafés. The level of UBR varies in different parts of the country and reflects local property values.

unique selling proposition (USP) is the particular benefit that one *product* or service is said by its promoters to have over another similar product or service, i.e. the reason why customers choose that item instead of all other competitors. The USP may be truly 'unique', for example a flight on Concorde, but is more likely to be a product feature that an organisation promotes to attract attention, e.g. a car hire company using the latest models of car.

unitary authority: a *local authority* body that provides a mix of services previously supplied by both district and county councils. The 47 unitary authorities in England and 22 in Wales are responsible for providing a range of services to the public at local level, including education, social services, leisure facilities, markets, museums, art galleries, planning, parks, open spaces and areas of countryside.

United Kingdom: refers to *Great Britain* and Northern Ireland.

United Kingdom Occupancy Survey (UKOS): a survey of the monthly occupancy rates of *serviced accommodation* in the UK, collected as part of the EU Directive on Tourism Statistics adopted in 1995. The responsibility for providing this data lies with the four National Tourist Boards.

United Kingdom Sports Council (UKSC): see *UK Sport*

United Kingdom Tourism Survey (UKTS) is a national consumer survey measuring the volume and value of tourism trips taken by UK residents. It is jointly sponsored by the *English Tourism Council, VisitScotland,* the *Wales Tourist Board* and the *Northern Ireland Tourist Board.* Up to 1999, the survey was based on face-to-face interviews in-home interviews using the Electoral Register as the sampling frame. Since 2000, telephone interviews with random digit dialling have been used. The survey is carried out by the British Market Research Bureau and is based on 50,000 interviews with adults per year. (See also *International Passenger Survey.*)

United Nations (UN): an organisation that was first established by charter in 1945 with the aim of promoting good international relations and maintaining world peace. Most countries of the world are members of the UN, which has its headquarters in New York. It has many operating divisions, including the UN Security Council, the International Monetary Fund and the United Nations International Children's Emergency Fund (UNICEF). The *World Tourism Organisation* has links with the UN and encourages developing countries to seek assistance for tourism projects through UN specialist departments, including the United Nations Development Organisation and the UN Environment Programme (UNEP). Weblink: www.un.org

unsocial hours refers to the times outside of the normal '9 to 5'; a person working in leisure, travel and tourism industry may well need to be on duty at such times.

upgrade is the movement of a passenger to a higher standard of *product* than he or she has paid for, e.g. allocating an economy class passenger to a business class seat on an airline, or a car hire company offering a customer a car in the next class up. It makes good business and *PR* sense to upgrade a customer if the situation allows and the company will not lose out financially.

Urban Development Corporations (UDCs) were established under the 1980 Local Government, Planning and Land Act to promote *urban regeneration* in areas of England and Wales which were suffering from the effects of the loss of their traditional industries. UDCs were set up in London Docklands, Merseyside, the Black Country, Teesside, Trafford Park (Manchester), Tyne and Wear, Bristol, Central Manchester, Leeds, Sheffield and Cardiff. UDCs have wide-ranging powers to acquire land and buildings, stimulate investment and develop infrastructure, in order to improve their immediate environments, create employment and promote regional prosperity. Many of the UDCs have seen the potential for *leisure* and *tourism* developments in their regeneration programmes, e.g. Albert Dock in Liverpool and the Black Country Museum.

urban regeneration: the process of revitalising derelict areas of towns and cities, often involving *partnership* arrangements between *public* and *private sector* organisations. Leisure and tourism often plays a significant part in urban regeneration projects, helping to create employment and add to an enhanced quality of life for residents and better facilities for tourists. Notable examples of urban regeneration schemes in the UK include the *Castlefields* area of Manchester, Bradford, Glasgow and London Docklands.

urban tourism: tourist facilities and services that are provided in towns and cities, for local residents, domestic visitors and overseas tourists. Tourist facilities in urban areas often contribute to *urban regeneration* and job creation.

USP: see *unique selling proposition*

vacation: another name for *holiday*.

validation: the process of making a travel ticket useable by stamping it with an official company imprint.

value added tax (VAT) was introduced in the UK in 1973 to replace purchase tax. It is an *indirect tax* levied on a range of goods, including household items and cars, and services, such as hotel accommodation and car hire. The current rate of VAT in Britain is 17.5%, although there are moves to harmonise the rates of VAT in all member states of the *European Union*, as part of the move towards *Economic and Monetary Union*. In Britain, certain products such as books, children's clothing, food, transport and newspapers, are currently exempt from VAT, although economic pressures at home or in Europe may force this position to change in the future.

variable costs: expenditure that fluctuates in line with the level of an organisation's business activity, rather than remaining stable as with *fixed costs* (see figure below). Variable costs in leisure and tourism include casual labour, telephone charges, publicity costs, postage, stationery and fuel for vehicles. (See also *semi-variable costs*.)

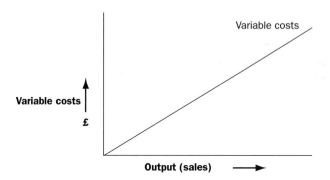

variance: the term used in budgetary control to signify the difference between actual and budgeted figures. Variances may arise in any items of revenue or expenditure, including labour costs, *sales revenue* and energy costs. The investigation of any differences between actual and budgeted figures is known as *variance analysis*.

variance analysis is the process by which an organisation investigates any variances in its budgets and takes corrective action. In the case of an *expenditure budget*, the terms 'unfavourable' or 'adverse' are used when actual costs are greater than budgeted costs. Where actual costs are below budget, the variance is said to be 'favourable'. The opposite is true of revenue variances, where favourable variances occur when actual sales are above budget. The aim of variance analysis is to highlight areas needing immediate attention. Minor variances are common and are unlikely to require detailed analysis, but when a variance is large, either in monetary or percentage terms, the situation will need attention. Variance analysis can be carried out manually, but is more often undertaken with the help of a computer *spreadsheet* package.

VAT: see *value added tax*

VDU: see *visual display unit*

venture capital is a source of finance available to leisure and tourism businesses to increase their *equity*. It is most appropriate for growing businesses that are not yet ready to raise funds on the stock market. Venture capitalists are prepared to invest in high-risk businesses, including many in leisure and tourism, in return for a say in the management of the operation and/or a high rate of return on their investment. Leisure and tourism companies sometimes turn to venture capitalists when traditional financing institutions consider their plans too risky.

Venuemasters: see *British Universities Accommodation Consortium (BUAC)*

verbal communication is the transfer of information using the spoken word. Learning to communicate effectively is an essential feature of working in the leisure, travel and tourism industries, given that staff come into regular contact with *customers, suppliers, professional bodies,* regulatory authorities and a host of other external bodies. Examples of verbal communication are meetings, telephone conversations, sales calls and advising customers face-to-face. (See also *written communication*, *electronic communication, non-verbal communication*.)

verbal warning: normally the first stage in a *disciplinary procedure* against an employee in the workplace, whose conduct, behaviour or performance does not reach suitable and acceptable standards. Should the problem persist, the member of staff is likely to receive a formal *written warning*.

vertical integration describes a process in which companies at different levels of the distribution chain are linked in some way to give *competitive advantage*. For example, *Thomson*, the UK's number one *tour operator*, owns the Lunn Poly *travel agency* chain, while JMC Holidays is part of the *Thomas Cook* Group. By working together, the companies hope to secure increased sales, thereby improving their *market share*. Thomson is a good example of a company that has taken the process a stage further, since it also owns its own airline, Britannia Airways, and *direct sell* operator Portland Holidays. Vertical integration can sometimes work against the public interest, by reducing choice in the marketplace. (See also *horizontal integration*.)

VFR: see *visiting friends and relatives*

video conferencing: an *electronic communication* technique which allows a group of individuals to hold a round table conversation by using telephone and video technology. Video conferencing allows the members of the group to see each other and communicate on a face-to-face basis at any distance, even from one country to another. Developments in video conferencing equipment are beginning to make an impact on the need for executives to travel to different parts of the world purely to attend meetings. (See also *teleconferencing*.)

videotext: another name for *viewdata*

viewdata: a computer-based interactive system used by travel agents to display information on *VDUs* and to access the *computerised reservation systems* of *principals*, mainly airlines and tour operators via a telephone line or *ISDN* connection. Many viewdata systems have now been upgraded to use *Internet* technology.

virtual reality is a technology that allows a user to enter and interact with images generated by a computer. Special graphics, video images and stereo sound make the pretend world seem real. The concept came into being in the 1930s when scientists created the first flight simulator for pilot training. Today, virtual reality has many uses in industry as well as in *leisure* and *recreation*. Many arcade games now use virtual reality, giving people the chance to experience the sensation of driving in a racing car or flying in outer space.

visa: a stamp in a *passport*, or other official document, giving a traveller the right of entry to a particular country. Countries use the allocation of visas as a way of discouraging travel, either for political, economic or socio-cultural reasons. The former Eastern bloc countries are beginning to relax their requirements for all visitors to hold a visa, resulting in a growth in tourism to such countries as Slovakia, Lithuania and Latvia.

visibles are manufactured items and goods whose value is shown on a country's *balance of payments*, i.e. those that can be seen or touched, for example cars, food, electrical components and raw materials. Such items brought into a country are known as imports, while those sent abroad are exports. (See also *invisibles*.)

visiting friends and relatives (VFR) is an important, if often overlooked, aspect of a nation's tourism industry. According to statistics from the *Star UK* website, UK residents made 36.5 million VFR trips in 2001 (22 per cent of all trips), spending £3 billion. Overseas visitors' VFR trips amounted to 5.9 million for the same period, with expenditure of £2.3 billion. It is sometimes difficult to understand just why VFR is important to tourism; how is it that a person who stays for free with friends or relatives can be contributing to the local tourism economy? The answer is that the visitor, although enjoying free accommodation, may well spend money on other goods and services in the locality, such as leisure facilities and restaurants.

visitor: a person who travels, for less than twelve months, to a place other than that of his or her usual environment and the main purpose of whose visit is other than the exercise of an activity remunerated from within the place visited. Visitors can be divided into those who travel between countries (international visitors) and those who travel within a country (domestic visitors/domestic tourists). A distinction can also be made between those who stay overnight (*tourists*) and those who do not (*excursionists*).

visitor attraction: see *attractions*

visitor centre: a custom-built facility which offers a range of services, the most important of which is an opportunity to learn more about its surroundings through a number of *interpretation* facilities, such as information displays, an audio-visual programme or a series of *guided walks*. Visitor centres are found in both town and country, e.g. the Wedgewood Visitor Centre in Stoke-on-Trent and the Brockhole National Park Centre in the Lake District *National Park*.

visitor management: the practice of controlling visitors and their vehicles so as to reduce their harmful effects on the environment and *host communities*. Visitor management employs a variety of techniques including *interpretation*, signage, demarketing and the encouragement of *public transport*.

Visitor Welcome Initiative (VWI) is a *customer care* programme co-ordinated in the 1990s by the *Countryside Commission*, designed to help the managers of sites in the countryside make sure that their visitors find a welcoming environment. The VWI provides a checklist of measures that sites should attempt to provide, from safe, off-road parking for the most basic sites, to a *visitor centre* and a children's play area at the largest.

VisitScotland: see *Scottish Tourist Board*

visual display unit (VDU): a screen, usually linked to a *computer*, giving access to information from remote *databases* and other computers on a linked *network*. VDUs are commonplace in leisure and tourism, e.g. in *travel agencies*, at airports, in hotels and at *tourist attractions*. VDUs are associated with a number of *front office* functions, such as making reservations and selling tickets, as well as *back office* routines, including accounting and *marketing*. The rise in the incidence of stress-related illnesses associated with the use of VDUs in the workplace led to the introduction of the Health and Safety (*Display Screen Equipment*) Regulations in 1993.

vocational qualifications are different to academic qualifications since they are directly related to the world of work. The government sees the introduction and development of *National Vocational Qualifications (NVQs)* in a wide range of industry sectors as a major step forward in bridging the skills gap in the UK. Vocational qualifications are increasingly being offered in schools and colleges, in areas such as business, health and social care, and *leisure* and *tourism*, with the introduction of the *Advanced Vocational Certificate in Education (AVCE)* and Vocational GCSEs. (See also *General National Vocational Qualifications*.)

voluntary code of practice: see *code of conduct*

voluntary sector body: see *voluntary sector in leisure, travel and tourism*

voluntary sector in leisure, travel and tourism: non-profit making sector that supplements both the private and public sectors, and is made up of organisations concerned with a range of activities, including:

- *heritage*
- minority groups
- youth organisations
- *conservation* of the environment
- community schemes
- clubs and societies.

Voluntary sector organisations vary greatly in their size and aims. At one extreme, a small group of like-minded people may decide to form a cycling club in their area, to improve their fitness and see the countryside. At the other end of the spectrum, large organisations such as the *National Trust, Youth Hostels Association (YHA)* and *Royal Society for the Protection of Birds (RSPB)*, all fall within voluntary sector leisure and tourism, each having its own distinct objectives and structures. Voluntary organisations at both national and local level often receive advice and *grant-aid* from the private and public sectors, sometimes in the form of *sponsorship*, the arts being a good example of this arrangement.

voluntary sector organisation: see *voluntary sector in leisure, travel and tourism*

VWI: see *Visitor Welcome Initiative*

Wales Tourist Board (WTB): this body was set up under the 1969 *Development of Tourism Act*. It is an independent statutory body, and is now financed mainly by direct *grant-in-aid* from the National Assembly for Wales. The Act requires the WTB to encourage people to visit Wales and people living in Wales to take their holidays there. It is also charged with encouraging the provision and improvement of tourist amenities and facilities in Wales. In order to fulfil these objectives, the WTB undertakes a wide-ranging programme of work, including:

- *promotion* and publicity in the UK and overseas
- providing advisory and information services
- providing financial assistance to any significant tourism project it believes will provide or improve tourist facilities and amenities
- promoting or undertaking *research* and giving advice on policy matters relating to tourism.

The 1969 Act debarred WTB from marketing Wales overseas; that was the responsibility of the *British Tourist Authority (BTA)*. However, since the introduction of the 1992 Tourism (Overseas Promotion Wales) Act, the WTB has been able to undertake overseas marketing activity to supplement the work of the BTA. In line with government policy, the Board has contracted certain activities to a number of companies and established four Regional Tourism Partnerships (RTPs) in 2001. The Board has recently launched its new Internet-based *destination management system*, which it hopes will further encourage tourism to Wales. Weblink: www.visitwales.com, www.wtbonline.gov.uk

Warsaw Convention: an international agreement, signed in 1929, which established minimum levels of *compensation* available to airline passengers in the event of death or personal injury resulting from their flight, or loss of personal possessions. The Warsaw Convention still applies today, although many countries e.g. the United States of America have introduced their own higher compensation levels.

WCTB: see *West Country Tourist Board*

WDA: see *Welsh Development Agency*

weaknesses: see *SWOT analysis*

website: a presence on the *Internet*, where an individual, organisation or company develops pages of information that are made available to 'surfers'.

Welcome Host is a *customer care* training programme first carried out in Britain by the *Wales Tourist Board*, from an original idea developed in Canada. The scheme has since been taken up by both the *Scottish Tourist Board* (now *VisitScotland*) and *English Tourist Board* (now *English Tourism Council*), with the support of *Learning and Skills Councils* and *ELWA* –

Education and Learning Wales. The programme aims to raise the standard of service and hospitality offered to visitors by training staff from a wide range of organisations, including hotels and guesthouses, restaurants, petrol stations, shops, *tourist information centres*, leisure facilities and *tourist attractions*. The key objectives of Welcome Host are professionalism and pride. The training concentrates on raising the level of communication when dealing with visitors, and focuses on the tourism attractions of the local area. At the time of writing, the 'family' of Welcome Host courses offered by the *English Tourism Council* is being revised and updated and will be known as Welcome to Excellence. The 'family' includes Welcome Host, Welcome All, Welcome International, Welcome Line and Welcome Management. The Welcome to Excellence programme will continue to be delivered at local level by the 10 *Regional Tourist Boards* in England.

Welcome to Excellence: see *Welcome Host*

Welsh Assembly: see *National Assembly for Wales*

Welsh Assembly Government refers to the First Minister and Cabinet of the *National Assembly for Wales*.

Welsh Development Agency (WDA): a *quango* established in 1976 and funded by the *Welsh Assembly*. Its main objective is 'to sustain one of the best business climates in Europe by aiding the growth of quality jobs and competitive industry for the benefit of people throughout Wales'. The WDA works to stimulate and support the economic prosperity of Wales, and sponsors a range of tourism-related projects in the Principality. Weblink: www.wda.co.uk

West Country Tourist Board (WCTB) is the official *Regional Tourist Board* covering Bath, Bristol, Cornwall and the Isles of Scilly, Devon, West Dorset, Somerset and Wiltshire. Weblink: www.wctb.co.uk

Which? magazine: the official publication of the *Consumers' Association*. (See also *Holiday Which?*) Weblink: www.which.net

white knuckle ride is a term use to describe an exhilarating ride at a *theme park,* such as *Alton Towers* or Oakwood. The name derives from the fact that passengers on these rides grip the safety bars so tight that their knuckles turn white from the pressure. Many white knuckle rides in UK *theme parks* are based on examples found in the USA.

WLRA: see *World Leisure and Recreation Association*

Wolfenden Report: an influential report published in 1960 with the full title 'Sport and the Community', which stressed the need for a greater range and distribution of better quality facilities for *sport* and indoor recreation for all people in their local communities.

word processing: the creation, storage, alteration and printing of textual information, including letters, reports, memoranda and other types of written communication, using a *computer software* package. Computers loaded with wordprocessing software, such as Microsoft Word, have all but replaced typewriters in the production of high quality documents in leisure and tourism organisations. A wordprocessing package allows text to be moved or enhanced, grammar and spelling to be checked, charts and diagrams to be added, and personalised documents created using a *mail merge* facility.

work equipment safety: the Provision and Use of Work Equipment Regulations 1992 were developed as a direct result of the *EU Directives on health and safety*, to pull together and tidy up the laws concerning equipment used at work. The regulations place general duties on employers and list minimum requirements for work equipment to deal with selected *hazards*, whatever the industry. Employers must ensure that the equipment they provide is suitable for its intended use and is adequately maintained. 'Work equipment' includes everything from a hand tool, machines of all kinds, to a complete plant such as a *leisure centre* or indoor arena.

working capital is the balance of *current assets* over *current liabilities* in an organisation. Often called the 'life blood' of a business, working capital is the amount available on a day-to-day basis to meet the normal financial requirements of running a business, e.g. buying stock, funding credit offered to customers and meeting overhead costs. Working capital is also known as net current assets.

Working Time Regulations 1998 implement the EU Working Time Directive in the UK, providing certain basic rights and protections to employees in respect of their time spent at work. These include a limit of an average 48 hours per week that a worker can be required to work, although staff can choose to do more hours if they wish, a right to 11 hours rest a day, and a right to four weeks paid leave per year. A number of sectors of interest to the leisure, travel and tourism industries were excluded from the Working Time Regulations, e.g. road, rail, air, sea, inland waterways and lake transport.

workplace conditions: the Workplace (Health, Safety and Welfare) Regulations 1992 were developed as a direct result of the *EU Directives on health and safety*, replacing a total of 38 pieces of old law and helping to make safety in the workplace a much easier topic to under-stand. The regulations cover four broad areas:

- the working environment – temperature, ventilation, lighting, etc.
- safety – use of materials in doors and partitions, opening of windows, etc.
- facilities – toilets, washing facilities, eating areas, drinking water, etc.
- housekeeping – cleanliness, maintenance, removal of waste, etc.

Employers were obliged to ensure that their premises met the requirements of the regulations by 1996 at the latest.

workplace rules exist to regulate staff behaviour and ensure the safety and welfare of all employees, their employers and the *customers* they are serving. Although workplace rules will vary between organisations, it is likely that they will include regulations concerning:

- health, safety and security
- hygiene
- punctuality and attendance
- sickness and absence procedures
- dress and personal appearance
- behaviour
- conduct and language in the workplace
- attitude to colleagues and customers.

All new members of staff should be introduced to the rules in their *induction* training and be issued with amendments as and when they arise.

workplace standards: see *occupational standards*

World Bank: the international organisation that provides aid and technical assistance to *developing countries* to help with capital projects, particularly *infrastructure* developments such as road building and airport construction. Weblink: www.worldbank.org

World Commission on Environment and Development: see *Brundtland Report*

World Heritage Site: a place designated by UNESCO as being of exceptional cultural, geological or historical interest. World Heritage Sites found in the UK include the City of Bath, Hadrian's Wall, Blaenavon and Ironbridge Gorge in Shropshire. Weblink: www.unesco.org

World Leisure and Recreation Association (WLRA): founded in 1952, the WLRA (sometimes referred to as 'World Leisure') is a worldwide, non-governmental association of people and organisations dedicated to discovering and fostering those conditions best permitting leisure to serve as a force for human growth, development and well-being. Members include leisure professionals from the public and private sectors, researchers, scholars, managers and concerned members of the community. Weblink: www.worldleisure.org

Worldspan: a US *computerised reservation system* introduced in 1990 by a number of major US airlines, including TWA, North-West and Delta. As well as its booking facility for airlines, hotels and car hire, Worldspan offers others features such as satellite ticket printing and a *local area network* facility. Weblink: www.worldspan.com

World Tourism Organisation (WTO): the established inter-governmental agency for *tourism* policies worldwide, representing public sector tourism bodies from the majority of the countries in the world. Linked to the *United Nations,* WTO exists to promote and support tourism *development* on a global basis in all sectors of the tourism industry. It is a major source of authoritative data on tourism developments and movements worldwide and is a major player in the move towards environmentally sound practices in the global tourism industry. It commissions *research* on all matters relating to world tourism, sponsors regional workshops and supports education and *training* initiatives in travel and tourism. Weblink: www.world-tourism.org

World Travel and Tourism Council (WTTC): an industry-sponsored *pressure group* representing the interests of the world's leading airline and tourist organisations. Formed in 1990, WTTC aims to marshal the resources of Chief Executive Officers of transnational commercial companies from all sectors of the *travel and tourism industry*, to lobby governments as to the economic, social and cultural importance of tourism to the world economy. Through the *World Travel and Tourism Environmental Research Centre*, WTTC also promotes environmentally sustainable management in the tourism industry. Weblink: www.wttc.org

World Travel and Tourism Environment Research Centre (WTTERC) was established in Oxford in 1991 with a mandate to create a worldwide database and information network to further environmentally compatible growth in the *travel and tourism industry*. Its founding sponsors were four members of the World Travel and Tourism Council (WTTC), namely *British Airways, American Express, Thomas Cook* and Steigenberger Hotels, together with the *British Tourist Authority*. Having developed its research database, WTTERC seeks to identify problem areas in respect of the environmental impacts of tourism and to promote *good practice* to further promote *sustainable tourism*. Weblink: www.wttc.org

World Travel Market (WTM) is a major international trade exhibition for all sectors of the *travel and tourism industry*. Held every year in London in November, WTM brings together *public* and *private sector* tourism organisations to develop new relationships and create new business opportunities. Linked to the exhibition are a number of training seminars to help keep industry representatives up to date with new developments and initiatives. Weblink: www.worldtravelmarket.co.uk

World Wide Fund for Nature (WWF) is an international organisation, founded in 1961, which is concerned with all aspects of man's relationship with the environment. With almost 5 million supporters distributed throughout five continents, WWF has over 28 national organisations, 24 programme offices and four associates. Since 1985, WWF has invested over US$1.2 billion in more than 1100 projects in 130 countries. As well as campaigning on issues of global concern, WWF is also committed to helping individuals and groups in the active resolution of environmental problems at local level. WWF projects of relevance to tourism industry include work on the destruction of coral reefs and water usage for tourism in *developing countries*. Weblink: www.wwf.org

World Wide Web (WWW) is a hypertext-based series of pages of information available on *personal computers*. WWW is currently the most popular system of navigating the *Internet*, giving access to global information on a vast range of topics, from *travel* to financial data.

written communication: a system of communicating that has the advantage of providing a permanent record of something that has taken place. Written communication methods are often more effective than, for example, verbal and electronic systems, since they enable complex information to be sent, e.g. statistical data, the quality of presentation can be altered to appeal to different audiences and they provide evidence of confirmation of a previous arrangement, e.g. the list of passengers on an aircraft. Common written communication systems used in leisure and tourism include letters, *brochures*, memoranda, press advertisements, *annual reports* and *press releases*. (See also *verbal communication*, *electronic communication*.)

written warning: the stage after receiving a *verbal warning*, of a *disciplinary procedure* against an employee who has continued with an unacceptable standard of behaviour or conduct, or poor performance.

WTB: see *Wales Tourist Board*

WTM: see *World Travel Market*

WTO: see *World Tourism Organisation*

WTTC: see *World Travel and Tourism Council*

WTTERC: see *World Travel and Tourism Environment Research Centre*

WWF: see *World Wide Fund for Nature*

WWW: see *World Wide Web*

YHA: see *Youth Hostels Association*

yield management: the process of controlling costs so as to achieve maximum yield at minimum outlay, as practised by companies such as *low cost airlines* and hotels.

Yorkshire Tourist Board (YTB) is the official *Regional Tourist Board* covering the county of Yorkshire and the area of Northern Lincolnshire. Weblink: www.ytb.org.uk

Youth Hostels Association (YHA) is a registered charity founded in 1930. Its aim is 'to help all, especially young people of limited means, to a greater, knowledge, love and care of the countryside, particularly by providing hostels or other simple means of *accommodation* for them in their travels, and thus promote their health, rest and education.' The YHA currently has 228 places to stay in England and Wales, many in coastal and countryside locations, others in city destinations, ranging from 17th century yeoman residences in the Peak District of Derbyshire, remote hillside cottages in Wales to state-of-the-art modern architecture in London's Docklands. With more than 300,000 members, the YHA makes an important contribution to the nation's tourism enterprise, as well as helping the economy of rural communities. Weblink: www.yha.org.uk

Youth Sports Trust: a registered charity established to assist with the development of sport in local communities. It helps implement a number of sport programmes for young people, which it calls TOP Programmes, to children from 18 months to 18 years. The Trust has also developed a number of projects to focus on specific issues, for example the inclusion of young disabled people, encouraging more teenage girls to take part in sport and supporting gifted and talented young sports people. More than 4.5 million young people had taken part in the Trust's programmes up to 2002. Weblink: www.youthsporttrust.org

YTB: see *Yorkshire Tourist Board*

'yuppie' stands for 'young urban professional', a term first used in Britain in the *Thatcher years* of the 1980s. Yuppies were people who benefited from the expansion of private enterprise, particularly the rise of the financial services sector of the economy. They were characterised as individuals working in banking who speculated on foreign exchange markets, drank in wine bars and enjoyed 'the good things in life'. In their leisure time, they took part in adventurous and glamorous pursuits such as hang gliding, motor sports and taking exotic holidays to *long haul destinations*. (See also *'dinky'*.)

zero-base budgeting: a financial technique that attempts to curb excessive annual *budget* increases by setting the coming year's budget at zero and asking managers to fully justify every element of their budget requests. It is a useful tool for identifying areas of activity whose budgets could be trimmed.

zoning has two meanings in leisure and tourism. The first is a *management* technique used to separate conflicting, or potentially conflicting, recreational activities, e.g. fishing, sailing and power boat racing on a reservoir. In this instance, the zoning can be physical (i.e. erecting physical barriers to prevent conflicts) or temporal (i.e. allowing each competing use a period of time when its activity has priority over all others).

The other meaning of zoning is a *planning* technique used to allocate different uses of land and facilities in a new *leisure* or *tourism* project.

LEARNING ABOUT KEY TERMS

As you can see from all the entries in this handbook, there's a lot to learn about leisure & recreation and travel & tourism! The following pages list the key terms from the following AVCE compulsory units:

AVCE/Vocational A level in Travel and Tourism

Unit 1: Investigating travel and tourism

Unit 2: Tourism development

Unit 3: Worldwide travel destinations

Unit 4: Marketing travel and tourism

Unit 5: Customer service in travel and tourism

Unit 6: Travel and tourism in action

AVCE/Vocational A level in Leisure and Recreation

Unit 1: Investigating leisure and recreation

Unit 2: Safe working practices in the leisure and recreation industry

Unit 3: The sports industry

Unit 4: Marketing leisure and recreation

Unit 5: Customer service in leisure and recreation

Unit 6: Leisure and recreation in action

You can use these lists as a guide to what's important to learn about in any particular unit. They can be used in a number of ways, including:

- as revision for any external tests you have to take
- to make sure you've covered everything in written assignments
- to make a good impression in any presentations you have to make
- to test yourself and your friends to see how much you really know!

And don't forget to use the weblinks and sources of information at the end of the book to get even more information.

Key terms for Vocational A Level (AVCE) Travel and Tourism

Unit 1: Investigating travel and tourism (advanced)

Accommodation

Air transport

Application form

Built attractions

Business tourism

Butlin's

Car ownership

Career development

Career opportunities

Catering

Center Parcs

Climatic changes

Commercial organisations

Computerised reservation systems

Consumer needs and expectations

Consumer spending

Currency fluctuation

CV

Disposable income

Domestic tourism

Domestic tourist

Economic impacts of tourism

Employment in travel and tourism

Environmental impacts of tourism

Environmental issues

Funding

General Household Survey

Government legislation

Guiding services

Health and safety at work

Holiday camp

Host communities

Impacts of tourism

Inbound tourism

Incoming tourism

Independent travel agent

Interview

Jet aircraft

Jobs in travel and tourism

Land transport

Leisure time

Leisure tourism

Long haul destinations

Multiple travel agency

Natural attractions

Negative impacts of tourism

Non-commercial organisations

Objectives

Outbound tourism

Outgoing tourism

Outgoing tourist

Package tour

Person specification

Personal qualities

Personal skills

Positive impacts of tourism

Private sector

Product development

Product

Promotion

Revenue generation

Sea transport

Self-catering accommodation

Serviced accommodation

Shareholder
Significance of UK tourism
Small and medium-sized enterprises
SMEs
Social impacts of tourism
Social Trends
Socio-economic
Stakeholder
Structure of the tourism industry
Structure of the travel and tourism industry
Technical skills
Technological developments
Tourism

Tourism development
Tourist attraction
Tourist board
Tourist destination
Tourist information
Tourist
Transportation
Travel
Travel agent
Travel and tourism industry
Unsocial hours
Vertical integration
VFR

Unit 2: Tourism development (advanced)

Access
Agents of tourism development
Asset
Commercial organisations
Community group
Consultancy
Cultural identity
Destinations
Developed countries
Developing countries
Development agencies
Economic development
Economic impacts
Ecotourism
Environmental auditing
Environmental education
Environmental impact assessment
Environmental impacts
Erosion
Good practice
Green tourism
Host community
Impacts of tourism development
Infrastructure
Local authority
National identity

National tourist board
Negative impacts of travel and tourism
Non-commercial organisations
Objectives of tourism development
Planning control
Political benefits of tourism development
Pollution
Positive impacts of travel and tourism
Pressure group
Private sector enterprises
Public sector organisations
Regeneration
Regional identity
Regional tourist board
Socio-cultural impacts of travel and tourism
Staff training
Staff development
Sustainable tourism
Tourism
Tourism development
Tourism education
Traffic management
Travel and tourism industry
Visitor management
Voluntary sector body

Unit 3: Worldwide travel destinations (advanced)

Accessibility

Accommodation

Brochure

Built attractions

Channel Tunnel

Charter flight

Climate

Continental Europe

Cultural destinations

Customer

Events

Exchange rate fluctuations

Gateway

Gazetteer

Historical destinations

Independent travel

Internet

Long haul destinations

Media coverage

Natural attractions

Natural disasters

Over-commercialisation

Peak season

Political instability

Political unrest

Pollution

Primary research source

Promotion

Promotional materials

Purpose-built resorts

Research

Research skills

Research sources

Scheduled flight

Secondary research sources

Self-catering accommodation

Serviced accommodation

Short break

Sources of information

Topography

Tour operator

Tourism management

Tourist board

Trade journals

Transport

Travel and tourism industry

Travel destinations

Unit 4: Marketing travel and tourism (advanced)

Advertising

Advertising campaign

Advertising regulatory bodies

AIDA

Branding

Business environment

Chain of distribution

Competition

Competitor activity

Consumer Protection Act 1987

Customer needs

Data analysis

Data Protection Act 1998

Direct mail

Direct marketing

Direct response advertising

Door-to-door distribution

Focus group

Internet

Location

Market research

Market segmentation

Marketing

Marketing communications

Marketing concept

Marketing mix

Marketing objectives

Marketing process

Mission

Niche marketing

Observation

Personal selling

PEST analysis

Place

Price

Price determination

Pricing policy

Primary research

Product

Product life cycle

Promotion

Public relations

Qualitative data

Quantitative data

Questionnaire

Quota sample

Random sample

Research objectives

Research strategy

Sales promotion

Sampling

Secondary research

SMART objectives

Socio-economic groupings

Sponsorship

Surveys

SWOT analysis

Telemarketing

Tour operator

Trade Descriptions Act 1968

Travel agent

Travel and tourism industry

USP

Unit 5: Customer service in travel and tourism (advanced)

After-sales service

AIDA

Attitude

Benchmarking

Closing a sale

Communication skills

Complaints

Customer loyalty

Customer needs

Customer service

Disability Discrimination Act 1995

Feedback

Focus group

Job satisfaction

Legislation

Mystery shopper

National tourism strategy

Non-verbal communication

Observation

Personal hygiene

Personal presentation

Personality

Product knowledge

Product

Public image

Quality criteria

Quality standards

Repeat business

Sales objectives

Selling skills

Sensory disabilities

Specific needs

Suggestion box

Surveys

Travel and tourism industry

Verbal communication

Written communication

Unit 6: Travel and tourism in action (advanced)

REVISION LISTINGS

Key terms for Vocational A Level (AVCE) Leisure and Recreation

Unit 1: Investigating leisure and recreation (advanced)

Active leisure activity

Ageing population

Arts and entertainment

Car ownership

Career development

Career opportunities in leisure and recreation

Catering

Central government

Consumer demand

Consumer needs

Consumer spending on leisure

Consumers

Countryside recreation

CV

Demographic changes

Disposable income

Employment application form

Fashions and trends

Funding

Heritage

Home-based leisure

Interview

Job opportunities in leisure and recreation

Leisure

Leisure and recreation industry

Leisure and recreation products and services

Leisure away from home

Leisure time

Local authority

Mobility

Objectives

Passive leisure activity

Personal skills

Physical recreation

Private sector organisations

Public sector organisations

Public transport

Recreation

Revenue generation

Shareholder

Skills

Socio-economic developments

Sport

Stakeholder

Technical skills

Technological developments

Unsocial hours

Voluntary sector organisations

Youth Hostels Association

Unit 2: Safe working practices in the leisure and recreation industry (advanced)

Children Act 1989

Civil prosecution

Control of Substances Hazardous to Health Regulations (COSHH)

Criminal prosecution

Customer service

Data Protection Act 1984

Disability Discrimination Act 1994

European Union Directives on health and safety

Fire Safety and Safety of Places of Sport Act 1987

Food Safety Act 1990

Fraud

Hazards

Health and safety at work

Health and Safety (First Aid) Regulations 1981

Health and Safety at Work Act 1974

Health and Safety Commission (HSC)

Health and Safety Executive (HSE)

Health and safety management

Institute of Leisure and Amenity Management

Laws

Legal requirement

Licensing laws

Local authority

Regulations

Risk assessment

Risks

Royal Life Saving Society

Royal Life Saving Society UK's 'Water Safety Code'

Sabotage

Safe working practices

Safety at Sports Grounds Act 1975

Secure environment

Security

Security measures

Special needs

Staff training

Voluntary code of practice

Working Time Regulations 1998

Unit 3: The sports industry (advanced)

Adventure activities

Ageing population

Annual spending on sport

Central Council for Physical Recreation

Central government

Charity

Economic impact of sport

Employment in sport

Facility provision

Funding of sport

Governing body of sport

GP referral scheme

Grant

Health and fitness

Health club

International Olympic Committee

International sports federation

Leisure and recreation industry

Local government

Mass media

Media

Merchandising

National Coaching Foundation

National Lottery

National Sports Centres

Organisation of sport

Outdoor activities

Personal fitness trainer

Personal trainer

Physiotherapist

Professional sport

Sky Television

Sponsor

Sponsorship

Sport

Sporting goods

Sports academy
Sports activities
Sports Aid Foundation
Sports coaching
Sports councils
Sports development
Sports development initiatives
Sports development officer

Sports injury clinic
Sports medicine
Sports participation
Sports-related gambling
Sports tourism
SPRITO
Structure of sport
Trends in sport

Unit 4: Marketing leisure and recreation (advanced)

Advertising
Advertising campaign
Advertising regulatory bodies
AIDA
Branding
Business environment
Chain of distribution
Competition
Competitor activity
Consumer Protection Act 1987
Customer needs
Data analysis
Data Protection Act 1998
Direct mail
Direct marketing
Direct response advertising
Door-to-door distribution
Focus group
Internet
Leisure and recreation industry
Location
Market research
Market segmentation
Marketing
Marketing communications
Marketing concept
Marketing mix
Marketing objectives
Marketing process
Mission
Niche marketing

Observation
Personal selling
PEST analysis
Place
Price
Price determination
Pricing policy
Primary research
Product
Product life cycle
Promotion
Public relations
Qualitative data
Quantitative data
Questionnaire
Quota sample
Random sample
Research objectives
Research strategy
Sales promotion
Sampling
Secondary research
SMART objectives
Socio-economic groupings
Sponsorship
Surveys
SWOT analysis
Telemarketing
Trades Description Act 1968
USP

Unit 5: Customer service in leisure and recreation (advanced)

After-sales service

AIDA

Attitude

Benchmarking

Closing a sale

Communication skills

Complaints

Customer loyalty

Customer needs

Customer service

Disability Discrimination Act 1995

Feedback

Focus group

Job satisfaction

Legislation

Leisure and recreation industry

Mystery shopper

National tourism strategy

Non-verbal communication

Observation

Personal hygiene

Personal presentation

Personality

Product knowledge

Product

Public image

Quality criteria

Quality standards

Repeat business

Sales objectives

Selling skills

Sensory disabilities

Specific needs

Suggestion box

Surveys

Verbal communication

Written communication

Unit 6: Leisure and recreation in action (advanced)

Adair's leadership groups

Appraisal

Belbin's team types

Budgeting

Business plan

Business skills

Communication

Contingency plan

Critical path analysis

Debriefing

Evaluation

Event

Feasibility study

Health and safety at work

Income

Insurance

Leadership

Legislation

Leisure and recreation industry

Marketing

Security

SMART objectives

Start-up costs

Team building

Team structure

Teamwork

Tuckman's 'forming, storming, norming, performing'

Travel & Tourism

For candidates wishing for high grades in their Advanced Level Travel & Tourism qualification, the following terms are all-important. Make sure to revise them with care, giving yourself time to discuss them with a tutor or fellow student, in case anything is unclear.

Accommodation

Attractions

Commercial organisations

Destinations

Economic impacts of leisure, travel and tourism

Environmental impacts of leisure, travel and tourism

Leisure time

Marketing

Non-commercial organisations

Objectives

Socio-cultural impacts of leisure, travel and tourism

Sustainable tourism

SWOT analysis

Tour operator

Tourism

Tourism development

Tourism management

Transportation

Travel agent

Travel and tourism industry

Leisure & Recreation

For candidates wishing for high grades in their Advanced Level Leisure & Recreation qualification, the following terms are all-important. Make sure to revise them with care, giving yourself time to discuss them with a tutor or fellow student, in case anything is unclear.

Arts and entertainment

Countryside recreation

Health and safety management

Heritage

Leisure

Leisure and recreation industry

Leisure time

Marketing

National Lottery

Objectives

Physical recreation

Private sector organisations

Public sector organisations

Recreation

Risk assessment

Sport

Sports development

SWOT analysis

Teamwork

Voluntary sector organisations

USEFUL ADDRESSES FOR FURTHER INFORMATION

England's Regional Tourist Boards

Cumbria Tourist Board
Ashleigh
Holly Road
Windermere
Cumbria LA23 2AQ
(Covers the county of Cumbria.)

East of England Tourist Board
Toppesfield Hall
Hadleigh
Suffolk IP7 5DN
(Covers the counties of Cambridgeshire,
Essex, Hertfordshire, Bedfordshire, Norfolk,
Suffolk and South Lincolnshire.)

Heart of England Tourist Board
Woodside
Larkhill Road
Worcester WR5 2EF
(Covers the counties of Derbyshire,
Gloucestershire, Herefordshire,
Leicestershire, Northamptonshire,
Nottinghamshire, Rutland, Shropshire,
Staffordshire, Warwickshire, Worcestershire,
the West Midlands and representing the
districts of Cherwell and West Oxfordshire.)

London Tourist Board
Glen House
Stag Place
London SW1E 5LT
(Covers the Greater London area.)

Northumbria Tourist Board
Aykley Heads, Durham
County Durham
DH1 5UX
(Covers the counties of Durham,
Northumberland, Tyne & Wear and the Tees
Valley area.)

North West Tourist Board
Swan House
Swan Meadow Road
Wigan Pier
Wigan
Lancashire WN3 5BB
(Covers the counties of Cheshire, Greater
Manchester, Lancashire, Merseyside and the
High Peak District of Derbyshire.)

South East England Tourist Board
The Old Brewhouse
1 Warwick Park
Tunbridge Wells
Kent TN2 5TU
(Covers the counties of East and West
Sussex, Kent and Surrey.)

West Country Tourist Board
60 St Davids Hill
Exeter
Devon EX4 4SY
(Covers Bath, Bristol, Cornwall & Isles of
Scilly, Devon, West Dorset, Somerset and
Wiltshire.)

USEFUL ADDRESSES

Yorkshire Tourist Board
312 Tadcaster Road
York
North Yorkshire YO24 1GS
(Covers the counties of Yorkshire and North East Lincolnshire.)

Southern Tourist Board
40 Chamberlayne Road
Eastleigh
Hampshire SO50 5JH
(Covers the counties of Berkshire, Buckinghamshire, East and North Dorset, Hampshire, Isle of Wight and Oxfordshire.)

National Tourist Organisations

British Tourist Authority
Thames Tower
Black's Road
Hammersmith
London W6 9EL
(Promotes tourism to Great Britain from overseas.)

English Tourism Council
Thames Tower
Black's Road
Hammersmith
London W6 9EL

Northern Ireland Tourist Board
St Anne's Court
59 North Street
Belfast BT1 1NB

VisitScotland
23 Ravelston Terrace
Edinburgh EH4 3EU

Wales Tourist Board
Brunel House
2 Fitzalan Road
Cardiff CF2 1UY

Isle of Man Department of Tourism and Leisure
Sea Terminal Buildings
Douglas
Isle of Man
IM1 2RG

Jersey Tourism
Liberation Square
St Helier
JE1 1BB

States of Guernsey Tourist Board
PO Box 23
St Peter Port
Guernsey
Channel Islands
GY1 3AN

Other organisations with interests in travel and tourism

Arts Council of England
14 Great Peter Street
London
SW1P 3NQ

Association of Independent Tour Operators
(AITO)
St Margarets Road
Twickenham
Middlesex TW1 1RG

Association of Leading Visitor Attractions
4 Westminster Palace Gardens
Victoria
London SW1P 1RL

Association of Scottish Visitor Attractions
Suite 6
Admiral House
Maritime Street
Edinburgh EH6 6SG

British Activity Holiday Association
Green Lane
Hersham
Walton-on-Thames
Surrey KT12 5HD

British Association of Leisure Parks, Piers
   and Attractions
25 Kings Terrace
London NWI OJP

British Hospitality Association
Queen's House
55–56 Lincoln Inn Field's
London WC2 3BN

British Institute of Innkeeping
Wessex House
80 Park Street
Camberley
Surrey GU15 3PT

British Resorts Association
8 Post Office Avenue
Southport
Lancashire PR9 0US

British Waterways
Church Road
Watford WD1 3QA

City & Guilds of London Institute
Giltspur Street
London EC1A 9DD

Countryside Agency
John Dower House
Crescent Place
Cheltenham
Gloucestershire GL50 3RA

Department for Culture, Media and Sport
4 Cockspur Street
London SW1Y 5DH

Edexcel
Stewart House
Russell Square
London WC1B 5DN

English Heritage
23 Saville Row
London W1X 1AB

Farm Holiday Bureau (UK) Ltd
National Agricultural Centre
Stoneleigh Park
Warwickshire CV8 2LZ

Federation of Tour Operators
170 High Street
Lewes
BN7 1YE

USEFUL ADDRESSES

Holiday Care Service
Imperial Buildings
Horley
Surrey
RH6 7PZ

Hospitality Association of Northern Ireland
108/110 Midland Building
Whitla Street
Belfast BT15 1JP

Hospitality Training Foundation
3rd Floor
International House
High Street
Ealing
London W5 5DB

Hotel Catering and International
Management Association (HCIMA)
191 Trinity Road
London SW17 7HN

Institute of Leisure and Amenity
Management (ILAM)
ILAM House
Lower Basildon
Reading
Berkshire RG8 9NE

Institute of Sport and Recreation
Management (ISRM)
Giffard House
36–38 Sherrard Street
Melton Mowbray
Leicestershire LE13 IXJ

Institute of Travel and Tourism
113 Victoria Street
St Albans
Hertfordshire AL1 3TJ

Museums Association
Clerkenwell Close
London EC1R OPA

National Trust
36 Queen Anne's Gate
London SW1H 9AS

Tourism Concern
Stapleton House
277–281 Holloway Road
London N7 8HN

Tourism Society
1–2 Queen Victoria Terrace
Sovereign Court
London E1W 3HA

TTC Training
The Broadway
7–11 Chertsey Road
Woking
Surrey GU12 5AR

Youth Hostels Association
Trevelyan House
8 St Stephen's Hill
St Albans
Hertfordshire AL1 2DY

SELECTED BIBLIOGRAPHY

Textbooks

Ashworth, G and Goodall, B (1990) *Marketing Tourism Places*, Routledge, London

Bull, A (1991) *The Economics of Travel and Tourism*, Pitman, Melbourne

Burkart, A and Medlik, S (1981) *Tourism: Past, Present and Future*, Heinemann, London

Burns, P and Holden, A (1995) *Tourism: A New Perspective*, Prentice Hall, UK

Burton, R (1995) *Travel Geography*, Pitman, London

Cooper, C et al. (1998) *Tourism: Principles and Practice*, (2e), Longman, London

Davidson, R (1998) *Tourism in Europe*, (2e), Longman, London

Davidson, R and Maitland, R (1997) *Tourism Destinations*, Hodder & Stoughton

English Tourist Board (1991) *Tourism and the Environment: Maintaining the Balance*, ETB, London

Gamble, W (1989) *Tourism and Development in Africa*, John Murray, London

Gibson, J and Wood, I (2000) *Vocational A Level Leisure and Recreation*, Longman, London

Gibson, J, Ferguson and Walton (2001) *Vocational A Level Leisure and Recreation Options*, Longman, London

Gunn, C (1994) *Tourism Planning*, Taylor & Francis, New York

Hall, C M (1994) *Tourism and Politics*, Wiley, Chichester

Hall, D (ed.) (1991) *Tourism and Economic Development in Eastern Europe and the Soviet Union*, John Wiley & Sons

Hall, M and Lew, A (1998) *Sustainable Tourism*, Longman, London

Holloway, C (1998) *The Business of Tourism*, (5e), Longman, London

Holloway, C and Robinson, C (1995) *Marketing for Tourism*, (3e), Longman, London

Horner, P (1996) *Travel Agency Practice*, Longman, London

Inkpen, G (1998) *Information Technology for Travel and Tourism*, Longman, London

Inskeep, E (1991) *Tourism Planning: An Integrated and Sustainable Development Approach*, Van Nostrand Reinhold, New York

Krippendorf, J (1989) *The Holiday Makers*, Butterworth-Heinemann, Oxford

Laws, E (ed.) (1997) *The ATTT Tourism Education Handbook*, Tourism Society, London

Lea, J (1988) *Tourism and Development in the Third World*, Routledge, London

Lickorish, L (1991) *Developing Tourism Destinations*, Longman, Harlow

Mathieson, A and Wall, G (1982) *Tourism: Economic, Physical and Social Impacts*, Longman, Harlow

Middleton, V (1994) *Marketing in Travel and Tourism*, (2e), Butterworth-Heinemann, Oxford

Mill, R and Morrison, A (1992) *The Tourism System*, Prentice-Hall International

Murphy, P (1985) *Tourism: A Community Approach*, Routledge, London

Pearce, D (1989) *Tourist Development*, Longman, Harlow

Pearce, D (1995) *Tourism Today: A Geographical Analysis*, Longman, Harlow

Pompl, W and Lavery, P (1993) *Tourism in Europe: Structures and Developments*, CAB International

Ryan, C (1991) *Recreational Tourism: A Social Science Perspective*, Routledge, London

Sharpley, S and Sharpley, J (1997) *Rural Tourism: An Introduction*, International Thomson Business Press, London

Smith, V (1989) *Hosts and Guests: The Anthropology of Tourism*, (2e), University of Pennsylvania Press, Philadelphia

Swarbrooke, J (1995) *The Development and Management of Visitor Attractions*, Butterworth-Heinemann, Oxford

Van Harssel, J (1994) *Tourism: An Exploration*, (3e), Prentice-Hall International

Watt, D (1998) *Event Management in Leisure and Tourism*, Longman, London

Witt, S, Brooke, M and Buckley, P (1995) *The Management of International Tourism*, Routledge, London

World Tourism Organisation (1994) *National and Regional Tourism Planning: Methodologies and Case Studies*, Routledge, London

Yale, P (1995) *The Business of Tour Operations*, Longman, London

Yale, P (1993) *Tourism and Leisure in the Countryside*, Elm Publications

Youell, R (1998) *Tourism: An Introduction*, Addison Wesley Longman, London

Youell, R (2000) *Vocational A Level Travel and Tourism*, Longman, London

Youell, R (2001) *Vocational A Level Travel and Tourism Options*, Longman, London

Journals

Annals of Tourism Research

Current Issues in Tourism

Insights (English Tourism Council)

International Journal of Tourism Research, John Wiley & Sons (formerly *Progress in Tourism and Hospitality Research*)

Journal of Sustainable Tourism, Channel View Publications, Bristol

Journal of Travel and Tourism Marketing

Tourism (Journal of the Tourism Society, London)

Tourism Management

Periodicals

Business Traveller

Travel Trade Gazette

Travel News

Travel Weekly

Leisure Management

Leisure Opportunities

Attractions Management.

SELECTED BIBLIOGRAPHY